Theodore Roosevelt

A BIOGRAPHY

Henry F. Pringle was born in New York City. After gradu-
ating from Cornell University in 1920 he worked as a reporter
for various New York newspapers until in 1927 he became a
free-lance newspaperman. In 1929 he went to the Columbia
School of Journalism as an instructor, and from 1936 to 1943 he
was a full professor there. His first book, *Alfred E. Smith: A
Critical Study* (1927), was followed by *Big Frogs* (1928) and
Theodore Roosevelt (1931), which received the Pulitzer Prize.
Seven years later he published *The Life and Times of William
Howard Taft*. He is an active contributor to such magazines as
the *Saturday Evening Post, Harper's,* and the *Saturday Review.*

THEODORE ROOSEVELT
A BIOGRAPHY

✳

By Henry F. Pringle

A HARVEST BOOK
Harcourt, Brace and Company
New York

B.2.59

For H.C.D.
with
devotion

FOREWORD

This is a carefully revised and—perhaps happily—shortened version of a biography first published almost a quarter of a century ago. The author said then, and reiterates now, that Theodore Roosevelt was polygonal. He was a man of many ideas, and few of them lacked brilliance. The book still attempts to tell the whole story of an extraordinarily full life. And within the limits of human fallibility, objectivity has been the goal. In all likelihood neither the adulatory friends of Roosevelt nor his foes will feel that the goal has been reached. For the storms which swirled around him while he lived have not yet spent their hurricane force in either history or in human memories.

The footnotes and the bibliography have been omitted, for the sake of space. Any who seek the sources can find them in the longer edition. The appendix is also missing, for the same reason. My debts therein expressed are still debts today. But there is a new and very deep one. This is to Elting E. Morison and his associates, who compiled the eight large volumes of Roosevelt letters with such industry and skill. They will long stand as a model for the publication of Presidential papers. I have naturally read them, word by word. They have confirmed much originally written and much in this briefer biography.

The pages which follow will have failed completely unless they prove that Theodore Roosevelt was never dull. He grew old in body only; at least a decade too soon. T.R. combined adult greatness with the endearing, if sometimes irritating, quality of being a magnificent child. The combination was a major reason why men followed and loved him, throughout a growing and changing land.

September 1955.

H.F.P.

CONTENTS

Foreword   vii

BOOK I   I. *Teedie*   3
         II. *Growth*   11
         III. *Thou Goddess, Indifference!*   18
         IV. *Especially Pretty Alice*   28
         V. *Butter and Jam*   39
         VI. *I Rose like a Rocket*   46
         VII. *Practical Politician*   56
         VIII. *Gentleman Cowhand*   64
         IX. *The Years Between*   74
         X. *A Job Once More*   84
         XI. *Sword of Righteousness*   93
         XII. *The Nation in Peril*   106
         XIII. *Lord of the Navy*   115
         XIV. *A Bully Fight*   126
         XV. *Reward for a Hero*   140
         XVI. *Yearnings and Consummation*   151

BOOK II I. *Middle of the Road*   167
         II. *The First Attack*   176
         III. *The Rights of Labor*   185
         IV. *The Big Stick*   196
         V. *Setting for a Melodrama*   211
         VI. *I Took Panama*   221
         VII. *Trimming Sail*   238
         VIII. *The Imperial Years Begin*   253
         IX. *Imperial Years*   261
         X. *The Japanese Menace*   280
         XI. *Malefactors of Great Wealth*   290

xii. *The Wicked Speculators*   303
xiii. *Substantial Justice*   314
xiv. *Handing Down the Law*   328
xv. *End of the Reign*   335

BOOK III   i. *The First Error*   351
ii. *Among the Kings*   358
iii. *Return Triumphant*   370
iv. *True Democracy*   379
v. *Battling for the Lord*   387
vi. *Drums of War*   400
vii. *The Final Blow*   412

Index   425

BOOK I

Chapter I

TEEDIE

✳

A day or so after October 27, 1858, a friend of the family called at the Roosevelt home in New York to offer congratulations on the birth of a son. Doubtless he hurried away as soon as possible. It was not until the night of June 21, 1905, that Morris K. Jesup, by then a man of seventy-one, publicly recalled the perfunctory visit of five decades before.

President Hopkins of Williams College was giving a small dinner at his home, a select small dinner at which the President of the United States was guest of honor. Theodore Roosevelt had come to Williamstown, Massachusetts, to receive an honorary degree, and around the dinner table were Elihu Root, soon to be Secretary of State, Joseph H. Choate, who had recently returned from the Court of St. James's, and Bishop William Lawrence of Massachusetts.

Elihu Root was closer to Roosevelt than anyone else at the dinner. But it was Mr. Jesup who took the opportunity to boast that he had known Roosevelt longer than the other guests. He told of his call in 1858 and said that Theodore Roosevelt, Sr., had taken him to the nursery to gaze upon the son and heir.

"You were in your bassinet, making a good deal of fuss and noise for a youngster of your age," he said, addressing the rugged and exuberant guest of honor. "Your father, however, lifted you out, and asked me to hold you."

Mr. Root looked up. "Was he hard to hold?" he demanded.

The President must have roared with laughter; it was such remarks that constituted one of the bonds between himself and Root. This time, however, accuracy had been sacrificed to wit. The infant had been all too easy to hold. Memories lasted through life of nights torn by asthma, when he had scarcely been able to breathe; recollections, half vivid and half vague, of nights when a rig had been

3

hurriedly summoned from a nearby stable. Then he had been bundled in rugs and had been held in his father's strong arms while the carriage careened through the silent streets, and the boy's lungs caught the wind as it passed.

When he was old enough, the boy detested his puny body. He was ashamed of eyes so weak that one failed entirely before he was fifty. In those days of childhood illness lies the clue to the evangelical vitality of later years. Theodore Roosevelt, by unending persistence, developed his body to outward strength. Anyone who did less was a weakling. Anyone who did less was no true patriot. So came the Gospel of Strenuosity, and the extraordinary rambles through streams and gorges in which the President of the United States led a file of panting, sweating, silently cursing diplomats, army officers, and Cabinet members.

The urge for physical fitness did not come for some years. He was an owlish, wistful boy; tall for his age at ten or eleven years, with a thin body and pipestem legs, with fair hair that was seldom combed, with blue eyes that took in, despite extreme nearsightedness, minute details of an absorbing world. He read constantly while his small brother and sisters played. At seven, he had decided upon the life of a naturalist and about him, until he went to college, clung odors of formaldehyde. The Theodore Roosevelt of later years was the most adolescent of men. He often said that the days of the Spanish War were the most glorious of his life. Failure to receive the Medal of Honor for his exploits had been a grief as real as any of those which swamp childhood in despair. "You must always remember," wrote Cecil Spring Rice in 1904, "that the President is about six."

But the boy was precocious. During a first trip abroad, he jotted down critiques of cathedrals and paintings. He gave way, sometimes, to faintly synthetic attacks of melancholy, and rather enjoyed his bad health.

The family made this foreign journey in 1869. Theodore, then called "Teedie," was not quite eleven. Elliott, his younger brother, was about nine, and Conie, the youngest, was seven. Anna, who was known as either "Bamie" or "Bysie," was an aging young woman of fifteen and thus was classed with the grown-ups. The others, however, were constantly together, and in Teedie's childhood diaries he refers to them as "We Three." One reason for the trip was the hope that Theodore's asthma might be relieved. The previous summer the family had taken a house in the

Catskills believing that the higher altitude would effect a cure. It did not. There is a diary note in August, written on "a cold and dreary day," when Teedie had "an attack of Asmer."

Nor did Europe aid greatly. In Bavaria, on October 8, 1869, "I had a dream that the devil was carrying me away and have collerer morbus, a sickness which is not at all dangerous." A day or two later, he wrote: "I was very sick last night and Mama was so kind telling me storrys and rubbing me with her delicate fingers."

2

Far from having an unhappy childhood, however, Theodore had an excellent time on the whole. There was money enough for all necessary comforts of life. In an age before psychoanalysis had been heard of, his parents had the innate wisdom to guide their frail son past the pitfalls of inadequacy. It is important that they were kind and affectionate. It is more important that they were wise. The dominant influence was the father, large where the son was small, strong where he was weak. His father, Roosevelt wrote in his memoirs, combined strength and courage with gentleness, tenderness, and great unselfishness. And then the ultimate tribute, written in the years when Roosevelt believed surrender to fear the deadliest of sins—his father had been "the only man of whom I was ever really afraid." It was impossible to believe, Theodore wrote at Harvard when his father died, that this source of enduring strength was gone.

The presence of his father never really left him. On the night of September 22, 1901, Roosevelt sat down to his first dinner, as President, at the White House. Mrs. Douglas Robinson, the Conie of "We Three," was there, and so was the other sister, now Mrs. Cowles. Mrs. Robinson recalled her brother's remarking, as the dinner began, that the date was his father's birthday.

"I have realized it," he said, "as I signed papers all day, and I feel that it is a good omen that I begin my duties in this house on this day. I feel as if my father's hand were on my shoulder and as if there was a special blessing over the life I should lead here."

So it was also, on another proud day, March 4, 1905. He had been inaugurated as President in his own right. All day the music of cheering thousands—the most celestial of music to the man in public life—had poured into his ears, and the length of Pennsylvania Avenue had echoed to the tread of the battalions gathered to do him honor.

"How I wish Father could have lived to see it too!" he wrote two days later.

3

But heredity, unless the mixing of many races added to his faceted character, had no perceptible influence in the shaping of Theodore Roosevelt. He talked about his Dutch, Scotch, English, Huguenot, and Welsh ancestors a great deal. It was convenient, when the day came to shake hands with assorted political supporters. In Washington there was a legend, unhappily without ascertainable basis in fact, that a Jewish caller was once presented at the White House. "Congratulations!" the President was rumored to have boomed automatically. "I am partly Jewish, too."

The paternal strain was Dutch, and the name is correctly pronounced Rose-y-velt, with the emphasis on the first syllable and the second slurred into the third. The Roosevelt forbears were excellent people. On his father's side they were among the early settlers in New Amsterdam, and were the mercantile folk of the new colony. It is recorded that Klaes Martensen van Roosevelt landed in 1644. The mother of Roosevelt's father was a Pennsylvanian and her ancestors were Welsh and English with Quaker leanings; Germans, and Scotch-Irish.

Theodore's mother was a Georgian, a gentle person who exerted much less influence than his father. The blood brotherhood between history and coincidence has rarely been better demonstrated than by the fact that one of her ancestors took part in an ill-fated attempt to colonize the Isthmus of Darien, just east of Panama. The dream of a canal, which finally came to fulfillment at Roosevelt's hands, dates virtually back to the discovery that land blocked the desired passages to the golden markets of the East. Men dreamed of linking the oceans, but no move was made until William Paterson organized, late in the seventeenth century, an expedition to plant a Scotch colony at Darien. Command of the isthmus, he knew, would guarantee for all time the commercial supremacy of Great Britain; when the time came for a canal, England would control the necessary land.

Paterson, however, received small backing from his government. Five vessels set out in 1698 with 1,200 people and soon afterward there was a second, and smaller, expedition. On board the *Rising Sun*, in this weak flotilla, was the Rev. Archibald Stobo, with his wife and daughter, Jean. They reached Darien to find that the first settlers had been dispersed by the combination of Spaniards, the climate, and fever, so the ship turned back along the coast until it reached Charleston, South Carolina. There the minister landed because an offer of a pulpit in the city had been made. From this point the connection with Theodore Roosevelt is direct. Jean Stobo became the bride of James Bulloch and moved to Georgia with her husband. Their great-grandson, James Stephens Bulloch, had a daughter, Martha, who in 1853 was married at Roswell, Georgia, to a Yankee from New York named Theodore Roosevelt. Thus the Jean Stobo of Darien was Roosevelt's great-great-great-grandmother.

Years later, in the days of his greatness, the son went back "to the home of my mother and of my mother's people to see the spot which I already know so well from what my mother and my aunt told me." The house had survived the war. Two of the old servants who had been with the Bullochs waited at the gracious, wide-verandaed home. The President dwelt on his devotion to the South and quite forgot that he had once branded Jefferson Davis a traitor comparable only to Benedict Arnold.

The hatreds of war were still unborn when Martha Bulloch began to receive beaus. She must have been a lovely person, with dark hair that took on russet shades in the sunlight, with a complexion "more moonlight-white than cream-white." Her half-sister, Susan Elliott, had entertained a youthful Philadelphia physician, Hilborne West, who was a brother-in-law of Theodore Roosevelt. Dr. West carried north tales of the charming Southern home, and later took Roosevelt to Roswell for a visit. It was not long before he had fallen in love with Martha and had taken his bride to New York.

4

The house on East Twentieth Street, where Theodore was born and spent his first years, was a comfortable three-story structure. It was solid, respectable, and a little complacent. His father had inherited some money, and carried on a profitable glass-importing business on Maiden Lane until American manufacturers started to compete with domestic glass. Then he went into banking.

The father of Theodore Roosevelt, like his fellow citizens of the upper middle class, had no particular interest in the movements for social reform which were beginning to get under way in the '6o's. But the elder Roosevelt was a kindly man, who took seriously the responsibilities of moderate wealth. He was a founder of the Orthopedic Hospital, the Newsboys' Lodging House, and the Young Men's Christian Association.

The house in which Teedie grew up was furnished, as he wrote later, "in the canonical taste of New York which George William Curtis described in the *Potiphar Papers.*" It was not, in the sense that some homes are, distinguished. Henry Cabot Lodge, who was eight years older than Roosevelt and who would be his closest friend for years, had listened to Longfellow and James Russell Lowell and Louis Agassiz; nearly all the important figures of the day had partaken of austere New England hospitality at Nahant. But the Roosevelts maintained no salon. Though they entertained well, small Teedie never heard history in the making. His father was concerned with business and philanthropy and his guests shared these tastes. Their social position was secure enough to make energetic participation in society both trivial and absurd. Their connection with politics was usually limited to futile fusion movements which sought, with slight success, to break the grip of Tammany Hall.

Even the Civil War could not disturb unduly the tranquillity of this home, a fact all the more remarkable since the sympathies of the father were with the North while Mrs. Roosevelt had relatives fighting for the hopeless cause of the South. Teedie's father was thoughtful and tolerant. He spared his wife the agony of having a husband fight against brothers, and engaged in noncombatant work during the struggle. But at no time, either as a small boy or as a man, was there any doubt of Theodore's own sympathies. An aunt, Anna Bulloch, was living with the Roosevelts at the time, and heard the ruthless Teedie pray for the Lord of Hosts to "grind the Southern troops into powder."

Teedie's impressions of the struggle must have been vague. But he sensed that his father was away, working among the Union troops. The cause that his all-wise father favored was right. The South was morally wrong, and merited slight consideration. He thought so as a young man. He thought so as President, although he disguised his true sentiments during political journeys into the South. To the historian James Ford Rhodes, he wrote on November 29, 1904, that "right was exclusively with the Union people, and the wrong exclusively with the secessionists." A few weeks earlier, he had written to George Harvey on the same subject:

Jefferson Davis was an unhung traitor. He did not, like Benedict Arnold, receive money for his treachery, but he received office instead. The two men stand on an equal eminence of infamy in our country.

On an occasion twenty years before, Roosevelt had exchanged communications with the President of the Confederacy. He had made the same comparison in 1885, in an article in the *North American Review,* and Davis had written in hot anger to deny the accusation of treason, to say that "the instincts of a gentleman, had you possessed them, must have caused you to make inquiry before uttering an accusation so libelous and false." Roosevelt, then twenty-seven years old, had pompously answered in the third person that "Mr. Roosevelt does not deem it necessary that there should be any further communication between himself and Mr. Davis." He may have held the same views in his years of comparative discretion but he regretted the rudeness of that retort: "I answered with an acerbity which, being a young man, struck me at the time as clever. It does not strike me as in the least so now."

5

In the early days Elliott, the younger brother, was the leader among the three children. Theodore took part in their games with enthusiasm enough, but he often wandered away with some older person and indulged in long conversations, usually on natural history. The trait grew stronger with time; even as a boy he was talkative. On the first ocean voyage in 1869 he found a fellow naturalist, a Mr. St. John, who proved to be "a most interesting gentleman." "We had," the diary reveals, "a long talk in the cabin after supper."

His interest was in animate things, in green fields and trees. At Rome, they drove one evening to a nearby villa where it was "so soft and balmy and we heard a nightingale." Another time he had been "rowed across Lake Coma [*sic*] by the light of a Golden Moon." Then, on Easter Sunday, in 1870, the family went to Versailles from Paris, where the children played in the groves "and picked cowslip and heard the cuckoo sing."

Conie and Ellie and Teedie—"We Three"—were normal young Americans. In Rome they wandered along the streets of the Pincian Hill frightening the inevitable dogs with a small, paper-cap gun. They exhibited the levity that a young American Protestant felt called upon to feel toward the Pope of Rome—behind his back, of course—when Pius IX chanced to come by with his retinue one day in January. "We saw the Pope as we walked along," recorded Teedie, "and he extended his hand to me; hem!! hem!!"

But traveling from hotel to hotel and living in strange cities did not appeal to Teedie, and sometimes he gave in, with fine histrionic appreciation of the melancholy which seized him, to introspective ponderings. While he was in Paris, word came from home that an uncle had died, and Theodore exclaimed that this "is the third relative that has died in my short life. What will come?" There came a Sunday in Dresden when the boy luxuriated in gloom:

I am by the fire with not another light but it. It is now after 5. All was dark except the fire. I lay by it and listened to the wind and thought of the times at home in the country when I lay by the fire with some hickory nuts. Again I was lying by the roaring fire (with the October wind shrieking outside) in the cheerful lighted room and I turned around half expecting to see it all again and stern reality forced itself upon me and I thought of the time that could come never, never, never.

Then he would shake off these dark moods and send the imps of melancholy scurrying to their lair. By November, "Hip, hurrah!," half of the trip had been completed and they could contemplate the return. Besides, Christmas was coming and Teedie knew that it would be as deliriously joyful abroad as it had been at home. When he was a man, Roosevelt remembered the almost insupportable happiness of those Christmas festivals and reproduced them, as exactly as possible, for his own children. In 1869, Christmas came while they were in Rome. "Tomorrow is Christmas!!! hip, hip, hurah!!!!" he exulted. The presents, he later explained, "passed our upmost expectations."

As spring approached, Teedie was much more cheerful, for he knew that they were to sail for New York in May. Still in Rome, he went to one of his first parties, and there is a note indicating awareness of that most baffling of creatures, the small girl. The experience had been rather pleasant:

We danced and when we had forfeits I was suddenly surprised by being kissed by Elliese Van Schaik as the boy she loved best in the room. I liked the dancing very much and have had a very nice time.

Chapter II

GROWTH

✳

The return from abroad in May, 1870, marked a definite change. Until then, Teedie had lived wholly without responsibilities. Now he faced two major problems. The first, and by far the more important, was building his health. The second was an education. His mother and aunt had taught him his letters, and he was an insatiable reader by the time he was ten. But his knowledge was scattered, and additional emphasis on some subjects was needed so that, in due time, he could begin preparations for college.

Getting rid of physical disability was vital; unless this was done nothing much could be achieved. So he was told by his parents. No evidence exists to show that Teedie, when he was seven or eight or nine, considered periodic illness as anything save a minor inconvenience. The boy, unlike the man, did not wish to emulate the warrior. He was far from believing, as he later did, in "those most valuable of all qualities, the soldierly virtues," or that "all the great masterful races have been fighting races." It is significant that, in front of the tomb of Napoleon in March of 1870, Teedie had been bored by the relics of military glory. "We saw numerous battle scenes," he wrote in his journal, "with russians, turks arabs crusades knights Charlemang passing the Alps. Napoleon doing the same."

He visited all the museums of natural history he could find in Europe. Being a naturalist required neither brawn nor muscle. Even handicapped by asthma, a scientist could work in the laboratory or ramble through the fields with a butterfly net. This was the life to which he looked forward, and he took his vocation with desperate seriousness. His mother once ordered a maid to divest a bureau drawer of dead mice; what hurt him most, said Teedie, was "the loss to Science! The loss to Science!"

The change was imperceptible at first. Roosevelt was, in a sense, a naturalist always. Few men have accomplished more toward the protection of wild life. But the search for strength brought a new phase. The strong man hunted. In Theodore Roosevelt the instincts of hunter and collector ultimately clashed. The naturalist kept the hunter from being a wanton killer. The hunter caused the naturalist to do strange things. At Oyster Bay when he was President, "I shot a specimen of the Dominican or yellow-throated warbler, and the skin is spoiled except for purposes of identification." Roosevelt worried about that incident a good deal, and a few days afterward expressed regret for having shot the song bird.

Looking back on his childhood, Roosevelt maintained that he had admired men of daring and particularly the soldiers of Valley Forge and Morgan's riflemen. More probably, however, these were enthusiasms formed later on and attributed in adult years to boyhood. At all events, on the return in 1870 to the house on Twentieth Street, his father told Teedie that he was a sorry physical specimen and that steps toward health were promptly to be taken. Anna, the older sister, was also unwell, and a gymnasium was constructed on the second floor.

"You have the mind but not the body," the father told his son, "and without the help of the body the mind cannot go as far as it should. You must *make* your body."

So began dreary hours with the punching bag, with dumbbells, and on the horizontal bars, and gradually Teedie's chest began to expand and muscle to form in his arms. It was two years later, however, during a visit to Moosehead Lake, that a humiliating incident aroused the first active, instead of perfunctory, interest in the journey to health. There had been another attack of asthma and for the first time Theodore was alone; until then, his more robust younger brother had been on hand to protect him when it was necessary. He was proceeding to his destination by stagecoach when four other youngsters made him wretched with teasing. At first merely unhappy, he finally decided to fight. But he found that any one of his tormentors could, without difficulty, hold him at arm's length. The boys did not hurt him, except mentally. There, he was deeply wounded. He began at once to take boxing lessons, and progress was swift. The following year, in a note to his aunt, he was "a bully boy with a black eye." The diary that had told of fields where the cuckoo sang was transformed into a "Sporting Calendar." There are records of victories, as he approached seventeen during the summer of 1875, in the dashes, the broad jump, and the pole vault. Teedie, the pet name of his small-boy years, was used less often. He was Theodore to most of those who knew him, although a few used Teddy, the name which was to be on the lips of men throughout the world. He detested the abbreviation; those who prated about "my good friend, Teddy," generally proved they did not know him well.

By the time he was sixteen or seventeen, the family had taken a house at Oyster Bay, where Theodore's grandfather had lived for some years. There, the boy learned to ride and shoot.

A second serious handicap was defective eyesight. This was bad from birth, and it constantly grew worse. On December 12, 1904, Dr. William H. Wilmer, then an eye specialist in Washington and later head of the department of ophthalmology at Johns Hopkins Hospital, was called to the White House. President Roosevelt told him that he had for some time noticed a dimness of vision in his left eye after violent exercise. A few days previously, he had been struck in this eye while boxing with a young army officer. Since then, black spots had floated in front of him. The President reminded Dr. Wilmer that he had always been nearsighted.

Examination disclosed a minor hemorrhage in the retina; Dr. Wilmer ordered that Roosevelt refrain from his more energetic exercises. Otherwise, he would lose the eye at once. The President protested vigorously. But when the specialist said that another blow might cause a cataract to form, he gave in. For a time he was careful, but during 1908 the growth developed and from then on Roosevelt was blind in his left eye. Not more than a half-dozen people in the country knew it, however. He was sensitive over the defect. He carefully and successfully avoided giving the impression that he was using only one eye.

2

The years of growth began with 1871. Part of the wistfulness—and also part of the charm—of the boy who signed his letters Teedie or T.D. faded. Slowly at first, but surely, he grew in self-confidence until finally the first green, very green indeed, shoots of a germinating ego began to appear.

The bent for natural history continued despite newly discovered joys in hunting. The notes in the diary grew more numerous, and also very much more learned. On a trip to the Adirondacks, "I picked up a salamander (*Diemictylus irridescens*). We saw a bald-headed eagle (*Halietus leuco-*

cephalus) sailing over the lake." Every living thing now had its Latin name. The boy had moments, too, when he wrote what he fondly believed exceedingly humorous letters. On a second trip abroad in 1873, for example, a communication was addressed to his Uncle Hilborne West, the same Dr. West who had brought Theodore's father and mother together. The letter was written in Paris:

From Theodore the Philosopher to Hilborne, Elder of the Church of Philadelphia. Dated from Paris, a City of Gaul, on the 16th day of the 11th month of the 4th year of the reign of Ulysses. Truly, O Hilborne! this is the first time in many weeks that I have been able to write to you concerning our affairs. In crossing the sea of Atlantis, I suffered much of a malady called sickness of the sea, but I am now in good health.

A good deal more followed, similarly sparkling.

The second trip to Europe began in the fall of 1872, with the children again filled with misgivings. There were occasional attacks of asthma, but Theodore's health had improved greatly, and for the first time there are signs of leadership. Elliott no longer dominated. Even Theodore's athletic father was finding it difficult to keep up with the pulsing energy of the hunter-naturalist, and he wrote from some point on the Nile that "I walked through the bogs with him at the risk of sinking hopelessly and helplessly, for hours. I felt that I must keep up with Teedie." Theodore's new energy was no unalloyed blessing. Elliott endured for some time joint hotel rooms in which there was an occasional elderly dead owl, innumerable partly dissected mice, ubiquitous and unpleasant odors. Finally he asked his father whether he could not have a separate room.

An aggravating factor was Theodore's interest in taxidermy, in which art he had taken a few lessons before leaving home. All normal boys are grubby, the theory being that the grubbier they are the more normal. Roosevelt, the adult, had few illusions about himself as a boy. He wrote in his memoirs:

The ornithological small boy is generally the very grubbiest of all. Doubtless the family had their moments of suffering—especially on one occasion when a well-meaning maid extracted from my taxidermist's outfit the old tooth-brush with which I had put on the skins the arsenical soap necessary for their preservation, partly washed it, and left it with the rest of my wash kit for my own personal use.

During the fall and winter of 1872-73, Theodore began to grow at an astonishing rate. He seemed, miraculously, to add an inch or two during the brief journey up the Nile, and when the expedition returned to Cairo a complete set of new clothing had to be obtained. Dutch thrift forbade discarding the old suit, and it was saved for second-best; so Theodore seemed a little out-at-the-elbows, a little gawky. He had not yet developed the flair for sartorial elegance that was to amuse his fellow legislators in the New York legislature, and to cause the first cartoons to portray him as a dude.

It was on this trip in Egypt that the instincts of the hunter first began the lifelong struggle with the naturalist. The family moved on to the Holy Land, and at Jericho there is a note in the diaries that "quails and partridges rose from the short grass, while doves, hawkes, finches, jays and verdons flew among the trees . . . but I happened to shoot very badly and procured only a bulbul and a warbler." It was not, though, a trip devoted only to hunting and collecting. A few galleries were visited. Theodore attempted some fine writing, noting that Egypt was "old when Rome was bright, was old when Babylon was in its glory, was old when Troy was taken! It was a sight to awaken a thousand thoughts and it did." Thereupon he had been overcome by a wholly novel speechlessness: "I *felt* a great deal but I *said* nothing. You cannot express yourself on such occasions." Thebes was "a glimpse of the ineffable, of the unutterable"; a phrase which seems to have pleased him greatly, since he used it in several letters.

3

The months from November until July of 1873 were pleasant and doubtless profitable, but the parents were worrying over the postponed education of their itinerant brood. Theodore's father had to return to the United States on business, and his mother conceived the not very happy idea of separating Corinne from the two boys so that the children would learn German instead of speaking English among themselves. The little girl was dispatched to the home of a Professor Wackernagel in Dresden, while the boys were left with Dr. and Mrs. Minckwitz in the same city. Mrs. Roosevelt went to Carlsbad for the cure.

The plan worked lamentably, because Conie was racked by loneliness. She wrote her mother that she could not en-

dure it and so she, too, was lodged at the Minckwitz establishment. Yet the children absorbed a good deal of German
that summer. Of chief importance, since Roosevelt was to
become head of a world power, was an affection for Germany that grew out of the months in Dresden. He admired
the capacity of these people for hard work, for their "sense
of duty," and for their pride in "the new Germany." In
later years, according to Roosevelt's critics, this admiration
extended to the German Kaiser. It was widely believed
that the President greatly resembled the Prussian ruler, and
also that Roosevelt was under his influence.

The theory is more false than true, although an element
of truth lies in it. Roosevelt liked the German Emperor and
thought him extremely capable. Returning from abroad in
1910, after prolonged conversations with Wilhelm, Roosevelt confided to intimates at Oyster Bay that "the Kaiser is
an able man, a *very* able man, but not so able as Elihu
Root!" The fact is that he could view the Kaiser far more
objectively than he did most men, and certainly far more
so than he did himself. But his wholehearted admiration
for Germany itself, a direct result of the Dresden experience, lasted until the World War destroyed it utterly.

Theodore was fifteen when the family returned from
the second European trip, and the change in him is apparent. He was healthier. The diffidence of childhood was
passing. His mother and father agreed that preparation for
college must start at once and be carried on with energy if
he was to enter Harvard at the proper age. Why Harvard
was chosen must remain unexplained; Theodore's father
had not been to college but had received an equivalent
education from tutors.

How much did the boy of fifteen know? It had been decided that he would enter Harvard in the fall of 1876, and
so he had less than three years in which to pass the necessary examinations. Naturally intelligent, Theodore had
absorbed considerable history and geography on his travels,
and he could speak a little French and German. Arithmetic
and spelling were largely mysteries still, but those branches
of learning, along with economics and finance, were to
bother him always. He was not much interested in them,
and leaned on others for advice when he was President.
Of greatest worth, aside from the general background obtained in travel, had been his love of reading. There is an
item in the diaries that on the first European trip, which
ended before he was eleven, "We Three" had read fifty
novels. Unfortunately, they are not named.

16

In his autobiography, Roosevelt dwelt on the importance of early reading. The naturalist in him was irritated by "the wholly impossible collection of animals" in the *Swiss Family Robinson.* He did not care for the first half of *Robinson Crusoe*, "although it is unquestionably the best part," but was fascinated by the second part, "containing the adventures with the wolves in the Pyrenees, and out in the Far East." The boy, as was the custom in those days, was not allowed to read dime novels. As was the custom, also, Theodore read them in secret. Unlike most boys, however, he found the forbidden fruit not wholly sweet. The moral sense and the righteousness that became so marked with the years were present even then: "I do not think the enjoyment compensated for the feeling of guilt."

It is not too safe to attribute the characteristics of adult years to the books and magazines of childhood. Nearly every boy and girl of the Victorian Era read the same moral rubbish. They read, in the '70's and '80's, such magazines as *Our Young Folks*, which Theodore Roosevelt still believed in 1913 "the very best magazine in the world." The admission makes it relevant to examine the files of that journal.

It was, if typical, pretty bad. Roosevelt recalled, in particular, an interminable serial entitled *Little Pussy Willow.* Therein, a poisonously sunny small girl did good deeds, month after month, and demonstrated conclusively the lamentable character of "Miss Emily Proudie," a rich and therefore discontented child. Another serial bore the lengthy title, *Good Old Times, or Grandfather's Struggle for a Homestead,* and began with the announcement that no subject was better suited to the attention of children than "the stern virtues and sterling worth and piety of the men who laid the foundations of the institutions which we enjoy." This sentence was destined to appear, almost word for word, in many a presidential public paper and state address.

The preparatory education of Theodore Roosevelt had a single goal, admission to Harvard, and everything was subordinated to that end. He had, some years previously, attended school at a "professor McMullen's" nearby on Twentieth Street, but the family had moved uptown, to Fifty-seventh Street just west of Fifth Avenue. Besides, it seemed wiser to have tutors. In consequence, Arthur H. Cutler, who later founded the Cutler School in New York, was engaged. Before his death, Cutler left a memorandum testifying to the "alert, vigorous quality of young Roosevelt's mind," adding that he had done exceedingly well in his work. He had particularly enjoyed history and modern languages, but he had not neglected mathematics or Latin and Greek. By the summer of 1874, the preparations for Harvard were going well, and were continued during July and August at Oyster Bay. So energetic did Cutler's pupil prove, in fact, that during the final two years he did the equivalent of three years of work. He passed his entrance examinations without difficulty, and during the summer of 1876 he made ready to leave for Cambridge.

Five years later, Roosevelt was a candidate for the legislature, his first political office. Dr. Cutler was one of those who received a circular, which Roosevelt had composed, asking for support in the approaching contest. After the victory in November, he offered his congratulations: ". . . but *do* write a grammatical circular next time," he pleaded. "You see, the pedagogue is still critical."

Chapter III

THOU GODDESS, INDIFFERENCE!

Dr. Oliver Wendell Holmes of the medical faculty was fascinated in 1871 by radical changes that were sweeping over Harvard College. On the whole, he approved of them; in particular, he looked with favor upon a young man named Charles W. Eliot who was facing a storm of unpopularity and causing such a buzz of discussion at Cambridge that the very leaves on the elms in the Harvard Yard seemed to flutter in the excitement.

"Our new President," wrote Dr. Holmes to a friend that year, "has turned the whole university over like a flapjack." He was "a sensation" who had demonstrated "an extraordinary knowledge of all that relates to every department."

The period of transition that was to change Harvard completely began with the elevation of Eliot to the presidency in 1869. It was still in progress when Theodore Roosevelt entered as a member of the freshman class in the fall of 1876. The struggle was between Harvard complacency and an energetic, ambitious, dissatisfied pedagogue without tact, with small patience. As an undergraduate, Theodore shared the general dislike for the president of Harvard. When Roosevelt became a national figure, Eliot disagreed violently with his growing imperialism. For his part, Roosevelt felt that Eliot had failed to appreciate in its full glory the future of the United States, that he was a theorist, and impractical. Harvard's president, Roosevelt would say, had tried to "Germanize the methods of teaching," a somewhat unfair criticism since Roosevelt could be fairly Germanic on his own part. The two men really were allies in the march of progress, but for twenty years they circled warily about each other, like street urchins in the preliminary stages of a fight. Suspicion and distrust, combined with personal dislike, kept them apart. In public, of course, they affected the most cordial of friendships.

Roosevelt, attempting to analyze his college career and weigh the benefits he had received, felt that he had obtained little from Harvard. He had been depressed by the formalistic treatment of many subjects, by the rigidity, the attention to minutiae that were important in themselves, but which somehow were never linked up with the whole. When at Harvard, he wrote from the White House in 1907, he had determined upon a career as "an out-of-doors fauna naturalist." But his professors had insisted on drab, indoor laboratory work, so he looked around for some other career. He might have been more generous toward Harvard if he had entered a few years earlier. It was a dreary place, a mere apology for a university. ". . . no one took Harvard College seriously," said Henry Adams, who had concluded this detail of his education in 1858. "All went there because their friends went there, and the College was their ideal of social self-respect."

Roosevelt would have found Harvard far more futile in Adams's day, or even in 1870. Under the pre-Eliot regime, A. Lawrence Lowell recalled, "all the students studied the same subjects." The elective system, perhaps the first admission that college students have minds, was just getting under way, and was viewed with deep suspicion. Little graduate work was done; a "good moral character" was the chief requirement for admission. Strenuous opposition arose in the medical school when written examinations were proposed; the professor of surgery protesting that the school would be wrecked in a year or two, that no one expected a medical man to be proficient in reading or writing.

Expansion of the elective system, in particular, aroused protests among parents who believed in a good, sound education pervaded by common sense. When rumors spread that, in addition, each student was allowed a number of absences from chapel, there was an outburst of moral indignation. Soon the idea would extend to classes, and then how would anxious parents know whether their sons were at Cambridge, where they belonged, or off on wild jaunts? At one time a report was circulated that many of the young men were actually spending the winter in Bermuda, far from the eyes of the too, too tolerant faculty. It was necessary for the authorities to point out that the roll was still being called each day.

2

Theodore, by now in moderate health, was no roisterer, however. Another young man arrived at Harvard, five years afterward, to live at Cambridge according to the popular formula of wild nights in Boston, chorus girls, collegiate pranks, and ultimate expulsion in a shower of beer. This was William Randolph Hearst of the Class of 1885, who did much to foment the war that advanced Roosevelt to the presidency, who yearned in vain for the eminence Roosevelt achieved. Theodore Roosevelt of the Class of 1868 did not smoke or drink, nor did he ever. He had small interest in any form of wickedness. He was elated to learn, he wrote in one of his first letters home, that of the eleven young men at his dining table "no less than seven do not smoke, and four drink nothing stronger than beer."

All men change in appearance, but faint traces of the adult are normally discernible in the fading photographs of childhood. Theodore, however, changed completely. The boy, thin-faced and anemic, was in no faint degree like the broad, overweight President, with publicized teeth and prominent jaw. Inner traits were developing, no doubt, but the Cambridge undergraduate was outwardly quite apart. His hair had lost its wild disarray. He wore reddish whiskers, carefully nurtured, which caused amusement in the Yard. A new fastidiousness in dress was creeping upon him.

Outwardly he might have been any well-bred young man arriving to begin his college career; certain of his position, aware that he need not mix with the rabble but would make the necessary clubs. Superficially, he conformed admirably to the pattern of the Harvard man of 1876; it was his preferences and tastes, his enthusiasms and squirming curiosity, his talkativeness and his nervousness, which soon made it apparent that he was a fish in a strange pond.

Theodore Roosevelt was different from his fellows, the greatest of crimes to the American college boy.

In 1876 the whole of Harvard College was almost as small as the Yard itself. The enrollment was about eight hundred. The center of Cambridge then, as now, was Harvard Square, but instead of traffic lights and streams of motors, a horsecar line led to Boston. In winter the cars were unheated, and straw on the floor was supposed to warm the feet of chilled passengers. The odors were not too pleasant. In fiction, the college man of the '80's was a fastidious youth who was twin to the dude of the comic supplements. Actually, he sometimes chewed tobacco, and the aroma of this blended with that of the damp and clammy straw. The cars bumped along, with wheels that screeched on the curves, toward the Parker House, which was the meeting place for Harvard men and from where they set forth on their juvenilities.

There was beauty for the eyes of those who could see. George Santayana, who came a few years later, found "old fashioned shabbiness and jollity [and] Boston and Cambridge in those days resembled in some ways the London of Dickens, the same anxious respectability, the same sordid back streets with their air of shiftlessness and decay." Santayana wrote that undergraduate life "drifted good-naturedly from one common-place thing to another," but outside, in Boston, and the New England countryside, there was beauty in "the brilliant sunsets and the deep snows . . . here and there a pane of glass, surviving all tenants and housemaids, had turned violet in the sunlight of a hundred years."

If Theodore felt any comparable appreciation, there is no hint of it in the letters home, no echo in his voluminous writings. The boy of eleven had mourned for October winds above the valley of a river. Perception of light and color and changing shadows returned when he saw the Far West, the "land of vast silent spaces, of lonely rivers, and of plains where the wild game stared at the passing horseman." But Cambridge marked a transition period.

A throb or two of homesickness came as he settled in private rooms at No. 16 Winthrop Street, a lane midway between the Yard and the Charles River. There were two reasons for this withdrawn existence; first, that his health was not yet perfect and only damp, first-floor rooms were available in the Yard. The second reason was that he intended to continue the collecting of natural history specimens, and the resulting disorder would not be tolerated in a dormitory. His older sister, Anna, had come to Cambridge some weeks ahead and Theodore wondered how he could have endured being away from home "if you had not fitted up my room for me." Not another boy in college, he said, "has a family who loves him as much as you all do me, and I am *sure* that there is no one who has a father who is also his best and most intimate friend." There was also a letter to the "Beloved Motherling" expressing gratitude because "in looking back over my eighteen years of existence, I have literally never spent an unhappy day, unless it was my own fault!"

He had arrived at Cambridge at a time of excitement so great that the normal Harvard languor was momentarily dispelled. This was over the election of 1876, the bitterly fought Hayes-Tilden contest, and it must have diverted Theodore's attention from thoughts of home. Student sentiment was largely, although not entirely, behind Rutherford B. Hayes, but that the youthful Roosevelt had much interest in the campaign is doubtful. Hayes well merited his support. The new President, whose election was at last confirmed, was to be a proponent of civil service reform. He was to fight the powerful bosses in New York against whom, not long after, Roosevelt was to struggle. He was to offer Roosevelt's father the appointment as Collector of the Port of New York.

"We saw to it," wrote Tom Platt smugly, "that the President's plan was foiled."

Theodore's participation in the campaign was limited, although he held Republican convictions, to a parade of Hayes adherents on October 27, 1876. Transparencies swayed in the hands of students whose political devotion had been warmed by beer and ale. They called for "Honesty in Politics, and Cribs in Examinations," for "Hard Money and Soft Electives," and for free trade, in which Theodore believed for some years, to his subsequent acute distress. This last principle was emblazoned on a banner reading "Free Trade, Free Press and Free Beer."

3

Only rarely did the young men of Harvard so forget themselves as to take part in the crudities that interested less fortunate men. In Henry Adams's day, and the change had barely started, Harvard made no effort to turn out leaders of men: ". . . the school," he wrote, "created a type but not a will. The graduate had few strong prejudices. Harvard

College was a negative force. If Harvard College gave nothing else, it gave calm."

It is not surprising that Theodore was unpopular, and an object of suspicion. Not enthusiasm, but indifference, was Goddess of the Yard. Men had been turned down by the better clubs, long before this, because they had been too eager. The spirit of Harvard in Roosevelt's day was expressed at a Hasty Pudding function in 1880, his senior year, when George Pellew, class poet, strummed his lyre:

> . . . We ask but time to drift,
> To drift—and note the devious ways of man,
> To drift,—and, probing life's recesses scan
> The truths that overarch and underlie
> The surface faiths whereby men live and die.
>
> Indifferent to all things, save the truth,
> We do not waste the fateful days of youth.

The Hasty Pudding poet may have been guilty of satirical exaggeration. But his caricature has the accuracy of approximate truth. The languorous Harvard man was typical in 1880, just as a few decades later the typical college youth was obnoxious in peg-top trousers, turtle-neck sweater, and drop pipe. The man who merely observes, who scorns ambition, who despises action: the portrait is the very antithesis of the Roosevelt whom Adams called "pure act."

William Roscoe Thayer, who was a class behind Roosevelt at Harvard and who later wrote an appreciation of him, remembered that he was considered a queer youth. He would drop in at the room of a classmate, ostensibly for conversation, and would become immersed in some book, to the disgust of his host. Thayer could see none of the "charm that he developed later . . . he was a good deal of a joke . . . active and enthusiastic and that was all."

Another sin in Roosevelt, Harvard '80, was a tendency toward too great an interest in what his instructors and professors said, and sometimes he made it worse by taking issue with them in the classroom. This seemed barbaric to young men who considered college mere exposure to thought and who had no serious apprehension of contamination. Henry Chapin Jones, later an instructor in the Public Latin School at Boston, heard Roosevelt insist on reasons for statements that professors made. He asked questions, and uttered protests, his eyes gleaming from behind his spectacles. He said that the matter at issue had not been clearly presented. In his chosen field of science this trait was particularly pronounced.

It was the Rev. Sherrard Billings, another classmate, who left a memorandum on the worst of Roosevelt's offenses: when "it was not considered good form to move at more than a walk, Roosevelt was always running."

Had Theodore not arrived at Harvard with an assured social backing, he might have had a lonely time. As it was he failed of election as class marshal in his senior year. On the whole, though, he was queer but eligible, and the latter asset was vastly more important than the handicap. In the end he made Porcellian, the loftiest of social honors. So far as he associated with the other undergraduates at all, he lived among the minority called the club set. He rarely appeared at Memorial Hall for meals, but ate with a group known as the Dining Club, whose number included young Bostonians of social position and a New Yorker or two.

"Unquestionably the evil development of Harvard is the snob, exactly as the evil development of Yale is the cad," Roosevelt wrote some fifteen years after graduation, "and . . . I think the cad the least unhealthy, though perhaps the most objectionable person."

He came closer to his fellows in athletics, perhaps, than in any other way, and this despite the fact that he was a very bad athlete. Participation was not an attempt to win prestige, for athletes received the mildest of homage in the '80's. Theodore's energetic, if unskilled, athletic activities were due to his continued determination to win complete health. Romantic stories were circulated of a grim young man in spectacles who battered his way to pugilistic eminence and by sheer grit overcame the handicap of being so nearsighted that he could barely see his adversary. The facts are less colorful. That he was plucky, there is no doubt. That he was not much of a boxer is probable. He did not wear his glasses in the ring.

In February, 1877, he was writing home that he was having almost a daily "set-to . . . with 'General' Lister, the boxing master," at the old Harvard gymnasium. During his sophomore year he "gave red-haired Coolidge a tremendous thrashing," and in 1879 was bending his energies toward the lightweight championship matches to be held in March. He entered at 135 pounds and he was again able to defeat Coolidge. His second opponent, however, was the formidable C. S. Hanks, who was "the better all through." The New York *Times* considered the events important enough for its sporting pages, and noted that Hanks had been "punishing Roosevelt severely." The *Times* added that the bouts had been well fought, brisk, and almost professional; and thereby aroused indignation on the part of the Harvard *Advocate.* This voice of student opinion regretted that the *Times* had crudely used the phrase "sparring bouts," and had failed to realize that these had been "friendly encounters between gentlemen." "Perhaps," the undergraduate editor loftily concluded, "it is all that can be expected from an average newspaper reporter."

Roosevelt felt no such ultradelicacy. As police commissioner of New York in 1896 he was criticized for permitting a fight between two gentlemen called Joe Choynski and Peter Maher. He retorted that boxing was a manly sport as long as the fighters were evenly matched. As for this bout having been brutal: ". . . when I was in Harvard . . . I suffered heavier punishment." He had been very much in earnest on that March day of 1879 in the Harvard gymnasium. The championship had been a greatly desired goal. An incident within five years after graduation offers proof of this, and also evidence of a curious aspect of Roosevelt's mind. Toward the close of his legislative career, an Albany newspaper requested an autobiographical sketch, and on May 1, 1884, he wrote that he had, at Harvard, "been very fond of boxing, being lightweight champion at one time." Ultimately Roosevelt recalled the facts correctly, but the error is characteristic. Another time, furnishing data for a similar sketch, he said that he was by profession a lawyer although actually he had stopped all study of the law soon after starting it. Other examples of this trait will be seen in subsequent episodes of his life, and they throw light on the belief held by so many that Roosevelt was careless with the truth. It can be demonstrated, I think, that he was not consciously a liar. That he stated facts incorrectly is beyond refutation, but egoism and not mendacity was the motivation. He had wanted very much to be boxing champion, and with the years it seemed impossible to him that he had not really achieved that eminence.

Aside from his boxing, Roosevelt's extracurricular activities at Harvard are of slight importance. He was elected to the *Advocate* editorial board. He belonged to the Natural History Society. He also exhibited momentary interest in the Finance Club, organized by Professor J. Laurence

Laughlin of the department of economics in the hope that the young men of Harvard would find fascination in obscure economic laws.

Other matters were taking up much of Theodore's time as the last half of his college course began. First, there was a girl at Chestnut Hill, the cousin of a classmate, whose beauty had awakened unaccustomed flutterings. Second, he had decided that no adequate history of the War of 1812 had been written and that he would therefore supply the need himself. He began work on it in his senior year.

4

He found other things besides the teaching of science to criticize in the curriculum, such as the uninteresting subjects assigned for treatment in themes and forensics. Looking back from adult years, Roosevelt declared this quite unsound, and contrasted Harvard with his beloved magazine, *Our Young Folks,* "which taught me much more than any of my textbooks." Roosevelt's quarrel with the pedagogical philosophy of the '80's was that it failed to instill into youth "the individual virtues . . . the necessity of character. . . ." Too, there was "almost no teaching of the need for collective action."

It might be deduced from this that Theodore, at twenty, was troubled by vague ponderings over social and political reform, and deeply concerned with the importance of individual and collective morality. This would be untrue. These impulses came later, years later. Like most undergraduates he took many of his courses without knowing why he had done so. He dodged the classes of Henry Cabot Lodge, then an instructor in history, because Lodge demanded too much of his students and graded their papers with undue severity.

Roosevelt was, however, a conscientious worker who maintained a rigid daily routine. During his first year he took the prescribed subjects: Latin, Greek, advanced mathematics, chemistry, and physics. He also sampled French, German, Italian, history, and philosophy. Most men would have forgotten such a smattering of culture before reaching thirty. But Roosevelt's unusual memory enabled him to retain a good deal of it. By voracious reading he added to his store of knowledge; by conversational dexterity he enjoyed a reputation as a man of profound culture. At Harvard he gave indication of competence but not of lead-

26

ership in his studies, and he stood twenty-first in a class of more than one hundred.

Of greater interest is Roosevelt's surprising failure to make human contacts at Harvard. He knew none of his professors or instructors intimately. The records at Cambridge reveal, for example, that the professor in charge of the anatomy class in Theodore's sophomore year was William James. It is true that James was still in his formative stage and had not yet deserted medicine for psychology. Yet Roosevelt, even as an undergraduate, would have found much to delight him in James.

"Isn't it abominable," James demanded of a friend long before Brander Matthews had converted Roosevelt to the perhaps rather foolish reform, "that everybody is expected to spell in the same way? Let us get a dozen influential persons each to spell after his own fashion and so break up this tyranny."

But Roosevelt did not know this rare spirit, nor did he have any but the most casual and official contacts with President Eliot. This, he conceded, had been his own fault.

5

As an upperclassman, a member of important clubs, and a young man of moderate wealth, Roosevelt was a well-known figure in the Harvard Yard. He may not have been popular, but he was pointed out as something of a personage. The metamorphosis from awkward precollege days had proceeded at an amazing rate and now Theodore was, undeniably, a man of fashion. "Please send my silk hat *at once*," was the peremptory demand to his family. "Why has it not come before?" An occasional "By Jove" began to creep into his letters. On an October afternoon in 1879 he was "going to drive Van Rennsaeler over to Chestnut Hill; tomorrow he and I take tea at the Lanes. Wednesday, Harry Shaw and I give a small opera party. Thursday six of us are going to take a four in hand and drive up to Frank Codman's farm, where we shall spend the day, shooting glass balls, etc." He was invited everywhere.

Dispute still rages as to whether Theodore Roosevelt actually drove a dogcart through Cambridge or whether this is merely legend. Wister, two years behind Roosevelt, recalled that he did. He remembered, too, a song written for the 1879 Dickey show in which there were references to Roosevelt: ". . . awful smart, with waxed mustache and hair in curls." His whiskers, which were to reappear during legislative days, had momentarily vanished, causing him to look, Theodore said, "like a dissolute Democrat of the Fourth ward . . . the front views giving me an expression of grim misery." Theodore was overcritical. The portraits of 1879 show a self-satisfied young man with a large mouth and the suspicion of a wave in his hair.

The comparative gaiety of the last two years at Harvard did not cause Roosevelt to neglect a responsibility he had assumed soon after going to Harvard. This was a Sunday-school class at Christ Church in Cambridge. It was an experience not unmarked by friction. The first arose when a boy appeared in class with a black eye, and explained that his small sister had been pinched in the arm by the neighborhood bully. Roosevelt gave the chivalrous youth a dollar, and was soon being criticized for encouraging fighting. In his senior year the rector of Christ Church, an Episcopal institution, learned that Roosevelt was not a member of that exclusive faith but had more common Presbyterian and Dutch Reform leanings. Theodore was asked to subscribe to Episcopalian doctrines, "but this I refused to do, and so I had to leave. I told the clergyman I thought him rather narrow minded."

In one respect, this must have been a relief. The class had taken a good deal of time, particularly since Theodore had been anxious to spend his week ends at Chestnut Hill. Each Sunday, after the service, he had been seen driving swiftly in that direction.

Chapter IV

ESPECIALLY PRETTY ALICE

"I first saw her on October 18, 1878," he wrote, "and loved her as soon as I saw her sweet, fair young face. We spent three years of happiness such as rarely comes to man or woman." So began a memorial to Alice Hathaway Lee of Chestnut Hill, Massachusetts, written by Theodore Roosevelt some time during 1884. She was remembered but rarely mentioned in the thirty-five years that followed.

October 18, 1878, was a week before Theodore's twentieth birthday, at the start of his junior year at Harvard. A good many years afterward he was to remark to his friend, Henry White, that women interested him very little, but this was not true in his boyhood and youth. The small boy traveling in Europe had noted in his diary that he sorely missed a playmate, Edith Carow. In the spring of 1876, while preparing to enter Harvard, he had attended a neighborhood party where he had enjoyed the company of "Annie Murray, a very nice girl, besides being very pretty, ahem!" And at Harvard he wrote of his pleasure in the company of two young ladies, "especially pretty Alice."

A tendency to lead the conversation into dull paths of natural science may have minimized his appeal to girls at first. Cambridge changed this. His intimates of Porcellian found him, though still overenthusiastic about botany and bugs, entirely acceptable. Their sisters, if amused, liked him. As Theodore's junior year ended he had even become a romantic figure; while his classmates worried about examinations and indulged only in sedate flirtations under a Victorian moon, he was in the throes of a turbulent love affair. It was known that he planned to be married immediately after graduation.

He met Alice Lee, that October, at the home of Richard Saltonstall, one of Theodore's closest friends. In November he wrote Conie that with Minot Weld, another intimate, he had driven to the Saltonstalls' home at Chestnut Hill and had "gone out walking with Miss Rose Saltonstall and Miss Alice Lee." Some weeks afterward he escorted Alice through the Harvard Yard and, while pointing out the beauties of the institution, discovered that it was time for lunch. He promptly took his guest to the Porcellian Club, never before polluted by the presence of a woman. The assertion that he did this was published while Roosevelt was alive, in a biography written by Jacob Riis and published with his approval. Presumably Roosevelt would have denied the incident had it been untrue. But no mention of it is found in any of his letters, and only conjecture is possible as to Theodore's reason for such radical conduct. It had been his invariable custom to lunch at the Porc house, and it may never have occurred to him that he was shattering precedent. He may have already been anesthetized by love. He may have believed the rule against women foolish nonsense, for he had strong feminist leanings in those remote days and his senior dissertation was on "The Practicability of Equalizing Men and Women Before the Law."

She walked the stage for so brief a moment, there are so

few who can remember and fewer still who will, that Alice Lee remains a fragment. But only partly. To Theodore she was "beautiful in face and form, and lovelier still in spirit," but she was lovely, too, to those who looked with less prejudiced eyes. It is known that she was seventeen on the October day when they met. She had light brown hair, with a touch of yellow in the sun. She wore it in curls that lay well back, over smaller curls which came down over her high forehead. Her nose tilted ever so slightly; her mouth was small and "peculiarly charming." She was about five feet seven inches in height and this, combined with an erect carriage, made her seem rather tall.

She was the daughter of George C. Lee of Chestnut Hill, and her family tree bore Cabots and Lees and Higginsons on all its branches. When Theodore met her in 1878 she had seen little or nothing of society, and her education had been the ornamentally fashionable one received by young gentlewomen of the day.

2

It was a turbulent courtship. Mrs. Robert Bacon, then sixteen, long recalled a function of the Pudding at which Roosevelt had walked up, had pointed across the room to Alice, and had demanded:

"See that girl? I am going to marry her. She won't have me, but I am going to have *her!*"

Mrs. Bacon remembered, too, that the gentle Alice was alarmed by the impetuosity of the young man who had suddenly precipitated himself into the circle of more decorous beaus. He had an overwhelming, gusty vitality and he insisted that she watch, from the gymnasium balcony, when he made his bid for the lightweight boxing championship. Alice was a little repelled, but wholly intrigued. Besides, there was no way in which she could avoid seeing him had she so desired. Richard Saltonstall, a cousin, was constantly bringing him to the house on week ends. He had a habit of throwing himself into a chair and telling thrilling stories about wolves and bears to her adoring five-year-old brother.

Alice sometimes discouraged the eager Theodore and then he was plunged into the deepest gloom. He was always to suffer periods of discouragement, when everything seemed black. These were moments of despair. One night, during the first winter of the courtship, a classmate telegraphed to New York in alarm that Roosevelt was somewhere in the woods near Cambridge and refused to come home. A cousin who was particularly close hurried up there, managed somehow to soothe him; and soon his confidence returned.

The courtship continued through the winter and spring of 1878-79, with Theodore becoming markedly possessive as the months passed. During the summer, beyond doubt, he wrote long and fervent letters, for it was his unfailing custom to do so on all subjects at all times, in private life as well as when he held office. That he suffered recurring attacks of jealousy is probable, particularly when Alice sent back accounts of picnics and festivities among the boys and girls of Chestnut Hill.

That he had already told his family about Alice is demonstrated by an invitation extended to the girl and her mother to spend the Christmas holidays at Oyster Bay. Theodore's mother seems to have been fond of Alice from the start; nor is this surprising. The young girl and the older woman had much in common. They were gentle and rather quiet. They had charm and grace. Both, for by now Alice's last defenses had been shattered, considered Theodore wholly magnificent. The brief days between Christmas and New Year's Day in 1879 must have been high marks in Theodore's life. He saw Alice, who affected heavy white brocades to set off her fair hair and blue eyes, standing in front of the open fire after dinner; Alice being very feminine, very attentive to the conversation, very timid about taking more than a sip of wine. He saw her, demure in furs and carrying a small muff, while she skated on nearby ponds and leaned deliciously on his strong arms.

Meanwhile, in the Yard, Roosevelt was a marked man. It now became apparent that he was neglecting his editorial duties on the *Advocate* because of more important activities at Chestnut Hill. Rumors of his preoccupation reached even the ears of the cloistered faculty. One morning, in the English and rhetoric class, Professor A. S. Hill, familiarly called "Ass" Hill, read aloud an unusually sentimental essay and cruelly asked Theodore to criticize it. His classmates assumed, from the fact that he blushed, that he was the author. The Dickey show, as far back as the previous year, had commented on his courting as well as on his elegant appearance.

At about this time Roosevelt's interest in the natural sciences began to flag. The evidence is not conclusive. Alice may have expressed distaste for squirrels and birds no longer alive but looking as dead as only an amateur taxidermist could make them look. A fragment of a letter remains, written in July of 1879, in which Theodore told his friend Harry Minot that he had done almost no collecting that summer, that "I don't approve of too much slaughter."

So Alice became his. She was an engaged girl. Her mind turned to the wedding, which had been tentatively set for the following October, and to such pleasant labors as her wedding gown and the countless linens that every young bride of that day considered essential. Theodore, even after the engagement was formally announced, could find no peace. He worried when some classmate, anxious to show polite attention to his fiancée, talked with her at a dance.

"Roosevelt," recalled a member of Alice's family, "seemed constantly afraid that some one would run off with her, and threatened duels and everything else. On one occasion he actually sent abroad for a set of French dueling pistols, and after great difficulty got them through the Custom House."

Theodore's honor was not impugned, however. No blood was shed. He managed to get his degree despite the distractions at Chestnut Hill. He became a Bachelor of Arts, by grace of Harvard College, on June 30, 1880. He took no prominent part in the exercises. Roosevelt did not attempt to begin the pursuit of a career that summer. The estate of his father had made him a young man of means, although not of wealth. There was no need to hurry. Meanwhile, a degree of ill health on Elliott Roosevelt's part offered excuse for a hunting trip that summer. The final note was that the trip had been a great success despite "a succession of untoward accidents and delays. I got bitten by a snake and chucked head foremost out of the wagon."

Then Roosevelt hurried to Chestnut Hill, and the marriage took place at Brookline on October 27, 1880. The day was Theodore's twenty-second birthday, while Alice was nineteen.

3

The honeymoon was delayed, apparently, until next summer, for the young couple went to New York to live with Theodore's widowed mother at No. 6 West Fifty-seventh Street, an address considered uptown and out of the way but which was beginning to be fashionable.

Having abandoned science, Theodore had decided to take up law, and this was the reason for postponing the honeymoon. He was not greatly interested in the law, but it was something to do and so he enrolled at the Columbia Law School and also did some reading in the office of his uncle, Robert Barnhill Roosevelt. The twelve months that followed Roosevelt's marriage constitute a period of uncertainty. He did a little work on his *The Naval War of 1812*, of which a chapter or two had been written at Cambridge. He started to take notice of local politics, also, but here, too, signs of active interest are lacking. He joined the district Republican Club in the fall of 1880 for the reason that "a young man of my bringing up and convictions could join only the Republican Party"; a curious statement, since both his uncle and father-in-law were Democrats. So life drifted, with frequent social affairs in which Alice and his mother were joint hostesses, and with life at home unmarked by the slightest friction between the mother and the daughter-in-law.

A trip to Europe, Theodore's third in less than fifteen years, provided a pleasant diversion during the summer of 1881. With Alice, he was in England in time for spring. They went north into Ireland and set off, one morning, in a jaunting car from Killarney. For a guide they had "a very nice old Irishman" who took them through the Gap of Dunlo and watched with Celtic melancholy their reaction to the Black Valley; "as dreary a place as I ever saw," Theodore wrote, "because of the black mist which rose from the peat bogs." Ireland was a beautiful country, but with an "under-stratum of wretchedness." Roosevelt had seen, for probably the first time in his life, actual hunger. They had run into a man on the Cork road who was weak from starvation and had helped him out with a shilling or two. It had been a depressing ending to the day.

Summer found them in Switzerland, where Theodore had a chance to demonstrate his physical fitness still further by some mountain climbing. Alice was, of course, left behind, for in those days women rarely joined in such strenuous diversions. Her husband seems to have agreed with the current attitude; at least, he does not mention missing Alice's company or express regret that she had not shared with him the majesty of the mountain peaks.

They continued without hurrying and made no attempt to emulate tourists anxious to see all of Europe in thirty days. By August they had been down the Rhine, and Roosevelt wrote to his sister that work on his book had suffered during their travels. He was, in fact, undergoing the discouragements that are the lot of authors. He was, characteristically, wondering whether his inability to get *The*

Naval War of 1812 written did not signify that he was to be a failure in other things. "I have plenty of information," he complained, "but I can't get it into words; I wonder if I won't find everything in life too big for my abilities. Well, time will tell." Fortunately for the progress of this pedantic history, Alice and Theodore spent some weeks with the Bulloch family at Liverpool. There Roosevelt had long conferences with the uncle who had been a captain in the Confederate Navy. Nautical mysteries were clarified. The book went on.

Before crossing the Channel, they had stopped in Paris, where Alice had done the inevitable shopping, and where they had looked at Napoleon's tomb. No longer was Theodore bored, as he had been eleven years before. His interest in war, in manly prowess, had grown. This time he experienced "a solemn feeling" in looking at the bier of "the mightiest conqueror the world ever saw." Then, in revulsion, he added: ". . . otherwise, I suppose, [he] was an almost unmixed evil."

They returned home toward the end of September, with Theodore expecting to continue his law studies. But within a few weeks he found himself the candidate of his party for election to the state legislature. He was soon making stump speeches while his friends alternated between amusement and indignation that a young man of good blood, with opportunity for a legal career before him, should stoop to the gutter of American politics. Alice and Theodore were still making their home with Mrs. Roosevelt, but after Election Day they prepared to move to Albany. He was now the Hon. Theodore Roosevelt, assemblyman-elect from the Twenty-first District.

4

Here, the story of Alice Lee becomes increasingly unsubstantial. It is known that during his first year at Albany, beginning in January, 1882, Roosevelt took rooms in a quasi-hotel where fellow legislators stayed. It is known that Alice was there with him the first winter and also that they returned to New York for most of their week ends. Isaac L. Hunt, an assemblyman from the northern part of the state, remembered her as "a very charming woman, tall and willowy. I was very much taken with her." On the whole, Alice must have been decidedly bored. She had little, if any, interest in politics. There must have been periods that dragged interminably until the summer of 1883. Then she knew that she was to have a baby, and Roosevelt, if his subsequent enthusiasm for quantity production of offspring is any indication, was delighted. Meanwhile, they had taken a house at No. 55 West Forty-fifth Street, and summers were spent at Oyster Bay, where a country home of their own, Sagamore Hill, where she would never live, was being planned.

Alice went into her ordeal cheerfully. She was not too well, but the doctors were suavely reassuring. There was a pleasant fluttering around the house on Fifty-seventh Street, where she spent much of her time while Theodore was at Albany. His sister Conie, who had become Mrs. Douglas Robinson, had a baby son, and the two young women had much in common. Alice enjoyed her new importance. She was playing the only vital part that a woman of her time could play—excepting, of course, the preposterous unsexed creatures who were beginning to talk about votes for women.

Roosevelt had been re-elected in 1882 and it would be necessary for him to campaign again in the fall of 1883. The star of his fame was rising rapidly. But he was tired. The work in the legislature was, "if conscientiously done, very harassing," and the 1884 session would be additionally so, since he was almost certain to become minority leader. Perhaps Roosevelt suffered, too, from a superfluity of feminine activity at home. Consequently, he decided to seek recreation in the West and arrived at Little Missouri, in the Dakota Bad Lands, on the morning of September 7, 1883. Again, he had a delightful time, and it was signally fortunate that he had gone to the Bad Lands during that summer. Less than a year later, when in a single night his life changed utterly, he had a place of refuge. He was back in New York in time to conduct his campaign for the Assembly and was, as usual, returned without difficulty.

As the day of her confinement drew near, Roosevelt's young wife left the house on Forty-fifth Street to stay with her mother-in-law on Fifty-seventh, where an apartment was furnished for her on the third floor. She waited anxiously each week for Friday to arrive, listening for the front door to open and close with a crash. Then she knew that Theodore had returned from Albany after the legislature had recessed for the week end.

The baby was expected about the middle of February and life at the house on Fifty-seventh Street moved on with this uppermost. Alice was happy, if physically wretched. Only one trivial incident is remembered of those weeks of waiting: an afternoon when Alice and Mrs. Roosevelt were to go driving. A member of the family dropped by and found Alice sitting, the personification of patience, in the drawing room on the first floor. She was wearing furs, for it was cold outside. She laughed when asked why she was sitting there. The Little Motherling, she explained, using Theodore's pet name for his mother, was "always late, but not generally so late as this time."

February 13, 1884, was a Wednesday. On the previous Friday Corinne Robinson and her husband had gone to Baltimore, and before leaving Mrs. Robinson had jokingly told Alice that she must not have her baby until they returned. "I promise," she said cheerfully. Conie then said good-by to her mother, who was in bed with what seemed a mild indisposition. On Monday a telegram went to Baltimore stating that no need to hurry home had developed, and so Mr. and Mrs. Robinson delayed their return until Wednesday morning. Then, just before they took the train, there was good news. A girl had been born late on Tuesday night, February 12; the doctors said that Alice had survived the ordeal well. So the journey back to New York was made in high spirits. They reached New York on Wednesday evening, glad that the period of suspense was over and wondering whether Theodore had yet arrived from Albany. Details of reaching New York that evening, quite unnoticed at the time, always remained etched on the minds of Corinne Robinson and her husband. They remembered that fog hung over the Hudson River that night, and that the ferry which brought them from New Jersey was delayed because of it. They went uptown on an elevated railway train and, since there was no reason to hurry, walked from the station to the house. Seeing a light in the window on the third floor, Mrs. Robinson again gave thanks that the baby had been born and that Alice's suffering was behind her. Then she went up the steps. The door opened. Mrs. Robinson saw her brother Elliott standing in the doorway, and knew from his face that something was wrong.

"If you want to see your baby," he said, "do so before you come into this house. He is over at your Aunt Gracie's. There is a curse on this house! Mother is dying, and Alice is dying, too."

It was then about 10:30. An hour later, Roosevelt came in, having been told only that a daughter had been born and having left the Assembly Chamber in the midst of effusive, good-natured congratulations. He found his wife barely able to recognize him, and all that night, save for one

36

brief moment, he sat at the head of the bed and held her in his arms. Just before 3 o'clock in the morning his mother, who had developed typhoid fever, died, and Theodore, standing by her bed, echoed the words of his brother: "There *is* a curse on this house." Then he went back up stairs. Dawn dragged into the next day. At 2 o'clock on February 14, 1884, her body weakened by Bright's disease, Alice died. A year later Roosevelt wrote:

She was born at Chestnut Hill, Massachusetts, on July 29, 1861; I first saw her on October 18, 1878, and loved her as soon as I saw her sweet, fair young face; we were betrothed on January 25, 1880, and married on October 27th, of the same year; we spent three years of happiness such as rarely comes to man or woman; on February 12, 1884, her baby girl was born; she kissed it, and seemed perfectly well; some hours afterward she, not knowing that she was in the slightest danger, but thinking only that she was falling into a sleep, became insensible, and died at two o'clock on Thursday afternoon, February 14, 1884, at 6 West Fifty-seventh Street, in New York; she was buried two days afterward, in Greenwood Cemetery.

She was beautiful in face and form, and lovelier still in spirit; as a flower she grew, and as a fair young flower she died. Her life had been always in the sunshine; there had never come to her a single great sorrow; and none ever knew her who did not love and revere her for her bright, sunny temper and her saintly unselfishness. Fair, pure, and joyous as a maiden; loving, tender, and happy as a young wife; when she had just become a mother, when her life seemed to be but just begun, and when the years seemed so bright before her—then, by a strange and terrible fate, death came to her.

And when my heart's dearest died, the light went from my life for ever.

5

On Saturday morning, February 16, two hearses moved side by side from the home on Fifty-seventh Street to the Fifth Avenue Presbyterian Church at Fifth Avenue and Fifty-third Street. Two rosewood coffins were carried in. The Rev. Dr. John Hall, who had been the family minister for years, could barely control himself as he made a brief address. One of the two women had done her work, he said, but the other was young. It seemed strange that she had been taken away. But Jesus was the Resurrection and the Life. Then he prayed for the husband and the little baby, three days old, and wept.

Theodore Roosevelt sat in a front pew, with Elliott Roosevelt, his father-in-law, and his sisters. The twin hearses moved again. The double interment was in Greenwood Cemetery.

Somehow, Roosevelt went on with his work; if proof were needed that he had courage and an iron will this fact alone would serve. On February 20 he was back at Albany to move for the passage of a reform bill. He stayed there until the end of the legislative session and went to the Republican convention at Chicago that summer, where he saw his opposition to the nomination of James G. Blaine fail. Then he fled to the quiet of the Bad Lands. At Albany, Assemblyman Hunt remembered, "you could not talk to him about it, you could see at once that it was a grief too deep. There was a sadness about his face that he never had before. He did not want anybody to sympathize with him. He hiked away to the wilderness to get away from the world. He went out there a broken-hearted man."

While he was in the West, Roosevelt wrote the memorial to his wife and mother, brief but deeply moving, which was printed in a limited edition and circulated among relatives and close friends. Roosevelt saw the relatives of his first wife whenever he was in Boston and the daughter, who was to become Mrs. Nicholas Longworth, frequently visited them. But if Alice Lee, whom he met on that October day in 1878, was ever mentioned, there is no record of it. A door was closed on the three years during which they lived together, a door that was never opened. There is not a word in the autobiography of Theodore Roosevelt to indicate that she had existed.

In time he may have doubted that she had. In December of 1886 he was married again, to the Edith Carow he had known as a child, and his married life was happy and complete. Five other children came. Four of them married and had children. One, the youngest, fell in an airplane behind the German lines. Honors came to Roosevelt; age came also. Only Alice Lee remains young and does not fade. She is forever fair; a figure on a Grecian urn.

Chapter V

BUTTER AND JAM

*

Roosevelt, while still at Harvard, knew that he must augment his private income after graduation. The estate of his father had to be divided among the four children. Theodore's share cannot be stated with exactness, but in 1880 it probably provided between $7,500 and $10,000 a year. During his days in the New York legislature, and while he was Civil Service Commissioner and Assistant Secretary of the Navy, Roosevelt was always mildly embarrassed for funds.

This was partly because he was reckless in personal financial matters. In later years Edith Carow effected salutary fiscal reforms, but at first Roosevelt was decidedly improvident. He cheerfully invested, out of his comparatively small resources, $20,000 for a limited partnership in G. P. Putnam's Sons. He felt that he wanted to be a publisher.

"He never had any idea where his money went," recalled Major George Haven Putnam. "When he came to us as partner, he gave me a check for $20,000. The check came back from the bank and the clerks said that he had only about half enough cash to meet it."

Fortunately he had an uncle, James A. Roosevelt, who was a banker. On this occasion, Mr. Roosevelt borrowed on his nephew's expectations to meet the overdraft. But as a financier should, he viewed all investments with a skeptical eye, and so he must have been even more irritated by another obligation incurred by the spendthrift Theodore. In September, 1883, on his first visit to the Dakota Bad Lands, Theodore paid $14,000 for a share in a cattle ranch. Most of the cattle died during the bitter winter of 1886-87.

It would have been necessary in any case for Roosevelt to supplement his income: "I had enough to get bread. What I had to do, if I wanted butter and jam, was to provide the butter and jam." By 1894 there were five children. "I am beginning to think," he confessed, "that this particular branch of the Roosevelt family is getting to be numerous enough." But three years later Quentin was born.

The last year and a half at Harvard having been devoted to the pursuit of Alice Lee, Roosevelt found himself in the summer of 1880 without definite ideas on the best way to procure the butter and jam. So he drifted into the study of law, and found that it was not to his taste. That Roosevelt was more popular at the Columbia Law School, or more widely acquainted, than he had been at Harvard, was demonstrated when he ran for the legislature in the fall of 1881. The loyal sons of the institution rallied to his support, as did even the famous Dean Van Amringe, the "old Van Am, with his snow-white hair" of the Columbia ballad. Van Amringe, who chanced to live in Roosevelt's district, offered his services as a campaign orator. He told Joe Murray, in charge as manager, that he would gladly electioneer in "the tough districts." But Murray was dubious about intellectuals in politics. "I am taking care of the tough ones pretty well," he answered. He told the dean that his services would be more valuable if he would work up Roosevelt enthusiasm among his own friends.

In 1913, Roosevelt felt that the innate idealism of youth had inspired his dislike for the law. The "teaching of the law books and of the classroom seemed to me to be against justice," he wrote in his memoirs. The law did not "discourage as it should sharp practice." This was written, however, after Roosevelt had found the law singularly unreceptive to some of his cherished reforms. Roosevelt's opinion of the law and the courts was at a low ebb when his autobiography was being written. It was at about this time that he referred to some jurist of the United States Supreme Court as an "amiable old fuzzy-wuzzy with sweetbread brains." William Howard Taft, who had ample opportunity to understand both Roosevelt's virtues and his faults, once chuckled to Archie Butt that his predecessor "did not like the delay of the law when he felt that the public weal was to be served."

Judge Taft might have gone even further. Sometimes, while President, Roosevelt looked upon the law as an adversary. He boasted of an occasion when a superior court had reversed the conviction of a man who had passed Confederate money. It was not, said the court, counterfeit money, and the man must be released from the penitentiary. A partner in crime, held guilty of the same offense, had failed to file an appeal, but Attorney General Philander Knox requested an order from Roosevelt for his release:

This I promptly refused to issue, and Knox and I then had an argument; he standing for the law and I for primitive justice. Knox's position was that, as the act committed by the man had been declared by the court not to be criminal, I could not keep him in prison. My position was that he was undoubtedly a scoundrel and morally a criminal. I certainly would not let him out of prison and as for saying that I could not keep him in, why, he *was* in, and that was all there was to say about it. I think Knox had the best of the argument as regards the law, but I had the final say-so as to the facts and the man stayed in jail for nearly a year longer.

It is just as well that T.R. abhorred Blackstone.

2

At Harvard, Roosevelt gave a passing thought or two to politics. He read a paper on "The Machine Age in Politics" before an undergraduate club. Soon after his marriage to Alice Lee in the fall of 1880, he joined the Republican district club near his home in New York City, and this caused amused surprise among the members of his family. A cousin, W. Emlen Roosevelt, remembered their reaction:

The Roosevelt circle as a whole has a profound distrust of public life. But we somehow knew that the boy was all-right; he was a boy then. To encourage him, I joined the ranks of the political workers. I dropped out after a year because I did not relish the personnel of that organization. But Theodore stuck to it. He had the personality and the spirit. He was able to impress those people. They didn't really care for him. He fought his way into their ranks.

No great reforms burned in Theodore's breast as he began the career that he was to follow with few interruptions until he died. It started, as so many do, partly by accident. In 1880, Roosevelt was not thinking of public office. A fairly typical New Yorker, he had one characteristic that set him apart. He wanted a hand in everything that was going on. He asked the men whom he knew how one took part in civic affairs. When they told him that this ambition was quite out of the question, that politics was a black trade which would soil the linen of a gentleman, Roosevelt retorted that he "intended to be one of the governing class," whether the men in control were crude or not. Consequently, although an object of suspicion to those who made their living by belonging to the "governing class," he became actively identified with the Twenty-first District Republican Club.

That he did this shows that Roosevelt, then twenty-two years old, had common sense beyond his age. He did not demand, as other youths fresh from the rarefied atmosphere of Harvard might have done, prompt election to the United

States Senate. He started at the bottom, and he was not dismayed by the difficulties. The district leader was Jake Hess, an able gentleman of German extraction who tolerated the reformers of the Union League Club in the hope of campaign contributions. Hess stood by the old-time leaders, and treated Roosevelt "with rather distant affability."

The Twenty-first Assembly District had a mixed population. The residents of the newly fashionable Madison and Fifth avenue areas were included, but so were dwellers of the tenement neighborhoods on the West Side. Having voters of wealth, it was known as the "Diamond Back" district, due to the popular theory that people of blue blood dined nightly on diamondback terrapin. In 1881, the Twenty-first was one of the few districts on Manhattan Island that was safely Republican. This was Roosevelt's first piece of good fortune, since it made election to the legislature possible. It also gave Jake Hess unusual power.

The meeting place of the district club was in a medium-sized room over a saloon at Fifty-ninth Street and Fifth Avenue, the present site of the Savoy-Plaza Hotel. It was furnished with a dais, chairs for about a hundred men, some funereal portraits, and capacious cuspidors, without which Americans of the "governing class" are still unable to think in comfort. Roosevelt doubtless reacted very much as had his cousin Emlen, who had not relished "the personnel of that organization." They were ward heelers, saloonkeepers, a cheap lawyer or two, perhaps a bail-bond shark. It is not difficult to visualize the meetings; men chewing on cigars, telling the type of dirty anecdote that always nauseated Roosevelt. But the young law student did not reveal his disgust. He made a speech or two on civil service reform, anathema to Jake Hess and his followers. In 1881, as later, Roosevelt was considered a dude, an amateur playing the political game for diversion. Yet there was something about him that these men liked despite themselves, and in the first months of his affiliation Roosevelt won the admiration and respect of a Hess Lieutenant named Joe Murray.

In September, 1901, when the death of McKinley precipitated Roosevelt into the White House, various claimants came forward as his political discoverer. The weight of the evidence is on the side of Murray, and Roosevelt gave him full credit in his autobiography. In 1880 Murray was active in the Hess club and in subsequent years, when Roosevelt had patronage to dispense, he was one of the few who could compete with the Rough Riders in obtaining appointment to public office.

"He is the one man I am most anxious to place," Roosevelt remarked in 1902, suggesting a post in the New York Custom House for Joe. "He has been very close to me and he is absolutely straight."

3

Roosevelt's participation in politics was spasmodic until after the summer of 1881, when he returned from abroad with Alice. He had intended to continue at law school that fall. He was putting the finishing touches on his naval history. He had no knowledge of a peculiar situation taking shape in the Twenty-first Assembly District. Jake Hess was troubled. He had been among those opposing the nomination of Garfield, whose days in the White House had been cut short by the assassin Guiteau that summer. Hess was learning with surprise that Chester A. Arthur was to continue the independent policies of President Garfield and that dark days, insofar as Federal patronage was concerned, had arrived. Hess, whose responsibilities included jobs for his loyal workers, had a disgruntled organization to control and he chose this unfortunate period to insist upon the renomination of Richard J. Trimble as assemblyman from the Twenty-first.

Joe Murray saw his opportunity to stage a revolt or, as Roosevelt described it, "to make a drive at Jake Hess." One can only speculate on Murray's real motives. His own explanation was that Trimble had not distinguished himself at Albany, that the "better element" was disgusted with machine methods, and that a stronger candidate had to be found. Then, according to a memorandum that Murray left, he asked Roosevelt whether he would run for the legislature. Roosevelt agreed that Trimble should not be returned, but demurred at his own selection. It would open him to the accusation of having joined the club for the sake of holding office. He said he would attempt to find another candidate, but failed to do so. Murray remarked that Trimble would have to be endorsed after all.

"The next night," Murray recalled, "I met him and he came up and shook hands with me. He said that he would accept."

All that remained was to keep the plan secret; to convert enough supporters to insure Roosevelt's nomination. This Murray did. Hess found that he was already beaten. He bowed to the candidacy of this novice, and gave his cordial support in the campaign.

Election Day was on November 9 that year. Roosevelt was praised by the New York *Times* as a "public-spirited citizen, not an office seeker." He was endorsed by the Council of Reform and other civic organizations, but all this was unimportant. The support that counted was the Republican machine. Roosevelt was sensible enough to place his destiny in the hands of its leaders. Murray became campaign manager and started work on accepted lines. With Hess and their youthful candidate, he undertook a tour of the district. Murray remembered:

We started in a German lager-beer saloon on Sixth avenue. The saloon keeper's name was Carl Fischer. Hess was well acquainted with him. I knew him slightly. We had a small beer and Hess introduces T. R. to Fischer and Fischer says, "By the way, Mr. Roosevelt, I hope you will do something for us when you get up to Albany. We are taxed much out of our proportion to grocers etc., and we have to pay $200 for the privilege."

"Why that's not enough!" said T. R.

After we got out on the sidewalk we came to the conclusion that we had better stop the canvass right then and there. I says, "Mr. Roosevelt, you go see your personal friends. Hess and I will look after this end. You can reach your personal friends, we can't."

Thus ably advised, Roosevelt swept the district.

4

It was all quite sudden. Roosevelt had no program of legislative or social reform beyond the vague one of believing that men of intelligence and honor, who did not seek a living from public office, should take an active part in government. The organization had supported him, but he remained an outsider. When, however, Jake Hess and Joe Murray found that Roosevelt was not a foolish visionary and did not intend to ignore the machine completely, their respect and their friendly attitude increased.

A more self-confident man than Roosevelt might have known, after the first few months had brought striking success, that public life was his destiny. Roosevelt, however, felt that he was fearfully handicapped by his high ideals. The ephemeral nature of his standing with the people became an obsession, almost from the start. It beats like a refrain in minor key through his letters. In April, 1884, after more than three years of signal accomplishment at Albany, he doubted whether anyone realized "the venomous hatred with which I am regarded by the politicians who supported me." After the 1884 presidential campaign he did not "expect to return to politics for many years, if at all."

Roosevelt was young and callow, and he knew very little. He had no sympathy for the aspirations of labor. He had only contempt for the mere acquisition of wealth, and so was not too cordial toward business. As for social legislation, "my attitude was that of giving justice from above."

Certain aspects of the period from 1881 to 1884 are most logically examined apart from Roosevelt's work at Albany. Membership in the legislature was not enough to occupy all of his time and energy. The term normally lasted only from January 1 until the late spring, and the week ended on Friday. The compensation, $1,500 a year, did little to make possible the "butter and jam" he intended to have. He planned to earn the money by writing. But "writing is horribly hard work to me," he confessed, and the returns were meager.

The Naval War of 1812 was published in 1882, and was favorably reviewed in the New York press. That it was a first-class study, scrupulously fair toward Great Britain as well as the United States, was indicated when the English publishers of Clowes's *History of the Royal Navy* invited Roosevelt to contribute the section dealing with the War of 1812. The history became a leading reference work on the second war with Great Britain and no student of the period can ignore it even today. The research gave Roosevelt his first interest in naval matters and was of great value when he became Assistant Secretary of the Navy.

His restlessness continued to seek further outlets though. One of them was the New York National Guard. Roosevelt was commissioned a second lieutenant in B Company of the Eighth Regiment on August 1, 1882. On February 3, 1883, he was promoted to a captaincy. T.R. was to advance this military record as a reason for being allowed to organize the Rough Riders in the Spanish War, and in his autobiography he insisted that three years of service with the regiment had been invaluable. It is to be doubted, however, that the National Guard in 1883 was an effective military unit. In June of that year, *Puck* described a drill in Union Square:

About 10 o'clock in the evening, there was a great rolling of drums, and a handful of undersized and slouchy men in uniforms trotted on the Plaza north of Union Square and proceeded to execute some strange maneuvers which, had there been anything like unanimity in the party, might have been taken for a military drill. But there was nothing military about the performance. The leaders, with much noise and exertion, got the men into two long, wavering lines and marched them back and forth. It looked like two snakes trying to roll down-hill. Every now and then someone cried "Halt!" and this took the lines by surprise, and they piled themselves up in irregular stacks. A man with a high, clear voice stood on the pavement and explained: "It's the Eighth Regiment, National Guard."

If Roosevelt was present at this exhibition, *Puck* made no mention of it.

It might have been better if the legislature had taken more of Roosevelt's time. At Harvard he had been taught "the *laissez-faire* doctrines—one of them being free trade"; in 1882 he was so indiscreet, in view of his political future, as to join the New York Free Trade Club. The association did not last for long, and it remained as virtually the only skeleton in Roosevelt's closet—to emerge and dismay him when he supported the high-tariff principles of the Republican party. One of the purposes of the organization was "the reduction of duties on raw materials."

On May 28, 1883, Roosevelt attended a dinner of the club and spoke on "The Tariff in Politics." He had been warned, he said, that it was political suicide to commit himself to free trade, and he expressed gratification that he was not dependent upon public office for his livelihood. As soon as important differences arose between himself and his constituents, he would gladly retire. As for the tariff, the success of free trade was only a matter of time. The present policy could not continue. The ultimate goal must be a tariff for revenue only. Obviously, Roosevelt had no national yearnings in 1883. A year later, when the club held its annual dinner, his name was not among those present. By then, he was planning to attend the Republican National Convention of 1884. He had begun a lifelong policy of evasion on the tariff.

His true profession began on January 2, 1882, the start of his first term in the legislature.

Chapter VI

I ROSE LIKE A ROCKET

The afternoon of December 31, 1881, at Albany varied but little from countless such afternoons lost in history. In 1881

the Delavan House was the gathering place for the honorable gentlemen who made laws for the sovereign state of New York. It was a Saturday. Outside it was snowing; the dry, sifting snow of a region inland from the sea. At about 5 o'clock a young man, wearing neither overcoat nor gloves, hurried through the lobby toward the cigar stand where a group of legislative correspondents loitered. They saw that he had sideburns, that his hair was sandy and his eyes blue, that his teeth were prominent when he smiled. They recognized Theodore Roosevelt. Roosevelt knew one or two of the reporters. He shook hands with them and doubtless they briefly discussed the oncoming session. But what he said was not important enough to justify space in the next day's dispatches.

The chance that Roosevelt would make himself known at Albany was remote. So many young aspirants had arrived only to sink into obscurity, and this one seemed peculiarly unfit as legislative material. In addition to his origin among New Yorkers of moderate wealth, he was a Harvard man. He wore eyeglasses on the end of a black silk cord. In brief, he was a dude; that creation born of American inferiority toward Great Britain. Even Isaac L. Hunt, who was also a new member and who fought at Roosevelt's side in many a battle, was to recall him as "a joke, a dude [in] the way he combed his hair, the way he talked—the whole thing."

It was an era when good manners were open to suspicion, and when the ability to speak grammatical English caused sarcastic comment. Virile men were rough men, who did not change their linen oftener than once a week. Undeniably, Roosevelt had a feeling for clothes, based on the exhibitionism that was part of his character. The young man, not yet twenty-four, was a decided novelty to his colleagues. His voice was high. He would call out, from the floor of the lower house, "Mr. Speak-ah! Mr. Speak-ah!" with such shrill determination that it made recognition imperative. He was filled with high purpose, although vague as to details. His curiosity caused him to sniff into everything and everybody crossing his path. At an early party caucus Roosevelt bolted over to Hunt, who represented a rural constituency.

"My name is Theodore Roosevelt," he said. "What's yours? You come from the country, don't you?"

Assemblyman Hunt was faintly annoyed, being "a little sensitive about being thought a countryman." However, he answered the avalanche of questions that followed.

Roosevelt's first speech in the lower house was on January 24, 1882. He spoke, Hunt remembered, "as if he had an impediment in his speech, sort of as if he were tongue-tied. But what he said was all right." On this occasion it concerned the efforts of the Democratic majority in the Assembly to elect their Speaker. The matter had been debated for three weeks, while the other business waited. Finally it was suggested that the Republicans, in the name of efficiency, join forces with the independents, but Roosevelt protested. The quarrel, he said, injured no one. The citizens of New York did not object to delays at Albany; if anything, they were pleased. The speech was duly noted in the New York *Sun* the next morning:

Young Roosevelt of New York made his maiden effort as an orator . . . he said that it was a family quarrel and the Republicans ought not to interfere. He had talked with conspicuous men in commercial and financial circles, he said, and they did not care whether the deadlock was broken or not.
"In fact," he said, "they felt r-a-t-h-e-r r-e-l-i-e-v-e-d."

But the legislators and newspaper correspondents, if they found Roosevelt amusing, conceded that he was active, that he was a striking exception to the usual young reformer. For his own part, he noted in a briefly kept diary, the legislative work was, at first, "both stupid and monotonous."

2

As his service in the legislature drew to a close in April, 1884, Roosevelt declared that his head had not been turned "by what I well know was mainly accidental success." That chance had been a factor in his rise was true. The disturbed situation in his local New York district had made possible his nomination in November, 1881. The lack of leadership at Albany in 1882 made his independence effective.

Roscoe Conkling had passed from power and Tom Platt himself, his reputation damaged by gossip of an unhappy incident in an Albany hotel, was also under an extremely black cloud. The situation was national; division between the Stalwart and Half-breed wings of the party had been causing dissension for years. It had been aggravated by enmity between James G. Blaine and Conkling, an enmity which never died after Blaine had accurately described Conkling's "haughty disdain, his grandiloquent swell, his majestic, supereminent, overpowering, turkey-gobbler strut." It was to end in the defeat of Blaine for the presidency in 1884 and the election of Grover Cleveland.

Both Platt and Conkling had desired the presidential nomination in 1876, and Rutherford B. Hayes had been a compromise candidate. They worked for the national ticket, of course; politicians—as Theodore Roosevelt soon learned—suppress their individual rancor during a campaign. But their enthusiasm was restrained. Save that he had voted for Garfield in 1880 and was morally aligned against the Platt-Conkling coalition, Roosevelt was not directly concerned with the national situation. It was the confused tangle in New York State that made possible his swift rise. Dreary days for the Republican party had begun in 1874 with the election of Samuel J. Tilden as governor. In 1879, Tammany Hall broke with the independent Democrats and Alonzo B. Cornell, a Republican, became governor. Yet the G.O.P. soon lost control of the legislature.

Amid such political confusion almost anything might happen, and a good deal did. Roosevelt, as soon as he had opportunity to identify his fellow legislators, found several other independent spirits. A partnership was formed with Hunt, who came from Jefferson County, with William T. O'Neill, another rural member, and with "Mike" Costello, an anti-Tammany Democrat. These three were allies in most of the struggles that brought Roosevelt to the attention of the public. They were greatly aided by George Spinney, legislative correspondent for the New York *Times* and in full sympathy with them. Without these four men, he might have failed, because in 1882 Roosevelt was particularly excitable, impatient to a degree that might have wrecked his career. In 1923 Hunt and Spinney recalled those days while a stenographer took down their remarks:

Hunt: He was the most indiscreet guy I ever met. Half the time George [Spinney], Billy O'Neill and I used to sit on his coattails. Billy O'Neill would say to him: "What do you want to do that for, you damn fool; you will ruin yourself and everybody else!"

Spinney: He was the leader, and he started over the hill, and here his army was, following and trying to keep him in sight.

Hunt: Yes, trying to keep him from rushing into destruction.

Spinney: If it had not been for you and Billy O'Neill, he would certainly have done some things most impulsively.

Hunt: He was the most impulsive human being I ever knew.

Roosevelt was fortunate in the associates that he chose. The success of any assemblyman depended, however, upon the committee assignments he received, and he was lucky in this also. An uncle, Robert Barnhill Roosevelt, was an influential Democrat in New York City. Before the session started he asked Michael C. Murphy, the Democratic chairman of the important City Affairs Committee to keep an eye on his impetuous nephew. This Murphy did, and also became deeply attached to the young man who opposed him on nearly every measure under debate. His seat was close by. His fatherly, "Now, Theodore . . ." was frequently heard. Of chief importance, however, was Murphy's influence with the Democratic Speaker of the Assembly. This resulted in Roosevelt's assignment to the City Affairs Committee.

3

It was fortunate for Roosevelt's political future that his diary jottings, as his legislative career began, did not leak into print. The "average Catholic Irishman . . . represented in this Assembly," young T.R. declared, "is a low, venal, corrupt and unintelligent brute," and the "average Democrat here seems much below the average Republican." A fortnight later he wrote down further, more specific, details regarding their deplorable characters. These and other forthright observations remained buried for decades, however. Until March, 1882, Roosevelt was known at Albany chiefly because of his eccentricities.

But on the morning of March 30, 1882, the name of Theodore Roosevelt appeared on the first pages of newspapers throughout the state. Plump businessmen, on their way to their offices, shook their heads in misgiving. On the previous afternoon Roosevelt had offered a resolution setting forth that charges had been made against former Attorney General Hamilton Ward and state Supreme Court Justice T. R. Westbrook. These related to their "official conduct [regarding] suits brought against the Manhattan Railway." The accusations had never been refuted. Since it was "of vital importance that the judiciary of this State shall be beyond reproach," the Judiciary Committee of the Assembly ought to investigate and report at the earliest possible moment.

"It was like the bursting of a bombshell," recalled Hunt. ". . . a dead silence fell on the whole Assembly for a while." The resolution had no sooner been offered than several members were on their feet demanding that it be tabled without consideration.

The incident marked Roosevelt's emergence from the ranks of fledgling assemblymen. Behind the resolution he had offered was a large amount of able work. The Westbrook scandal, as it became known, had been simmering since December. Headlines in the New York *Times* had pointed to "The Stock-Jobbing Scandal of the Elevated Railroad," and the articles under them declared that Jay Gould, Russell Sage, and Cyrus W. Field had obtained control of the Manhattan Elevated Railway Company by depressing its securities. Attorney General Ward, whose term had expired on December 31, 1881, had abandoned a suit started by the state to brand the action illegal. Judge Westbrook had aided in the scheme by holding court in the private offices of the stock speculators.

Roosevelt visited the offices of the *Times,* where Henry Loewenthal, the city editor, gave him the evidence in the possession of the newspaper. Various letters were placed in the young legislator's hands and in one of these, addressed to Gould, Westbrook had promised to "go to the very verge of judicial discretion" to aid him. In the receivership proceedings in which the Manhattan Railway had become involved, two Gould henchmen were named by Westbrook as receivers. Thus fortified, Roosevelt returned to Albany and drafted the resolution calling for an inquiry.

Organization members of neither party desired to see an examination of the activities of Gould or Westbrook. On April 5, however, Roosevelt spoke for some minutes, emphasizing the strange conduct of the former attorney general and the Supreme Court justice. He was aware that the demand for an investigation should have been made "by a man of more experience than myself," but no one had arisen for that purpose. His speech was received in silence. Then Thomas G. Alvord, a Republican who had been Speaker the year that Roosevelt was born, got up with an air of kindly tolerance. Delay was essential, he said, so that the Honorable Gentleman from the Twenty-first would have opportunity to ponder the wisdom of his action.

That night Roosevelt's speech was the main topic of discussion in the Delavan House lobby. The forces allied against righteousness, as he would later have described them, made plans to block passage of the resolution and the Tammany members prepared to work with the Republican Old Guard.

"By Godfrey," Roosevelt sputtered, "I'll get them on the record yet."

Six days later, he did. Editorial approbation of the resolution had been too much for the organization men. The resolution was adopted and the Judiciary Committee began its hearings in the St. James Hotel in New York City. That its findings would be a vindication of the Gould interests was apparent at once. The majority report insisted that there had been no wrongdoing.

But Roosevelt's reputation had been made. He was no longer a society man and dude. The New York *Evening Post* declared that "Mr. Roosevelt accomplished more good than any man of his age and experience has accomplished in years." On June 12, 1882, there was a dinner in his honor at Delmonico's at which Roosevelt voiced a good many bromides about "pluck, honesty and private morality in public life."

If Roosevelt was well pleased with himself, there was basis for it. "I rose like a rocket," he subsequently confided to his son Ted. "I was reëlected next year by an enormous majority in a time when the Republican Party as a whole met with great disaster." Thereupon, he candidly added, he had lost his sense of proportion and was far less valuable during 1883.

The interests he opposed decided that Roosevelt was dangerous to their welfare. They made efforts to ensnare him with women and thereby ruin him. These enemies, whoever they may have been, were more vicious than astute. They could not have used worse bait. One night, during the height of the Westbrook excitement, Roosevelt was in New York, walking toward his home, when a woman fell to the pavement in front of him. He placed her in a cab, but he became suspicious when she asked him to escort her to where she lived. Instead, he paid the driver and made note of the address. Detectives later learned that several men had been waiting to confront him.

4

Although in 1882 he had few illusions regarding the party to which he belonged, Roosevelt supported Charles J. Folger, the Republican candidate for governor. Folger was a distinguished jurist, but public discontent and the festering feud between the two wings of the party sent Grover Cleveland to Albany with a majority of 192,854 votes. Roosevelt's record of the previous year, combined with preponderant Republican strength in the Twenty-first District, made his own re-election foreordained. In a campaign speech he promised again to carry "private morality into public office." Roosevelt had no forebodings of the crisis that the rise of Cleveland was to cause in his own soul, or that in little more than a year he would be forced to choose between party discipline and his private conceptions of morality.

The records do not bear out Roosevelt's confession that he was less effective in 1883 because of undue self-satisfaction. It is true that he was more quiet. The Democratic majority had been increased by Cleveland's victory and greater harmony between the Tammany and anti-Tammany wings prevailed. But when the balloting for Speaker, the most important office in the state aside from that of governor, took place, Roosevelt was his party's choice. Election was impossible, due to Democratic control, but he automatically became minority leader. It was a distinction virtually without precedent for one so young.

The degree to which Roosevelt and Cleveland worked together has been exaggerated. By the time Cleveland became a presidential probability, and a threat to Republican rule in national affairs, Roosevelt had convinced himself that the governor was corrupt. On several major matters, however, they did have common views. The first was opposition to a bill to reduce the fare on the New York City elevated railroads from ten to five cents. It was one of the familiar "strike bills," so named because its purpose was to extort bribes from the traction interests in return for negative votes.

Cleveland could not be dissuaded that the bill was flagrantly unconstitutional. He refused to play to the gallery and killed it with his veto. Roosevelt was no less courageous. He was recorded against the bill.

The assassination of Garfield by a disappointed office seeker had accelerated demands for civil service reform. Cleveland, in his annual message, sponsored the program of the Civil Service Association of New York. He knew, however, that the Tammany delegation would combine with the machine Republicans to block, as Tom Platt phrased it, "the impossible civil service reform system." If the change was to come, the independents of both parties would have to fight for it, and the governor called Roosevelt, O'Neill, Hunt, and one or two other assemblymen to his office. A bill establishing the merit system was introduced early in 1883. Hunt contrived to get it out of the Judiciary Committee, and the politicians were too timid to oppose it on the floor. So it was passed.

It had been apparent from the beginning of his term that Cleveland could not work with Tammany. By October, 1883, he had broken with the New York City Democratic organization. Again, the truism that party quarrels alone bring defeat was proved. On Election Day the Republican party, welded into momentary unity by bitter adversity, regained control of both houses of the legislature. Thereupon, Roosevelt began a vigorous campaign for elevation to the post of Speaker.

Like his canvass for the mayoralty of New York City in 1886, this was one of Roosevelt's defeats. It was as 1884 approached, rather than in 1883, that Roosevelt gave way to self-satisfaction. In December he toured the rural districts to obtain backing for the speakership. The city-bred assemblyman found campaigning in the hinterlands a novel experience. One cold November evening he arrived at Garbuttsville, a small village in Monroe County, in search of Assemblyman Philip Garbutt, after whose forebears the place had been named. It was dark. No cabs were visible at the railroad station, so he trudged up the winding road to find that the assemblyman was not in. According to a contemporary account, the women of the Garbutt household were somewhat alarmed by the stranger who stood at their door: ". . . his eye-glasses and New York accent might have been the make-up of a bunko steerer or other predatory person." They hastily told Roosevelt that the Honorable Garbutt had left the house a moment before; if he hurried, he might overtake his man. So Roosevelt, whose bad eyesight made it difficult for him to recognize anything, stumbled over the country road in the dark looking for a rig pulled by "a sorrel horse with a white spot on his forehead." After hailing team after team with a "Hello, there!" he found his man and obtained a promise of support.

"I don't like to boast," he said as the party caucus for Speaker drew near, "but I think my chances are good." His campaign was a plea for harmony between the opposing Republican factions, and his friends were on hand at Albany immediately after Christmas, 1883, to arrange the last details. Undoubtedly, Roosevelt talked too much. Perhaps the machine leaders never intended to permit so young a man to become Speaker and thereby increase his standing among the independent voters. The party caucus was held on New Year's Eve, and Assemblyman Titus Sheard of Herkimer County was chosen for the office.

"This will not be a happy New Year to the exquisite Mr. Roosevelt," said the New York *Sun*. "But Mr. Roosevelt is young and Time is a kind physician."

Time was rather exactly that.

5

In Roosevelt's final year he did useful work at Albany, but the accomplishments were overshadowed by the sorrows of the death of his bride and his mother. His demands for an investigation of the city government in New York resulted in the appointment of a committee. Roosevelt was made chairman and at the hearings which followed he learned much that was useful in future years. For one thing, he came into contact with police methods and qualified himself for the post on the Police Board that he was to hold a decade later.

Other incidents of 1884 are more revealing. Roosevelt's attitude toward labor legislation indicates that he was both ignorant and prejudiced, that the doctrines of the upper middle class still dominated him. He had little sympathy for the groping aspirations of labor to better its condition by organizing. He had no sympathy, either, for laws that sought to remedy other social abuses. It is true that Samuel Gompers, who was laying a foundation for the American Federation of Labor, obtained his support for a bill to abolish work in the tenements. As a member of the City Affairs Committee, Roosevelt investigated conditions in tenement sweatshops. When he saw cigars being manufactured amid filth and disease, he was revolted by it and demanded that it be stopped. His indignation, however, did not spring from concern over the predicament of the workers; he looked at the problem in terms of public health. It was the correct attitude of a well-bred young gentleman.

Roosevelt's real feeling toward labor legislation became obvious when he spoke on a bill to forbid streetcar employees from working more than twelve hours a day. He opposed the measure on principle. It demonstrated the spread of communistic ideas. The law of supply and demand, he explained, could no more be repealed than could the law of gravitation. It was un-American for the streetcar conductors and motormen to demand such protection; no men who asked to be coddled by law were worthy of their sex. In all this, Roosevelt merely echoed the best sentiment of his day. The previous year, when sociologists called for abolition of contract labor and conditions of virtual slavery in state prisons, he had disclaimed "maudlin sympathy for convicts." So, also, he had opposed increasing the pay of New York City firemen to $1,200 a year, as well as pensions for teachers in the city schools.

On such matters, Roosevelt had done little thinking, although he was to ponder on them at length in the years ahead. In 1884, continuing as best he could with his legislative work but thinking of Alice Lee, he was conscious that his political horizon was beginning to expand. During most of the session he was preparing for an occasion that was to mark, although he did not know it, the turning point in his life. He was to choose between being a nice young man in politics and a professional politician. He decided to become, if never quite wholly, a professional. The Republican National Convention of 1884, to be held at Chicago in July, was his major interest.

Chapter VII

PRACTICAL POLITICIAN

✳

It was not a harmonious gathering which assembled at Utica, New York, on April 22, 1884, to select delegates for the approaching Republican National Convention. Roosevelt would again benefit from party discord.

T.R., as a delegate to the state convention from the Twenty-first District, was exceedingly busy. It was rumored that he nursed a personal grudge against the leaders who favored either Blaine or Arthur for the presidential nomination and that he proposed to defeat their plans. It was further rumored that he had joined forces with another foolish visionary, Henry Cabot Lodge of Massachusetts, to nominate Senator George F. Edmunds of Vermont for the presidency.

That Roosevelt had plans and possibly aspirations in the field of national politics had been demonstrated during recent weeks. In January, for example, he abandoned completely his ill-considered advocacy of a tariff for revenue. He said that "anything approaching a free trade platform is certain to be defeated." The influence of the East alone was enough to bring repudiation to any party that favored it.

Roosevelt was still an object of suspicion. But he was greeted with applause when he took his seat as the state convention opened on April 23. Before the end of the day he had been named a delegate at large from New York to the national convention, and this in the face of his announced preference for Edmunds. Before the convention adjourned he had shaken an excited fist in the face of United States Senator Warner Miller of New York, who was on record for Blaine.

The incident is a key to the motivation for Roosevelt's conduct on other, more important occasions. Only twice, in all the years of his political activity, did he seriously contemplate breaking the bonds which held him to the Republican party. The first time was in 1884, after the Chicago convention had nominated Blaine, whose record he had described as "decidedly mottled." The other time was in 1912. In 1884 he remained within the party, after considerable anguish of soul.

Only a forced parallel can be drawn between the two situations, yet the impulses in 1884 and in 1912 were identical. Roosevelt acted from personal considerations, not from principle. The statement is made in analysis and not in criticism. Roosevelt had been planning revenge on the machine for rejecting his candidacy for the speakership. His opportunity came at the state convention when four delegates at large for the national convention were chosen. Two main factions prevented harmony; one seeking a term in his own right for President Arthur and the other favoring Blaine. A small group of independents objected to the nomination of either, and so could be swung to some other candidate.

Edmunds was incidental; as far as can be learned Roosevelt had never met him. But Senator Miller, his hated enemy, was for Blaine. Roosevelt exhorted the independents and the less enthusiastic Arthur men to throw their support to the Vermont Senator. By gradual metamorphosis, characteristic of his career, the advocacy of Edmunds became a righteous cause. His rage when the Vermont Senator was defeated at Chicago nearly caused him to break with his party.

2

Roosevelt possessed to an unusual degree the political asset of self-hypnosis. Without it he could not have labored for the success of the ticket in 1884; indeed, he could hardly have continued his affiliation with the Republican party. The stench of scandal and corruption had permeated the party for years. It had been so since the Civil War. The ghastly struggle had demonstrated, among other things, that this was to be an industrial nation. Soon the fires that never burned out and the clouds of smoke that no winds could dispel marked a dozen booming cities between the Atlantic and the Rockies. An unprecedented era of railroad expansion began. Adventurous promoters risked all they had; and sometimes won and sometimes lost. But smart men, risking nothing, profited the most. They began the alliance between big business and politics, an alliance that was to flourish undisturbed until the voice of Bryan echoed the grievances of millions in the West. When occasional complaints arose, if the farmer or the laborer protested, the politicians were commanded again to wave the bloody shirt, to point to the glories of the war to free the slaves, and to send another well-intentioned and easily misled major general to Congress or the White House itself.

The historian Rhodes felt that Blaine had "probably prostituted his position as Speaker of the House for the purpose of making money." Doubtless, he had. Yet Blaine, even if all the accusations were true, was a gentle sinner compared with certain other members of his party. These scoundrels were forgotten wholly by Roosevelt, who also convinced himself in time that Blaine was honest enough to be President of the United States, and campaigned in his behalf.

The Chicago convention was devoid of enthusiasms. Blaine had greatly desired the nomination in former years, but now even he was none too eager. He feared defeat. He attempted to persuade General William T. Sherman to become a candidate, but that explosive warrior retorted that he would be "a fool, a madman, an ass, to embark anew, at sixty-five years of age, in a career that may at any moment become tempest-tossed by the perfidy, the defalcation, the dishonesty or neglect of any one of a hundred thousand subordinates." He would have none of it, and for once men believed that a presidential nomination could sincerely be spurned.

Prospect of a Democratic victory, with Cleveland as the candidate, hung over the Chicago gathering. Innumerable dark horses were trotted out and their fine points declaimed by their managers. Edmunds of Vermont received the most attention because Roosevelt, Lodge, and others were his noisy backers. He was a curious figure to win Roosevelt's support. He was devoted to the theory that "this is a government of law, not of men," whereas Roosevelt always believed it a government of men, and not of law. But Edmunds was eligible for the nomination. He had no enemies. He was unique among the political figures of his day because scandal had never touched him. Campaign press agents might have been able to do something with Edmunds. He was a man of "pure morals," of simple tastes, who believed in a sound currency and a high tariff, whose career in the United States Senate had been admirable but not colorful.

Fundamentally, that is to say politically, Roosevelt was not a major figure at the convention which assembled in Chicago on June 3, 1884. He was, however, very conspicuous. Everyone knew who he was. Everyone was filled with admiration or indignation or scorn as he rushed about in behalf of the austere Senator whose candidacy he supported. Memories were born at Chicago. The path of Roosevelt first crossed the trails of men he was to meet again in the busy years ahead. Nicholas Murray Butler was there—"Nicholas Miraculous," as Roosevelt was to call him, until finally they differed and their friendship cooled. Joseph B. Foraker of Ohio was on hand to recall with irritation in his memoirs the impression that Roosevelt made. Another Ohioan, Congressman William McKinley, was sharing a hotel suite with Marcus Alonzo Hanna, a Cleveland businessman who admired him greatly but saw no presidential possibilities as yet. To all of these men, whether they sympathized with his convictions or not, Roosevelt in 1884 was merely a lively young man exuding idealistic notions.

3

So the Grand Old Party, which had boasted of his virtues through a thousand campaign orations, assembled at noon on June 3, 1884, and once more claimed the heritage of the sad-eyed Lincoln, whose flag-draped portrait looked down from its quadrennial place of honor on the platform. The selection of a temporary chairman was the first order of business. Cabot Lodge nominated Thomas R. Lynch, a Negro from Mississippi, an unusual member of his race then to be in politics, for he had integrity and honor. Immediately, from the center of the New York delegation, came a falsetto demand for attention, and Roosevelt was recognized. He tossed aside a straw hat, scrambled to his chair and insisted that "the great Republican Party [which] nominated Abraham Lincoln of Illinois choose to preside one of that race whose right to sit within these walls is due to the blood and treasure so lavishly spent by the founders of the Republican Party." Lynch was elected by 427 votes to 385.

The next two days were uneventful, although Roosevelt continued to visit various delegations to plead the cause of Edmunds. On June 5, came the platform, boasting of the accomplishments of the party. It emphasized "purity in legislation, integrity and strict accountability in all departments of the Govermnent, the elevation of labor, legislation [another genuflection to the Negro vote] such as will secure to every citizen, of whatever race or color, the full and complete exercise of all civil and political rights." The platform called for a high tariff, the gold standard, railroad regulation, extension of civil service reform, and the rest of the panaceas offered every four years. The New York *Times,* which was still a Republican journal, called the platform an "insincere and senseless hodge-podge." Even the gold plank was dishonest.

On June 6, on the fourth ballot, Blaine was nominated. The Edmunds vote had started at 93 and had dwindled to 41. Word flashed through the country that the "Plumed Knight" had become his party's candidate for President. Roosevelt left the convention hall in a towering rage, and Democratic leaders in a hundred cities decided, though they hated Cleveland and distrusted his party loyalty, that the governor of New York offered the long-sought chance for victory that fall. That there would be a revolt against Blaine became apparent immediately. How widespread would it be? What would Roosevelt the reformer, the hope of the independent voters, the new influence in American public life, do?

His first public action was to issue the stilted statement of the politician:

To say that I am satisfied with the nomination of Mr. Blaine would be false. I have participated in a Republican Convention, and by all the usages of the party, I would be expected to support the nominee. I should suppose, from what I have heard many independents say, that they would not give Mr. Blaine any support whatever; and I believe they will keep their promise.

4

The rebellion began, appropriately, in Boston. On June 7, the Massachusetts Reform Club heard Charles Francis Adams, Jr., express the hope that the Democratic party would nominate Cleveland. Another meeting was held in the nation's intellectual capital on June 13, when President Eliot of Harvard and William Lloyd Garrison supported resolutions censuring the Massachusetts delegation because it had not stood firm against Blaine. Dr. Eliot wished that a new political party would be formed, "a party of principle." On June 18, the independents met in New York City, with Carl Schurz, Thomas Nast, George William Curtis, J. Henry

Harper of *Harper's Weekly,* George Haven Putnam, and Henry Holt among the more prominent protestants. Roosevelt must have been perplexed as he read this list; another who was present was his old supporter, Dean Van Amringe of Columbia.

Meanwhile the New York *Times,* which in March, 1884, had regarded "a Democratic Administration, no matter who might be its nominal head, with very serious apprehension," declared that it could not tolerate Blaine for reasons "perfectly well understood by everybody." Among the other influential journals that turned from Blaine were the New York *Herald,* the Brooklyn *Union,* the Rochester *Post-Express,* the Boston *Advertiser,* the Boston *Transcript,* the Springfield (Massachusetts) *Republican,* and the Chicago *News.*

Certainly no young man beginning a political career ever found himself in a sadder position than Roosevelt in June, 1884. These were dark days, indeed. He had to suffer the contempt of those who had been his closest friends. Why did he not express his scorn for the party nominee? Instead, left Chicago almost stealthily for his ranch in the Dakotas. His friends heard nothing until one of the press associations circulated an interview, given in St. Paul, Minnesota, on the morning of June 10. It seemed unbelievable, and the New York *Times* refused to print it. It quoted Roosevelt as saying that he would support the candidate, that "I have been called a reformer, but I am a Republican."

The New York *Evening Post* promptly telegraphed Roosevelt to ask whether this was genuine, and on June 12 he answered that he had said nothing "for publication," that the dispatch was erroneous. So the perplexity continued.

That October, after Roosevelt's support of Blaine had become known, Horace White of the *Evening Post* wrote a letter to the New York *Times.* At midnight on June 6 at Chicago, said White, he had been drafting a dispatch predicting a revolt against Blaine. As he was doing so, Roosevelt came in and read what he had written. Was it, White asked, strong enough?

"No," answered Roosevelt. "If I were writing it I would say that any proper Democratic nominee will have our hearty support."

The White letter was widely reprinted, and Roosevelt soon disavowed its contents.

I utterly fail to recognize my own words. I fully realized that I did not wish to commit myself in the excitement of the moment and therefore positively refused to say anything in public until I had carefully considered the matter.

There is no possible doubt that Roosevelt was disgusted with the nomination of Blaine. He wrote to his sister, en route to his ranch, that "the voice of the people might be the voice of God in fifty-one cases out of one hundred; but in the remaining forty-nine it is quite as likely to be the voice of the devil, or what is still worse, the voice of a fool."

The matter is barely mentioned in his autobiography; merely that Blaine had been the choice of the party and merited support. The most detailed explanation was offered by Cabot Lodge; that he had conferred with Roosevelt in New York City in May of that year. They both agreed, according to Lodge, that it was their duty, whatever the outcome at Chicago, to work for the candidates selected.

Lodge denied that he influenced Roosevelt; to have refrained, however, would have taken unusual self-control. Lodge was then chairman of the Massachusetts State Committee and a candidate for Congress. A bolt would have been fatal to him in 1884; defection on Roosevelt's part alone would have hurt his prospects. It is, at least, significant that Roosevelt's first definite statement followed a hurried journey east and a conference with Lodge at Boston. He announced on July 19, 1884, his party fidelity.

So great was the excitement that the staid Boston *Transcript* abandoned its customary reserve and issued an extra. When it appeared that Roosevelt had already made up his mind, he was branded a "backsliding reformer, [who] in attempting to fly off on the wings of his ambition has met with a terrible fall!" The virulence of the rebels may have done much to cement Roosevelt's faith in the justification for the position that he took. His hatred for the Mugwumps, as they were called, lasted through life. They became, in his eyes, futile and wrong-headed, even effeminate. "The bolt is very large among the dudes," he confided to Lodge in July. Such men as Putnam and E. L. Godkin of the *Nation* were suffering "from a species of moral myopia, complicated with intellectual strabismus."

In short order, a monopoly of righteousness was held by those who campaigned for Blaine.

5

By midsummer, Roosevelt grew confident that Cleveland, duly nominated by the Democrats, was corrupt. "I can oppose Cleveland with a very clear conscience," he told Lodge.

Roosevelt could not remain on the side lines in so bitter a contest, and he left his beloved West to go on the stump. At St. Paul he dropped off the train to tell a reporter that Cleveland, as governor of New York, had been "very inimical to reform legislation." Then it became known that a decade earlier Cleveland had had an affair with a married woman. There had been a child whose identity had been kept secret and Cleveland had declared, when rumors spread, that the truth must be told. The revelation was a shock to the independent-reform group that had rallied to his banner. Their candidate had committed the worst of sins for an American in the '80's. He had erred and been caught. A conference of his backers received the news with dismay and adjourned to the University Club for dinner; Carl Schurz and George William Curtis pondered whether it was worthwhile to go on. At this point one of those present, his identity unfortunately lost, remarked:

From what I hear, Mr. Cleveland has shown high character and great capacity in public life, but that in private life his conduct has been open to question, while, on the other hand, Mr. Blaine in public life has been weak and dishonest while he seems to have been an admirable husband and father. The conclusion I draw is that we should elect Mr. Cleveland to the public office which he is so admirably qualified to fill and remand Mr. Blaine to the private life he is so eminently fitted to adorn.

Roosevelt joined in the personal attacks to the extent of remarking smugly that Cleveland was no man for the presidency, not merely because of his public career, but "for private reasons as well."

He had no deep interest in the issues. Roosevelt might have argued, with logic, that it was absurd to expect a man just beginning a political career to bolt his organization. The Democrats would have welcomed him for campaign purposes, but they would have had small use for him after Election Day. He would have been the saddest of public figures, a politician without a party. If only he had said something to that effect—not publicly, of course, but in private—it would be possible to pay Roosevelt the tribute of sincerity. He was thinking, however, of his future.

When he arrived east in October it was suggested that he might run for Congress from the First District on Long Island, where his home at Oyster Bay made him eligible. He said, according to the formula of politicians, that he was reluctant. If in "any honorable way" he could avoid it, he would do so. It did not prove difficult. The demand was less than overwhelming and this was just as well, for he probably would have been defeated. Election Day brought disaster. Grover Cleveland became President-elect. Even Cabot Lodge, whose strength in Massachusetts was great, was defeated for Congress.

After it was over, Roosevelt felt sure that he had been facing personal defeat whatever the outcome. The Blaine men, had they won, would have given him nothing. He consoled Lodge with the thought that "it may be that we have had our day; we have both of us fought the losing fight grimly to the end. What we have been cannot be taken from us; what we are is due to the folly of others and to no fault of ours." Their action in urging the election of Blaine, Roosevelt wrote, had been dictated by duty and unselfishness; ". . . by bolting we could have done an immense amount for ourselves." This was nonsense. What Roosevelt really believed on the subject of dishonest candidates for office he revealed in a speech eleven years later:

> It is bad enough to allow a man who is dishonest to stand as the representative of your party in any position. You can, however, invent excuses for it. I do not think they are valid excuses, but they often have weight.

Chapter VIII

GENTLEMAN COWHAND

❋

Undoubtedly Isaac Hunt was right; Roosevelt "hiked away to the wilderness to get away from the world, went out there a broken-hearted man." Cattle ranching had been no more than a potentially interesting avocation when, in 1883, he made arrangements to buy a herd. Even after his domestic tragedy in February, 1884, and the bitter disappointment of the Chicago convention, Roosevelt went west for only one reason; he had nothing else to do. A neighbor asked whether he intended to make ranching his business.

"No," he answered. "For the present I am out here because I cannot get up any enthusiasm for the Republican candidate, and it seems to me that punching cattle is the best way to avoid campaigning."

He sought peace, and never quite found it, in the jagged prairies of the Dakota Bad Lands. He told Bill Sewall, a

Maine guide whom he had known for years and whom he attempted to transform into a Western cowhand, that his future was a matter of no concern. He might do a little writing; he made it plain that life stretched on as barren as the dusty prairie. Sewall disagreed. He pointed out that Roosevelt had an infant daughter "to live for."

"Her aunt can take care of her better than I can," was the answer.

There were, however, qualities in Roosevelt that halted introspection soon after it had started. He could surrender momentarily to depression, but it could not prevail against an innate robustness. Roosevelt's contradictions speak for themselves. It must have been in the summer or fall of 1887, in one chapter of a book published the following year, that Roosevelt voiced his true philosophy: "Black care rarely sits behind a rider whose pace is fast enough."

Roosevelt could erect barriers against thoughts, and memories too, that troubled him. Not primarily an optimistic person, he none the less tinted the past with colors of the rose.

"Ah," remarked James Bryce, one day, when Roosevelt's name had come into a conversation with Owen Wister, "but Roosevelt wouldn't always look at a thing, you know."

It was wiser not to look at things in late 1884 as he faced a life remote from the one he had known. It was better to soften retrospection with a note of the whimsical, to live for the moment, to purchase the gaudiest of cowboy outfits and mount his horse.

"My cattle are looking well," he wrote to Lodge, "and in fact the Statesman (?) of the past has been merged, alas, I fear for good, into the cowboy of the present."

Soon melancholy had quite vanished, and sorrow became as blunted as the sorrow of a child in the face of a new excitement. Yet for all that the West exhilarated him, Roosevelt went quickly back to public life when the opportunity came. The roar and the turmoil and the strife of politics were in his blood—and even the whirl of the roundup and the stalking of a grizzly could not take their place for very long.

2

Life in the open had been part of the program whereby, as a boy, Roosevelt had built up his health. During a college recess in 1876 he went to the Maine woods with two cousins. William Wingate Sewall, the Maine woodsman whom he was to take west in 1884, was engaged as guide for the party. He recalled an eighteen-year-old youth who was "not remarkably cautious about expressing his opinion," but who was courageous and plucky. Sewall had been warned that the boy must be protected against overexertion, but the protection was declined. Roosevelt was already finding great satisfaction in physical pre-eminence. "I could carry heavier loads and travel farther and faster than either of them," he boasted, regarding his cousins, "and could stand rough work better." Sewall was even more impressed by the manner in which the studious-appearing youth "got right in with the people" wherever he went. He established contacts with woodsmen, lumberjacks, and trappers.

Roosevelt first saw the Far West in September, 1883, when he dropped off the train at the station called Little Missouri in the Dakota territory. He then had no idea of becoming a cattleman. He had gone to Little Missouri because of a letter written by Howard Eaton, who subsequently became famous as a dude rancher. This had declared the country unequaled for buffalo hunting, and Roosevelt's first demand was for a guide. The important thing about this trip, however, was contact with Joe Ferris, his brother Sylvane, and the latter's partner, A. W. Merrifield. He also met Gregor Lang, who dwelt on Little Cannonball Creek, some fifty miles distant. These four men infected Roosevelt with enthusiasm for the cattle business. Before returning east that fall he had invested $14,000. A year later he added $26,000, and in April, 1885, he wrote a third check, this time for $12,500. He was to lose nearly every cent of this $52,500, but he never regretted the venture. The dividends were paid in intangibles.

"It was still the West in those days," Roosevelt wrote in his memoirs, and it was. By 1884, a boom was in progress. This was the land of plenty, enthusiasts said. This was the land where, somewhat mysteriously, since there seemed to be no grass, cattle would grow fat. The region was served by a great transcontinental railway that would ship cattle to such markets as Kansas City and Chicago at rates with which Texas and the rest of the Southwest could not compete. So men dreamed.

Little Missouri, which called itself a town, had a hotel, the Pyramid Park, near the railroad tracks. As in every frontier community there was a ramshackle general store, in this case run by a Swede who supplied comic relief to the scene. A few houses dotted the barren landscape. How the residents of this prairie metropolis made a living remains a mystery. Some were guides, waiting for just such prey as young Roosevelt. Others lived by such wits as they possessed, and often went hungry. Little Missouri itself viewed with a jaundiced eye the optimistic boosters who were to make the land flow with honey. They viewed with particularly acute suspicion a young Frenchman who arrived in March, 1883. He explained that he was Antoine de Vallombrosa, the Marquis de Mores. He was the son of a duke, the husband of Medora von Hoffman, who was the daughter of a New York banker. The marquis had heard of Little Missouri, he said, through a friend who had hunted there.

The marquis had large ideas. He told those who would listen that he intended to build an abattoir at Little Missouri and ship steers and hogs east after they had been slaughtered. The savings would be great. De Mores said that he had at least $10,000,000 behind him, and before long he had formed the Northern Pacific Refrigerator Company. Little Missouri, however, had no use for a business prosperity that might bring sheriffs and jails and thereby disturb the accustomed routine of life. Co-operation was not forthcoming and so, in disgust, De Mores started a new community on the other bank of the river. With true Gallic sentimentality, he named it Medora, in honor of his wife. This was on April 1, 1883, and the future seemed bright.

3

Roosevelt became the owner of two ranches, the first at Chimney Butte, seven or eight miles from Little Missouri's cluster of shacks, and more generally known as the Maltese Cross because of its brand. The other was the Elkhorn Ranch twenty miles down the river. Sylvane Ferris and Merrifield had, when Roosevelt suggested it in 1883, agreed to become his partners in a cattle enterprise.

Ferris and Merrifield took care of Roosevelt's interests during the winter of 1883-84. They were at the Medora station when he returned on June 9, 1884. On the following morning all three rode to the Maltese Cross together and Roosevelt began, in earnest, the life of gentleman cowhand. He had arranged to do some literary work between roundups. The cottonwoods showed their fluffy green against the gray of the prairie. The river, neither the raging torrent of early spring nor the sullen trickle of the hot summer, flowed gently through its valley in front of the ranch. In the early dawn Roosevelt could stand at his cabin door and gaze off across his domain and breathe the varied scents of the desert. In the evening he could sit on the veranda, watch the sunset, and turn the pages of some book.

The love of beauty, which had so marked Theodore Roosevelt as a child, and which had been so strangely lacking at Harvard, had returned. But he remembered, as much as the beauty, the vigorous life of his years in the West. He established himself with the cowboys, whose riding, recklessness, and exhibitionism he admired extravagantly. That Roosevelt, wearing eyeglasses and christened Four-Eyes, was able to win their respect is no small tribute to his character.

His somewhat precise tones, still flavored by exposure to Harvard culture, rang strangely in their ears. He did not smoke or drink. His worst profanity was an infrequent "Damn!" and his usual ejaculation was "By Godfrey!" The first time he took part in a roundup, some time during the summer of 1884, one or two hardened cowboys nearly fell from their saddles as he called in his high voice to one of the men:

"Hasten forward quickly there!"

The phrase became a classic in the Bad Lands. Riders passing distant ranches relayed it with profane guffaws. Strangers in Medora and Little Missouri saloons were puzzled as some thirsty customer ordered the bartender to "hasten quickly" with his drink. Roosevelt's conception of a cowboy costume aroused additional merriment and, in all fairness, in T.R. as well. "You would be amused to see me," he wrote to Lodge—one of the few instances in which Roosevelt gave way to understatement—"in my broad sombrero hat, fringed and beaded buckskin shirt, horsehide chaparajos or riding trousers, and cowboy boots, with braided bridle and silver spurs." In addition to his colorful clothing he had a "pearl hilted revolver and [a] beautifully finished Winchester rifle. I feel able to face anything." On his return east in July, 1884, he was excessively patronizing to the effete young men of his acquaintance:

It would electrify some of my friends who have accused me of representing the kid-gloved element in politics if they could see me galloping over the plains, day in and day out, with a big sombrero on my head. For good, healthy exercise I would strongly recommend some of our gilded youth to go West and try a short course of riding bucking ponies and assisting at the branding of a lot of Texas steers.

Meanwhile, in the Bad Lands, there were demands that Roosevelt serve as one of the first Congressmen from the territory soon to become a state. The Mandan (Dakota) *Press* praised "this vigorous young Republican of the new school" and said that, should he run for office, signal honors would be his. Roosevelt had no desire for it. Either he still had aspirations in the East, which is probable, or he was disgusted with public life. His letters reflected merely his reluctant conclusion that he must assist in the Blaine campaign.

4

Grover Cleveland, Blaine, the Mugwumps, the tariff—all these must have seemed remote as Roosevelt watched the Bad Lands locked in winter. He had returned from his campaigning in November, 1884. The spectacle of nights that "seem never-ending [when] all the great northern plains are changed into an abode of iron desolation" gave power to his pen. It could be a very expressive pen:

Sometimes furious gales blow out of the north, driving before them the clouds of blinding snowdust, wrapping the mantle of death round every unsheltered being that faces their unshackled anger. All the land is granite; the great rivers stand still in their beds, as if turned to frosted steel. In the long nights there is no sound to break the lifeless silence. Under the ceaseless, shifting play of the Northern Lights, or lighted only by the brilliance of the stars, the snow-clad plains stretch out into dead and endless wastes of glimmering white.

Roosevelt would have been far more contented had he remained in the West throughout the winter of 1884-85. He did some hunting. He was active in organizing an association of stockmen to inaugurate law and order and put down the cattle thieves. He was still restless, however. On December 20, 1884, he went east again, in order to be with his daughter at Christmas. While there, he began work on his series of hunting and ranching essays. He also dressed up in his cowboy costume and had some photographs taken. Facing the studio camera, with a painted backdrop behind him, he leaned on his trusty rifle, assumed a fiercely Western expression and gazed out across imaginary prairies. He also found time, while in New York, to complete a lengthy article for the *Century* on

"Phases of State Legislation." This described his experiences of the past three years, and it did not increase his standing with the Republican machine in New York.

During the next two years he was to be pulled this way and that way. Should he accept a nomination for the mayoralty in New York? Should he spend a winter in Dakota or stay at home trying to write? Where was happiness to be found—in the Western country that he professed to love so or among the milling crowds of the cities, whose allure he could never shake off? For the moment, in the spring of 1885, he was occupied with his literary work and his ranch. The cattle had survived the winter. At the Maltese Cross a half-dozen men were now busy and Roosevelt's optimism rose again. He enjoyed the hard work. He treasured the respect that, despite his eccentricities, he had won from his hands.

By summer, Medora was prospering. One pioneer had built a roller-skating rink where cowboys would stop after exhilarating hours in Bill Williams's saloon and delight their companions with plain and fancy skating. Bill Williams was the town bad man, its resident villain. He ran the faro game. He represented Sin, and sometimes he would stand in the doorway of his place and discharge his six-shooter into the night.

Excessively moral himself, Roosevelt never failed to be fascinated by wickedness in others. "I am not in the least sensitive as to the past career of one of these Vikings of the border," he confided. He was particularly intrigued by "Hell Roaring Bill" Jones, so called to distinguish him from several other Bill Joneses in the community, who was sheriff at Medora during the boom days. Bill's profanity was an art study in purple. Roosevelt never forgot this sheriff, who in leisure moments had worked on the Maltese Cross as cowhand. In the summer of 1903 the President met the former guardian of the law, somewhat fallen in estate owing to liquor, driving a team near Yellowstone Park. Memories came back of the days in Medora, the days when there had been straight-shooting villains and all the world was adolescent. On his return to Washington, T.R. told his Secretary of State, John Hay, about Hell Roaring Bill, and so entranced that connoisseur of good stories that he demanded a written version. It was duly supplied, and Hay read the letter "by a crackling brick fire, while a thunder storm played a fitting obligato" at his country place in New Hampshire. Roosevelt had recalled a three-cornered conversation at Medora, some time in the '80's, with Sylvane Ferris and the sheriff:

There was also a good deal of talk about a lunatic, and some cross-questioning brought out a story which cast light on the frontier theory of care for the insane. Sylvane began—"Well, the way was this. That lunatic was on the train and he up and shot the newsboy, and at first they wasn't going to do anything about it because they thought he just had it in for the newsboy. But someone said 'Why, he's plumb crazy and is liable to shoot one of us.'—and they threw him off the train."

It was at Medora where this incident occurred and Sheriff Bill Jones came forward. Here he took up the tale himself: "The more fool I! Why, that lunatic didn't have his right senses. At first he wouldn't eat . . . you know Snyder, don't you? (Snyder was a huge, happy-go-lucky cowpuncher, at that time Bill Jones's deputy) well he's plumb stuck on his running and he's soft-hearted, too. He'd think that lunatic looked peaked and he'd take him out on the prairie for an airing and the boys they'd josh him as to how much start he could give the lunatic and then catch him again. Well, he always did catch him."

5

It has been said profoundly that Theodore Roosevelt's life was the ultimate dream of every typical American boy: he fought in a war, killed lions, became President, and quarreled with the Pope. The years in the Bad Lands constituted an earlier role that nearly every boy plays in imagination. Roosevelt wore gaudy clothes. He was a deputy sheriff. He caught some thieves. The final adventure was with the Marquis de Mores, whose impressive plans had been progressing none too well. That Roosevelt and the Frenchman irritated each other is clear. Like Roosevelt, De Mores exulted in gay costumes. He had arrived at Little Missouri first and he was by far the most vital figure when Roosevelt came. A minor clash or two occurred during 1884. The influence of the marquis diminished after Roosevelt's arrival, partly because he was a foreigner. It was soon a matter for barroom gossip that he resented Roosevelt's presence in Medora.

Naturally enough, Roosevelt's friends made De Mores the villain in the friction that followed T.R.'s colorful advent. They insisted that he had allied himself with the evil element. They told of a shooting scrape in 1883 in which one Riley Luffsey had been killed, the implication being that De Mores was behind it. Gregor Lang, one of Roosevelt's close associates, was an outspoken critic and said bluntly that the killing had been unnecessary—a western euphemism of the day. The matter slumbered for two years.

One dream after another in which De Mores had envisioned the future of Medora failed. On August 26, 1885, although no further evidence had been uncovered, he was indicted for the murder of Luffsey and concluded: first, that his business enemies were responsible; second, that Roosevelt was behind it. There is ample evidence for the first and none for the second. The marquis was brought to trial at Mandan and was promptly acquitted. On September 3, he addressed an angry letter to Roosevelt. Joe Ferris, he said, had been instrumental in the prosecution. He had furnished money to witnesses:

The papers also publish very stupid accounts of our quarreling. Is this done by your order? I thought you my friend. If you are my enemy, I want to know it. I am always on hand as you know and between gentlemen it is easy to settle matters of this sort directly.

Roosevelt reached Medora from the East in October. Rumors were immediately current that he had been challenged to a duel by the marquis and had replied that rifles would be his choice of weapons, that they would meet at twelve paces and fire until one of them dropped. It is impossible to sift fact from fiction in weighing the exploits of Roosevelt in the Bad Lands. Inevitably, as Medora joined the ranks of cow towns that had failed, he became a legend; the stories about him may have been embroidered by repetition. The marquis is mentioned only once or twice in all the magazine articles and books written by Roosevelt about the Bad Lands. No reference is made to a duel. No letter suggesting rifles at twelve paces has survived. He did preserve, however, the communication from De Mores, and on the back of this, in Roosevelt's writing, was drafted a reply:

Most emphatically I am not your enemy; if I were, you would know it, for I would be an open one, and would not have asked you to my house nor gone to yours. As your final words, however, seem to imply a threat, it is due to myself to say that the statement is not made through any fear of possible consequences to me; I, too, as you know, am always on hand, and ever ready to hold myself accountable in any way for anything I have said or done.

Perhaps the choice of weapons was made in a subsequent draft, actually delivered to De Mores. Undoubtedly Roosevelt, quick to accept any challenge, had interpreted the letter from the marquis as a demand for satisfaction on the field of honor. Nor was he without basis in so believing. But there was no duel. The marquis, according to the reminiscences of those who were then in Medora, hastened to say that he had been misunderstood.

The differences between Roosevelt and De Mores were soon forgotten in common disaster. T.R. spent a good part of the winter, including Christmas, in Medora that year. Late in 1885, he had been gratified by appointment as a deputy sheriff of Billings County. In March, 1886, he captured three thieves who had stolen a boat belonging to his ranch and fled down the river. He told his friends and family in the East about this exploit and was quickly informed that it would be wiser not to make it the subject of a magazine article. There had been alarm lest Theodore's narratives of life among the bold, bad men of the West seem extravagant in the East. "I shall take good care," he added plaintively, "that the pronoun 'I' does not appear once in the whole piece. His mentors were adamant, however. The account was not published until 1888.

The winter of 1886-87 is still remembered in the Bad Lands. Roosevelt was not there to see the snows that started in November and continued with ferocity for weeks. Woodsmen and hunters had been predicting, as they watched the leaden skies, that a hard winter was coming. The birds and beasts that could migrate had fled earlier than usual. The wolves and coyotes grew longer coats. The cattle died by tens of thousands. Men searched for them in the storms and never returned. In one or two cabins, cut off by the blizzards, insanity added to the horror. When spring came, the melting snows uncovered desolation. Roosevelt went out in April, 1887, and reported that the losses were terrific.

So ended the adventure in the West. So ended Medora. The pleasant clink of glasses in the Williams saloon died away. The bad men, the cowboys, and the cattlemen departed for more lucrative fields, and in their wake trudged the ladies of easy virtue who had furnished Medora's quota of sin. Roosevelt spent part of the summer in 1887 at the Elkhorn Ranch, winding up his affairs and selling the remnants of his cattle at a loss.

Theodore Roosevelt, nominee for the vice-presidency,

saw the Bad Lands again on September 12, 1900. He had been on a long and exhausting tour in praise of McKinley and the Republican party. Synthetic cowboys, hired for $2.50 a day to ride in parades in the Middle West, had greeted the commander of the Rough Riders. Now Roosevelt was leaving these imitation horsemen; his train was crawling across the prairies. When it stopped at Chamberlain, South Dakota, some real cowboys galloped up. A brass band from the Crow Creek reservation played "Annie Laurie" with peculiar rhythm. At the clapboard station were buckboards, ponies, men and women on horseback.

Hastily, while the train waited, a small reception was held. Roosevelt leaned from the platform and shook hands, managed a joke or two. But he seemed subdued. Then the train made its way toward Medora, through the country Roosevelt knew so well. For some minutes the cowboys spurred their horses after it, whooping and shouting. They were dim specks on the horizon as Roosevelt, his arms clasped over the brake handle and his chin on his wrist, continued to sit on the observation platform and watch the steel rails recede toward the infinity where parallel lines meet. An hour later a member of the vice-presidential party looked for him and found the door blocked by a colored Pullman porter.

"The governor don't want to see nobody for a while," he said apologetically.

Later the train stopped again, this time at Medora. Roosevelt mounted a horse and rode, by himself, into the broken contours of the Bad Lands.

Chapter IX

THE YEARS BETWEEN

✳

The episode of the Bad Lands would have ended even if the herds of the Maltese Cross had flourished and multiplied. The winter of 1886-87 merely accelerated the end. The West had brought Roosevelt a measure of tranquillity. But his fundamental interests were more and more in the East, where two factors, in particular, drew him back. The Bad Lands, having served their purpose, became touched with sentimentality. Roosevelt had no desire to return, had it been possible, to the land "of scattered ranches, of herds of long-horned cattle, and of reckless riders who unmoved looked in the eyes of life or of death."

The more important of the influences that turned his face east was the fact that he was to be married again. The first mention of his engagement to Edith Kermit Carow was on November 1, 1886, when he told Cabot Lodge. The story of Edith Carow goes back virtually to the beginning of Theodore's own story, however. She belonged to the group of boys and girls who played in the yards of the ample houses off Gramercy Park and Union Square. The daughter of Mr. and Mrs. Charles Carow, who lived near the Fourteenth Street mansion of Theodore's paternal grandfather, she was an intimate companion of Corinne, the youngest of the Roosevelt brothers and sisters. She was three years younger than Theodore.

When the Roosevelt family went abroad in the summer of 1869, the children were homesick. They missed all their New York friends a good deal, and they longed to see Edith. Teedie, gave voice to their sentiments. On November 22, 1869, he noted in his diary:

In the evening Mama showed me the portrait of Eidieth Carow and her face stirred up in me homesickness and longing for the past which will come again never, alack never.

The boy and girl friendship between Theodore and Edith continued through the years of tutoring and the second journey abroad. During Roosevelt's freshman year at Harvard she went to Cambridge, accompanied by Corinne, to visit him. That she was in his mind that year is shown by a letter to his sister, dated February 5, 1877, in which he told of some sleighing party in Boston: ". . . one of the girls," he said, "looked quite like Edith only not nearly so pretty as her ladyship."

Was a childhood love affair behind all this? It would be natural, in view of the outcome, to assume that there was. Mrs. Robert Bacon, who knew Edith and Theodore and also Alice Lee well, felt confident that such had been the case. If it was so, Edith suffered because she remained at home while Theodore went to college. In October, 1878, he met the fascinating Alice Lee. There is little to support any theory regarding them; my own is based on the degree to which, in the years of their married life, Edith Carow took care of the violently adolescent person who had become her husband and risen to such heights. She was not a power behind the throne. Rather, she watched over his welfare.

She persuaded him to put on dry clothing when he returned from some ridiculous tramp in the rain. To all the familiars Mrs. Roosevelt was a gracious woman who never made mistakes, who saw that things moved properly at some White House function, who brought up the children and paid the bills.

My theory is, then, that the small Edith of the '70's represented a degree of the maternal to the sickly Teedie. She remained so until he died. "Was he ever wholly aware," asked Wister, "of what she did for him?" The evidence is strong that he saw and treasured it; he could be amused by his own defects and the balancing influence of the woman who presided over his home. In the civil service days at Washington he wrote of a dinner they had given to some notables:

Bill of fare, crabs, chicken and rice, claret and tea. Springy [Cecil Spring Rice] nervous and fidgety; I, with my best air of oriental courtesy, and a tendency to orate only held in check by memory of my wife's jeers.

Mrs. Cowles, Roosevelt's older sister, accompanied him to London, where the wedding took place. Spring Rice, who described him as "the boss Republican young man," was the best man at the ceremony on December 2, 1886, at St. George's Church in Hanover Square. The two men had become fast friends, and Mrs. Cowles had moments of anxiety, on the morning of the wedding, because "they were intensely occupied in a discussion over the population of an island in the Southern Pacific." The London fog was thick, and she felt that they must get started if Edith Carow was not to be kept waiting at the church.

The honeymoon was spent in England and on the Continent, and Roosevelt's letters reflected contentment and happiness. His sole worry was over his financial situation. Calamitous reports had reached him from the Bad Lands. He wrote Mrs. Cowles that it might be impossible to keep the home he had built for the vanished Alice at Oyster Bay.

On March 28, 1887, uncertain as to his future, he returned from abroad and went at once to Medora.

2

The other influence that drew Roosevelt back from the Bad Lands was an opportunity to re-enter public life. Politics, he had written in March, 1885, had "reached a stage best described as the Apotheosis of the Unknown." In October of that year he addressed a Republican meeting in Brooklyn and with rare self-control, said he would not scold "Mr. Cleveland for his numerous short-comings" as President of the United States. The fundamental issue was civil service reform. Regarding the two great political parties the young man who was "out of politics" said:

Throughout the North the bulk of the honesty and intelligence of the community is to be found in the Republican ranks. If the Republicans take a false step it is usually because the politicians have tricked them into it; while if the Democrats make a good move it is almost always merely because the astute party leaders have been able for a short time to dragoon their dense-witted followers into the appearance of deference to decent public sentiment.

The party thus holding a monopoly of virtue continued, however, to be tossed by trouble. David B. Hill, the Democratic candidate for governor of New York, was elected, and the gloom was deeper than ever. Thomas C. Platt was to make capital out of the discord. He dreamed of returning to the United States Senate, from which he so ignominiously retired. It was still too soon, he decided, and he supported Levi P. Morton instead. Among those who opposed his plan was Theodore Roosevelt, still "out of politics," and the outcome was the elevation of William M. Evarts, the distinguished attorney who had defended President Andrew Johnson in the impeachment proceedings.

Platt continued to hope and yearn, with 1887 as another year when he could run for the Senate. That Roosevelt had fought him made no difference to this objective statesman. He decided that Roosevelt could be useful. The state elections in 1886 were unimportant; interest centered in the New York mayoralty campaign. Historically, it was a contest well meriting attention. But in Roosevelt's memoirs, for reasons understandable enough, it is dismissed with three lines of type.

Slowly and with slight support from the politicians, the American labor movement had been making progress. For a decade there had been acute labor disputes. In the spring of 1886 a bomb exploded in Haymarket Square in Chicago, killing one policeman and wounding others. The outrage, although no proof of the responsibility of labor was offered, aroused the respectable people who had been paying no attention to organized labor or its plans. At this point Henry George became labor's candidate for mayor of New York, with Abram S. Hewitt and Theodore Roosevelt as his opponents. Where Roosevelt stood on the matter of the Haymarket riots was expressed in a letter from his ranch:

My men are hard working, laboring men, who work longer hours for no greater wages than most of the strikers; but they are Americans through and through. I believe nothing would give them greater pleasure than a chance with rifles at one of the mobs. When we get the papers they become more furiously angry and excited than I do. I wish I had them with me and a fair show at ten times our number of rioters; my men shoot well and fear very little.

The workingman had found very little prosperity in the American garden. When times were good, he worked long hours for low wages. When a panic swept the country, as it did periodically while the politicians in Washington fumbled with finance, he joined the bread lines or starved. Labor had no voice. It controlled very few votes. It seems not to have occurred to its leaders to organize for action in their political districts, to seek relief through the ballot, to storm the national conventions.

Meanwhile, that strange and scholarly figure, Henry George, had arisen. Millions read his writings. He pointed to still another utopia. George is remembered chiefly as a fanatic who advanced some absurd, undoubtedly socialistic, idea called the single tax. He was a famous man in 1886, but his views were either misunderstood or distrusted by the respectables. Roosevelt had probably met George, since they were fellow speakers at the dinner of the New York Free Trade Club in May, 1883. He had, however, no sympathy for his ideas and had probably read none of his books. Ultimately he was dismissed, as Roosevelt usually dismissed those whose philosophies he could not appreciate, as "an utterly cheap reformer."

To the laboring man, whether organized or not, George's ideas offered hope. He said that financial depression was caused by the speculation that came from increases in the value of land. If these increases, through taxation, became the property of the government, a new and just distribution of wealth would result. The only way, in the United States, in which "the redress of political and social grievances" could be obtained was through the ballot.

Then came the demand that he run for mayor, and on October 5, 1886, Henry George consented. Immediately there was consternation among the leaders of Tammany Hall and the machine Republicans. They saw their comfortable alliance in danger of disruption. Richard Croker was the first to act, and he did so with skill. He forced his lieutenants to agree to the nomination of Abram S. Hewitt, an independent Democrat of great wealth. Croker, who cared nothing whatever for the rights of labor, was wise enough to know that the George candidacy would alarm great numbers of Republicans and independent Democrats. If the proponent of the single tax could only be painted as a black enough menace, their votes would go to Hewitt.

The Republican bosses, had they been interested in defeating George, would logically have endorsed Hewitt. They had, however, more fundamental interests. In the first place, it was necessary to keep their machine in operation. It did not seem possible, with so honest a man as Hewitt the candidate of Tammany, that the usual division of spoils with Tammany could be made. Too, the Republican leaders felt that George would draw more heavily from the Democratic side, which pretended to be the party of the workers. A nominee of their own might win. Consequently, Roosevelt was approached.

"I was visited by a succession of influential Republicans," he told Lodge. "With the most genuine reluctance I finally accepted" the Republican nomination for the mayoralty.

Elihu Root, Levi P. Morton, and Chauncey M. Depew were among the Republicans who attended the county convention at the Grand Opera House on the night of October 16. It was a routine affair at which the decision of the bosses was confirmed. Mr. Depew placed Roosevelt's name in nomination and dwelt on the extent to which Hewitt, surely an honorable man, would be handicapped by his *mésalliance* with Tammany. He was about to swing into his eulogy of Roosevelt when former Assemblyman Isaac Dayton, known locally as Uncle Isaac, shoved his way toward the platform screaming that the man they were about to nominate was a free trader.

Depew was suave. Mr. Roosevelt, he said, "has had the rare courage to acknowledge that he has recovered from the errors of his youth." He admitted that their candidate, when fresh from college, might have subscribed to this economic heresy. He might even have "believed in the strange and extraordinary theories of Henry George; he may even have had doubts of orthodox religion." Mr. Depew permitted a look of horror to pass across his face.

"But today," he added emphatically, "he stands cured."

Roosevelt, thus purged, was nominated by acclamation. He pledged himself to honesty in civic affairs, to war "against the spoilsmen who are eating up the substance of the city." He branded as "deliberate untruth" accusations that he favored low wages and had no sympathy for the workingman. Only by "that capacity for steady, individual self-help which is the glory of every true American" could the problems that tortured labor be solved. Roosevelt was still to become socially minded. He did, however, see clearly the obstacle to his own election: the probability that many Republicans would vote for Hewitt through fear that Henry George and his "strange and extraordinary theories" would otherwise blight their prosperity.

"If we stand together," he said in one speech, "we can and will win."

Even the New York *World,* taken over by the liberal Joseph Pulitzer, joined in the outcries of alarm over the Henry George menace. Unlike its contemporaries, though, the *World* appreciated the significance of the George movement as "a protest—a deep, disgusted protest, not wholly free from anger—against the evils, abuses and corruptions that are rooted in our politics." This was true, but the evils were deeper in their source than politics. It was the squalor, the abject poverty, and the disease in New York City that caused the theories of Henry George to win so many converts. Well-bred residents of New York ignored these conditions until, four years later, a newspaper reporter named Jacob Riis wrote a book, *How the Other Half Lives,* and shocked a few of them into action. Roosevelt was among the number.

That Democratic and Republican henchmen combined on Election Day to defeat Henry George is possible. The vote was close enough to justify suspicion of an alliance against the common enemy. Hewitt won with 90,466 votes. George received 67,930, while Roosevelt was third with 60,477. Roosevelt had been apprehensive that he would not do well. He told Lodge that he had made "a rattling canvass, with heavy inroads on the Democratic vote; but the 'timid good' are for Hewitt." He was correct about the "timid good." Roosevelt's vote of 60,000 compared badly with the normal Republican vote of between 75,000 and 80,000. This demonstrated that some members of his own party had preferred Hewitt to Roosevelt.

"I do not believe," recalled Brander Matthews, "that we were really more afraid of Henry George than we were of Theodore Roosevelt's youth."

Roosevelt found consolation in the belief that "at least I have a better party standing than ever before." It is doubtful whether he had. A good many years were to pass before the demand again came that he run for office. *Puck*, in May, 1887, published the political obituary of Theodore Roosevelt:

Be happy, Mr. Roosevelt, be happy while you may. You are young—yours is the time of roses—the time of illusions. You see not the rouge on old cheeks, the powder on the wrinkled forehead. Do not let it annoy you if we smile. You have heard of Pitt, of Alexander Hamilton, of Randolph Churchill, and of other men who were young and yet who, so to speak, got there just the same. Bright visions float before your eyes of what the Party can and may do for you. We wish you a gradual and gentle awakening. We fear the Party cannot do much for you. You are not the timber of which Presidents are made.

3

Although not quite as dark as the editor of *Puck* believed, Roosevelt's political future was dubious as he returned from his honeymoon in the spring of 1887. Three defeats within two years had damaged his standing; the inability to block the nomination of Blaine, the defeat of Blaine after Roosevelt had supported the party nominee, the unhappy mayoralty campaign. The last was the most serious. It revealed that there was no magic in the Roosevelt name. So, as he had before sought to lose himself in the Bad Lands, he now attempted to submerge his yearning for public life in his writing.

Again, his efforts were futile. Roosevelt's gnawing hatred of the Mugwump independents made it impossible for him to withdraw into a literary cloister. He was yearning to "take a hack at the estimable Godkin," to "give the Mugwumps something to howl over. I am in for war to the knife with the whole crew." By his truculence and too obvious wrath, Roosevelt delivered himself into the hands of Godkin, and during spring and summer of 1887 that vitriolic editor made the most of it. It had been a mistake "even to take him seriously as a politician; his chatter-box abuse of the Mugwumps continues." Roosevelt made one address that summer, an attack on Henry George, who had been nominated for secretary of state on an independent ticket. He said that "it is only a step from land confiscation to anarchy," that it was to the common interest of all Americans that "the Chicago dynamiters be hung." It did not matter to him that George had never suggested land confiscation and at no time had urged clemency for any who might actually be guilty of the Haymarket bombing.

Roosevelt's literary output between 1884 and 1889 was large but not distinguished. His *Hunting Trips of a Ranchman* appeared in 1885 and received enough attention, partly through surprise that an American politician could be an author of any kind, to earn a friendly review in the London *Spectator*. In March of 1886, Roosevelt was working feverishly, far too feverishly for a historian, to complete a biography of Thomas Hart Benton. In 1888 came another biography, that of Gouverneur Morris. During this period, also, he was completing *The Wilderness Hunter* and a *History of New York*. All in all, unlike *The Naval War of 1812* or the three-volume study, *The Winning of the West,* which were based on sound research, these studies reflect small credit on Roosevelt as a historian. They were too superficial. More serious was Roosevelt's loss of the objective touch that, in judging the work of others, he believed essential to history. Hatred of the Mugwumps poisoned his pen; he attempted to find in political history precedents for the conduct of Lodge and himself in 1884. In the life of Benton there were numerous thinly veiled reflections upon the miscreants who had dared to vote for Cleveland. In the same book, Roosevelt's growing jingoism was so apparent that *The Nation* commented upon it.

To imply that Roosevelt was unhappy during these years would be inaccurate. He was busy. He was enjoying his new home, Sagamore Hill. He had his horses and he organized a polo club among friends on Long Island. Cecil Spring Rice, attached to the embassy at Washington, was a frequent guest and permitted Roosevelt to feel elated over his inadequate horsemanship. An insatiable interest in every subject under the sun made it impossible for Roosevelt, under any circumstances, to feel bored. "Do you see how the Newport cads have taken up the Duke of Marlborough?" he demanded of Lodge, as the young British nobleman was preparing to wed Consuelo Vanderbilt in return for a sizable dowry.

4

Suddenly, in December, 1887, hope stirred in the breasts of Republican leaders. President Cleveland's annual message had branded the current tariff schedules as "vicious, inequitable, and illogical sources of unnecessary taxation." For a President to take so emphatic a stand on the most controversial of issues just before a campaign year was unthinkable; Cleveland's conduct constituted a horrible example to Roosevelt, and he was careful to avoid this error in later years. The storm that resulted—for the President already was unpopular with the practical politicians of his own party—gave the G.O.P. its first basis for optimism in long and weary months. Whom could the party nominate in 1888 now that chance of a victory loomed? The answer again came from the worshipers of James G. Blaine:

> Blaine, Blaine, the man from Maine,
> We've had him once, and we'll have him again.

"It is unfortunate, but it is true," said Roosevelt, that Blaine was still the choice of the party. He convinced himself anew that "the Republican party, and the Republican party alone" was capable of handling the financial and business problems that faced the nation. He thought that minor tariff revisions might be instituted, but the treasury surplus that worried Cleveland should be used for additional warships. So developed Roosevelt the jingo. His interest in the political scene heightened. Curiously, since Cleveland was to renew his appointment as Civil Service Commissioner in 1893, he said that the President was no true friend of the merit system, that his ruthlessness in discharging faithful government servants "would have done no discredit to Andrew Jackson; he has signally failed to make good his pledges."

This time Blaine was not to win the nomination. He withdrew from consideration while the convention was in progress at Cleveland. He suggested that General Benjamin Harrison, another of the Civil War military men, be selected instead. This was done, with Levi P. Morton as the vice-presidential choice. Although Roosevelt did not attend the convention, he watched its progress and was relieved when Harrison was nominated. He believed that Harrison was both able and honest. Roosevelt took the stump in October and November and his speeches were typical of this stage of his career. He condemned Cleveland and praised the high tariff, the leading issue of the campaign. Astutely, in view of America's anti-English complex in the '80's, the position of Cleveland was twisted to appear as favoring free trade. Protection was christened the "American tariff"; the other was British. The patriotism of the American people was not found wanting, and Harrison was elected.

The campaign had done little to lift Theodore Roosevelt out of the obscurity into which he had fallen. Yet 1888 marked the beginning of the era in which he was to grow great. In March, old Emperor Wilhelm died. Frederick III came to the German throne for a few brief weeks and left it to another man of destiny with a withered arm, a man less fortunate than Roosevelt. The decade that was closing would give way to one in which the United States abandoned her policy of isolation and assumed responsibilities in distant seas. Roosevelt was to typify the imperialism, the yearning for expansion, the new American ego, during the years that followed.

In domestic politics the leadership was shifting. Matthew S. Quay of Pennsylvania was rising. Platt himself was again powerful in New York. William McKinley was becoming increasingly prominent in Congress and Mark Hanna looked upon him as the hope of the future. The Old Guard was giving ground to younger men. In time these, in their turn, would constitute still another Old Guard; and the day would come when they would meet defeat at the hands of the young man who now seemed either insignificant or amusing.

To Roosevelt, the immediate importance of Harrison's election lay in the chance of some Federal appointment. He was heartily weary of private life.

Chapter X

A JOB ONCE MORE

✳

In political life, among the virtuous as well as among the corrupt, the enemies of yesteryear are the allies of today. Roosevelt was wholly aware of this, although he often denied its implications. He never permitted hostilities of the past to interfere with subsequent harmony—if harmony was what he sought.

In 1889, the Harrison administration was under obligation to James G. Blaine and he was appointed Secretary of State. Misunderstanding regarding Roosevelt's real opinion of the "Man from Maine" is not possible, but Blaine had the ear of the President. So Roosevelt permitted him to urge upon the President his desire for a Federal appointment. "I hope you will tell Blaine how much I appreciate his kind expressions," he told Lodge in March, 1889.

Roosevelt was even willing to serve as Assistant Secretary

of State under the man whose integrity he had questioned. The correspondence with Lodge reveals his disappointment when the appointment was not offered. "I would like above all things to go into politics," he said in the same letter. He added despondently that since this was not to be he would "go in for literature." Lodge, however, continued to press Roosevelt's eligibility. He reported that General Harrison seemed cordial, that Speaker Thomas B. Reed was also bringing pressure on the White House.

Ultimately, Harrison admitted that Roosevelt constituted a minor obligation. He had a reputation for civil service reform, and the President won credit for the administration and satisfied Roosevelt's friends by tendering appointment to the United States Civil Service Commission. The post paid only $3,500 a year. It controlled no patronage. No one in the capital expected, or desired, that the commission would accomplish more in the future than it had done in the past. It was an office that normally went begging, but Roosevelt accepted. He began work on May 13, 1889, temporarily leaving Mrs. Roosevelt and the children at Oyster Bay.

The United States Civil Service Commission was a pleasantly quiet government bureau in the Concordia Building at Eighth and E streets. It had been drifting along in comfortable tranquillity with only one commissioner, Charles Lyman, holding office. Mr. Lyman, who was nominally president of the commission, was a Presbyterian elder, a grave and decorous gentleman whose Republicanism was based on inheritance rather than conviction. On May 13, Matthew F. Halloran, the commission's executive secretary, heard an unusual commotion in the outer offices. Roosevelt came bounding in:

"I am the new Civil Service Commissioner. Have you a telephone? Call up the Ebbitt House. I have an engagement with Archbishop Ireland. Say I will be there at 10 o'clock."

This all came without a pause for breath. During the coming months the executive secretary was to be fascinated by his contacts with the new member. Roosevelt would summon him to take dictation and would "walk up and down emphasizing important points by driving his right fist firmly into his left hand." The clerks wondered idly how, with all this jumping about, he contrived to keep his eyeglasses perched on his nose.

President Cleveland had done much to advance the merit system. The bill sponsored by Senator George H. Pendleton of Oregon, who was, incidentally, a Democrat, gave protection to about 14,000 government employees, and 7,000 were added to the classified lists by Cleveland's executive orders. The President, it is true, disappointed the more extreme among the civil service reformers, but this was partly because politicians of both parties threw every possible obstacle in his path.

In a speech in 1900, General Harrison intimated that Roosevelt and he had worked together in harmony for the advancement of civil service. Roosevelt had become governor, and the former President of the United States was a shade patronizing. "The only trouble I ever had with managing him," he said, "was that he wanted to put an end to all the evil in the world between sunrise and sunset." Certainly Roosevelt felt that the White House was unreceptive to his plans. Harrison had no desire for drastic reforms. Another member, former Governor Hugh S. Thompson, was appointed to the Civil Service Commission on May 13, 1889. The fourth, like Thompson a Democrat, was John R. Proctor. To his surprise, Roosevelt found that both the Democrats supported his policies.

At first, he had no doubts regarding the work ahead. "I have made this commission a living force," he observed six weeks after taking office. He had already encountered opposition, and the party protests had been sufficient to alarm the President:

"But I answered militantly that as long as I was responsible the law should be enforced up to the handle everywhere, fearlessly and honestly."

2

Another flaming cause had been born in Roosevelt's breast. As President, Roosevelt was to learn that loopholes in the civil service regulations could be useful. In May, 1889, however, he infused moral qualities into the merit system. It was extremely satisfactory to face no longer the compromises of the Blaine campaign, of the mayoralty canvass.

Roosevelt's work as Civil Service Commissioner marked his first prolonged exercise of extraordinary gifts as propagandist. Until he began to roar, the merit system had been a subject that concerned only a small fraction of the intelligent minority. Roosevelt started to fight. The people became interested in civil service, once prosaic and dull, because they read in newspaper headlines about Roosevelt's violent quarrels with those who dared to stand in his way. One of the first men he attacked was John Wanamaker—

wealthy merchant, patron of Sunday schools, benefactor of the Republican party.

Mr. Wanamaker was a good man, a godly man. He was Postmaster General in the Harrison Administration. According to his official, yet innocently frank biographer, Wanamaker was exceedingly valuable. He was able

to prevent his chief from making the irreparable blunder of accepting the drastic program of Civil Service reformers, most persuasive of whom was young Theodore Roosevelt. Much to the joy of the party leaders, the new Postmaster-General insisted that the President give full weight to the Congressional claims for patronage. He had no profound objection to the theory that to the victors belong the spoils.

Such being Mr. Wanamaker's philosophy, the Post Office Department was an ideal Cabinet office for him to fill. It has always been the fountain of rewards for faithful service. By the end of May, 1889, the "good of the service" had required the removal of 985 Democratic postmasters. By November, 1889, 30,000 fourth-class postmasters had been replaced by deserving Republicans, and the *Civil Service Chronicle* excoriated the Postmaster General:

One day in the week he exhorts a large Sunday School to acts of Christian Charity and on the next he affords an object lesson on an enormous scale of sly intolerance, cruelty, and meanness that would be shocking to a barbarian.

T.R. could not remain aloof in such a situation. The chance to attack the Postmaster General came toward the end of 1890. Charles J. Bonaparte of Baltimore, later to be in Roosevelt's Cabinet and for many years an active civil service proponent, presented evidence regarding corruption among postal officials in his city. Bonaparte assisted Roosevelt in an investigation. The outcome was a recommendation that twenty-five Harrison appointees be dismissed. Not long after this Roosevelt arrived, flushed with anger, at a meeting of the Civil Service Reform Association in New York City. Carl Schurz and other of its leaders were there. Roosevelt closed the door behind him, stared grimly at the older men, and asked whether newspapermen were present. He was assured that they were not.

"Then," said Roosevelt, "damn John Wanamaker!"

President Harrison, naturally enough, had no desire to irritate so generous a source of campaign funds as Mr. Wanamaker. He must have felt, very early in Roosevelt's civil service career, that the appointment of the hustling New Yorker was a grievous error. When appointed, Roosevelt had been confident that "the old boy is with us," that Harrison would, at least, remain neutral in the row with Wanamaker. Disillusionment came soon. He learned that the President had no real convictions regarding civil service. "Heavens, how I like positive men!" he exclaimed after one interview at the White House.

By July, 1891, Roosevelt felt that "the President has never given us one ounce of backing." He was continuing to fight and was "battling with everybody [while] the little grey man in the White House [looks] on with cold and hesitating disapproval, but not seeing how he can interfere."

For the friction that arose, Roosevelt was partly to blame. He seemed devoid of tact or diplomacy. He gave so many interviews that his mentor, Cabot Lodge, was moved to protest. "Edith thoroughly agrees with you," said Roosevelt humbly, "so I cry peccavi and will assume a statesmanlike reserve of manner whenever reporters come near me."

In time, he was able to spread his data on the Baltimore scandals, and on Wanamaker, before the House Civil Service Committee. By then, the Democrats had obtained control of the House and so Roosevelt was cordially enough received. He flatly accused Wanamaker of attempting to shield subordinates guilty of "slanderous falsehoods." The majority of the House committee, in its report on June 22, 1892, upheld Roosevelt, while the Republican minority did an elaborate straddle. It said that Commissioner Roosevelt had probably uncovered wrongdoing in Baltimore, but it was "quite probable that he had in mind the influences prevalent in that city, for many years under Democratic auspices."

It was rather late for these findings to be important. In general, the press applauded and agreed that Roosevelt had been vindicated in his charges. The committee's report did prove of use in the 1892 campaign. Mr. Harrison was to be defeated, and Mr. Wanamaker had to return to his stores and his Sunday school.

3

Life as Civil Service Commissioner was not always filled with pleasant excitement and quarrels. The six years from 1889 to 1895, when Roosevelt retired to become head of the Police Board of New York City, might have bored him excessively had it not been for the social life that he found in Washington. He came to know William Howard Taft, Henry Adams, and Thomas B. Reed intimately. He was constantly with Cabot Lodge and his lovely wife. He saw something of Rudyard Kipling and Richard Harding Davis. During one summer he lived with Cecil Spring Rice. To Roosevelt's home, and to Lodge's, came the men and women of the day who enjoyed conversation and laughter and charming people. It did not matter, in the light of all this, that Roosevelt's standing with the administration was anomalous, that President Harrison never once invited him to the White House.

In the summer of 1886, alone on his ranch in the Bad Lands, Roosevelt had looked forward to a day when he and his sisters and his daughter would gather around them "society men who take part in politics, literature and art, and politicians, authors and artists whose personal habits do not disqualify them for society."

In 1891, in a letter to Bamie, he told of some guest who had just dined with them; nice, "but, oh, how dreadfully common-place and middle-class British dull! I never can be intimate with that enormous proportion of sentient beings who are respectable but dull. I will work with them, or for them; but for pleasure and instruction I go elsewhere." During the civil service years, however, Roosevelt achieved the salon of which he had dreamed in the West, although some of his guests were unkind enough to intimate that he monopolized the conversation.

"I dined with Theodore and did *all* the talking myself," wrote Spring Rice, in triumph, to Mrs. Roosevelt in 1894.

Life at Washington had the charm and advantage of simplicity at this time, and it was well that this was so. Roosevelt's finances still suffered from his ranching reverses. The family had been increasing. Theodore, the first son, had been born in 1887, and Kermit in 1889. Ethel came in 1891. Roosevelt had been further handicapped by inability, because of his public duties, to continue the literary work that had been bringing in from $700 to $800 a year. His brother-in-law, Douglas Robinson, shocked him in 1893 with a warning that there had been a $2,500 deficit in his personal accounts that year. He grew pessimistic and again considered the sacrifice of Sagamore Hill.

The Roosevelts lived in a small house off Connecticut Avenue. They learned that Washington, in those days, was not in the least concerned with wealth. William Dudley Foulke, a civil service enthusiast, recalled dining "in the little house on a side street" where Roosevelt was "the most hospitable of men," where Speaker Reed and Cabot Lodge were often to be found. It was a small town in the '90's;

to Roosevelt it was "just a big village, but a very pleasant big village." The Roosevelts saw the people they wanted to see. They dined out three or four times a week, and people came in once or twice. Those whom they saw were "mostly those who stand high in the political world, while there are enough men of letters or of science to give a pleasant and needed variety." Roosevelt had resumed his *The Winning of the West,* and when they did not entertain the nights at home were pleasant: "Edith sews while I make ineffective bolts at my third volume."

"Theodore Roosevelt was at Lodge's," wrote Henry Adams on March 19, 1889. "You know the poor wretch has consented to be Civil Service Commissioner and is to be with us in Washington next winter with his sympathetic little wife." The New Englander was to find the "poor wretch" a singularly entertaining foil for his own aloofness. At Henry Adams's home, No. 1603 H Street, Roosevelt was always welcome. Spring Rice was constantly there, and so was Cabot Lodge. John Hay, who was alternately amused and awed by Roosevelt, was at his best in the presence of the somewhat austere but appreciative Adams. It was a brilliant circle. Occasionally Henry Watterson of the Louisville *Courier-Journal* would come up from Kentucky to listen to the Three Musketeers of Culture, as he called Hay, Lodge, and Adams.

During the summer of 1891, awaiting the birth of Ethel, Mrs. Roosevelt left Washington for Oyster Bay, and her husband and Springy moved into the vacant Lodge home to keep each other company. They were having "great fun," Roosevelt reported, ". . . he is *so* gentle and pallid and polite." They entertained "in a mild way. Millie, the colored one, cooks very well and we have California claret for the guests—twenty-five cents a bottle. None of the guests have died yet." But Spring Rice, Roosevelt added, was inclined to be "querrelous toward America. He oughtn't to be a diplomat; he is too serious."

Springy's irritation was only natural. His country was constantly the subject of criticism in the United States. Even Roosevelt shared the general antipathy toward Great Britain, and his dislike was to continue well into his term as President—". . . certain people," he told Dr. Matthews, could be placed only "in the category of feeble folk, with subdued Anglo-maniac tendencies." Another letter was filled with abuse of Rudyard Kipling, whom Roosevelt had recently met. A third indicated his anger toward Richard Harding Davis because that journalist had dared to defend the English. In time, as did the more extreme phases of his Anglophobia, Roosevelt's dislike for Davis and Kipling vanished. The former was to stand with him at Las Guasimas, in the Spanish War. Kipling and Roosevelt were soon good friends. One of the British author's diversions was to drop in at the Cosmos Club, where Roosevelt held forth, in the lounge, on politics, literature, world affairs.

"I curled up on the seat opposite," he said, "and listened and wondered until the universe seemed to be spinning around and Theodore was the spinner."

4

Propagandizing for the merit system was not Roosevelt's only activity as Civil Service Commissioner. In the face of repeated objections he revised and improved the examinations whereby men and women applicants were placed on the eligible lists. His constant endeavor was to eliminate the theoretical examination. He felt particularly competent, in view of his experiences in the West, to arrange new tests for customs officials and members of the border patrol.

Marksmanship and the ability to ride horseback were more essential than skill in spelling and arithmetic, Roosevelt said. The men who were to halt the smuggling of cattle across the border should be able to read brands. He enlarged on this until it almost seemed that candidates for these posts were to be eliminated at a government rodeo where competition in roping, bulldogging, and riding was to be required. Roosevelt did, in fact, introduce marksmanship and told of it, with great pride, at a dinner of civil service proponents in Baltimore in 1892. In crisp, emphatic sentences, he explained that the applicants had eliminated each other by shooting at a target.

"It seems to me," said Mr. Bonaparte, who spoke next, "that Mr. Roosevelt has been very remiss. He did not get the best men. He should have had the men shoot at each other, and given the jobs to the survivors."

That Roosevelt was in disfavor at the White House was publicly known during the closing months of the Harrison Administration. The newspapers were filled with rumors of his pending resignation. He felt himself that "that fool Wanamaker" was likely to bring it about. Meanwhile, the tide of public favor had turned again toward Grover Cleveland. He was still detested by Tammany Hall. The bosses were, however, unable to halt the demand for his nomination. He became the Democratic candidate for President at Chicago on June 23, 1892, on a platform calling for lower tariffs and evading the perplexing question of silver and gold coinage.

The Republican party was forced to renominate Harrison, although no real enthusiasm for him existed. Many causes for Cleveland's victory in November might be cited: the Homestead riots that year, the bitter animosity of labor, the tariff, the unrest in the West. They all come down to the same essential fact—the people were dissatisfied. They did not have enough worldly goods. As they do so often, they voted against the man who was in the White House rather than affirmatively for his opponent.

What did the election mean to Roosevelt? He was elated when, in 1893, the Massachusetts legislature sent Cabot Lodge to the United States Senate. He had, however, viciously and publicly abused Grover Cleveland. He must have hesitated before making any request that the Democratic President-elect continue his appointment as Civil Service Commissioner. No other post was in sight, though, and return to private life was a greater evil. On January 4, 1893, Carl Schurz informed him that Cleveland had been most cordial. He hoped that Roosevelt would continue to work for reform. So the offer was made, and the acceptance was immediate.

For a time he "got on beautifully with the President, who is really very cordial with me." It must gradually have dawned upon Roosevelt that Cleveland was, in fact, a sincere believer in the merit system. Unlike his Republican predecessor, he listened when Roosevelt told his tales of villains in their midst. The President refused to sanction a proposal of John G. Carlisle, his Secretary of the Treasury, which called for removal of Republican officeholders.

The fights continued, but their flavor was gone. Roosevelt was a little bored, increasingly restless, during 1893 and 1894. Besides, his imperialistic tendencies were growing and the President persisted in quaint notions regarding the virtues of peace. As 1894 gave way to 1895, Roosevelt was again looking for a job. He felt that he had done his work as Civil Service Commissioner. The thought of becoming head of the New York Police Board fascinated him.

Chapter XI

SWORD OF RIGHTEOUSNESS

✳

The appointment of Theodore Roosevelt in 1895 to the Police Board of New York, which brought friction and fighting enough to surfeit even his restless spirit, may be traced back to two events some years before. The first was a legislative investigation in 1884, which initiated Roosevelt into certain irregularities practiced by guardians of the law. The second took place on Sunday, February 14, 1892, when the Rev. Charles H. Parkhurst told his congregation that New York was "a very hotbed of knavery, debauchery and bestiality." Subsequent fulminations by the pastor of the Madison Square Church resulted in 1894 in the momentary downfall of Tamanny Hall.

A member of the state legislature in 1884, Roosevelt had led in the fight for the passage of four or five bills backed by civic organizations in New York. It was their hope that the legislation would put an end to graft and corruption in police and other municipal circles. Enthusiastic rallies were held at which orators pointed to Assemblyman Roosevelt as their champion. One of the reform bills called, specifically, for an inquiry into the city's police force. In due time Roosevelt was presiding over public hearings, and before him passed witnesses who told unsavory stories of police incapacity and dishonesty.

Roosevelt was convinced, after the hearings in 1884, that police reform was vitally needed in New York. His reports to the legislature called for civil service and for a single police commissioner to take the place of the bipartisan board, so-called, of four members. These utopian changes were slow in coming, however. The board, of two Republicans and two Democrats, still existed when Roosevelt was appointed eleven years later. The police alliances with vice and crime were as strong as ever.

Ultimately, feeling the stings of Dr. Parkhurst's shafts himself, Roosevelt's enthusiasm for this extremely active clergyman began to cool and he referred to him as "that goose." But for a time their relations were most cordial, and Roosevelt watched with approval the pastor's efficient campaign against Tammany and sin. Parkhurst was a handsome man of fifty when he fired his first salvos; very vigorous, with hair that he permitted to grow moderately long. He wore rimless spectacles from behind which his indignant eyes flashed.

No restraints clouded the meaning of the sermons in which he described disorderly houses and gambling dens that "flourish almost as thick as the roses of Sharon." The Parkhurst exposures resulted in the appointment of another legislative committee, the famous Lexow tribunal, and this proved far more effective than the one Roosevelt had commanded in 1884. Its hearings substantiated, with additional lurid details, the charges that Parkhurst had made, and in 1894 the prophets of Tammany Hall foretold defeat. William L. Strong, a respected businessman, received fusion support and was elected mayor of New York. He found it an unhappy role and a brief one; reform mayors of New York usually find it so.

Roosevelt's letters to Lodge reveal that the mayoralty nomination had been offered to him before it had gone to Strong, but it is not clear whether the suggestion came from Platt and the Republican machine or from the far less influential fusion leaders. Not improbably, Platt would have preferred Roosevelt to Strong, whom he viewed with suspicion as "another of the fellows who wore a little bunch of whiskers under his chin." Strong was a man of standing, whose place in the community had long since been assured. Roosevelt was young and ambitious. This might make him more amenable to party discipline.

But Roosevelt was in no position to accept the nomination. He had no money for campaign purposes, so he watched the contest with deep interest from Washington. "The stars in their courses fight for us," he told Lodge, and perhaps found satisfaction in the knowledge that Strong, if elected, would doubtless offer some appointment. He declined a first suggestion, to become street cleaning commissioner, because he felt no special qualification for the post. On the other hand, the "work of the Police Department was in my line; I was glad to undertake it."

2

Police headquarters was still on Mulberry Street in 1895, a gloomy building with subterranean dungeons where rats and vermin assisted the persuasive effectiveness of the third degree. The patrolman of the day could barely read and write. His convenient conscience made strict obedience to the commands of his political sponsor easy, and he saw that wealth and a life of ease could be achieved by emulating the accepted methods of grafting upon saloonkeepers, gamblers, and prostitutes.

The arrival at Mulberry Street of any new commissioner was a crisis in police circles. It meant promotions and demotions, and the shifting of favorites from warm inside posts to pounding of cold pavements. The arrival of Roosevelt in May, 1895, was doubly unsettling because it was known that Mayor Strong desired his selection as president of the Police Board. Too, there were rumors of his incorruptibility, his daring courage, and his independence. Naturally enough, his appointment had been viewed with mixed emotions. To the notorious Tom Byrnes, superintendent of the department, it was the end of happy, influential days. To Jacob Riis, whose excursions into New York's slums had produced *How the Other Half Lives*, the appointment seemed divine deliverance from an era of corruption. Riis was a newspaper reporter at headquarters.

At the first meeting of the new board, Roosevelt became its president, and in due course the other commissioners blocked his program. Before two years of his five-year term had ended he was weary and discouraged and was hoping that President McKinley would call him back to Washington. At first, though, optimism ruled. The New York *World* proclaimed "the substitution of the reform idea for the spoils system."

The general approbation did not extend to the other three members of the board: Frederick D. Grant, son of the Civil War general, Andrew D. Parker, an anti-Tammany Democrat, and Avery D. Andrews, the second Democratic member. Roosevelt got along amicably with Andrews. Parker, however, was to be his bitter opponent, and Grant he considered easily misled. For the bipartisan board, destined to be the center of unending friction, only the politicians had any use.

A secondary cause of disharmony in the Police Board was the spotlight focused on Roosevelt, a spotlight so white and continuous that the other three commissioners found themselves in comparative shadow. The new president of the board was none too considerate of the feelings of his colleagues. He came rushing into headquarters on the first day, had himself elected chairman, and demanded as soon as he could get his breath, "What'll we do now?" He assumed, from the start, that his position was superior to the standing of the other three commissioners, although, in law and in fact, each had equal power.

But Roosevelt could not be blamed, at the beginning, for the public attention he attracted. Later he may have been responsible, because of his Haroun-al-Raschid prowlings through the city, often accompanied by a reporter. He had no way of avoiding the pen portraits of such journalists as Arthur Brisbane, then a feature writer on the New York *World*. "Sing, heavenly muse," began Brisbane's prose poem, "the sad dejection of our poor policemen. We have a real Police Commissioner. His teeth are big and white, his eyes are small and piercing, his voice is rasping. He makes our policemen feel as the little froggies did when the stork came to rule them. His heart is full of reform, and a policeman in full uniform, with helmet, revolver and night club, is no more to him than a plain, every day human being."

Everyone agreed that the new police head had brought color and action to Mulberry Street. His flair for dressing up led him to wear, on hot summer days, a remarkable black silk sash in place of a vest. This, combined with a pink shirt and with its tasseled ends dangling to his knees, was a constant source of astonishment to visitors at headquarters. In May, 1895, Roosevelt was not quite thirty-seven years old. He was heavier than he had been before, a development that worried him a good deal. But his health was excellent; he was determined to make good, and he saw in the post of police commissioner the opportunity for limitless pleasant excitement.

Action began immediately, with Roosevelt as the spokesman for the board. An early sensation was the appointment of a young woman as secretary to the president of the Police Board, a selection not entirely due to feminist leanings on Roosevelt's part. She was a protégée of Joe Murray. A woman in the excessively male atmosphere of police headquarters, however, was hailed in the press as "another illustration of the onward march of women."

The first crisis faced by the new board lay in the person of Superintendent Byrnes. "I think I shall move against Byrnes at once," Roosevelt wrote Lodge on May 18. Less than ten days later the policeman who had been in the department since 1863, who had caught the notorious Manhattan Bank robbers, and who had earned the gratitude of prominent financiers by orders that thieves were not to operate, as such, in Wall Street, packed his things and departed. Inspector Peter Conlin, who was ultimately to protest that he was weary of "being used as a missle, thrown by one commissioner at the other," was made acting chief. Conlin, too, quickly fell under Rooseveltian disapproval.

3

It was early in the police commissioner days that Roosevelt's teeth grew famous. It became part of the New York credo that delinquent patrolmen watched uneasily for the approach at night of a dark figure with gleaming molars. Some time passed before Roosevelt appreciated the humor in this, and he was offended when some reporter disguised himself with a broad-brimmed hat and circled the town frightening policemen by chattering his teeth at them. Still later, peddlers appeared with small whistles supposed to be replicas of "Teddy's Teeth," and a loyal policeman arrested one of the hawkers for *lèse majesté*. But by this time, Roosevelt's sense of humor had returned and when shown one of the novelties he remarked that they were "very pretty."

"I suppose it is more habit than anything else," said Roosevelt in 1900, when asked to explain his extraordinary dental display. "All short-sighted men have some facial characteristic of which they are unconscious. I cannot be blamed for having good teeth, or this characteristic of a short-sighted man."

The unhappy police considered Roosevelt's eyesight all too good during the summer of 1895. He arrived one drowsy June afternoon at a station house in the lower part of the city, and interrupted the meditations of the sergeant on the desk. He watched appreciatively while an ambulance surgeon sewed up the cuts in the hand of a Mr. John Sullivan, suddenly brought in. This diversion over, the commissioner went back, with the sergeant as a nervous escort, to the cell block in the rear of the station house. In one of the cells an intoxicated woman was engaged in the absorbing occupation of hauling on a string which disappeared out of a window. While the sergeant watched in horror, and Roosevelt very sternly, a whisky flask appeared on the end of the string. But the sergeant was a man of action. He entered the cell, battled with the inebriated lady, and emerged with the remnants of the bottle and a badly cut hand. Roosevelt made a note of his heroism and departed, remarking that he had had "a very pleasant time." This was life in the raw.

The excursions at night gave Roosevelt the greatest pleasure. There was a fantastic note to the program of dining at someone's home and then, at midnight, sallying forth with a black cloak over his evening clothes and a wide-brimmed hat pulled down over his face. He prowled through dark streets in the hope of finding a patrolman asleep, off his beat, or engaged in diverting conversation with a friendly prostitute. Disguised as he was, the commissioner could often lead some unwary patrolman into insolent defiance when questioned. Then Roosevelt would reduce the wretch to incoherent servility by explaining that he was president of the Police Board.

Variety sparked the nights. He spied a policeman at the side door of a saloon, drinking a glass of beer. The man tossed his glass into the saloon and started to run, but after a chase of fifty yards, Roosevelt had him by the collar, and he was cited to appear for trial the next day. So the ramblings would continue until well toward dawn. Then Roosevelt would appear at Mike Lyons's restaurant on the Bowery, eat a hearty meal of ham and eggs, and retire to a couch at his office nearby for an hour or two of sleep. By 10 o'clock he was refreshed and energetic once more, ready to pass judgment on the trembling victims of the night's excursion.

The citizens of New York, as they read of these exploits, glowed with vicarious satisfaction. They had yearned to humble insolent policemen themselves. The approval was entirely unanimous and Roosevelt was the subject of commendatory comment in Philadelphia, Chicago, Baltimore, and other cities. Before the end of the year, Cabot Lodge was painting alluring pictures of the United States Senate, even of the White House itself.

But in New York, at least, the applause began to die when Roosevelt announced that he intended to enforce the Sunday excise law and that, in due time, even beer would be impossible to obtain on the Sabbath. This was not reform; it was interference with personal liberty.

4

Fundamentally, Roosevelt was not a prohibitionist nor did he really care whether beer or anything else was sold on Sunday. He started with the sound position that violations of the excise law led to extortion by the police and that if the department was to be cleansed, it was necessary to enforce the law. He soon became enmeshed in a web of inaccurate thinking, however, and he demanded that all laws, good and bad, be enforced. He delivered himself into the hands of his enemies, because of this surplus of zeal, and his career as police commissioner ended largely in failure.

Roosevelt's views on prohibition itself can, fortunately, be set forth in his own words. He expressed himself as forcibly opposed on at least three occasions while in public life; in 1884, in 1905, and in 1908. Excessive use of alcohol, he said over and over, could not be controlled by law. It was not until the last year or so of his life that Roosevelt was persuaded to endorse the dry movement and he then did so with qualifications and misgivings.

"I cannot sit still and hear the arguments in favor of prohibition," said Assemblyman Roosevelt on January 24, 1884, "without at least raising my voice against it." The occasion was a debate over a resolution calling for a referendum on a state prohibition amendment, a resolution that met defeat partly because of Roosevelt's argument. Roosevelt added that he respected the motives of many of the sincere prohibitionists, but the extremists among them did "quite as much harm to decency and morality as the extremists of the other side." As for the political aspects, he voiced a challenge to the fanatics who said that the Republican party must adopt prohibition as its cause or be destroyed as the Whigs had been destroyed by the Abolitionists.

But the struggle for morality by legislative fiat gathered force. The support of the churches had soon been enlisted and the alarm of the politicians increased. Curiously enough Roosevelt, whose paternalistic tendencies were pronounced and who believed in a Federal divorce law, continued to feel that alcohol was an individual problem.

Had Roosevelt, as police commissioner, recalled the speech he had made in the legislature in 1884, he would have avoided great difficulty. But he was facing an extremely complicated situation. New York had been drifting along comfortably under a law that forbade the sale of liquor on Sunday. The front doors of the saloons were closed, but the workingman knew that a side or rear door would swing hospitably inward at the slightest touch. Virtuous vestrymen, passing the corner saloon on their way to church, saw with satisfaction that all was outwardly decorous. They knew that at their clubs, after the morning service, refreshment could be obtained. Despite this tranquillity, however, the Sunday closing law was a source of evil; the police enforced it against the saloonkeepers who refused to buy protection. Roosevelt had not been in office for more than a few weeks before he attempted to solve the insoluble. His declaration of war read:

I do not deal with public sentiment. I deal with the law. I am going to see if we cannot break the license forthwith of any saloon keeper who sells on Sunday. This applies just as much to the biggest hotel as to the smallest grogshop. To allow a lax enforcement of the law means to allow it to be enforced just as far as the individual members of the police force are willing to wink at its evasion. Woe be to the policeman who exposes himself to the taint of corruption.

Accompanied by columns of newspaper prediction that the day would be dry, the Roosevelt program of enforcement started on Sunday, June 23, 1895. Early on that day a small steamer, the S.S. *Sarah,* anchored in the Harlem River with a large sign over the side bearing the words: "No Whisky or Beer Aboard, but Plenty of Water. Try the Water. It's the Kind You Like." Whether word of this prehistoric Rum Row had been passed about, or whether they were merely curious, large numbers of men were soon pulling for the vessel in rowboats, and three stout policemen in uniform promptly hired a skiff of their own. The skipper of the *Sarah* saw them, however, and pulled anchor in time to steam away. Later in the day he returned, probably for additional customers anxious to sample the water. This time Roosevelt's men used guile. In plain clothes they rowed to the *Sarah* once more, boarded her, and made their arrest.

By the middle of July, 1895, the uproar was incessant, and Roosevelt had been transformed into an extremely unpopular figure. His men continued to arrest saloonkeepers, the town was measurably more arid than it had been, and the weather was exceedingly hot. The workingman, deprived of his beer, demanded to know why the upper classes, enjoying the cool recesses of the Union League Club, could obtain anything they wanted to drink.

"They are united," complained Roosevelt, "in portraying me as spending my Sundays drinking heavily in the Union League Club."

The Sunday closing law, like the Federal prohibition amendment that was to follow it, struck at the beer drinker more than at the whisky drinker. The saloonkeeper could sell a pint of hard liquor to be smuggled home. The man with the tin pail known as a "growler" was certain to be seen emerging from the side door. The beer drinker of the '90's faced perils, in fact, that no longer exist, for his long mustaches offered a clue to what went on behind the swinging doors. The police waited in plain clothes on the corner near a suspected saloon; when a citizen appeared wiping his mustaches with the back of his hand, they made a raid.

That New York was much more dry on Sunday during that summer is undoubtedly true. That it was as dry as Roosevelt believed it—"I have, for once, absolutely enforced the law in New York"—is improbable. That it was dry enough to irritate the citizenry to new heights of indignation is clear. The Germans were particularly outraged. Favorite beer parlors and gardens, where they had spent quiet days with their wives and children, were closed. After an arid summer, and knowing that the state elections were but a few weeks distant, they organized a parade of protest. It was scheduled for September 25, 1895. It was known that the atmosphere would be stolidly hostile. But someone made the mistake of sending an invitation to Roosevelt, supposing that he would appreciate the heavy sarcasm implied and would decline. Instead, he promptly accepted. It was a tactical error on the part of the Germans, for Roosevelt enjoyed himself hugely and, with the amazing talent for the picturesque that helped carry him to the White House, the police commissioner transformed the angry demonstration into a minor personal triumph.

He laughed uproariously when a coffin labeled "Teddyism" was trundled by, when signs appeared proclaiming "Roosevelt's Razzle Dazzle Reform Racket," when Germanic drinking societies solemnly held empty beer steins aloft. Then a rotund German, his blue eyes peering through heavy lenses, trudged past and, looking up at the reviewing stand, asked in a loud tone:

"*Wo ist der Roosevelt?*"

The police commissioner leaned far over, grinned and screamed back:

"*Hier bin Ich!*"

There was a burst of laughter, from marchers and spectators alike. Next day's newspapers agreed that Roosevelt had survived his supposed ordeal very well indeed.

But the enemies of reform had, before this, devised a master stroke which spelled ultimate defeat. It aggravated the growing friction in the Police Board. It supplied ammunition that even Roosevelt's personality could not turn aside. Their latest move, Roosevelt wrote on July 14, 1895, "has been, through various lawyers, to revive obsolete blue laws, and bring cases before magistrates. The blue law business is puzzling." Instead of ignoring the ordinances against soda fountains, florists, delicatessen keepers, and bootblacks, Roosevelt vacillated between agreeing that these ancient statutes must be enforced and insisting that he was not interested. He told a Good Government Club on July 16 that "the law will be enforced in every particular." He permitted the police to close soda-water parlors. He indignantly denounced as a lie the story that orders had gone out against flower-selling; but so friendly a journal as the New York *Times* commented on the arrest of a peddler who had sold five cents' worth of violets to a detective.

Tammany Hall was probably back of these arrests, made to embarrass Roosevelt. He had placed himself in a position where such blows could be struck. It was next rumored that ice could no longer be sold on Sunday, and Charles F. Murphy, then a Tammany leader on the East Side, dispensed ice water free of charge from two liquor stores on Avenue A. The attacks went to the extreme of stating that ice was being denied the sick and dying, and Joseph Pulitzer's New York *Evening World* thereupon reached a new low mark in journalistic depravity. It published an account, giving neither names nor dates nor place, of a mother who had vainly sought a small piece of ice for her sick child. The dealer had declined to sell, since it was a Sunday morning, but had given the woman some ice. At this moment a patrolman came by, refused to listen to their stories, and took them both to court. The *Evening World* concluded this obvious fabrication by describing the mother's return to the bedside of her child:

"I was kept away, darling. I couldn't get the ice because . . ."
Suddenly the words died on her lips. She knelt by the bed and took a little wasted hand in hers. Then, raising her face, she gazed up with dry eyes that yet saw nothing and whispered:
"Thy will be done, O God! Thou knowest best!"
For the child was dead!

Roosevelt continued his onslaughts. He insisted that "the sole weapons of our foes are mendacity and misrepresentation." "Talk as little as possible," was the futile advice from his friend Cabot Lodge. Roosevelt talked a great deal, but sometimes there were moments of deep depression. He wrote Lodge in December, 1895:

. . . It really seems there *must* be some fearful shortcoming on my side to account for the fact that I have not one New York City newspaper or one New York City politician on my side.

During 1896 public attention was shifted from Roosevelt's police activities. Bryan, with his heresies of free silver and rights for the masses, caused a chill of fear in the East, and Roosevelt joined in the heroic efforts whereby the invader was thrown back across the River Platte. But his unpopularity as police commissioner increased and, as 1896 progressed, he succeeded in alienating nearly every faction essential to success. The reform element, once his staunch ally, was irritated by the constant bickerings at meetings of the Police Board. Welfare workers were horrified when he sanctioned the use of a small boy to obtain evidence against a saloon where liquor was sold to minors. Sporting enthusiasts were indignant over his attempts to control conditions in the prize ring; even more furious protests arose in conservative circles when he went to a prize fight himself and said he enjoyed it because it had been an honest contest. Mayor Strong had meanwhile grown weary of the blue-law and excise activities, as he made clear in December, 1895. The mayor said that a citizen of an upstate town had recently asked whether one of the four heads of the police department could not be lent to assist in cleaning up a local crime wave.

"I told him," the mayor said, "all four were busy watching the girls who sold flowers and the poor devils who sold ice on Sunday."

Roosevelt declined to reply to this, saying he knew that the mayor could not be serious. But as early as October he had been writing to Lodge that Strong had been asking him "to let up on the saloon, and impliedly threatening to turn me out if I refused!" The cruelest defection was that of Dr. Parkhurst himself. In September, 1895, he had promised to stand by Roosevelt "until death." In January, 1897, he was scolding him for his part in the Police Board quarrels and insisting that the board, "by the indignity of its demeanor is doing more to depress than elevate the tone of the force."

The indictment was all too accurate. New York was to wait twenty years for a repetition of such rows among city officials. The other three commissioners, it will be recalled, were Grant, Parker, and Andrews, of whom only the last supported Roosevelt. The president of the board was probably in the right in most of his contentions; certainly he was far the ablest and most active member. Never too competent a judge of men, being warmhearted and anxious to believe the best of his fellow citizens, Roosevelt had at first placed full confidence in Parker and Grant.

Wrangling in the Police Board began in August, 1895, when Commissioner Grant took exception to the trial of a police captain against whom charges had been brought by Parkhurst's men. On August 16, Grant criticized the excise campaign and said that "crooks take advantage of the police being at saloon doors." On February 18, 1896, Commissioner Parker remarked that Roosevelt was receiving from $100 to $250 for speeches he was making outside of New York. This seemed unnecessary, since the president of the Police Board was a man of private means—the intimation being that Roosevelt was neglecting his duties. In March the rupture was interfering with police matters. Parker was absent from many meetings. He was working with Chief Conlin to block promotions and appointments.

"Your manner," snapped Parker to Roosevelt at a meeting in April, "conveys the impression that your desires and wants are law."

The year ended with open disagreement over excise enforcement, with Mayor Strong urging Roosevelt to soften his blows. But in April, 1896, a still more serious complication arose through the passage at Albany of the Raines Law, a statute which turned out to be the greatest boon to commercialized vice in the history of New York. Ostensibly a liquor-control measure, the Raines Law continued the provision that hotels could serve liquor on Sunday and defined a hotel as a structure with ten bedrooms and facilities for serving meals. Soon hotels were springing into existence at an astonishing rate. Competition became excessively keen as hundreds of new ones appeared; the ten rooms required by law were used for prostitution in order to pay the overhead. Previously Roosevelt's problem had been merely to see whether, in places where intoxicants were served, there had actually been dining rooms. Now his men had to judge whether the hotels themselves were genuine. That many were not was indicated by the offer of a furniture firm to furnish all of the ten rooms for $81.20.

Had Roosevelt begun a crusade against this evil, a drive as vigorous as his excise campaign of the year before, he would have found public opinion squarely behind him. Commercialized vice, even in the '90's, was far different from beer drinking on Sunday. But Roosevelt, it would seem, had no heart for another fight. He had been pulling wires for some weeks in the hope of an appointment from President

McKinley. His effectiveness, also, had been further damaged by violent quarrels with Comptroller Ashbel P. Fitch, who had objected to the manner in which certain police funds had been allocated. At a city hall hearing on May 5, 1896, Roosevelt had exploded that Fitch was no fighter and would run away. The following intellectual exchange then ensued:

Fitch: I would never run away from you!
Roosevelt: You would not fight.
Fitch: What shall it be, pistols or—
Roosevelt: Pistols or anything you wish.
Mayor Strong: Come, come. If this does not stop I will put you both under arrest.

The year closed, and 1897 began, very much on this note. Charges were finally brought against Parker for neglect of duty, with Roosevelt as a leading witness for the prosecution. On March 17, 1897, Mayor Strong screwed his courage to the sticking point and dismissed Roosevelt's adversary, but not until Seth Low had pleaded with him to end the disgraceful scenes at board meetings and to "bring some or all the commissioners to trial." The last few months of 1896 were devoted by Roosevelt almost entirely to the campaign against Bryan and to negotiations for appointment as Assistant Secretary of the Navy.

The police commissioner years were years of immaturity, but there was growth, too. If they ended in a degree of failure, they were not without influence on Roosevelt and his career. Of chief importance is the fact that he came into contact, for the first time, with social problems on an extended scale. It was during the Mulberry Street days that Roosevelt absorbed so much of the philosophy of Jacob Riis and abandoned the attitude of aloof noninterference that had marked his legislative years. He became "more set than ever in my distrust of those men, whether business men or lawyers, judges, legislators or executive officers, who seek to make of the Constitution a fetich for the prevention of work of social reform."

Nor had Roosevelt damaged himself politically, even by his crusade for righteousness. The Platt machine abhorred him more than ever. It seemed as though all the factions were united against him. But Roosevelt was the child of fate. Tom Platt was forced to nominate him, less than two years later, for governor of New York. He was forced to support him, not a decade later, for a second term in the White House. The police commissioner years made Roosevelt a national figure; even an international one, inasmuch as the London *Times* carried lengthy accounts of his activities on Mulberry Street. He had earned a just reputation for vigor and for honesty, if not for good sense or diplomacy, and this was of value when the lightning struck.

His retirement to Washington was accompanied by customary polite editorial regret. It was said, with truth, that Roosevelt had brought a new conception of honesty to the police department. A degree of civil service had been instituted and the novel idea of promotion for merit had made its first, faint impression. The reform element was to regret, perhaps, that it had been of so little faith and had supported so half-heartedly the man who had been its hero.

Chapter XII

THE NATION IN PERIL

The winds from the West were ominous and chilled the bones of respectable people. They grew to gale proportions as 1896 approached; the respectable people whispered of the danger of revolution. They penetrated the office of Theodore Roosevelt in police headquarters on Mulberry Street and filled him with a curious tangle of exhilaration and alarm. He agreed that danger existed, but danger brought with it excitement. Had he not been an officer in the New York National Guard? Could he not, metaphorically speaking, take down his sword to defend his country against the menace from within? But Mark Hanna, who was to be the Horatius of 1896, preferred campaign contributions and declared this chatter of revolution nonsensical.

"You're just a lot of damn fools," he said, at luncheon, in the Cleveland Union League Club.

The winds began to blow in 1886, with the explosion of the bomb in Haymarket Square in Chicago. They stirred uneasily until four of the anarchists, as they were conveniently called, had been hanged in November, 1887. They gathered new force, in 1893, when Governor John P. Altgeld of Illinois, knowing it to be political suicide, pardoned two of the men whose sentences of death had been changed to life imprisonment because the evidence against them was even less substantial. Altgeld, as he had foreseen, paid the penalty of courage. He vanished from public life.

These winds were from Illinois; there were others. In May, 1892, Henry Clay Frick of the Carnegie Steel Company notified his superintendent that, "with a desire to act toward our employees in the most liberal manner," a number of wage reductions had been put into effect. On June 25, he wrote to Robert A. Pinkerton of New York for three hundred armed guards. They were needed, he said, to maintain order at the Homestead plant near Pittsburgh and they would be moved up the Ohio River on the night of July 5. They were shipped according to schedule, and in the battle which resulted ten men were killed and seventy wounded. On July 23, Alexander Berkman attempted to assassinate Mr. Frick and wounded him severely.

The Haymarket bombing, the Homestead rioting, the attack on a great industrialist—all these were placed at the door of organized labor. Then came the panic of 1893, the bread lines, and bitterness. Then, in 1894, the Pullman strike in Chicago brought more disorder and President Cleveland used Federal troops to move the mails. This time Eugene V. Debs went to jail because he had ignored a sweeping injunction. Debs became a martyr, as the four men who had been hanged were martyrs. It must have been fear which caused people of wealth and breeding to strike back so viciously at their enemies. The respectables still had power. By the summer of 1896 they had found a third scapegoat for the friction and the turmoil of a decade. He was William Jennings Bryan, who stood for the income tax, for railroad regulation, and for free coinage of silver.

There were other scapegoats in addition to Altgeld, Debs, and Bryan. Another was General Jacob Coxey of Massillon, Ohio. Coxey's "Army of the Commonwealth of Christ" had started to mobilize, in the dismal jungles of the hobo world, and in 1894 the dreary march to Washington began. They came to demand an issue of $500,000,000 in paper money.

"Messrs. Bryan, Altgeld, Debs, Coxey and the rest," said Roosevelt in October, 1896, when urging the election of McKinley, "have not the power to rival the deeds of Marat, Barrère, and Robespierre, but they are strikingly like the leaders of the Terror of France in mental and moral attitude."

2

The national crisis, as Roosevelt sincerely viewed the Populist movement, interrupted pleasant dreams of greatness.

Lodge had been painting his future with the bright hues of optimism. "The day is not far distant," wrote this friend from Paris in August, 1895, "when you will come into a large kingdom." Roosevelt's fight for excise control might have annoyed the Republican machine leaders, but it had afforded new strength in the rural parts of New York State. "The Senatorship," added Lodge, "is getting well into sight, my dear boy." Roosevelt, of course, could not abandon his usual pessimism. "Platt's influence is simply poisonous," he replied. It was impossible for an "honest man of sincerity"—an idealistic notion he would eventually abandon—to work with this boss. The chance of "future political preference for me is that of lightning striking." Lodge, however, persisted. "I do not say that you are to be President tomorrow," he wrote. "I do not say that it will be—I am sure that it may and can be."

Roosevelt would have been inhuman had he failed, with such visions floating before him, to ponder the future. He had, however, a firm foundation of common sense. This, combined with his knowledge of the uncertain nature of politics, caused him to shrink from such ponderings. One day in 1895 at police headquarters, Jacob Riis came to his office with Lincoln Steffens. They asked whether he was a possible candidate for President of the United States, and Roosevelt leaped to his feet, red with rage.

"Don't you dare ask me that!" he almost screamed. "Don't you put such ideas into my head. No friend of mine would say a thing like that. Never, never, must either of you remind a man on a political job that he may be President. It almost always kills him politically. He loses his nerve; he can't do his work; he gives up the very traits that are making him a possibility."

Thus at thirty-seven, Theodore Roosevelt intuitively appreciated a political truth men twice his age had never learned. Roosevelt went on with the job at hand, but the campaign of 1896 was to make him, as Lodge hoped it would, far better known to the people. Oddly enough, the leading issue was to be an economic one, and Roosevelt knew precious little about economics.

The issue was free coinage of silver, and Roosevelt's position on it, unlike McKinley's, had been consistent. The men closest to him saw clearly the peril inherent in the Sherman Act. On March 7, 1891, he addressed the Federal Club in New York City and said:

. . . the demand for the unlimited coinage of depreciated silver is simply the phase in the struggle against honest money which happens to be uppermost at the moment. During the last year there has been a perfect craze on this subject, which has swept over the West and South and has affected somewhat the Middle States. Fortunately for the honor and good faith of the country, it was the Republican Party which was in power, and the Republican Party steadfastly withstood the demand.

In making such a statement, Roosevelt was misinformed. The Sherman Act required the Treasury to buy 4,500,000 ounces of silver each month and to issue certificates, redeemable in either gold or silver, in payment. The difference between such a law and unlimited coinage was so slight as to be nonexistent. The silver output in 1890 was little more than 4,500,000 ounces a month. Harrison, a Republican President, had approved the bill. The truth is that free silver, like nearly every important issue in American history, cut across both parties. The Democrats were to bear the onus for it because of Bryan.

Grover Cleveland, a Democrat, accomplished repeal of the dangerous Sherman Silver Purchase Act. He returned to the White House, in March, 1893, to face the task of saving his country from financial ruin. Against an impassioned plea by Bryan and others, the law which was draining the treasury of its reserves was repealed on August 28, 1893. The President preserved the nation's credit, and ruined himself in doing so. "Staunch old boy! Great old character!" remarked the amiable McKinley during the fight. Prosperity and contentment did not come, however. The wheels of industry slowed down until they almost stopped. The farmer burned his grain because he could not sell it.

More than three years passed. On November 10, 1896, a Victory Luncheon was held in New York City at which those who had defeated Bryan and his silver battalions gathered to congratulate themselves. Jacob Schiff, of Kuhn, Loeb & Company, was there with Isaac Seligman, of J. & W. Seligman & Company, Cornelius N. Bliss, James McCreery, the merchant, and John A. Stewart. They thanked God, as they ate, for Mark Hanna. Mr. Hanna, receiving congratulations for his part in the victory, was modest, although he agreed that prosperity would soon return. Theodore Roosevelt was a shade obscure among these local great.

Toward the end of the luncheon Carl Schurz, who had campaigned for the gold standard after his years of error as a Democrat and a Mugwump, arose. He proposed a toast to the President of the United States, "a bulwark against all financial heresies!"

The toast was drunk. After all, Mr. Cleveland was still

President. But there were no cheers. One or two of the celebrants, as they left, remarked that it had been excessively bad taste to introduce Mr. Cleveland's name at such a moment.

3

Speaker Thomas B. Reed, who had reorganized the rules of the House so that troublesome minorities could be stifled with ease, was a man to stir enthusiastic approval in the breast of Theodore Roosevelt. He did things. He, too, was "pure act"; or so Roosevelt believed until he later learned that Reed could be rather too cynical. In 1891, it will be recalled, there had been an abortive boom for his nomination. Roosevelt and Cabot Lodge then started to work for his selection as Republican presidential nominee in 1896.

Tom Platt, however, viewed Reed with distaste. The speaker had been too domineering and had antagonized influential members of his party before the St. Louis convention in the summer of 1896. In this, Platt's diagnosis was correct. Spring Rice, who saw Reed constantly and liked him, referred to him as "that fat, sarcastic man." Mark Hanna, nursing the aspirations of McKinley, had brought Reed to Ohio for the 1891 campaign and then had dismissed him from consideration as a presidential possibility. The speaker's manner had been alien to the great mass of Republican voters whom Hanna intended to control. He was eastern. He was not given to bombastic oratory. So Hanna went on with his plans to nominate McKinley and held that wavering warrior to support of the gold plank ultimately adopted. Reed, bitter and unhappy, addressed a letter to his friend Roosevelt. What remained for the future? he asked. He had twice been Speaker; a Cabinet post did not appeal:

> In a word, my dear boy, I am tired of this thing and want to be sure that my debts won't have to be paid by a syndicate. Moreover, the receding grapes seem to ooze with acid and the whole thing is a farce.

This was a reference, which Roosevelt doubtless deplored, to the fact that in 1893 a syndicate headed by Hanna had subscribed $100,000 to save McKinley from financial ruin.

The nomination of Hanna's man had been conceded when the convention assembled. All that remained was a plank calling for the gold standard. It was adopted on the third day, June 19, 1896, and as the vote was being taken a score of free silver delegates left the hall in disgust. They were watched with satisfaction by William Jennings Bryan, who was in the press section as the correspondent of the Omaha *World-Herald*. Roosevelt, who had not achieved election as a delegate to the convention, scribbled a note to Lodge from Sagamore Hill. McKinley was an honorable man; the platform was excellent. He congratulated his friend for his part in bringing about the gold plank.

The voice of the people became the voice of God; the voice of the Republican party was the voice of Wall Street. Such was the issue as the Democrats prepared to gather at Chicago for their own convention. The first was true only in the minds of oppressed men and women. The second was true, in fact. It was the "plain people," whose support Roosevelt cherished as President, who in 1896 turned to the magnetic figure of Bryan. Quite apart from the merit of free silver, their grievances were real. The ones who wanted jobs could not find them. Those who had farms could not sell their products. The final insult had been a five to four decision of the Supreme Court that an income tax provided by Congress in 1894 was unconstitutional.

The story of Bryan is the story of one man's voice. His first juvenile achievements were in debates and oratorical contests at school, beginning when he was fifteen with "Give me liberty or give me death!" His gifts were similarly displayed at Illinois College. In 1890, having studied law and started to practice at Lincoln, Nebraska, he was sent to Congress from a district that was normally Republican. Mrs. Bryan, who met him during his junior year at college, remembered that his "face was pale and thin; a pair of keen, dark eyes looked out from beneath heavy brows; his nose was prominent—too large to look well, I thought."

From 1890 until he died, the voice of Bryan was never still. He was well known in the silver country months before the 1896 convention. In April he was dreaming of having his name presented as the presidential nominee. It was his voice, when the chance came to debate the silver plank from the platform, which brought him to the goal of his aspirations. Bryan labored most of the night before the debate on July 9. He worked over old speeches, and decided that a phrase successful on many earlier occasions—the "cross of gold and crown of silver" phrase—was the most effective in his repertoire. On July 10 he was nominated for the presidency. The hostile factions of the Democratic party seemed reconciled.

Roosevelt, watching events from Mulberry Street, felt that the Republican party would win, although Bryan was formidable in the West, the Middle West, and the South. He called on Mark Hanna, the new chairman of the Republican National Committee, to offer his services and reported to Lodge that Hanna was a "good-natured, well-meaning, rough man, shrewd and hard-headed, neither farsighted nor very broad-minded." This was in July, 1896.

4

Emotion faced emotion. Hysteria fought hysteria. The respectables, at first, shared Roosevelt's opinion that Bryan could be beaten. At the same time, disquieting reports spread eastward and could not be ignored. Men were rallying under the banners of free silver. Toward the end of July, the McKinley followers were alarmed because of the vast crowds that greeted Bryan wherever he appeared. Then their alarm turned to terror; Bryan became anti-American, even anti-Christ, as terror was sublimated into hatred.

It grew fashionable, as the decades passed, to sneer at William Jennings Bryan. Roosevelt did so, although he borrowed many a platform plank from the man he professed to hold in contempt. In part, Bryan justified the sneers. He was too often a candidate for the presidency. He talked too much. He ate too much. His fanaticism led him to causes which were absurd; the Scopes evolution trial was the worst and the saddest. But in 1896, he spoke for millions who had no other spokesman. Inexhaustible in energy, he would make as many as thirty-six speeches in one day. He probably addressed 5,000,000 people on a tour that covered 16,000 miles. Never a clear thinker, never a student, and often ignorant, Bryan was deeply in earnest, and newspapermen on his campaign train noted that he would kneel in prayer each night.

The respectables did not sneer at Bryan during the summer of 1896. Fearing him, they denounced him. The Rev. Dr. Robert S. McArthur of Calvary Baptist Church in New York and the Rev. T. DeWitt Talmadge of Brooklyn, and, of course, Dr. Parkhurst were among the clergymen who offered sonorous warnings. The Rev. Cortland Myers of the Baptist Temple in Brooklyn admitted that the pulpit was "absolutely non-partisan" but said that he could not be silent:

I must be heard and will be heard against all dishonesty and anarchy and kindred evil. I love the blood-stained banner of the Cross and it is in danger. I must speak every Sunday from now

112

on until November. I shall denounce the Chicago platform. That platform was made in Hell.

The New York *Tribune*, when victory came at last, stated with journalistic complacency that Bryan had been defeated because "right is right and God is God":

He was only a puppet in the blood-imbued hands of Altgeld, the anarchist, and Debs, the revolutionist, and the other desperadoes of that type. He goes down with the cause and must abide with it in the history of infamy. He had less provocation than Benedict Arnold, less intellectual force than Aaron Burr, less manliness and courage than Jefferson Davis. He was the rival of them all in deliberate wickedness and treason to the Republic.

The editorial expressed, with fair accuracy, Roosevelt's own views as the campaign got under way. Through July and August he preserved his balance well enough. In September he told Lodge that the situation in the West was far from hopeless. On September 11, he addressed the Commercial Travellers' Sound Money League in New York City and set forth some rather novel views on free silver. This, he said, would not injure the wealthy man because "his lands, his factories and his homes would still be his." The man of wealth, enjoying credit and paying his bills by check, would get along well enough. The poor man, using cash, would suffer because of depreciated silver dollars. If such reasoning normally marked Roosevelt's economic and financial policies it is not to be wondered that he preferred to deal with other subjects.

"The silver craze surpasses belief," he wrote in a private letter. "Bryan's election would be a great calamity."

The vigor of his expression, if not the accuracy of his ideas, caused Roosevelt to become a major figure in the campaign. Mark Hanna, aroused by the success of Bryan's tour, was leaving nothing undone. He arranged for private trains, by the simple process of sending memoranda initialed M.A.H. to the managers of the leading railroads. Printing presses poured forth literature emphasizing the fallacy of free silver, denouncing the tariff for revenue only, predicting another panic if Bryan won. By October 28, Hanna was so confident of the outcome that he returned a superfluous check. At that, he had raised $3,350,000.

Roosevelt was faintly nauseated by Hanna's program of advertising McKinley "as if he were a patent medicine." He was, however, gratified when the national chairman asked him to speak in the localities where Bryan had been receiving the most enthusiastic plaudits. His ardor grew as he sniffed the air of the battlefield, and at several small towns in the Middle West he remarked that Bryan and Jefferson Davis were very much alike. At Chicago he announced that the danger to the nation was the greatest since the Civil War, that the honor of the United States was in the balance, that Bryan and Altgeld embodied "the negation of the two commandments, 'Thou shalt not steal' and 'Thou shalt do no murder.'"

He reached New York on October 27 to report that those who had heard Bryan in the West had done so from "curiosity." The Democratic nominee had a "hold on the unintelligent and the vicious" alone. On the following day, in a dispatch to the New York *Journal* from Chicago, appeared an account of a conversation between Willis J. Abbot, then an editor of the *Journal*, and Roosevelt. Mr. Abbot was not named in the dispatch.

Roosevelt was quoted as saying that the purpose of the "Propocratic Party" was, whatever its pretensions, "revolution." He had known Bryan well, and had a feeling of "commiseration" for the Democratic candidate. Toward Altgeld he felt much more bitter. He would refuse to meet him.

"Because, sir," Roosevelt said, "I may at any time be called upon to meet the man sword to sword upon the field of battle. When war does come I shall be found at the head of my regiment. I speak with the greatest soberness when I say that the sentiment now animating a large proportion of our people can only be suppressed, as the Commune in Paris was suppressed, by taking ten or a dozen of their leaders out, standing them against a wall, and shooting them dead. I believe it will come to that. These leaders are plotting a social revolution and the subversion of the American Republic."

Roosevelt promptly denied that he had used such a phrase as "sword in hand"; he had talked to Mr. Abbot on a train en route to Chicago. He had supposed the conversation a private one. Denial was followed by counterdenial, with Roosevelt insisting finally that the whole interview was a "tissue of falsehood," with Abbot pointing out that he was "willing to put my reputation for truth against yours."

In the end, righteousness triumphed and the Devil was rebuked. McKinley received 271 electoral votes to 176 for Bryan. On March 5, 1897, the New York *Tribune's* headline on the account of the inauguration was: "Republicans Take the Helm. Under Bright Skies and with Fair Winds, the Ship of State Sails for the Haven of Prosperity."

Chapter XIII

LORD OF THE NAVY

✳

"The truth is, Will," complained President-elect McKinley to William Howard Taft after Election Day in 1896, "Roosevelt is always in such a state of mind."

The appointment of Theodore Roosevelt as Assistant Secretary of the Navy was one of the many perplexities which faced Mr. McKinley. The head of the New York Police Board was clearly entitled to reward for his valiant services against Bryan, but was it wise to assign him to the Navy Department? There had been continuous rows in the Police Board. Perhaps the President-elect had read a recent magazine article in which Roosevelt had hailed "the rugged fighting qualities" without which no nation could "achieve real greatness," and had spoken with scorn of the "timidity of wealth" and its distaste for war. Mr. McKinley may have reflected that timid wealthy men had raised $3,350,000 for his campaign chest. Besides, he was a man of peace and Roosevelt was a jingo.

"If I can only go out of office with the knowledge that I have done what lay in my power to avert this terrible calamity I shall be the happiest man in the world," McKinley remarked to Cleveland on the night before his inauguration, regarding the Spanish War.

Roosevelt was the avowed opponent of peace, but the pressure calling for his appointment as Assistant Secretary of the Navy was great. Lodge had gone to Canton, Ohio, where the President-elect discussed policies and expressed the friendliest feeling for his friend Roosevelt.

"I hope he has no preconceived plans which he would wish to drive through the moment he got in," McKinely said. And Lodge, perhaps with a cough, assured him there was no need for concern on this score.

Lodge might have been denied, but there were other appeals. Myron T. Herrick of Ohio, an important Hanna lieutenant, dropped in to say that the Bellamy Storers of Cincinnati, who had contributed $10,000 to the fund which had mollified McKinley's creditors some years before, also desired Roosevelt's appointment. John Hay, Taft, and Hanna himself agreed that he deserved the post.

Maria Longworth Storer, whose nephew would one day be married to Princess Alice of the White House, had met the Roosevelts during the civil service period. In 1896, the two families were on terms of intimacy. T.R. would be grateful "if you would care to say anything for me, old fellow," he wrote to Bellamy Storer on November 19, 1896. "I should rather have you speak than anyone in the United States." On December 5, he told Mrs. Storer that he was disinclined to go to Canton to plead his own ambitions before McKinley:

He saw me when I went there during the campaign, and if he thinks I am hot-headed and harum-scarum I don't think he will change his mind now. Moreover, I don't wish to appear as a supplicant.

Any indictment that brands Roosevelt a jingo and an imperialist is supported by ample evidence. In 1886, elated by headlines predicting trouble with Mexico, he had offered to organize his Medora ranch hands into a cavalry battalion. He felt that there was "some good stuff among these harum-scarum riders." That same year, at a Fourth of July celebration in the West, he said that he hoped "to see the day when not a foot of American soil will be held by any European power." In 1892 he watched with eager interest the friction with Chile and approved the American demands that an indemnity be paid for injuries to sailors in Valparaiso.

"Do you remember," asked Mrs. Roosevelt of Spring Rice, "how we used to call Theodore the Chilean Volunteer and tease him about his dream of leading a cavalry charge?"

By October, 1894, Roosevelt was demanding the annexation of the Hawaiian Islands and the construction of an oceanic canal through Nicaragua. He told the National Republican Club on May 28, 1895, that he favored the establishment of "a navy that will sustain the honor of the American flag. I want to see the Monroe Doctrine upheld in its entirety. I believe in these policies with all my heart and soul."

Roosevelt reached his point of highest excitement later that year when Great Britain declined to concede the rights of the United States in the Venezuela boundary dispute. The emphatic position taken by President Cleveland won his enthusiastic praise. He told a reporter that England never permitted "a consideration of abstract right or morality [to] interfere with the chance for her national aggrandizement or mercantile gain." As for war, let it come:

American cities may possibly be bombarded, but no ransom will be paid for them. It is infinitely better to see the cities laid level than to see a dollar paid to any foe to buy their safety. Moreover, a great many of our friends seem to forget we will settle the Venezuela question in Canada. Canada would surely be conquered, and once wrested from England it would never be restored.

Similarly wild utterances could be quoted almost indefinitely. "This country needs a war," he informed Lodge on December 27, 1895, but added that "the bankers, brokers and anglomaniacs generally" seemed to favor "peace at any price." These Rooseveltian furies aroused President Eliot of Harvard to ask whether anything could be more offensive "than this doctrine of Jingoism, this chip-on-the-shoulder attitude of a ruffian and a bully." Both Lodge and Roosevelt, he said, were "degenerated sons of Harvard."

McKinley's hesitation in appointing Roosevelt is not surprising. Mark Hanna, his most valued adviser, was frank in his contempt for those who desired war with Spain. Both the President and Hanna, however, seem to have been persuaded by Roosevelt's promises that he would suppress his jingo tendencies. "I should have been entirely loyal and subordinate," he wrote Lodge in March, 1897, when it seemed probable that he was not to be selected. A few days later, hope having revived, he asked his friend to explain to John D. Long, the Secretary of the Navy, that no peril lurked in having him as assistant:

I want him to understand that I shall stay at Washington, hot weather or any other weather, whenever he wants me to stay there, and go wherever he sends me, and my aim should be solely to make his administration a success.

Another obstacle, however, was standing between Roosevelt and his ambiton. Tom Platt of New York saw no reason to reward him with public office.

2

The antagonism between Roosevelt and Platt, periodically suppressed for political reasons, had been increased by Roosevelt's unbending attitude as head of the Police Board. The New York Republican leader knew that so much righteousness was certain to return Tammany Hall to power.

Cabot Lodge, who was at least Roosevelt's equal in political practicality, had no scruples against going to Platt, telling him that Roosevelt wanted the appointment, and asking for his reaction. Platt's answer was evasive. He had nothing but the friendliest personal feelings toward Roosevelt, he said. He would be glad to consider it.

In February, 1896, Roosevelt had complained of the "absolutely cynical disregard of decency" which Platt had exhibited. He was quite "as bad a man as Hill or Croker." But Roosevelt had been willing in 1888 to use Blaine, and he was now just as ready to bow to Platt. Rumors were soon current that he would be neutral in a contest for the United States Senate between Platt and Joseph H. Choate. Choate had been among Roosevelt's supporters since the very beginning of his career. On the night of December 16, 1896, however, Roosevelt attended a "harmony" dinner at which it was agreed that Platt could have the New York senatorship. Two weeks later the Rev. Dr. Parkhurst referred, without mentioning Roosevelt, to "those who consent, spaniellike, to lick the hand of their master." It was plain that Roosevelt, in return for Platt's influence, had withdrawn his opposition.

"I refused to speak at the Choate meeting," he reported to Lodge.

Platt appears to have been singularly dull. It did not dawn on him until the end of March, 1897, that Roosevelt in the Navy Department would be far less annoying than Roosevelt in New York. At last he agreed to the appointment and McKinley sent Roosevelt's name to the Senate on April 5. It was confirmed three days later. That night Roosevelt arrived in Washington and called upon Platt at the Arlington Hotel to express his gratitude. Roosevelt subsequently repaid the debt by writing "a very strong letter" to the board of governors of the Metropolitan Club in Washington. He had been "much annoyed over the alleged opposition to Senator Platt's election to the club."

3

It was pleasant to be back in Washington, although Henry Adams was mourning the dissolution of the group of intimates that had meant so much between 1889 and 1895. On this, "McKinley laid his hand heavily." John Hay had gone to London as ambassador. Spring Rice was in Persia. Only the Lodges and the Roosevelts remained, "but even they were at once absorbed in the interests of power." T.R.

plunged at once into the absorption of work, but he also missed the friends who had made life delightful during the comparatively dull civil service years. He demanded of Spring Rice why he had not written. Had he disapproved of his friend's "supposititious jingoism"? Was he " 'mad' about the arbitration treaty"?

> Oh, Springie, Springie! I fear you are forgetting your barbarian friends on this side of the water. As you see, I am now Assistant Secretary of the Navy. My chief, Secretary Long, is a perfect dear.

The "perfect dear" gazed upon his young assistant with misgivings softened by affectionate admiration. Mr. Long was a splendid old gentleman, who had been governor of Massachusetts. He was about sixty years old as Roosevelt took office. Long was inclined to be conservative and cautious. Roosevelt's "ardor sometimes went faster than the President or the department approved," the Secretary of the Navy remembered. It was only human for him to feel irritated when Roosevelt became the more prominent figure. He may really have replied, as the gossips reported, "Why 'Assistant'?" when someone asked him about his new Assistant Secretary.

Roosevelt might have lived up to his pledges of good conduct, made in all sincerity, had he served in less exciting times. For him to submerge his truculent ideas was, under the circumstances, quite beyond his power. He seemed to personify all of the forces that demanded a show of arms on the part of the United States. The navy must be enlarged. The chance of a war with Spain over Cuba must not be forfeited through interference by timid pacifists. Such was the stream of thought that swept on toward war in 1897. McKinley, who hoped for peace, had brought to Washington a young man who, within the decade, had been favorably inclined toward war with Mexico, Chile, Great Britain, Spain, and all European powers so arrogant as to hold colonies in the western half of the world.

In addition, Roosevelt desired expansion in the Pacific. A canal across the isthmus at Nicaragua or Panama would certainly be built some day and Cleveland, he felt, had erred sadly in declining to annex Hawaii. Now, in 1897, the Japanese were looking at the Hawaiian Islands with covetous eyes. On April 22, while Acting Secretary of the Navy in the absence of Long, Roosevelt assured President McKinley that the U.S.S. *Philadelphia* was already at Hawaii and that other war vessels could steam there swiftly. Ten days later he wrote Capt. A. T. Mahan, the naval authority whose views influenced him profoundly:

If I had my way, we would annex those islands tomorrow. If that is impossible, I would establish a protectorate. I believe we should build the Nicaraguan Canal at once, and should build a dozen new battleships, half of them on the Pacific Coast. I am fully alive to the danger from Japan.

But his superior, the Secretary of the Navy, was "only luke-warm" on building up the fleet. The new Assistant Secretary, seething underneath, controlled his public utterances until June 2, 1897, when he addressed the Naval War College at Newport. He cast to the winds any promise that he would be subordinate. It was an excellent address, and it must have delighted the naval officers who dreamed, as they listened, of battle and glory and advancement in rank. No danger existed, said Roosevelt, "of an over-development of warlike spirit; the danger is of precisely the opposite character." A wealthy nation,

slothful, timid or unwieldy, is an easy prey for any people which still retains the most valuable of all qualities, the soldierly virtues. Peace is a goddess only when she comes with sword girt on thigh. The ship of state can be steered safely only when it is always possible to bring her against any foe with "her leashed thunders gathering for the leap."

Clearly the burden of proof rested upon peace.

The rest of the address constituted a plea for a strong navy, "not merely for defense," and included a veiled reference to Cuba: ". . . if we mean to protect the people of the lands who look to us for protection from tyranny and aggression," he said, an adequate navy was essential. Otherwise, the United States might as well "abandon all talk of devotion to the Monroe Doctrine or to the honor of the American name."

This speech showed power. It was one that Roosevelt, at the height of his career, would have been content to make; it offers an accurate outline of the philosophy that molded Theodore Roosevelt during the greater part of his life. Let the thing be done, and worry about the law and the details afterward. Only cowards evade the cost of a just war, and war is usually just. Let not this country place too much faith in its bankers and industrialists, its brokers and its merchants: ". . . a thousand rich bankers," he said, "cannot leave such a heritage as Farragut left."

Public reception of the speech was divided. Dana of the *Sun,* who had been agitating for the liberation of Cuba, endorsed such views heartily. *Harper's Weekly* criticized Roosevelt's "bellicose fervor." One or two more belligerent speeches were made during the summer of 1897 and these so distressed Navy Secretary Long that Roosevelt, again, promised to reform. All he had done, he pleaded in August, was to hold forth on the need for additional ships.

As the summer wore on the country drifted closer to war with Spain, and Long, a little apprehensive, left Washington for a rest, and permitted his assistant to command the Navy Department. Further reassurances from Roosevelt probably convinced Long that a disquieting dispatch in the New York *Sun* was exaggerated. This said that the Assistant Secretary had "the whole Navy bordering on a war footing. It remains only to sand down the decks and pipe to quarters for action."

"The Secretary is away, and I am having immense fun running the Navy," he had written with naïve delight.

4

The fervor of a nation for war is often confused with the fervor of its war party. In time, there was popular enthusiasm enough for the war with Spain, but a debate on April 6, 1897, in the House on the plight of Cuba aroused little interest. Noisy minorities, however, continued to express sympathy for the insurgents who had rebelled against Spanish rule in February, 1895.

The war so greatly desired by Roosevelt finally came as the result of various causes. With several of them, he can have had little patience. American trade with Cuba, for instance, had reached nearly $100,000,000 by 1894 and it dropped to almost nothing because of the turmoil. Aware that economic arguments could effectively supplement appeals to America's idealism, the insurgents contributed at least their share to the destruction of sugar plantations in which American capital was invested. Then, through press agents, they placed the blame on Spain. It was not entirely true, as Roosevelt had declared, that the financial interests of the nation shrank from war. In all probability, however, it never would have come had not Joseph Pulitzer and William Randolph Hearst been anxious to increase the circulations of their newspapers. Hearst had entered the New York newspaper field as the owner of the New York *Journal* on November 8, 1895. He decided, as soon as the campaign of 1896 ended, that a war would provide opportunity for the maximum number of headlines, and so he proceeded to produce the war. Pulitzer, his rival, followed his trail of red ink and gigantic type. The owner of the New York *World* did his best, but he never equaled Hearst as a maker of war. In six months a contest with Spain seemed probable.

Spain, during the autumn of 1897, was making every effort to conciliate the United States. The jingo factions might have been disappointed, despite Hearst and Pulitzer, had not the Spanish ambassador, Señor Don Dupuy de Lôme, addressed a letter in January, 1898, to a friend living in Havana. A traitorous embassy clerk in league with the revolutionists notified their propaganda headquarters in New York and the letter was intercepted by another spy in the Havana postoffice. When De Lôme heard from his friend that the letter had not been received, he waited for the blow to fall. It had referred to McKinley as "weak and catering to the rabble; a low politician who desires to stand well with the jingoes of his party." On February 9, 1898, the *Journal* published the letter, and Richard Olney wrote to Cleveland that "poor Dupuy must realize how much worse a blunder can be than a crime."

The letter was not only insulting. It was stupid. McKinley was ardently hopeful for peace. But Hearst called it "the worst insult to the United States in its history," and De Lôme's prompt recall in disgrace did little to quiet the resulting indignation. On February 15, 1898, the U.S.S. *Maine* was sunk in Havana Harbor.

It is not easy to draw a line between Roosevelt's anxiety to build up the navy, which was legitimate preparedness, and his lust for war. His letters of 1897 and early 1898 indicate confusion in his own mind. He convinced himself, indeed, that a war with Spain was merely part of the preparedness program itself, a triviality to be taken lightly. On August 3, 1897, in remarking that it would be well to take "firm action on behalf of the wretched Cubans," he added: "It would be a splendid thing for the navy, too." In September, he was pleading with Secetary Long that "we will have our hands full, and the greatest panic would ensue" if "we wait to receive the attack." But "if we move with our main force on Cuba and [dispatch] a flying squadron against Spain itself," the affair would "not present a very great difficulty." This was prior to the De Lôme indiscretion of February, 1898, and, of course, before the sinking of the *Maine*.

On November 18, 1897, in the most outspoken of his private letters, the Assistant Secretary of the Navy repeated his desire to have the Asiatic Squadron steam for the

Philippines as soon as war had been declared. He would have a fleet ready at Key West for action off Cuba. In this communication, to use his own descriptive phrase, he had summed up the situation "with a frankness which our timid friends would call brutal":

I would regard a war with Spain from two viewpoints: First, the advisability on the ground both of humanity and self-interest of interfering on behalf of the Cubans, and of taking one more step toward the complete freeing of America from European domination; second, the benefit done to our people by giving them something to think of which isn't material gain, and especially the benefit done our military forces by trying both the Army and Navy in actual practise. I should be very sorry not to see us make the experiment of trying to land, and therefore to feed and clothe, an expeditionary force, if only for the sake of learning from our blunders. I should hope that the force would have some fighting to do. It would be a great lesson, and we would profit much by it.

The military-spiritual adventure that Roosevelt desired would mean, of course, the loss of many lives, but this was a detail that never bothered him. He was not, he wrote in 1902, "in the least sensitive about killing any number of men if there is adequate reason."

5

Conditions in Cuba grew worse after January 1, 1898. American citizens were imprisoned. Riots had occurred in Havana, and at the request of Consul General Fitzhugh Lee the second-class battleship *Maine* was dispatched to Havana Harbor. In accordance with diplomatic custom among nations officially at peace, this was announced by McKinley as "an act of friendly courtesy" and Spain, equally observant of the amenities, replied that she considered it proof that such was the sentiment in the United States. The commander of the vessel, Capt. Charles D. Sigsbee, conducted himself admirably in Havana, even attending a bullfight to propitiate Castilian sensibilities. No attention was paid to disgruntled murmurings against the presence of the warship. There was nothing to prepare Secretary Long for the shock on the morning of February 16, 1898, when, at 1:30 o'clock, he was awakened by his daughter with a dispatch announcing that the *Maine* had been blown up. Having shared the hope of the President that war might be averted, the Secretary of the Navy felt that this was "the most frightful disaster, both in itself and with reference to the critical condition of our relations with Spain." Two officers and 264 men had been killed in the explosion.

"I would give anything," wrote Roosevelt that morning, "if President McKinley would order the fleet to Havana tomorrow. The *Maine* was sunk by an act of dirty treachery on the part of the Spaniards." This was before any details had been received and while Captain Sigsbee, who had survived the disaster, was asking the public to suspend judgment until "further report."

Roosevelt, not McKinley, sensed correctly the temper of the country. The rantings of Hearst had been effective. A really proud nation might have scorned war with Spain, a power that was almost bankrupt and had a population of only 18,000,000 as against 75,000,000 in the United States. All other sentiments, however, were swept aside by the winds of the war fever. Theater managers in New York City, always prompt in wrapping themselves in the flag, displayed the national emblem from the stage. The "Star-Spangled Banner" was sung after all performances. It was announced that De Wolf Hopper, playing in *El Capitan* at the Fifth Avenue Theater, would give a "patriotic speech" at each performance. Roosevelt watched with contempt the efforts of McKinley to avoid the struggle. The President, he told his intimates, "has no more backbone than a chocolate éclair."

At this crisis, wearied by the excess of burdens, Secretary Long decided to take an afternoon off. He did so on February 25, and regretted it exceedingly. The next day he wrote in his diary that "the very devil had seemed to possess" his assistant:

I find that Roosevelt, in his precipitate way, has come very near causing more of an explosion than happened to the *Maine*. Having authority for that time of Acting Secretary, he immediately began to launch peremptory orders. He has gone at things like a bull in a china shop. It shows how the best fellow in the world—and with splendid capacities—is worse than no use if he lacks a cool head and discrimination.

The criticism may have been partly justified, but by no means entirely. For some time, Roosevelt had been watching with admiration the naval career of George Dewey. He persuaded the commodore to use what political influence he possessed to have himself designated admiral of the Asiatic Squadron. This was done. The admiral sailed for Japan on December 8, 1897, and took with him all available data on waters adjacent to the Philippine Islands. He arrived at Hongkong just in time to hear by cable that the *Maine* had gone down. On February 25, he received the famous cable sent by Acting Secretary Roosevelt. This ordered him to coal his ships and to make certain, "in the event of declaration of war," that the Spanish squadron did not leave the Asiatic coast. He was also to begin "defensive operations" in the Philippines. This cable, sent by Roosevelt while Long was resting at his home, made possible the naval victory at Manila Bay.

Highly excited, Roosevelt continued his pleas to Secretary Long for war preparations. A month prior to the explosion in Havana Harbor he had suggested a "flying squadron" which would slip through Gibraltar at night, destroy Barcelona, and strike Cadiz. His letters do not, however, bear out the accusation that he desired an attack on Spain's fleet, rumored to be about to cross the Atlantic, before war had been declared. As President, Roosevelt denied any such intention. He did believe that the sailing of the fleet should be regarded as an act of war and notice to that effect given to Spain. In the interim between the sinking of the *Maine* and the declaration of war on April 21, Roosevelt had exhorted Long to get ready and had even, as he described it, "told the President in the plainest language" that war alone was "compatible with our national honor."

"We will have this war for the freedom of Cuba," he insisted, shaking a fist toward Senator Hanna, at a Gridiron Dinner on March 26, "in spite of the timidity of the commercial interests."

Roosevelt was right. The diplomat, as he had urged in his address before the Naval War College, had become "the servant of the soldier." By March 20, 1898, McKinley knew that the court of inquiry would declare that the *Maine* had been destroyed by a submarine mine; this meant that war was inevitable. The report was handed to Congress on March 28, at a time when every member had "two or three newspapers in his district printed in red ink shouting for blood." McKinley surrendered to the war party. "Remember the *Maine!*" became the battle cry of the nation. A strong President could have avoided the war; on April 10, the day before McKinley sent his message to Congress, the American ambassador at Madrid notified the State Department that Spain would go "as far and as fast as she can" to insure peace. Even Rhodes, friendly as he was to McKinley, referred to it as "this unnecessary war."

In 1903, Governor Long wrote that the reason for it "remains yet to be solved"; the destruction of the *Maine* is, to this day, a mystery. The United States did not permit Spain to take part in the investigation nor would it consider an international court of inquiry. Thus in 1898, as well as in 1911 when the wreck was raised, the examination was scarcely impartial. Battleships, badly constructed in those years, not infrequently blew up from internal causes. Quite possibly, the *Maine* was so destroyed. Some Cuban fanatic, aware that it would mean war, may have brought about the disaster.

All this is irrelevant. Roosevelt had his war. He had been agitating for it for a long time, and he announced that he would take an active part.

"I abhor unjust war," he wrote in his autobiography. "I should never advocate war unless it were the only alternative to dishonor.

Chapter XIV

A BULLY FIGHT

This was the adventure glorious. "San Juan was the great day of my life," said Theodore Roosevelt two decades later. It was then that he personified his own ideal—the sickly boy who had been afraid of bullies had vanished forever into the limbo of forgotten things. War, in 1898, was still romantic.

There were reasons enough why, the war with Spain an accomplished fact in April, 1898, he should have refrained from active participation. Their fifth child, Quentin, had been born in November and Mrs. Roosevelt was so ill in January that Dr. Alexander Lambert, their New York physician, was summoned to Washington. During the months when Roosevelt was calling with enthusiasm for war, he was embarrassed for funds. In addition to all this, one of the small boys had been sick.

Secretary Long, aware of these domestic complications, was astonished and distressed when his assistant announced his intention of resigning. He felt that Roosevelt would merely "ride a horse and brush mosquitoes from his neck in the Florida sands." But even as Mr. Long so commented in his diary on April 25, 1898, he wondered whether Roosevelt might not be right. How absurd his words would sound "if by some turn of fortune he should accomplish some great thing!" Years passed. Mr. Long turned back the pages of his journal and scribbled across the entry for April 25, 1898: "Roosevelt was right. His going into the army led straight to the Presidency."

As far back as September 14, 1897, while driving with President McKinley, Roosevelt said that if war came he would go. His efforts did not cease until he had been commissioned as lieutenant colonel of the Rough Riders, the most picturesque of all the regiments. But he constantly protested, so vehemently that the remarks might have been addressed to his own conscience, that "I shouldn't expect to win any military glory," that "I say quite sincerely that I shall not go for pleasure . . . if I should consult purely my own feelings I should earnestly hope that we would have peace." On April 18, 1898, he admitted that his "family and friends" were unanimously opposed to his going to war and denied that he was doing so "in a mere spirit of recklessness or levity." His purpose was to practice what he had preached. He had been a leading advocate of war with Spain and it was his duty to take part in it. Then, in one of those flashes of honesty which illumine Roosevelt, he added:

"I don't want you to think that I am talking like a prig, for I know perfectly well that one never is able to analyze with entire accuracy all of one's motives."

"Really, we are all fake heroes," he wrote a fortnight later.

Roosevelt was not a coldly calculating person. Nowhere, even in the most confidential of his private letters, is there any sign that he was then thinking of political preferment. In due time he accepted the fruits of glory and became governor of New York; to have done otherwise would have been the action of a hypocrite. Not shrewdness but adolescence was behind his desire to become a soldier in the Spanish War.

"I shall chafe my heart out if I am kept here instead of being at the front," he said in March, "and I don't know how to get to the front."

The prospect was dark for some time. Immediately after the *Maine* went down, Roosevelt appealed to the adjutant general of the New York National Guard. "I have had a good deal of experience in handling men, and I can do my part well," he wrote. On March 9, he offered to raise a regiment in New York; would the governor authorize this and, if so, could he bring a young officer named Leonard Wood with him? On April 7 he was hoping that he might go as lieutenant colonel in a regiment that he would help to raise.

"We will have a jim-dandy regiment if we go," he said.

It is not difficult to picture the family conferences, with all the banker and lawyer uncles and cousins heavily disapproving, as Theodore persisted in his mad intention of going to war. Cabot Lodge, also, was against it, in addition to Mrs. Roosevelt herself. Roosevelt was more easily influenced by these two people, perhaps, than by any others on earth. But "this was one case," he told McKinley, "where I would consult neither."

His chance to go to the war came a few days after the declaration of hostilities against Spain on April 24, 1898. On April 30, he telegraphed to Brooks Brothers in New York City for a "blue cravenette regular Lieutenant-Colonel's uniform without yellow on the collar and with leggings," to be ready in one week. Congress had authorized three cavalry regiments to be recruited in the Southwest and in the Rocky Mountain country. Secretary of War Russell A. Alger had offered Roosevelt the command of one of these, but he had refused on the ground that it would probably be a month before he had mastered the science of war sufficiently. By that time, the war might be over.

He elected to serve, instead, as lieutenant colonel under Wood, then an army surgeon with the rank of captain, who shared Roosevelt's yearnings for war. Telegrams were dispatched to the territorial governors of Arizona, New Mexico, and Oklahoma asking for men who were "young, good shots and good riders." Wood and Roosevelt were overwhelmed with applications, and by May 1 a camp was being prepared at San Antonio, Texas, for preliminary training.

2

Roosevelt's anxiety to get into action was a little ludicrous. "I suppose it will be two or three days before I get off. I am awfully afraid we shall miss the first expedition," he complained to his brother-in-law. Such phrases as "it will be awful if we miss the fun" appeared, during the anxious days while he waited in Washington in letters to his older sister. On May 10, he wrote Colonel Wood that, "drill or no drill," it was vital to "get our troops down with the first expedition." This letter disclosed apprehensions that the navy might unfortunately terminate the war by sinking the Spanish squadron supposed to have started across the Atlantic.

As Roosevelt wrote, rumors were current that the Spaniards had turned back.

"I don't want to be unpatriotic," he admitted, "but I feel like saying 'Thank Heaven.' If true, this means that instead of Admiral Sampson ending the war, we will be put in to end it in Cuba."

Roosevelt at last completed his preparations at Washington. He had obtained smokeless powder for the Rough Riders, a detail upon which Wood had insisted, since it would give his men added protection from the enemy. He had telegraphed for "a couple of good, stout, quiet horses for my own use . . . not gun-shy . . . trained and bridle-wise; no bucking." With military foresight he had looked ahead toward the predicament in which he would find himself, due to his bad eyesight, in the event that he lost or broke his glasses. He ordered his optician to make up a dozen pairs of steel-rimmed spectacles. These were stowed in all parts of his uniform, while several were fastened with light thread into the lining of his campaign hat. As Lieutenant Colonel Roosevelt went into action at Las Guasimas, his first skirmish, he placed two or three additional pairs in his saddlebags, further to avoid the dread possibility that he might not be able to see the enemy he had come so far to annihilate.

It promised, from the start, to be a lovely war as far as the First Volunteer Cavalry was concerned. Wood was the commanding officer, but it was Roosevelt's outfit from the start, and an air of charming informality nullified the more customary military austerity. At the railroad station, to welcome incoming recruits, was a sign proclaiming, "This Way to the Roosevelt Rough Rider Camp." Often a band was present, laboring with its one tune, "There'll Be a Hot Time in the Old Town Tonight."

Never, probably, had so novel a military organization been gathered together. Mingling among the cowboys and momentarily reformed bad men from the West were polo players and steeplechase riders from the Harvard, Yale, and Princeton clubs of New York City. They arrived wearing derby hats, and in clipped tones, foreign to San Antonio, where the regiment mobilized, they gave directions at the railroad station that wagonloads of smart leather trunks and hatboxes were to be transported to the camp. Within a few days, however, they were indistinguishable in their enlisted men's uniforms. They had not asked for commissions.

San Antonio was not greatly impressed by the First Volunteer Cavalry. They drilled badly; they were poorly equipped. In truth, it was a mob rather than a regiment during the first weeks. One cowboy took a solemn oath to salute no one. Another saluted every noncommissioned officer and added pleasantly: "How are you, Captain?" A third, having been criticized for crudity in executing the manual of arms, practiced in secret for several days and then snapped to attention with "Pretty nifty, eh, Captain?" as the officer of the day passed.

Roosevelt, a little sensitive over the name Rough Riders, which the newspaper correspondents had evolved, protested that the regiment was not "to be a hippodrome affair." His protest was futile. He arrived at San Antonio on May 15, 1898, a week after the news of Dewey's victory, to find a brass band and most of his command at the station. There were cheers and demands for a speech and the lieutenant colonel's efforts to throw cold water on this improper cordiality were without effect.

Colonel Wood, having been in the regular army, had slight sympathy with the eccentricities of this aggregation. Roosevelt had too much. He wanted them to drill well, but he won the frantic adoration of his troops by his willingness to talk with them as man to man instead of as officer to recruit. He went further. It was hot in Texas, and after one mounted drill on the shimmering prairies, the troop rode back to the fair grounds past a resort called Riverside Park. Roosevelt turned in his saddle and gave the order to dismount.

"The men," he bellowed, "can go in and drink all the beer they want, which I will pay for!"

That night Roosevelt was summoned to the headquarters of Colonel Wood and the enormity of his offense was pointed out. An officer who drank with his men was not fit for a commission, said Wood severely, although he was finding it difficult to keep from laughing. Roosevelt saluted and disappeared. He returned a few minutes later, the expression on his face showing that he had been plunged in thought.

"Sir, I consider myself the damnedest ass within ten miles of this camp," he said. "Good-night, sir." That he used profanity demonstrated that Roosevelt was deeply agitated, but the rebuke failed to effect a complete cure for nonmilitary vices.

Two sources of irritation kept Roosevelt from complete happiness during the training period in Texas. The first was his ever-present fear that the war might be over before he got to Cuba. The second was disgust with the War Department. He had started a diary before leaving Washington and on May 21 he noted that the "blunders and delays of the ordnance bureau surpass belief; there is no head, no energy, no intelligence in the War Department. The President is of course really to blame." On May 19, he begged Lodge not to permit consideration of peace overtures until Puerto Rico had been taken, Cuba liberated, and the Philippine Islands seized. These details, presumably, would prolong the war.

News that the Rough Riders would leave for Tampa on May 29 was received with mixed emotions at San Antonio, but her citizens decided to show their good will by a farewell concert on the night of May 24. It was duly held in one of the parks and Professor Carl Beck, the local bandmaster, gave his program a military flavor by including a number listed as "Cavalry Charge (A Descriptive Fantasy)." To provide realism mere drums could not supply, Professor Beck arranged to have a small saluting cannon located on the outskirts of the crowd.

All was orderly among the members of the First Volunteer Cavalry, who had been given seats of honor, until the first cannon shot in the "Cavalry Charge." This was far too realistic. "Help him out, boys!" cried one of Roosevelt's bully men, and several pistols cracked into the night air. Officers barked orders in vain while ladies screamed and men and children ducked under the seats. A moment later, the electric cable was cut and in the darkness the Rough Riders vanished to continue their merrymaking in town.

Unwept by the better element, the Rough Riders entrained for Tampa, where, it was supposed, a transport would promptly carry them to the Caribbean. It was, however, June 7 before orders came to embark on the following morning. They reached the quay at Port Tampa at about dawn, discovered after great difficulty that they had been assigned to the U.S.S. *Yucatan*, and then Wood and Roosevelt found to their inexpressible horror that she had previously been allotted to two other regiments, which would fill her to the gunwales. It seemed as though they might yet arrive in Cuba too late, but Roosevelt was equal to the emergency.

I ran at full speed to our train; and double-quicked the regiment up to the boat, just in time to board her as she came into the quay, and then to hold her against the Second Regulars and the Seventy-first, who had arrived a little late, being a shade less ready than we in the matter of individual initiative. There was a good deal of expostulation, but we had possession.

Such was the first victory of the Rough Riders. They sweltered in Tampa Bay for almost a week, having anchored in the center of a stream of sewage from the city. The heat was terrific; there was no ice, no fresh meat. The vessel sailed on June 13, and that night one of the troopers wrote in his diary:

When Colonel Roosevelt heard the news he could not restrain himself and entertained us all by giving an impromptu war dance.

3

It was pleasant, Roosevelt wrote, "sailing southward through the tropic seas toward the unknown." On the morning of June 22, the *Yucatan* steamed in toward shore and the order came to land. Opposite lay a small hamlet called Daiquiri, where there had once been a sugar plantation or two, and behind it the hills of Cuba. A heavy surf was running; there were few boats. The landing was like everything else in this most amateurish of wars—a mad scramble. The maddest of the scrambles was that of the brigade under Brig. Gen. S. B. M. Young, which included the Rough Riders. Wood and Roosevelt had rejoiced at their assignment to Young's command. They had discussed the possibility with him the previous winter and he had guaranteed "to show us fighting" if war came. Still another gamecock was on board the convoy which arrived on June 22, Maj. Gen. Joseph Wheeler, whose last deeds of valor had been as an officer in the Confederate Army. His old nostrils quivered as he smelled gunpowder again. He rushed into the fighting before Santiago shouting, "The Yankees are running! Dammit! I mean the Spaniards!"

Time was the essence of this war. It was important to defeat the Spaniards. It was even more vital to get ahead of the other brigades, and General Wheeler, who commanded the cavalry, co-operated to the utmost in seeing that the Young-Wood-Roosevelt contingent obtained at least their share of the glory. The brigade was landed at once, two men being drowned in the heavy surf. Horses brought down for the officers—the rest had been left in Tampa—were thrown overboard to swim ashore as best they could. By the afternoon of June 23, the advance was under way.

Cuban scouts reported that the Spaniards had just evacuated Daiquiri for the safety of Santiago. If Wheeler's unmounted cavalry was to strike the first blow, it was necessary to pursue, with all vigor, the flying Castilians. Young was assigned to the job. "Ain't it grand to have a horse?" jeered irreverent infantrymen as the footsore cowhands of the First Volunteer Cavalry trudged along the beach toward Siboney, another wretched town eleven miles west.

Now arose a new source of rivalry. General Young announced that he would personally command two regiments of regular cavalry. Wood and Roosevelt would lead their volunteers. The Spaniards were supposed to have intrenched at a point called Las Guasimas, some four miles inland, and the attack would be made at dawn. Young would advance through a valley road to the right. The Rough Riders would take a hill trail further inland. As a result of the skirmish on June 24, an argument arose that has never been settled. The regulars insisted that the Rough Riders were ambushed. The volunteers countered hotly that nothing of the sort occurred. The truth may well remain as one of the minor controversies of military history, but certain facts are conceded.

The advance took place as scheduled. Wood, his mind on Young's men to his right, pushed his men so fast that even Roosevelt was inclined to protest until he realized that "otherwise we should have arrived late." After an hour's march through the sultry jungle, the order came to halt. Immediately there was a crash of rifle fire and the skirmish was on. Very much confused, but standing their ground admirably, the Rough Riders fired back at an enemy they could not see, and in the end the Spaniards continued their flight toward Santiago.

The point in dispute is solely whether the First Volunteer Cavalry was ambushed. The first shots had killed Sergeant Hamilton Fish, Jr., who led the outpost in conjunction with a Cuban scout or two, and Captain Allyn Capron, who came just behind. Several men were badly wounded. Roosevelt claimed that "we struck the Spaniards exactly where we expected"; which was hardly complimentary to the soldierly skill of the men who died. Two newspaper correspondents, Edward Marshall and Richard Harding Davis, were with the First Volunteer Cavalry, but their testimony conflicts. Marshall's opinion was that it was "not technically an ambush although the American troops met the Spaniards before they expected to."

Davis telegraphed the New York *Herald* that the Rough Riders were "ambushed by receding Spaniards with the advantage all on the side of the enemy." In a letter written at about the same time, immediately after the fight, he said that "we were caught in a clear case of ambush." But Richard Harding Davis and Roosevelt soon became close friends. Did Roosevelt's recollections of the battle persuade Davis that he had been mistaken? In 1910 he was certain that "so far from anyone running into an ambush, every one of the officers had full knowledge of where he would find the enemy."

Sixteen men were killed in this brush and fifty were wounded. Roosevelt admitted that the Spanish loss was not as heavy as the American; obviously the little skirmish had not the slightest military significance. However, as Roosevelt boasted, "we wanted the first whack at the Spaniards and we got it."

4

If the American Navy, operating in the Caribbean, had been able to keep the Spanish fleet under Admiral Cervera from slipping into Santiago Harbor, there might have been no skirmish at Las Guasimas, no battle in front of the hills at San Juan, and no glory for Roosevelt. The Spanish admiral, however, entered the harbor on May 19, 1898. This was while the Rough Riders were still in San Antonio.

The objective of the Cuban campaign was to drive the Spaniards off the island. This might be done by a naval bombardment of Santiago, which would force Cervera into action, by the slow process of starvation, or by military operations. The convention of history is that the army and the navy were engaged in bitter rivalry for the honor of taking the offensive and that, in the end, both branches of the service performed untold feats of heroism. Unhappily, the evidence shows that the desire for action was less keen. The navy did not want to scratch its pretty ships. The army, under Maj. Gen. W. R. Shafter, felt that the navy should somehow save the day after the advance before Santiago had been blocked. The impatience of Young, Wood, and Roosevelt for deeds of valor was hardly shared by the high command nor was it echoed in Washington.

Roosevelt did not have a high opinion of his commander in chief. He told Lodge, following Las Guasimas, that Shafter had not yet come ashore from his transport. After San Juan, he said that he was "too unwieldy to get to the front," an accusation not without truth, since Shafter weighed three hundred pounds, was given to gout, and was ill from the heat. He was sixty years old. When the Dodge Commission held its investigation at Washington into the conduct of the war, Shafter's testimony was a recital of woe:

I was nearly prostrated; when I would sit up it would make me dizzy. I had a beastly attack of gout so that I could not wear a boot for a week, and had to wear a gunny sack on my foot, and I could not climb my horse, and would have to build a platform to climb up on.

But to Roosevelt, aside from irritation over the War Department and Shafter, the struggle was glorious. He may have been reckless in sending his men to death and have judged the success of an engagement by the length of its casualty list, but between battles he was indefatigable in caring for his troops. The commissary department, like nearly all the other departments of the army, had collapsed under the unaccustomed strain of war. For days, after June 24, there was little or no food. Roosevelt thereupon organized foraging parties which went back to the coast and obtained food by paying for it with funds he supplied. The lieutenant colonel spent $300, all his available cash, and borrowed $100 more.

Las Guasimas had merely whetted Roosevelt's appetite. Due to the illness of Young, and the consequent elevation of Colonel Wood to brigade commander, Roosevelt became colonel of the First Volunteer Cavalry. On June 30, he wrote, the "men were greatly overjoyed" because orders had come for the advance on Santiago. Throughout that day they tramped through the jungle toward the Spanish stronghold. That night, they slept on their arms.

Against the sky, as they waited for morning, could be seen the reflected glow of the city's lights. The morning of July 1, the day of Roosevelt's crowded hour, dawned. To the right was a village called El Caney. To the left was San Juan Hill. The strategy of the American command was based upon the theory that El Caney would be captured in short order by a brigade of regulars, with Wood acting as support and reserve. The expected capture of El Caney was delayed, however, by stubborn resistance and, "under orders of the vaguest kind," Wood and Roosevelt were commanded to advance. They went into the valley and lay under sickening fire from the fortifications above. It was an extremely bad spot, directly in front of the Spanish batteries, and with retreat blocked by masses of troops congesting the road. The culminating blunder was the raising of an observation balloon that revealed the exact location of the American forces.

Whether, during the charge that followed, Roosevelt and his men stormed San Juan Hill, became another subject of heated controversy, if a matter of small importance. Roosevelt referred loosely to the "San Juan charge" on many occasions, but in all his more formal accounts of the fight he stated clearly that the hill he had stormed had been the one to the right of the San Juan forts. It was christened Kettle Hill immediately after the battle because some sugar kettles were found there. The Spaniards had entrenchments on Kettle Hill.

That Roosevelt was both brave and reckless is beyond question. "The percentage of loss of our regiment," he wrote, "was about seven times that of the other five volunteer regiments." To those who watched the engagement it seemed remarkable that any of the men survived. To Davis it appeared as though "someone had made an awful and terrible mistake." Roosevelt was a dashing figure; mounted on his horse, shouting encouragement, easily distinguishable because of a blue polka-dot handkerchief that he had draped on the brim of his sombrero and which floated in the breeze like a guidon. But the line of men that followed seemed pathetically thin, and a good many dropped on the way up the hill.

To Roosevelt, it was the ultimate in warfare. "Are you afraid to stand up when I am on horseback?" he demanded of one or two reluctant troopers. "Let my men through, sir!" he commanded a regular army officer. Other pleasant details lingered in Roosevelt's memory, through all the long years, until he died.

"I waved my hat and we went up the hill with a rush," he wrote in his autobiography.

"The charge itself was great fun," he wrote home from Santiago.

"I rose over those regular army officers like a balloon," he said twenty years later.

In retrospect, the battle of July 1, 1898, assumed in Roosevelt's mind the aspects of a pleasantly dangerous sporting event. He forgot that on the two days which followed, while the First Volunteer Cavalry waited in the trenches, there had been moments of great discouragement. On July 3, he scribbled a note to Lodge pointing to the need for re-enforcements: ". . . we are within measurable distance of a terrible military disaster; we *must* have help —thousands of men, batteries and *food* and ammunition . . . we lost a quarter of our men . . . how I have escaped I know not." It was on that day, a Sunday, that Shafter telegraphed to Washington his intention of retreating. Ill and disheartened, the commanding officer was urging Admiral Sampson to save the army by forcing an entrance into Santiago Harbor. But on that day Cervera ventured out and was destroyed. Santiago fell and no further fighting had to be done by the land forces.

In April, 1899, Gen. Joseph Wheeler protested regarding some book which attempted to take credit from the cavalry brigades. "I do not think you and I need pay any attention to all these small vermin," answered Roosevelt suavely on April 25. "If any of them gets in my way I stamp on him."

When, however, Finley Peter Dunne put into the mouth of Mr. Dooley certain observations on the Rooseveltian ego which permeated his memoirs of the war, he was torn between indignation and amusement. ". . . If I was him," Mr. Dooley had been made to say, "I'd call th' book 'Alone in Cubia.'" Roosevelt, who preferred a club for his own use, could recognize the rapier thrust.

"I regret to state," he wrote Dunne from the Executive Mansion at Albany, "that my family and intimate friends are delighted with your review of my book."

5

War without action had no interest for Roosevelt. He wrote to the Secretary of War on July 23, 1898, hoping that his regiment would be sent to Puerto Rico. When there was no indication that further excitement lay ahead, and when yellow fever began to sweep through the humid camps, his only desire was to get home. Besides, Cabot Lodge was writing that he was a hero, and thoughts of political preferment doubtless made war seem less attractive. The sickness among the men resulted in the round robin which constituted the third great controversy of the Spanish War. Roosevelt's part in it aroused the War Department to apoplectic wrath; it has always been the official view that death to thousands is preferable to a breach of military etiquette. By the end of July, Wood had been made military governor of Cuba, and Roosevelt was an acting brigadier. The responsibility for the safety of the men was squarely on his shoulders. "I am determined," he told Lodge, "that my skirts shall be kept clear of this particular form of murder."

The round robin was greatly to Roosevelt's credit. A day or so before the end of July, General Shafter called a staff meeting at which everyone agreed that the troops must be moved. Some of the regular army officers, nervous about their careers, suggested that Roosevelt, being a volunteer, should write the letter setting forth the facts. This he immediately agreed to do. The letter was drafted, and then the other officers decided they would sign an appeal of their own. Meanwhile, the correspondent for the Associated Press had heard of the plan and went with Roosevelt to Shafter's headquarters. The letter was presented. The major general waved it away in the direction of the newspaperman, saying that he did not want it. Presumably this was to escape responsibility. This version, which is Roosevelt's, is fully confirmed by the dispatches which appeared throughout the country on August 5, 1898.

War Secretary Alger was indignant. He made public a letter Roosevelt had written on July 23 containing disparaging remarks about National Guard regiments. It could only have been done with malicious intent, to embarrass Roosevelt in his political ambitions. It was intimated that the affliction at Santiago might not be yellow fever or malaria at all, but "homesickness." But the swivel-chair warriors at Washington backed down. The regiments at Santiago were called home. They landed at Montauk on Long Island from the transport *Miami* on the morning of August 15, and Roosevelt remarked, as he looked at his disease-shaken troops, "I feel disgracefully well!"

The great adventure was over. Two weeks or so were needed to muster out the troops. The Rough Riders, sauntering through the streets of New York during this interval, were the heroes of the town. On September 4, at the Montauk camp, the colonel bade farewell to his army. "We are knit closer together than any body of men I know of," he said. "I would honestly rather have my position of colonel than any other position on earth." Then he thrust his chin forward, and saved himself from showing undue emotion by offering a moral precept to his men.

"Don't get gay and pose as heroes," he warned. "Don't go back and lie on your laurels; they'll wither."

Roosevelt never forgot his Rough Riders nor, indeed, did these heroes forget their colonel. By 1899 he was governor of New York and found himself besieged with petitions for jobs by veterans who "looked upon the governor as their chief and only adviser and friend." It was impossible to take care of all of them, but he did his best as long as he held office. A Rough Rider, to him, was always better qualified for some appointment than the other aspirants. Roosevelt was aware of this weakness. In 1906, when Secretary of War Taft asked for the nomination of a Yale man to some post in the Southwest, the President wrote:

> I guess Yale '78 has the call, as there seems to be no Rough Rider available and every individual in the Southern District of the Indian Territory (including every Rough Rider) appears to be either under indictment, convicted, or in a position that renders it imperatively necessary that he should be indicted. Let us, therefore, appoint George Walker, Yale '78, charge to Taft, and see if the Senate (God bless them!) will confirm him.

The epic of ex-Sergeant Benjamin Franklin Daniels, once sheriff of Dodge City, Kansas, indicates that even incarceration in the penitentiary did not disbar a Rough Rider from sharing Roosevelt's bounty. On entering the White House, President Roosevelt had been anxious to do something for Daniels, who had been a brave soldier, and he meditated appointing him United States marshal of Arizona. The plan had to be abandoned, however, when it developed that Daniels, at the moment, was in the territorial prison because of some minor homicide. Roosevelt kept Daniels in mind, however, and shortly afterward Lieutenant Colonel Brodie, another cherished trooper, was selected for governor of the Territory of Arizona. A note to Cabot Lodge on June 4, 1902, revealed that Roosevelt had found a post for Daniels as well; one which the overmeticulous Senate could not pass upon. The President had persuaded Brodie to install the sergeant as warden of the penitentiary in which he had recently been an involuntary guest.

"When I told this to John Hay," said Roosevelt, "he remarked (with a brutal absence of feeling) that he believed the proverb ran, 'Set a Rough Rider to catch a thief.'"

Roosevelt's chief source of information regarding the peacetime tribulations of his Rough Riders was Major W. H. H. Llewellyn, whose valor had been rewarded with the post of United States attorney in New Mexico. The major wrote:

> I have the honor to report, that Comrade Ritchie, late of Troop G, is in jail at Trinidad, Colorado, on a charge of murder. It seems that our comrade became involved in a controversy and it appears that the fellow he killed called him very bad names, even going so far as to cast reflections on the legitimacy of our comrade's birth. He killed the fellow instantly, shooting him through the heart.
>
> Also have to report that Comrade Webb, late of Troop D, has just killed two men at Bisbee, Arizona. Have not yet received the details of our comrade's trouble but understand that he was entirely justified in the transaction.

. . . was out at the penitentiary yesterday, and had a very pleasant visit with Comrade Frank Brito whom you will remember was sent to the penitentiary from Silver City for killing his sister-in-law. He is very anxious to get out. You will doubtless recall that he was shooting at his wife at the time he killed his sister-in-law. Since he has been in the penitentiary, his wife ran away with Comrade Coyne of Troop H, going to Mexico. This incident has tended to turn popular sentiment strongly in Brito's favor.

Roosevelt hugely enjoyed these reports from Llewellyn. The major, he told Hay, was "a large, jovial, frontier Micawber type of person, with a varied past which includes considerable man-killing." Nor was Llewellyn forwarding news solely about the murders so lightly undertaken by Rough Riders. On December 27, 1904, he wrote:

Comrade Johnson, late of Troop G has been converted and is now a full-fledged Evangelist, laboring in the Lord's vineyard among the Swedish and Norwegian sailors. One of his illustrations of the presence of Our Savior and of the fact that Our Savior sees everything and knows everything is as follows:

"I tell you boys that Jesus Christ sees us all the time; I tell you boys He has an eye just as sharp as a rat."

You will doubtless be glad to know that at least one of the men of your regiment is not in the penitentiary or a candidate for office.

Chapter XV

REWARD FOR A HERO

❋

During August, 1898, Senator Platt was, as he described it, "doing a heap of thinking." The governor of New York, Frank S. Black, was entitled to another term, but he had alienated large numbers of voters by permitting undue extravagance in repairs on the Erie Canal. Suggestions were constantly being made that Theodore Roosevelt, the hero of the Spanish War, should receive the gubernatorial nomination, but the G.O.P. leader was even more dubious about Roosevelt. He was "a perfect bull in a china shop."

Among the many influential Republicans who called upon Platt that summer was Chauncey M. Depew. Mr. Depew said that he had been thinking of the spellbinders who would take the stump that fall. Almost certainly they would suffer from embarrassing questions "about the canal steal," and these might be difficult to answer unless, as Depew urged, Roosevelt was nominated. In that happy event, the campaign speaker could turn upon the heckler with "indignation and enthusiasm." Mr. Depew even heard the words of rebuke that the spellbinder would utter:

I am mighty glad you asked that question. We have nominated for Governor a man who has demonstrated that he is a fighter for the right. If he is elected every thief will be caught and punished.

And then, added Depew, the speaker would "follow the Colonel leading his men up San Juan Hill and ask the band to play the 'Star Spangled Banner.' "

Roosevelt was still in Cuba as these conversations were held. Lodge had been writing that the newspaper accounts of his exploits had started a boom for governor. The colonel of the First Volunteer Cavalry replied that his popularity was undoubtedly merely temporary and said that he would prefer to be in national, not state, politics.

Roosevelt was careful, however, to let the New York leaders know that he was subject to persuasion on the governorship. He declined to commit himself, but a few days later inspired dispatches from the Rough Rider camp on Long Island indicated that Roosevelt would listen to the voice of the people. It is doubtful whether he seriously considered declining the nomination. The only thing worse than an office which he did not want, as he demonstrated when the vice-presidency faced him, was no office at all.

All that remained was for Roosevelt to call upon Platt at the Fifth Avenue Hotel, which he did on September 17, and to decline a nomination tendered by a group of independents. He repulsed the reform element on September 24. A week later Dr. Parkhurst returned from Europe and expressed disbelief that Roosevelt had sworn allegiance to Platt:

I do not believe that Teddy Roosevelt—I call him Teddy because I know him so well—has so far humbled himself as to go to Mr. Platt. Mr. Platt must have gone to him.

The clergyman-politician rather betrayed himself in his reference to "Teddy," the name which Roosevelt loathed. He forgot that his hero had already bowed to Tom Platt. Besides, Roosevelt had sacrificed only a fraction of his honor in return for the governorship. Letters exchanged with Lemuel E. Quigg, a Platt henchman, reveal that he had agreed to work with the organization only to the extent that his sometimes elastic conscience would permit. On September 14, all the details having been arranged, Quigg wrote Roosevelt that he might well begin making speeches:

I think that this invitation of the Brooklyn Sunday School Association would be a first rate one to accept, although it would probably have to be followed by an address to the Brooklyn Association of Amalgamated Liquor Dealers or something of the sort.

A curious and really unimportant fact is that Roosevelt was, in 1898, probably ineligible for the office of governor or even to vote in New York State. The state constitution required residence in the state for the five years immediately preceding election, and Roosevelt had recently signed two affidavits: one to avoid payment of taxes in Oyster Bay and the other to escape payments in New York City. In the second of these he swore that his residence was in Washington, D. C. The tangle marked Roosevelt's closest approach to a personal scandal, for his personal honor was beyond reproach. He was badly worried until the astute mind of Elihu Root had swept aside the alleged disqualification; the whole matter was actually an outgrowth of Roosevelt's chronic carelessness regarding his financial affairs.

In 1897, while Assistant Secretary of the Navy, he was the owner of Sagamore Hill at Oyster Bay and also maintained a town house at 689 Madison Avenue in New York. On August 14, 1897, he wrote to his uncle, James A. Roosevelt, that the personal tax assessed in Oyster Bay was heavier than it had been in New York and

I adhere to New York as my place of abode. I shan't pay in Oyster Bay. I have been voting in New York for the past two years and that has been my residence.

An affidavit to this effect was deposited with the town clerk of Oyster Bay on August 24, 1897, and the taxes were waived. Thereupon came the distractions of the approaching war, the birth of Quentin, and the illness of Mrs. Roosevelt. Six months passed, filled with busy days in the Navy Department. On January 20, 1898, Roosevelt asked his brother-in-law, Douglas Robinson, whether it would be necessary for him to pay levies on $50,000 in personal property. This assessment had been filed in New York City. "I live at Oyster Bay where I vote and pay my personal tax," he wrote. In a second affidavit, deposited in New York City, Roosevelt said, "I have been and am now a resident of Washington."

All this would hardly have come to light had it not been

that Superintendent of Insurance Lou F. Payn and one or two other Republicans were supporting Governor Black for renomination. Through useful Tammany Hall friends in the New York City tax offices, they exhumed the second of the two affidavits. It was published on the eve of the Republican State Convention at Saratoga. All details for the selection of Roosevelt as the party's candidate had been arranged, and at first there was consternation at Republican headquarters. Then came reassurances from Mr. Root. Letters were available showing that Roosevelt had not intended to lose his voting residence. At Saratoga, following a grandiloquent oration in which Chauncey Depew placed Roosevelt's name in nomination, Root made a long and plausible address. He explained, to the satisfaction of the delegates, that their candidate was a resident of Oyster Bay. But he did not mention the first affidavit, as yet unknown to Payn and the other Black adherents, in which Roosevelt had disavowed his home on Long Island.

Roosevelt had certainly given way to the universal urge to avoid tax payments. Had his enemies pressed their claims, he might really have been declared ineligible by court action. They did not do so. The Republican machine, meanwhile, had been further reassured by the knowledge that an attorney general elected on the same ticket would hardly start proceedings against his own governor after the inauguration. The New York City taxes were paid, on October 3, 1898, by Roosevelt's check for $995.28.

2

The Democrats, lacking a hero comparably as great as Roosevelt, rather hopelessly gave the nomination to Augustus Van Wyck, a brother of the Tammany Hall mayor of New York City. Platt, meanwhile, was carrying out the suggestion of Depew that patriotism was to be the keynote of the campaign. With Roosevelt's willing assistance, almost nothing was discussed except San Juan Hill and national issues. Before Election Day the orators were proclaiming that a vote for Van Wyck was close to treason.

Roosevelt's first important address was at Carnegie Hall on "The Duties of a Great Nation." A dozen Rough Riders were escorted to the platform. The meeting opened with cheers for San Juan and for its hero. The hall was smothered in flags. The candidate for governor began with generalities on integrity in government. He said not a word about the canal steal, and was soon in the midst of an appeal for the new imperialism. "The guns of our war-ships have awakened us to the knowledge of new duties," he said. "Our flag is a proud flag, and it stands for liberty and civilization." Then he praised the army and the navy.

Seven Rough Riders were on the special train on which Roosevelt began a tour on October 17. At each stop a bugler appeared on the rear platform to sound the cavalry charge. At Fort Henry, New York, a small upstate town, the candidate began his address as the notes of the bugle died. "You have heard the trumpet that sounded to bring you here," he said. "I have heard it tear the tropic dawn when it summoned us to fight at Santiago."

Huge crowds turned out to see Roosevelt at these patriotic rallies, to marvel at his energy and the fury with which he waved a wide-brimmed black felt hat, similar in shape to the campaign hats of the First Volunteer Cavalry. The Fourth of July excitement was continuous. When he was not talking about patriotism, which was seldom, Roosevelt admitted that he had been a degree uncharitable to labor in the past and announced that he had seen the light. He defended the Raines Excise Law, although as police commissioner he had learned that its provisions stimulated commercialized vice.

Yet the campaign was going badly. "New York cares very little for the war," Roosevelt mourned. The public, if interested at all, was merely disgusted with the manner in which the Republican party had mismanaged things. The Republican candidate did not escape criticism for his evasion on State issues, while Carl Schurz was again attacking his imperialism. And the National Guard remembered his earlier disparagements. Meanwhile a whispering campaign to the effect that Roosevelt had not stormed San Juan at all was in full swing. The truth, as Roosevelt earlier would have admitted, was that no commanding officer had any real idea of where he fought and charged.

Under these bludgeonings, he made frantic appeals for the Medal of Honor to which he believed himself entitled. His pleas to have Lodge use his influence to hasten the award started in July, 1898, and increased during the campaign. On October 25, Lodge addressed a personal petition to President McKinley, pointing out that "just now it would have a very important meaning and would put at rest many stories being circulated by the Democrats." He felt that "in view of the immense importance of the New York election," the award of the Medal of Honor should be made "in the course of the next few days." But the War Department, perhaps recalling the round robin and Roosevelt's other criticisms, failed to come to the rescue of the New York G.O.P. The award was never authorized, and ten years later, Roosevelt agreed that the authorities had taken "exactly the right position."

Roosevelt would probably have been defeated had it not been that Boss Croker of Tammany supplied an effective issue by publicly expressing contempt for the principle of a nonpartisan judiciary. Supreme Court Justice Joseph F. Daly, who had been on the bench for twenty-eight years, failed to receive a renomination from Tammany, and Croker insanely explained that this was because of undue independence. "Mad, indeed, is the brain that conceives the punishment of a just judge," exclaimed Daly, and his challenge gave new life to the discouraged Republicans. Then Croker added to the indignation of the voters by baldly stating that Daly had been placed on the bench by Tammany, and "Tammany Hall has a right to expect proper consideration at his hands."

"This gave me my chance," exulted Roosevelt, and it did. Out of the justifiable anger of New York citizens of both parties, and the protest meetings attended by thousands, grew the small majority by which he triumphed over Van Wyck. His majority was only 17,794. On November 22, 1898, Roosevelt wrote:

I have played it in bull luck this summer. First, to get into the war; and then to get out of it; then to get elected.

3

Until he led his hosts at Armageddon in 1912 and battled for the Lord, no banners proclaiming radicalism marked the onward march of Theodore Roosevelt. He stood close to the center and bared his white teeth at the conservatives on the right and the liberals of the extreme left. In his legislative messages as governor of New York may be found most of the principles he advocated as President. He seemed to be radical because his roar was so loud. Bromides? "I have to use bromides in my business," he told Owen Wister at luncheon one day.

Platt, being rather dull, was far from comprehending the man whom necessity had forced upon him. In May, 1899, he confided to Roosevelt the apprehensions he had felt when the new governor took office:

I had heard that you were a little loose on the relations of capital and labor, on trusts and combinations . . . on those numerous questions affecting the security of earnings and the right of a man to run his own business in his own way, with due respect, of course, to the Ten Commandments and the Penal Code.

The friction between Roosevelt and Platt was based on fundamental disagreement regarding these two admirable if contradictory codes. Platt felt that the Ten Commandments could sometimes be amended or even ignored. On his part, Roosevelt sought to strengthen the penal code. His first message to the legislature in January, 1899, can have caused no alarm to Platt, however. In all probability the leader had been consulted on the recommendations it contained; in 1900 Roosevelt sent Platt a copy in advance and hoped that he would "make suggestions and criticisms with the utmost frankness."

The message reiterated Roosevelt's new solicitude for organized labor. It called for tax reform, an improved civil service law, economy in government, and reform of the municipal machine in New York City. The governor again evaded the noxious evils of the Raines law. He recommended biennial sessions of the legislature. The message did not refer to a tax on corporation franchises which was to be Roosevelt's principal accomplishment that year.

In claiming credit for franchise taxation, Roosevelt neglected to mention that the bill providing it had been drafted and introduced by State Senator John Ford, a Democrat. He also forgot to point out that he had first been quite oblivious to its importance. As late as March 27, 1899, he was urging the legislature to appoint a commission to study the matter and report back the following year.

Roosevelt's assumption of credit was not wholly unjustified, however. If tardily, he awoke to the importance of a bill that would bring in millions of dollars in legitimate taxes. His messages to the legislature on April 27 and 28, 1899, declared this "the most important [bill] before the legislature this year." Platt's legislators were hastily summoned to oppose it, but the best they could do was to amend the bill in the hope that Roosevelt would be influenced to veto it. The worst of the alterations was one providing that assessments under the new law should be in the hands of the local authorities, which meant that Tammany in New York City would have new power over honest Republican businessmen. The governor called a special session for the purpose of having this defect removed. Then the machine made plans to emasculate the measure beyond all recognition.

Governor Roosevelt was master of the situation, however. He gave notice that unless an adequate bill was passed at the special session he would sign the existing measure. Frank Platt, son of the Republican boss, was permitted to take part in framing the new bill, but Roosevelt's threats were effective. "Three cheers!" was the rather ironical telegram which Roosevelt dispatched to Platt after the amended bill had become law. It was an effective measure; "Governor Roosevelt," said the New York *World*, "has not yielded an inch. The people honor him for it."

On other grounds, as well, Roosevelt was pleased with his first year as governor of New York. The civil service law was "the best statute of that character . . . enacted by any State or by the nation." He felt that much had been done to add to the welfare of the workingman, that the primary law had been improved, that "not a single law [has] been put on the statute books which ought not to have been made." Roosevelt had, however, been a pallid friend of home rule for the large cities of the state. Despite his assertion, he had bowed to Platt on many an appointment, and his only important step toward punishment of the guilty in the canal frauds was to arrange for further investigations.

Only one unpleasant incident marred the summer of 1899. Roosevelt had been persuaded to make a tour of the state fairs late in August. He was speaking at Hornellsville, New York, on integrity in government, when some farmer in the audience crudely interrupted to ask about the canals. The governor shot back that his questioner was "not quite sober" and that the accusations against canal officials were "infamous lies and slanders." He did not mean that. The following day he admitted that the canal administration had not been "what it ought to have been." Even the staunchly Republican New York *Tribune* chided him for minimizing the loss of $9,000,000.

"It was unquestionably a mistake to make it," Roosevelt wrote regarding his outburst at Hornellsville.

4

In 1900, the term of office of the governor of New York was two years. Since the election was concurrent with the presidential campaign, it was the duty of the Republican candidate for governor to carry his state for the national ticket. Roosevelt, as his second year began, knew that Mc-Kinley would be renominated for the presidency. He was handicapped in his program by demands that nothing be attempted that might alienate essential sources of support.

Benjamin B. Odell, as Roosevelt prepared his second message to the legislature in December, 1899, urged a policy of caution. The Republican state chairman added that it would be "very unwise" to suggest further liability for employers in cases where workmen were so clumsy as to injure themselves. As for a suggestion that members of the judiciary should not be assessed for campaign purposes, there was no reason, wrote Odell, why judges "should not pay their proper proportion as well as the governor or any other official." As a final warning, the state chairman asked modification of the trust-control section of the message. Publicity regarding corporate earnings would merely drive industry out of New York State.

The receipt of such advice, as he formulated his plans for the year, was decidedly embarrassing to an honest and able governor. Quite apart from his personal ambitions, Roosevelt desired another term in order to complete his program. To accomplish much in two years was impossible. But Odell's advice represented the views of the party leaders who could refuse the renomination. The result of the conflict was the inevitable one; a compromise in which expediency nullified certain of Roosevelt's convictions. He did not, however, surrender entirely. The recommendation for publicity on corporate earnings was retained. He deprecated contributions by judges to campaign war chests.

Interest in the message was overshadowed by the governor's announcement that Lou Payn would not be reappointed to the post of superintendent of insurance. Roosevelt had no personal love for Payn, who had assisted in bringing to light the unfortunate tax affidavits, but there is no evidence that this was the motive for demanding his head.

"Like the population of Poker Flat," he wrote, "I only venture to draw the line against individuals whose immorality is professional; but in Mr. Payn's case it *is* professional."

The term of the superintendent of insurance expired in February, 1900, and Roosevelt's plan to oust him was common knowledge in November of the previous year. Barnes had said that he would not object, but that Platt was the leader and would have to be obeyed since he controlled the Senate, which must confirm any substitute. The governor then said that he would turn Payn out while the Senate was in recess and so would have his own man in office for the greater part of 1900. The Albany *Evening Journal,* the voice of Bill Barnes, echoed these conversations and praised Payn's administration.

Payn was one of the numerous links between financial New York and the legislature. He had previously been a lobbyist for such eminent citizens as Jay Gould, and his appointment as superintendent of insurance augmented his value to these gentlemen. As Roosevelt phrased it, "being a frugal man, out of his seven thousand dollars a year salary he has saved enough to enable him to borrow nearly half a million dollars from a trust company, the directors of which are also the directors of an insurance company under his supervision."

The right was preponderantly on Roosevelt's side. He might have lost his fight, however, had not an unrelated petition been filed at Albany pointing out that the State Trust Company of New York City had made improper loans to the extent of $5,000,000. One of them, for $435,000, was to Lou Payn. The revelations regarding the State Trust Company spelled doom for Payn and victory, of a sort, for Roosevelt. Francis Hendricks of Syracuse was confirmed as the new superintendent of insurance. But Roosevelt's elation must have been dampened by the fact that Elihu Root, his friend and adviser as well as Secretary of War in McKinley's Cabinet, had been identified with the State Trust Company as counsel and director. Roosevelt had the wisdom this time to say nothing, however, and the whole affair was quickly forgotten. Smart men in business circles were constantly engaged in this sort of activity; no one cared. Mr. Root remained in public life, to do invaluable service for many years to come. Roosevelt promptly forgot that Root had been in any way involved. His only recollection was of the wisdom with which he had handled Tom Platt. It was the Lou Payn affair that inspired his most famous apothegm. He had been, he told a friend, "entirely good humored [and] cool" in his dealings with Platt:

"I have always been fond of the West African proverb: 'Speak softly and carry a big stick, you will go far.'"

5

"I think I have been the best Governor within my time, better than either Cleveland or Tilden."

Roosevelt's own estimate of his services was a shade

overenthusiastic. Aside from the fact that he improved civil service requirements and emphasized through the franchise tax the need for corporation control, his term provided no outstanding legislation. The governor claimed credit, however, for a law ending prize fighting, a tenement house bill to relieve congestion in the crowded city districts, and excellent game law amendments. The reason, he said, that more had not been accomplished in 1900 was "the very fact that so much was done in 1899."

Another reason was Roosevelt's preoccupation with the problem of the vice-presidency and the 1900 campaign. A third was the domination of Platt. Roosevelt was under constant fire, particularly from the independent Republicans, whose nomination for governor he had rejected in 1898, because he consented to see a great deal of the Easy Boss during his term. The theorists, whom he despised, proclaimed that a truly courageous governor would have defied the machine. He was questioned on his independence during the Barnes trial in 1915, and the attorney for William Barnes caused Roosevelt to grow rather excited during cross-examination on his political philosophy:

Q: You stand by righteousness, do you not?
Mr. Roosevelt: I do.
Q: With due regard for opportunism?
Mr. Roosevelt: No sir, not when it comes to righteousness. I say emphatically that you must have a due regard for opportunism in the choice of the time and method in making the attack. Just exactly as I did when I was Governor.

This was an accurate analysis of Roosevelt's political theory—always remembering that he drafted his own definition of "righteousness." Without compromise, nothing was accomplished. Opportunism could be one of the major virtues. In the *Century* for June, 1900, appeared an article written by Roosevelt which expressed again his contempt for those men "with slightly disordered mentalities who champion reforms as a kind of tribute to their own righteousness." On occasion, he said, it might be necessary to "cut loose and stand alone for a great cause; but the necessity for such action is almost as rare as the necessity for revolution." Sometimes, "it is a sign of the highest statesmanship to temporize."

On the other hand, not all of Roosevelt's temporizing while governor of New York was precisely statesmanship.

Chapter XVI

YEARNINGS AND CONSUMMATION

※

Three paths to the presidential nomination in 1904 opened
before Roosevelt while he was governor of New York.
One was to seek re-election. The second was to achieve appointment as Secretary of War under McKinley. The third,
and in Roosevelt's mind the least promising, was the vice-
presidential nomination.

Any governor of so important a state as New York is a
possible candidate for President. Public comment on Roosevelt's presidential aspirations started in March, 1899, to the
annoyance of the party leaders pledged to a renomination
for McKinley. Depew said in May that the President was
certain to be named and that Roosevelt did not want the
vice-presidency. He would continue as governor of New
York for two more years, "but look out for him in 1904."
Depew did not hint that Platt might refuse to tolerate another term at Albany for Roosevelt.

Roosevelt did not deceive himself about 1900. He told
Lodge in April, 1899, that McKinley would be chosen. In
June, however, he attended a Rough Rider reunion in New
Mexico and was astonished at the throngs which greeted
him "exactly as if I had been a presidential candidate."
The New York *Times* was amused over the enthusiasm being shown for Roosevelt, and intimated that he was debating his presidential chances. Had the governor of New York
no consideration for poor Mr. McKinley, no feeling for "a
weary President who, when he read of these exploits wondered how it is that with 7,000,000 people to look after,
Governor Roosevelt can't find enough to keep him busy at
home"? Mark Hanna, a little worried, said that Roosevelt
had made a fine governor, "but he is too ambitious." The
national chairman, hoping that this might put an end to the
presidential talk, said that the governor of New York deserved another term.

Roosevelt had enough consideration for McKinley to issue a statement when he returned from the West. He was
not a candidate for President, he said. Everyone he had
seen on his trip was behind McKinley; his renomination

was assured. This relieved the tension at the White House, but it was lamentable political strategy for Roosevelt to withdraw. He might have had any post he desired had he refrained from speaking out. As it was, he soon found himself being maneuvered toward the vice-presidency.

In July, 1899, Lodge analyzed possible programs which would bring victory in 1904. Two years more as governor had much to be said for it, the flaw being that the term would end in 1902 with the national convention still two years off. The ideal solution, Lodge felt, was for Roosevelt to become Secretary of War, where "your services will make you President without serious opposition." But this hope vanished when McKinley appointed Elihu Root. The third possibility was the vice-presidency. Lodge did not agree that this was a blind alley: "I have thought it over a great deal and I am sure I am right."

Roosevelt was puzzled. He had preferred the War Department. He recognized the disadvantages in another term as governor. He replied that he was aware that his hold on the voters was "entirely ephemeral" and could hardly last until 1904. He was inclined, although his wife disagreed, to share Lodge's belief that the vice-presidency offered the best chance.

The winter was one of indecision. On January 27, 1900, Lodge remarked with faint asperity that it was time for him to make up his mind. By February, Platt was joining in the chorus, and Roosevelt, suspicious that he was being placed on the political shelf by his enemies in New York, started to back away. "I would greatly rather be anything, say a Professor of History," he told Platt. At about the same time he protested that his finances would not permit acceptance.

Roosevelt thereupon announced that he would not accept the nomination if it was offered. His statement of February 6, 1900, was as conclusive as such a statement could be, although he later denied that he had closed the door.

"It is proper for me to state definitely that under no circumstances could I or would I," he said, "accept the nomination for the Vice-presidency. My duty is here in the state whose people chose me to be governor. I am happy to state that Senator Platt cordially acquiesces in my views in the matter."

If Roosevelt really believed that Platt agreed, he was mistaken. Meanwhile, the board was being prepared for a contest at the Republican National Convention on which

Roosevelt was to be merely a pawn. Mark Hanna, obsessed by forebodings, could forget neither the excited utterances which Roosevelt had voiced during the 1896 campaign, nor his anxiety for war. "Your reasoning in the political situation in New York seems to be good," he wrote to the governor, "and I think should be conclusive." Some weeks later, in an interview, he said the predictions that Roosevelt would be nominated vice-president came from "sources unacquainted with the facts." Hanna, hoping that the governor of New York would not be chosen, was not acquainted with all the facts either. He did not know that two men who disliked him heartily—Matt Quay and Boies Penrose of Pennsylvania—were soon to conspire with Platt to bring it about.

As the national convention, due to open in Philadelphia on June 19, approached, Roosevelt's resolution faltered. If you go as a delegate, Lodge warned, you will be nominated. "I would be looked upon as a coward if I didn't go," Roosevelt answered, and permitted himself to be chosen as a delegate at large. "By the way," he wrote on April 23, 1900, "I did *not* say that I would not under any circumstances accept the vice-presidency." His preference was still to be governor of New York for the next two years, but he was also afraid that he might be retired to private life. His friends, meanwhile, saw him being forced into an office that meant the end of presidential dreams; no vice-president had ever been elected to the presidency.

"I think you are unduly alarmed," remarked John Hay, "there is no instance of an election of a Vice-president by violence."

On a June night, just before the delegations began their migrations to Philadelphia, Chief Judge Alton B. Parker of the New York Court of Appeals dined at the Executive Mansion in Albany. After dinner he found himself alone with Mrs. Roosevelt, and the conversation turned to the approaching convention. He told the governor's wife that she would enjoy watching the ridiculous sessions, but he was not reassuring when Mrs. Roosevelt asked whether Theodore could avoid the vice-presidency. Judge Parker did not believe that her husband was so very anxious to avoid it. He described, with uncanny vision, Roosevelt's arrival at the convention hall:

And then—just a bit late—you will see your handsome husband come in and bedlam will break loose, and he will receive such a demonstration as no one else will receive. And being a devoted wife you will be very proud and happy. Then, some two or three days later, you will see your husband unanimously nominated for Vice-president of the United States.

2

The Republican National Convention of 1900 had been called to order at 12:30 o'clock with the usual formalities. Then, "just a bit late," as Mark Hanna was thumping for order, a burly figure strode down the aisle toward the New York delegation. He was wearing the wide-brimmed black hat that had attracted attention during his campaign for governor. Its similarity to the campaign hat of a Rough Rider was obvious, and Wayne MacVeagh, who had been attorney general under Garfield, looked at it with amusement.

"Gentlemen," he whispered to his neighbors, "that's an Acceptance Hat."

Why Roosevelt wore the hat must be left to the psychoanalysts. He paid no attention to the applause which swept the convention as he made his entrance. His jaw seemed to be set in determination. He did not even remove his hat during the long two minutes while he made his way toward his seat. He froze into military immobility, the hat against his heart, as the band struck up the national anthem. But on the platform a smile on the round face of Mark Hanna faded.

A strange clairvoyance of disaster apparently gripped the national chairman at Philadelphia. Mr. Hanna said something about a different situation this year, about the possibility that the nominee would be a presidential candidate in 1904.

"At this convention, if ever," he added, "the vice-presidential nomination should be made a serious question and a man chosen who would . . . give the country an administration equally as good as that of McKinley if he should, by any mishap, ascend to the first place."

Roosevelt's perplexities were unending. Would Boss Platt, at the last moment, push forward Odell and refuse him even the vice-presidency? Would he then be denied a second term as governor? There were indications that some such plot was in the air. Before the delegation left New York, Odell had intimated that he would not decline to run with McKinley. On reaching Philadelphia, Platt denied any intention of pushing Roosevelt against his will; Odell would "fill the place to a dot." On the other hand, from

154

western delegations knowing nothing of the conspiracies behind the scenes, came demands that Roosevelt bow to the will of the people and accept the nomination. Under the strain, Roosevelt was ferocious in private and cautious in public.

The phrases which marked another declination were: "I appreciate all this to the full." "I understand the high honor and dignity of the office, an office so high and so honorable well worthy the ambition of any man in the United States." But Roosevelt felt, he protested, that his "best usefulness to the public and to the party" lay in his renomination as governor. He asked that "every friend of mine in the convention respect my wish and judgment in this matter."

Roosevelt was entirely sincere when, the convention over, he told his sister that "the great bulk of the Republicans" had brought about his nomination, that he would be "both ungrateful and a fool not to be deeply touched by the way in which I was nominated." This much of his belief was true; public demand for Roosevelt's nomination made the Platt-Quay-Penrose conspiracy possible. The evidence points to the probability that the whole matter had been settled a day or so before the convention met. Even "Buttons Bim" Bimberg, a peddler of buttons and other souvenirs and a familiar figure at state and national conventions, had ordered thousands of emblems proclaiming a McKinley-Roosevelt ticket.

"If it isn't Roosevelt," he said, "there will be a dent in the Delaware River caused by Bim committing suicide."

Roosevelt was nominated for the vice-presidency, against his faltering will, because Matt Quay nursed a grudge against Mark Hanna. Just when Quay, with Penrose, his aide, first planned their revenge on Hanna, whose apprehensions regarding Roosevelt they well knew, is not clear. Just when Platt, who bore no ill will toward Hanna and desired to get Roosevelt out of New York State for reasons of his own, joined the conspiracy is also unknown. Platt's own account is a suavely untruthful one, but he does say that he agreed with Quay "to combine forces" for Roosevelt.

The details are not essential. Quay despised Hanna because the Ohio Senator had, in 1899, blocked his admission to the Senate. He waited anxiously for revenge, and his chance came when he perceived Mark Hanna's alarm over Roosevelt. The attack was launched on June 20, the second day of the convention. Quay must have been quietly amused when he arose from the Pennsylvania delegation to suggest an amendment to the rules. He proposed that state representation at national conventions be based on the size of the Republican vote in the latest election. This was an ancient proposal, never taken seriously, which would have stripped Southern Republican leaders of their power. It would have eliminated the Negro delegates who adorn every Republican gathering. It was a step toward honesty in politics, a consummation in which Quay was wholly uninterested. His purpose was not misinterpreted. This was a blow at Mark Hanna, who controlled the Southern delegates. The excitement was intense as the clerk read Quay's motion. Southern leaders climbed to their chairs and shrieked for recognition. Then the Pennsylvania boss suggested that discussion be delayed for a day or two.

Hanna knew that it was the end. When the convention recessed, the delegates from the South flocked to the headquarters of the national chairman to ask what the amendment meant. They said, as Hanna knew they would, that Quay had promised to withdraw it if they swung their support to Roosevelt. Hanna could do nothing except bluster and surrender. "Don't any of you realize," he demanded, his forebodings returning in full force, "that there's only one life between this madman and the White House?"

Nothing further marred the harmony of the day. McKinley was unanimously nominated, with Roosevelt making one of the seconding speeches. This was followed immediately by the nomination for vice-president.

3

Mark Hanna, making the best of a defeat which had been a blow to his prestige, informed Roosevelt that the main burden of the campaign would fall on his shoulders. The President would make an address or two from his home at Canton. The arduous work of crusading in doubtful states would be done by the candidate for vice-president. Roosevelt assured the national chairman that he was "as strong as a Bull Moose and you can use me up to the limit." He felt distaste, however, for appearing as "a second-class Bryan," and he doubted the wisdom of too many speeches.

In April, 1900, Roosevelt had been seriously alarmed by the possibility that Admiral George Dewey would be the standard-bearer of the Democratic party. The hero of San Juan, whose military renown had resulted in election as governor of New York, had once written that "popular sentiment is just when it selects as popular heroes the men who have led in the struggle against malice domestic or foreign levy." But he was now less certain. Bryan, said Roosevelt on April 9, was preferable to Dewey, whose candidacy would be merely ridiculous were it not that "the unthinking under the glamor of his naval glory" might support him. The presidential aspirations of the admiral were, in fact, absurd. "I am convinced," he had said, "that the office of President is not such a very difficult one to fill." The novelty of the Spanish War heroes had diminished, however, and Dewey was forgotten when the Democrats assembled in Kansas City in July. Bryan decreed another defeat for his party by demanding the nomination and insisting on a free silver plank.

For all his magnetism, and despite the fact that he perceived current evils with a kind of emotional vision, William Jennings Bryan always spoke for disorganized minorities. They did not seek some common end; they disagreed violently among themselves. He recommended corporation control, and one group believed in him. He added free silver and this dropped away. He spoke against "manifest destiny," against the imperialists who sought the acquisition of distant lands, but he also harped on the worn-out theme of sixteen to one. The anti-imperialists left him in disgust.

They were fascinating phrases, these phrases of imperialism. They intrigued a nation which had, until 1898, never been admitted to adult standing among the powers of the world. They furnished glowing perorations for the orators who, at the same time, promised the Full Dinner Pail and appropriated once again for the Republican party the issu of prosperity. Against the beating of such words, the warnings of Carl Schurz and Godkin and the rest were impotent. Mark Hanna had changed his mind on the unwisdom of the war with Spain and was talking about "the march of Christianization and civilization of the world." So much the better, remarked Senator E. O. Wolcott of Colorado, if the new island possessions of the United States were "rich in all the products of the tropics, in mineral wealth, and in the possibilities of future development."

In the face of this pleasant combination—inflation of the national ego by conquest and the prospect of selling goods to the conquered—Roosevelt should have been confident of victory. But he was not. A Messianic urge again gripped him and gave him strength to indulge in one of the most vigorous campaigns in the annals of presidential circuses.

A good deal of doubt existed as to the "paramount issue"

of the campaign. To Mark Hanna it was the Full Dinner Pail. To Bryan it was imperialism, legislation against the trusts, and the bondage of gold. To Roosevelt the paramount issue was the depravity of those who disagreed with the Republican administration. The vice-presidential nominee's party shared his apprehensions over the outcome. Senator Hanna was constantly insisting that danger lay in overconfidence. Roosevelt was afraid that the voters were "busy and prosperous" and so would not perceive the danger. On the other hand, the prosperity so proudly claimed was more apparent than real. Some of the dinner pails were rather empty. It took heroic efforts on the part of Mark Hanna, and the assistance of J. P. Morgan, to halt a strike of the anthracite miners in September. It would have been an exceedingly embarrassing strike, coming at the height of the campaign, and the operators were frightened into granting a ten per cent wage increase.

Roosevelt ignored these reflections on Republican beneficence. His first important address was at St. Paul on July 16, and he then described the "fearful misery, fearful disaster at home, shame that is even worse-flinching from the great work we have begun" that would follow a Republican defeat. He rattled the metallic skeleton of free silver that "would paralyze our whole industrial life." He said that the Democratic convention had "reasserted the doctrines of anarchy." He cited the Louisiana Purchase by Thomas Jefferson, although Roosevelt detested Jefferson on every other subject, as proof of the necessity for expansion.

The exertion of this campaign proved too much for the constitution of even a Bull Moose, and by the middle of October Roosevelt was complaining that his voice was giving out, that he felt like "a football man who has gone stale." There were other irritations. He was criticized for neglecting his duties as governor of New York. His opponents read with critical eyes the lives of Benton and Cromwell which he had written; and Roosevelt learned that a literary career, when combined with politics, had unsuspected disadvantages. He was forced to state that he had meant no offense when he wrote that the Quakers, being unwilling to fight, should be denied citizenship. A good many Republican Quakers had protested to the national committee over this. Roosevelt explained:

. . . were I to rewrite the sentence, I should certainly so phrase it that it could not be construed as offensive to the Society of Friends, a body whose social virtues and civil righteousness justly command universal respect.

The reward of his zeal was victory on November 6. The McKinley-Roosevelt ticket received 292 electoral votes to 155 for Bryan. The plurality was 849,000, the largest since 1872.

Roosevelt found it difficult to be too elated over the result. Cynicism was a mental vice that he deplored, and which rarely overcame him, but there is a trace of it in a letter to Root on December 5. He was inviting the Secretary of War to attend a dinner in honor of J. P. Morgan:

> I hope you can come to my dinner to J. Pierpont Morgan. You see, it represents an effort on my part to become a conservative man in touch with the influential classes and I think I deserve encouragement. Hitherto I have given dinners only to professional politicians or more or less wild-eyed radicals. Now I am at work endeavoring to assume the vice-presidential pose.

Mr. Morgan must have been gratified by this hospitality, as well as reassured. It perhaps dispelled lingering doubts induced by Roosevelt's fight for the franchise tax as governor. It enabled Mr. Morgan to proceed with entire confidence with his plans for the organization of the United States Steel Corporation. Sometimes history is written on the inside pages of the newspapers as well as in headlines. The headlines told of the enthusiasm for Theodore Roosevelt on Inauguration Day, March 4, 1901, and mentioned the contrasting obscurity of the President of the United States. They said that the question on everyone's lips was whether Roosevelt would be taking the oath as President four years later.

On the financial pages, however, appeared an announcement that J. P. Morgan & Company were syndicate managers for the new United States Steel Corporation. Mr. Morgan had correctly interpreted the vote on November 6, but the new Vice-President was, after all, a very real adversary; one whom the fates were watching.

4

As President, Roosevelt did not entertain a high opinion of the Senate; it was a body that opposed his will. He had sympathized with the reforms instituted by Speaker Reed in the House and preferred limited debate. Curiously, he heard cloture discussed during his brief service as president of the Senate, and listened while the inevitable denunciations greeted the suggestion.

The Senate was in session from March 5 to March 9, 1901, to pass upon presidential appointments, and this, although a debate or two on other matters took place, was the only official business. Vice-President Roosevelt was nervous about his ability as presiding officer of this august assemblage; a clerk was at his side to prompt him. On one of the first motions, Roosevelt revealed his innate belief that Democrats were fundamentally obstructionists. "All in favor will say Ay," he called, bowing in the direction of the Republican members. Then, while the Senate chuckled audibly, he turned toward the Democrats: "All those opposed say No," he added.

Fortunately, when the Senate convened again, Roosevelt was President of the United States.

Facing months of idleness until Congress convened in December, Roosevelt consoled himself with plans for studying law and with dreams of the presidential nomination in 1904. At the same time he gave consideration to occupation as a historian. Would it be possible, he asked, for him to take a position "in a college where I could give lectures on United States History to graduates"? He would find it pleasant to do "some serious, scholarly work—which should go on the shelves at least with Charles Henry Lee and John Fiske."

Concurrently, although indicating his belief that his political future was dark, Roosevelt worked actively for the 1904 nomination. "I want you to be very careful," Cabot Lodge had warned during the 1900 campaign. Everything should be considered in the light of the future and "nothing finds lodgment in the human mind so easily as jealousy." Roosevelt must, therefore, subordinate his position to that of McKinley. This would insure the support of the Federal machine "four years hence."

"I have no doubt that you will be the nominee in 1904," wrote Taft in January, 1901.

In all probability, these plans would have reached fruition. Innumerable letters came to Roosevelt pledging support. As early as March, 1901, virtual endorsement had been obtained from Governor Henry T. Gage of California, and it was suggested that Roosevelt arrange a tour of the country the following year. Clearly, the boom was to have been started in California, thus avoiding the impression that Roosevelt was in any manner allied with Tom Platt of New York.

Other friends were equally busy. William Allen White of Kansas said that he would "be glad to undertake the job of passing the hat" in his state. Could the support of Hanna, Quay, and Platt be counted upon? From Illinois came assurances of Roosevelt sentiment, and Charles G. Dawes, returning from a journey through the Southwest, brought similarly encouraging news. Roosevelt then told Editor White that Hanna seemed to be more friendly, that

I do not believe he thinks me the bull in the china shop which he once did; and my opinion of him has changed enormously for the better.

When it comes to Quay, I am really at a loss what to say. There are certain things which he has done of which I cannot in any way approve. Were I President I should certainly endeavor to do what the two Pennsylvania Senators wished in the matter of patronage so far as I honorably could.

Now about Platt. As I told you, Platt informed me that if I decided to become a candidate for the Presidency, he would support me.

Politically, the nomination depended largely on control of the Southern delegates, who were, in 1901, still in Hanna's hands. In his posthumously published autobiography, Speaker Cannon declared that Roosevelt had arranged to visit Tuskegee Institute in the early fall and that Dr. Booker T. Washington, the Negro educator, had agreed to build a new Republican organization in the South, an organization based on character instead of patronage and bribery. This was to be for Roosevelt. It was also on the program to have the Vice-President visit his mother's home at Roswell, Georgia, where he could appropriately hold forth on the Southern blood that flowed through his veins.

Part of the story, but not all, is confirmed by Roosevelt's letters. A trip to Tuskegee had been scheduled for some time in November, 1901. Dr. Washington told the Vice-President that a reception would be held at Atlanta, not far from Roswell, and a visit to the old homestead could easily be arranged. The letters also reveal that the Negro was entertained by Roosevelt either at Oyster Bay or in Washington prior to the famous dinner at the White House. On September 1, Washington wrote that he was "delighted to have the privilege of meeting Mrs. Roosevelt and the members of your family."

Nothing in the correspondence, however, indicates a plan to enlist Washington's aid for 1904, and it is doubtful that one existed. Any attempt to reform Republican political methods in the South would have failed, as Roosevelt learned when he attempted it as President.

5

The summer of 1901 was rather dull, the principal diversion being a trip to Colorado in August, on which the cheers for Roosevelt were encouraging. In May he attended the opening of the Pan-American Exposition at Buffalo, New York, and spoke on the probable blessings of the new century. President McKinley, who was to visit the exposition in September, sent a message expressing his hope for its success.

"May there be no cloud," he telegraphed, "on this grand festival of peace and commerce."

On September 6, in the Temple of Music, McKinley was shot twice by Leon Czolgosz, an anarchist. He died in Buffalo in the early morning of September 14.

Roosevelt, on September 6, was attending an outing of the Vermont Fish and Game League on the Isle La Motte in Lake Champlain. It was toward dusk. A reception was being held at the home of former Governor Nelson W. Fisk of Vermont, when a telephone message from Buffalo was received. No one knew, as yet, how serious McKinley's wounds were. The Vice-President hurried to Burlington, and boarded a special train for Buffalo.

However ambitious he may have been, Roosevelt was a decent and affectionate person. He was also a patriot. The shock of the news swept aside consideration of its momentous meaning to his own career. On the trip across the lake to the train someone was so gauche as to remark that he might, at any moment, become President of the United States. Roosevelt rebuked this with the answer that everyone would think only of the stricken Chief Executive. It appears to have been the unanimous judgment that the Vice-President conducted himself with dignity and restraint. He told Lodge, who was in Paris, that "at first the news seemed literally incredible," that the attack had not been on corporate wealth, but

simply and solely on free government, government by the common people. McKinley comes from the typical hard-working farmer stock of our country. In every instinct and feeling he is closely in touch with the men who make up the immense bulk of our nation.

This was not quite an accurate picture of McKinley's political philosophy, but it indicates Roosevelt's feeling toward the President during the days of tragic uncertainty. McKinley, who had been taken to a private home, had rallied after the first day and optimistic reports were issued by the surgeons on September 9. On the following day, the Vice-President left Buffalo as an assurance to the nation that the danger had passed. He was to join his family in a remote part of the Adirondack Mountains near Mount Tahawus. Before leaving, however, Roosevelt left his itinerary with Ansley Wilcox, at whose residence he had been staying in Buffalo.

Some time after midnight on the morning of Friday, September 13, Mr. Wilcox was awakened by a messenger. The President was worse, much worse, he was told. Roosevelt must be summoned immediately. Within two hours a courier had started from Albany, but when he arrived at the Tahawus Club he found that Roosevelt had left to spend the day mountain climbing. It was late that afternoon before the Vice-President began his descent and met a guide who had started up with telegrams. Then came a wild ride of fifty miles on a buckboard to the nearest railroad station, where a special train waited. All of that day, as the messages to Roosevelt must have made clear, there had been no hope that McKinley could live. At 2:15 o'clock on Saturday morning, September 14, 1901, while his hack careened on toward the mountain railroad station, Roosevelt became President of the United States. He boarded the train at dawn, learning that the President was dead.

He reached Buffalo at 1:30 o'clock the next afternoon and was driven to the house where McKinley's body lay. Again, he was deeply affected by the tragedy. An hour and a half later the oath of office was administered at the Wilcox home. The house had been dismantled for the summer and in the library, where the small group gathered, the chairs were still shrouded in dust covers. Except for Secretary of State Hay and Secretary of the Treasury Gage, all the members of McKinley's Cabinet were present. Secretary of War Root addressed the new President and asked that the oath of office be taken at once.

Roosevelt's face was nearly expressionless. His eyes were fixed straight ahead. He bowed to the Secretary of War and spoke in the crisp, staccato sentences that already were so familiar.

"I am at one mind with the members of the Cabinet," he said. "I will show the people at once that the administration of the government will not falter in spite of the terrible blow. I wish to say that it shall be my aim to continue, absolutely unbroken, the policy of President McKinley for the peace, the prosperity, and the honor of our beloved country."

That was all. The President asked that the members of the Cabinet remain in office. Then he excused himself and went out into the September afternoon, talking earnestly to Mr. Root.

Roosevelt had returned when a carriage drove up, and Mark Hanna stepped out. Loiterers pointed toward Hanna as he leaned on his cane, his normally cheerful face gray, the torment in his mind apparent. This was the man, they whispered, who had warned the Republican National Convention of 1900 that to make Roosevelt Vice-President would place but a single life "between this madman and the Presidency." Well, this was the end of Mark Hanna, once so powerful and so blunt. But the Senator from Ohio knew more about Roosevelt than he had known in June, 1900. He now learned that graciousness was a part of the make-up of the young politician who had sometimes puzzled and alarmed him, but who had more often been merely amusing. The President of the United States had seen the carriage drive up. He hurried from the house with outstretched hands. Mark Hanna removed his hat.

"Mr. President, I wish you success and a prosperous administration," he said. "I trust that you will command me if I can be of any service."

BOOK II

Elihu Root ⎫
Cabot Lodge ⎭ ?

Chapter I

MIDDLE OF THE ROAD

✳

The news from Buffalo on September 6, 1901, reached New York after the stock market had closed, but important figures in the financial world remained at their desks and made plans to halt the bear raids certain to occur when trading began in the morning. In the large brokerage houses, telegraphers gossiped in dots and dashes over private wires, and told their employers how word of the attempted assassination had reached J. P. Morgan. It was shortly after 5 o'clock; the colossus was passing from the building when a newspaper reporter halted him.

"What!" exclaimed Morgan, grasping the journalist's arm. He hurried back into his office and ordered assistants to telephone for confirmation. Just then another reporter came in, with a copy of the first extra under his arm. Morgan read it slowly, muttered something to the effect that it was "sad . . . sad," and declined further comment. Charles M. Schwab, of the newly organized United States Steel Corporation, abandoned his customary optimism to say that business would surely suffer if the President died.

So McKinley must not die, and on September 7 reassurances came from the surgeons. These, combined with preparations during the night, prevented serious stock depressions. "The financial situation," said Morgan, "is good. There is nothing to derange it. The banks will take care of that."

But Friday, September 13, brought additional frightened chattering on the tickers. The President was sinking. His death was a matter of hours only, and Henry Clews tried to explain away another impending slump. Roosevelt, he said, would continue McKinley's policies. The nation had "no cause to fear any serious happenings through Theodore Roosevelt." Perhaps Mr. Clews had heard of a conference being held that day by Douglas Robinson, Roosevelt's brother-in-law, and Major George Dunn, chairman of the

Republican State Committee. Toward evening, Robinson dictated a lengthy letter to Roosevelt, a letter so important that it was rushed to Buffalo by special messenger and was waiting when he arrived on Saturday. Meanwhile, McKinley had died. Robinson wrote:

I feel I must be frank . . . [if] when you start you will give the feeling that things are not to be changed and that you are going to be conservative . . . it will take a weight off the public mind.

Mr. Dunn told me today that either he or I must get to you to impress upon you the fact that you must, no matter how much you are pressed and badgered, be as close-mouthed and conservative as you were before your nomination for Governor.

When Roosevelt digested this practical and valuable advice, he was already President of the United States. He followed it literally for a time; in his statement to the Cabinet, in the assurance to the country that McKinley's policies were his own. The suggestions made by Mr. Root at Buffalo must have been along similar lines. Finally, there was counsel from Mark Hanna.

They conferred at the Wilcox home in Buffalo, and T.R.'s reports of their meeting were calm and objective. Hanna had "in very manly fashion" said that he would not necessarily work for Roosevelt's nomination in 1904. No break between Hanna and Roosevelt occurred in 1901; the stories to that effect were inaccurate. On October 18, 1901, the President told the national chairman that he would not give consideration to Southern appointments until a consultation had been held. A few days later, Hanna wrote his famous letter asking Roosevelt to "go slow." The President would be deluged with opinions. "*Hear* them all patiently but *reserve* decision," Hanna begged.

"It would not be possible to get wiser advice," Roosevelt answered, "and I shall act exactly upon it. I shall go slow." The cordiality of their relations increased rapidly: "To *the* Senator" was the italicized greeting on December 20. "Many thanks, old man, your note gave me real pleasure. All good wishes to you and yours."

"As regards Hanna, I like him," he had already confided.

The new President was to be docile enough, for the moment, but the disquietude of the respectables had some basis. The lush prosperity of the days just after the Spanish War was beginning to diminish. The settlement of the coal strike during the summer of 1900 had been a compromise and further trouble was probable. Most disturbing of all, although the full significance was appreciated by a limited few, was the election of Robert M. LaFollette as governor of Wisconsin. He was the outspoken foe of the railroads and other corporate interests. He was dangerous because he was effective.

There were other dangers, such as the apparent success of the newspaper which Joseph Pulitzer had purchased from Jay Gould in 1883. For a time, the New York *World* had been lightly dismissed as "yellow," but by 1901 it was winning readers by the thousand because it dared to become a voice for the lower middle classes. Pulitzer was sounding the reforms less ably advocated by Bryan: income and inheritance taxes, corporation control by the Federal Government, a tariff for revenue. The red glow of Progressivism, in the full glare of which Theodore Roosevelt was one day to stand, was just perceptible over the horizon.

2

Expediency had demanded the conciliation of Mark Hanna. Roosevelt was too wise to emulate that other ruler, with whom he was often unfairly compared, and send ashore a skilled pilot. Hanna was the Bismarck who could do much for party harmony. "Of course," Roosevelt remembered, "I very earnestly desired his support and felt that it would be a great calamity to the party and therefore to the public if there was a break."

But Roosevelt was only forty-three years old, the youngest President in history. The death of McKinley was not the only sad note attendant upon his accession. The government had been in the hands of men who were old or elderly and so, as Roosevelt became President, an epoch passed. It was a time of change and it was felt most, perhaps, by John Hay, who had been private secretary to Abraham Lincoln, minister to Great Britain, and who was now Secretary of State. Hay's worst enemy, if his greatest charm, had been his tongue. He had never been able to suppress amused comments on the career of the young man who now was President.

John Hay had been irritated, as well as amused, during Roosevelt's rise. In February, 1900, he received a lengthy letter from the governor of New York protesting against the Hay-Pauncefote Treaty, which, said Roosevelt, did not protect the rights of the United States in relation to a canal across the isthmus at Panama or Nicaragua. Presumably, Hay felt that this did not concern a mere governor, and he resented the interference because the treaty was very close to his heart. There was a touch of malice in his amusement when, in June of that year, Roosevelt went to Washington to beg that the vice-presidency might not be forced upon him. He told Henry White about it:

Teddy has been here: have you heard of it? It was more fun than a goat. He came down with a sombre resolution on his strenuous brow to let McKinley and Hanna know once for all that he would not be Vice-president, and found to his stupefaction that nobody except Platt had dreamed of such a thing.

Hay must have pondered, as he read the tragic news from Buffalo, the effect on his position as Secretary of State. His apprehensions vanished, however, when the funeral train arrived in Washington on Monday night, September 16, for "in the station, without waiting an instant, [he] told me that I must stay with him—that I could not decline or even consider." On Sunday, Hay had written a letter to Roosevelt, which the President had probably not yet received, in which he had expressed his "sincere affection and esteem for you, my old time love for your father." This letter would certainly have moved the emotional Roosevelt, even had he not already promised to retain the McKinley Cabinet. Sorrow had come in overwhelming measure to the man whose charm can never be exaggerated. His son, Del Hay, had recently died. Nicolay, who had been co-secretary to Lincoln, was dying. Clarence King, a close friend, was seriously ill in California. Hay's letter to Roosevelt was deeply moving:

. . . from the depths of the sorrow where I sit, with the grief for the President mingled and confused with that for my boy, so that I scarcely know, from hour to hour, the true source of my tears—I do still congratulate you. With your youth, your ability, your health and strength, the courage God has given you to do right, there are no bounds to the good you can accomplish. . . .

Roosevelt, never too analytical about his fellows and rarely a keen judge of men, was not one to resist the pathos of this, or to suspect that John Hay may have been surrendering to the cruel pleasure of literary melancholy. The end had not really come, although Hay had passed the crest of his career. He was again to be gay and charming, again amused at the strutting figures of the pageant. It may be doubted, however, that Roosevelt and Hay ever trusted each other completely. Hay's role, unlike that of Elihu Root, was always subordinate. But his personal relations with the President were extremely cordial and it became Roosevelt's habit to stop, each Sunday, on his way home from church, at the house of John Hay. This continued until Hay's death in 1905.

Roosevelt was not generous in his appraisal of the services rendered by John Hay. Shortly before his term in the White House ended, the private letters of Hay were published and old resentments crowded back into Roosevelt's consciousness. Hay had been "the most delightful man to talk to I ever met," he wrote Lodge in January 1909. He made

out of hand those epigrammatic remarks which we would all like to make. He was the best letter writer of his age. But he was not a great Secretary of State. For instance, he was not to be mentioned in the same breath with Root. In public life during the time he was Secretary of State under me he accomplished little . . . his usefulness to me was almost exclusively that of a fine figure-head.

The heartache of the older men lay in the truism that the adolescent had become all-powerful. He might be an adolescent still, but everything was in focus no longer. In a single week, time had moved far too swiftly; the outlines were very blurred. Henry Adams, returning from Europe in December, 1901, saw all this. He felt that Hay was glad to remain in the Cabinet, "if only to save himself the trouble of quitting." But to Adams himself, as he resumed his brooding in the house on Lafayette Square, "all was pure loss." He wrote of the men who were passing:

To them at sixty-three, Roosevelt at forty-three could not be taken seriously in his old character, and could not be recovered in his new one. Power, when wielded by abnormal energy, is the most serious of facts, and all Roosevelt's friends knew that his restless and combative energy was more than abnormal. Roosevelt, more than any other man living showed the singular primitive quality that belongs to ultimate matter—the quality that medieval theology ascribed to God—he was pure act.

But when seven and a half years had passed, and Roosevelt was leaving the White House, Henry Adams was singularly depressed. No better proof lies anywhere, perhaps, of Roosevelt's charm or, more important, of his capacity for growth.

3

Various gentlemen, some of them in public life and others affiliated with finance and industry, were reassured by the receipt of messages from the White House during September and October, 1901. The President, it is clear, had taken to heart the advice from Mark Hanna that it was best to "go slow." Letters went out, while Roosevelt worked on his first message to Congress, to Senators Hale of Maine, Foraker of Ohio, and Fairbanks of Indiana. A preliminary draft was sent to Hanna. On November 10, 1901, the Republican national chairman wrote that certain sections might "furnish ammunition to the enemy in a political contest," that he had been "thinking hard" over the part relating to the trusts. Hanna felt, he told the President, that even the labor unions were not greatly interested in corporation control, "and I do not believe they want to see it made a political issue." He was particularly doubtful regarding a passage relating to overcapitalization. On the following day, Roosevelt sent word to Hanna assuring him that this feature had been eliminated.

The message contained nothing new in so far as Roosevelt's policies were concerned. The pressure upon the White House, in fact, demanded that he disavow the principles he had recommended as governor of New York. It was a verbose document of more than twenty thousand words with quantity more apparent than quality. If it proved nothing else, it demonstrated that Roosevelt was not inevitably impulsive. Control over large corporations was needed, but caution was essential or business unrest would result. Organized labor was entitled to protection, but it must not be allowed to abuse its privileges. Perhaps the tariff should be lowered, but not at the expense of industry. McKinley, in the speech made on the day before he was shot, had called for downward revision by means of reciprocity agreements with other nations. Excellent, said McKinley's successor, but "reciprocity must be treated as the handmaiden of protection." Mr. Dooley was vastly amused as he read Roosevelt's message:

"Th' trusts," says he [Roosevelt], "are heejoous monsthers built up be th' enlightened intherprise iv th' men that have done so much to advance progress in our beloved country," he says. "On wan hand I wud stamp thim undher fut; on th' other hand not so fast."

The message must be judged in the light of Roosevelt's anxiety to prevent party discord and with consideration for the influences which surrounded him. He did not wholly retreat from the positions he had taken in the past. Out of the excess verbiage of this first presidential state paper grew the more definite principles which he made his own.

A Department of Commerce and Labor should be created with power to investigate corporate earnings and to guard the rights of the workingman. Immigration should be limited to those fit to enter the United States. Consideration should be given to subsidies for ships under the American flag. Granting of rebates by railroads must be halted. In addition to all this, there were paragraphs dealing with conservation and reclamation, Hawaii, Puerto Rico, Cuba, and the Philippine Islands. The only reference to a canal connecting the Atlantic and Pacific was the insistence that this work begin at once. Roosevelt did not recommend a route. He asked for a stronger navy and said that the Monroe Doctrine was the basis of the foreign policies of all nations of North and of South America. The doctrine, he added naïvely, "has nothing to do with the commercial relations of any American power."

The public, intrigued by the novelty of the first colorful President in decades, was more interested in Roosevelt's personality than in his messages. This phase fascinated equally the Washington correspondents. They sent dispatches pointing to the astonishing fact that he was at his desk by 8:30 in the morning and had visitors for breakfast, luncheon, and dinner. He would, they predicted, collapse unless he took things more easily. They told of his irritation over the constant attendance of secret service men and of his attempts to escape on solitary horseback rides or walks. Cartoonists everywhere were elated because no longer would they be lost for ideas.

"I am going to curb my desire for hunting," he told one of the correspondents. "I do not want the people to get the idea that they have a sporting President."

Roosevelt did not live up to this resolution, however. He went on several hunting expeditions. Because of these, which were reported at length, and for other reasons also, he was one of the few Presidents undimmed by the aura of dignity that normally surrounds the Chief Executive. The people had a fair approximation, although certain aspects were exaggerated, of what the man was really like. This was, on the whole, fortunate for his career.

It was, however, the tangles in which Roosevelt became involved that made his countrymen love him. There were many of these: Booker T. Washington, the Bellamy Storers, simplified spelling, nature-faking, the Brownsville riot. Any one might have meant ruin to a less gifted public official. They began as soon as he assumed the presidency.

The assassination of McKinley had made obsolete any plans that Roosevelt may have had for a new and more honest group of Southern Republicans who would support him for the 1904 nomination. He continued to yearn, however, for a new era in the South, and he pursued the illusive dream of instituting appointments based on merit. He wrote Lodge on October 11 that he wished to have the Republican standard as high in the South as in the North. This rivaled simplified spelling as Roosevelt's most quixotic ambition, and its realization was quite as impossible. If anything, the President retarded rather than advanced the day of a purified party below the Mason-Dixon Line. He blundered into a complicated situation and left it worse than it had been before. On September 14, the day on which he took the oath of office at Buffalo, Roosevelt wrote Dr. Washington that he wished to discuss appointments. The Negro educator, in response to this command, visited the White House during the last week in September and offered advice.

On October 7, 1901, the President announced the appointment of Thomas Goode Jones of Alabama as a United States district judge. The significance lay in the fact that Jones was a Democrat, and his selection had been recommended by Washington. Roosevelt had promised that he would name a Democrat if a competent Republican could not be found, and his only reluctance had been based on the fact that Judge Jones had once supported Bryan.

"I guess I'll have to appoint him," he said, "but I'm awfully sorry he voted for Bryan."

Dr. Washington, recalling the days when he had been summoned to the White House, felt that Roosevelt "wanted to help not only the Negro, but the whole South." Undoubtedly he did, but when the President invited Washington to dine at the White House, he demonstrated lamentable ignorance of Southern opinion. For the President of the United States to entertain "a nigger," as Southern gentlemen classed all members of the race, was unforgivable. Having done so, Roosevelt could no longer hope that the South might be reconciled to the G.O.P.

The facts regarding the occasion when Washington was at the White House have been clouded by conflicting versions. The invitation was premeditated, and it was a dinner, not a luncheon. After the appointment of Judge Jones,

Roosevelt again asked Dr. Washington to come to the capital. He arrived in the afternoon and went to the home of a friend, also a Negro, and there found an invitation for dinner that night. In the Roosevelt papers there is a note in Dr. Washington's hand, dated October 16, 1901:

Dear Mr. President: I shall be very glad to accept your invitation for dinner this evening at 7:30.

The head of the Tuskegee Institute went to the White House at the appointed time and there dined with the President and the members of his family. "We talked at considerable length concerning plans about the South," he wrote in his memoirs. He took a train for New York the same night.

The South had applauded the selection of Judge Jones, but this was far different. "White men of the South, how do you like it?" demanded the New Orleans *Times-Democrat.* "When Mr. Roosevelt sits down to dinner with a Negro, he declares that the Negro is the social equal of the white man." The Memphis *Scimitar* screamed that Roosevelt had perpetrated "the most damnable outrage ever." The editor of the Richmond *Times,* giving way to total hysteria, portrayed the President as believing that white women should receive attention from Negroes, that the two races might even intermarry.

One may question the sincerity of the defamation directed toward Roosevelt. Certainly Democratic leaders in the South had already been alarmed by his efforts to fumigate the Republican party in their stronghold. They rejoiced, perhaps, at his discomfiture. The issue of free silver had, moreover, alienated many Southern Democrats. It was not, said Josephus Daniels, then a member of the Democratic National Committee, "a precedent that will encourage Southern men to join hands with Mr. Roosevelt." Nor was it; the President had injured his cause.

Roosevelt blustered that he would have Dr. Washington "to dine just as often as I please," but he never repeated the error and he never publicly commented, while President, on the unfortunate incident. He was obviously chagrined by his mistake. A few weeks later, while the storm still raged, he invited Finley Peter Dunne to dinner and ruefully added: ". . . you need *not* black your face."

To Lodge and to others, Roosevelt explained that he had asked Washington to dine as "a matter of course," that he had not considered the political effect. The confusion which has marked the affair may have been caused by Roosevelt's desire to make it appear that the hospitality to Dr. Washington had been impulsive. On at least one occasion he insisted that the Negro chanced to be at the White House at luncheon time and was asked, on the spur of the moment, to remain. He may, from time to time, have convinced himself that such had been the fact.

Chapter II

THE FIRST ATTACK

*

The financiers who found basis for optimism in the President's first message to Congress had failed to note certain passages which revealed antagonism toward stock speculation. A moral fervor marked Roosevelt's disapproval of "the men who seek gain, not by genuine work, but by gambling." Jay Gould, an adversary in years long past, had been a gambler. In time, although in 1901 their personal relations were cordial, Roosevelt was to convince himself that E. H. Harriman was another.

Arduous toil could be included among the cardinal virtues. Roosevelt did not oppose great wealth in itself; his guns were to be trained upon the "malefactors of great wealth." Stock manipulators were inimical to the public good at all times; the industrialists when they became too arrogant.

"I know the banker, merchant and railroad king well," he told Brander Matthews in 1894, "and *they* also need education and sound chastisement."

Roosevelt had concluded, as 1902 began, that a degree of chastisement was in order. The previous year had been marked by excessive speculation and also by arrogance on the part of such promoters as Pierpont Morgan. The President made his plans quietly. He turned a deaf ear when Jacob Schiff of Kuhn, Loeb & Company pointed to possible dangers during a visit to the White House early in 1902.

The financier had urged a "careful and prudent administration of difficult economic problems" as the best safeguard against financial disturbance.

But in 1902, prudence could be variously interpreted. In the mind of Mr. Morgan there was no need for it. The past fifteen months had been thoroughly satisfactory. He had accomplished the organization of the United States Steel Corporation. This, by its very size, had brought adverse comment. Such nonradical influences as the *Review of Reviews* and President Hadley of Yale had pointed to the necessity for control of large corporations by some agency of the Government. Morgan felt, however, that these voices could be ignored. He went ahead with other plans.

On November 13, 1901, as Roosevelt was putting the finishing touches on his message, attorneys for J. P. Morgan & Company arranged for the incorporation of the Northern Securities Company at Trenton, New Jersey. The capital of the new concern was placed at $400,000,000. Its charter provided for the purchase or sale of the securities of certain railroads. It was set forth in the news accounts that the real purpose was a railroad monopoly in the northwest, controlled by the Harriman–Union Pacific interests, with Kuhn, Loeb & Company as bankers, in conjunction with the Hill–Great Northern interests. Morgan was James J. Hill's financial agent.

This was the first important holding company and it marked, in Morgan's mind and in the opinion of a good many others, a constructive step forward. No longer were there to be violent battles, such as the Harriman-Hill contest in May, 1901, when each sought desperately to control the Northern Pacific and the stock soared dizzily to $100 a share. The plan represented peace, a fitting continuation of the reorganization of the nation's transportation systems that started in 1885 when Morgan felt he must "do something about the railroads." The effect of his interest had been salutary. Thousands upon thousands of miles in the East had been placed on a sound basis. Harriman had combined the Union Pacific and the Southern Pacific. Jim Hill, the only practical railroad man among the three, had created the Great Northern in 1889.

These men dreamed of transcontinental lines that would link the great producing centers of the United States with the markets of Asia. They looked toward a day when steamship lines would connect with their railheads and reach toward the golden East, which had moved so much closer because of the Christian Imperialism forced upon McKinley. The Northern Securities Company was formed to carry out these plans, and skilled attorneys gave assurance that the Sherman Anti-Trust Law of 1890 offered no obstacle. This law had never interfered seriously with the operations of the large corporations. In 1902, its standing was additionally dubious because of a decision by the Supreme Court seven years before. The American Sugar Refining Company had acquired a virtual monopoly of the production of sugar and President Cleveland ordered dissolution proceedings. But in 1895, in the Knight case, the highest court ruled that a monopoly of manufacture was not a monopoly of commerce. Not a single indictment was found under the Sherman Act, as a result of this interpretation, during the McKinley Administration.

"This decision," wrote Roosevelt, with pardonable pride, "I caused to be annulled by the court that had rendered it."

2

The legality of the Northern Securities Company would undoubtedly have been tested in the courts, if only to insure the validity of its securities. It was not so much the fact that Roosevelt inaugurated a suit which aroused applause and resentment, as the manner in which he did so. He consulted no one, except Attorney General Knox, and this was a severe blow to the pride of important gentlemen who had been boasting of their intimacy with the President. The aura of secrecy was little short of insulting. When appeals were made to Mark Hanna, however, the Republican national chairman would do nothing to dissuade the President. "I warned Hill," he said, "that McKinley might have to act against his company. Mr. Roosevelt's done it." New legends circulated regarding Pierpont Morgan. It was said that he had been entertaining guests at dinner on the night in February, 1902, when word was received, and had expressed surprise and disappointment. It was unfair that he had not been informed; he had felt quite certain that Mr. Roosevelt would do the gentlemanly thing.

The motives that inspired Roosevelt to action in 1902 will become more clear as consideration is given to his second term in the White House. The essential point is that he failed to share Mr. Morgan's confidence in the beneficent rule of the United States by its business interests. Understanding of Theodore Roosevelt must always take into account the apprehensions which tossed him. He seldom looked ahead save with foreboding. The more acute his foreboding, the greater was his desire to do something. So he passed through life, feverishly active because he was so constantly worried.

A more personal reason was Roosevelt's desire for

power. "I did not usurp power, but I did greatly broaden the use of executive power," Roosevelt wrote of his years as President. His critics exaggerated his conviction that "I am the State," but the accusation has some basis. He was first alarmed, then irritated, and finally moved to strike by the industrialists who complacently assured themselves that their power was greater than that of the Federal Government. A phrase or two from Roosevelt's memoirs will offer light on his attitude to the forces which challenged his power. He was writing of conditions when he became President:

> The total absence of governmental control had led to a portentous growth of corporations. In no other country was such power held by the men who had gained these fortunes. The Government [was] practically impotent. Of all forms of tyranny the least attractive and the most vulgar is the tyranny of mere wealth, the tyranny of a plutocracy.

To Roosevelt, the formation of the Northern Securities Company was a step toward the tyranny of a plutocracy, and it was challenged. He appears to have believed that most of his advisers would disagree with him, and so he consulted only Attorney General Knox. An editor once asked the President to state which of his Cabinet officers had been the most valuable. "Elihu Root," Roosevelt answered. "He is the only one who will fight with me." It was a sincere tribute, repeated in varying versions on other occasions. He did not, however, inform his Secretary of War about the impending suit. Root had been a corporation attorney; "He has not the view that Taft and I take about corporations . . . about Mr. Whitney and Mr. Ryan, and so forth," Roosevelt said in 1905. Perhaps Roosevelt felt that it was safer not to consult this able, if too conservative, counselor.

On February 19, 1902, the stock market reflected no uneasiness. But after the market closed, the tickers carried disturbing news from Washington. Attorney General Knox had announced that "in a very short time" dissolution of the Northern Securities Company would be demanded by the Federal Government. Knox had just informed Roosevelt that, in his opinion, the company had transgressed the limitations of the Sherman Act.

The shock was acute because it was so unexpected. On February 20, stocks slumped badly and the *Tribune* said that the market had not been similarly rocked since the assassination of McKinley. At the offices of Mr. Morgan reassurances were offered that the courts would sustain the Northern Securities Company. Three days later an imposing group of gentlemen, including Morgan and Hanna, descended upon the White House under the chaperonage of United States Senator Depew. "It was a social call," explained Depew, and denied that the Northern Securities matter had been so much as mentioned. It was rumored at Washington, however, that Morgan might return that same day for a less public conference. He did so. The President had a vivid recollection of the conversation.

"If we have done anything wrong," said the financier, "send your man [meaning the Attorney General] to my man [naming one of his lawyers] and they can fix it up." Roosevelt had answered that this was impossible, and Knox added that the purpose of the suit was not to "fix up," but to stop illegal mergers. Then Morgan inquired, doubtless anxiously because the steel trust was much closer to his heart, whether the President was going to "attack my other interests." Not, said Roosevelt, "unless we find out they have done something that we regard as wrong."

The interview must have been soothing to the presidential ego. When Morgan had left, Roosevelt turned to Knox and remarked that this had been an excellent example of "the Wall Street point of view." Morgan "could not help regarding me as a big rival operator, who either intended to ruin all his interests or else could be induced to come to an agreement to ruin none."

The suit was filed in St. Paul on March 10, 1902. The slow grind of the national judicial machinery began.

3

The Northern Securities suit under way, Roosevelt was content to lay aside his Big Stick for a time. Certain of the large Chicago packing houses were challenged, but the President refrained from identifying himself too closely with the litigation. He did, on the contrary, a characteristic thing—reassured the nation that the suit against the railroad merger marked no departure from caution and conservatism. This was partly, but not entirely, due to the approaching congressional elections.

From the very start of his first administration, Roosevelt followed a policy of taking action and then justifying his conduct by going directly to the voters. He was constantly asking for a vote of confidence. That his method was wise was demonstrated by the frequency with which he won the endorsement that he sought. Roosevelt's attempts to justify the Northern Securities suit began in April, 1902, when he visited Charleston, South Carolina. He pointed to the "sweep and rush, rather than the mere march, of our progressive material development." This had brought problems, and they could be solved only by "resolute fearlessness." On the other hand, "we are certain to fail if we adopt the policy of the demagogue who raves against the wealth which is simply the form of embodied thrift, foresight and intelligence."

In August Roosevelt departed on a tour that was to take him through the New England states and the Middle West. At Providence, Rhode Island, he denounced those who "go into wild speculation and lose their heads." But the conciliatory spirit of his message to Congress the preceding December was also present in his speeches. He disavowed any sympathy for the radicals who "in a spirit of sullen envy insist upon pulling down those who have profited most in the years of fatness." It was not true, although the President offered no statistics, that "the poor have grown poorer." It was obvious, however, that "some of the rich have grown very much richer."

Much of the alarm aroused by the Northern Securities suit must have vanished in the face of these presidential assurances. In August, 1902, however, Roosevelt was doubtful of his standing. The Congressional Campaign Committee "have been in to see me," he told John Hay, "feeling decidedly blue." Contributions had been coming in rather slowly.

"My plutocratic friends in New York," Roosevelt added, "hardly feel toward me with sufficient benevolence to warrant my writing to them."

Would Hay do what he could?

4

The potency of Government, with regard to corporation control or any other problem, depended on the degree to which its three branches worked in harmony. It seldom occurred to Roosevelt that the duty of the executive was to carry out the mandates of the legislative. In so far as he was able, he reversed this theory. Congress, he felt, must obey the President. The third branch, the judiciary, was of even greater importance because it had the last word.

"The President and the Congress are all very well in

their way," said Roosevelt in 1906. "They can say what they think they think, but it rests with the Supreme Court to decide what they have really thought."

Roosevelt invariably denied any desire to control the judiciary. He was, however, shaken to the depths of his nature by the extent to which the courts nullified Rooseveltian conceptions of what was right. His fury toward the courts was to lead him, conservative that he really was, into strange bypaths of political thought. More than anything else this was responsible for the final break with three of the men who had been closest to him; Taft, Root, and Nicholas Murray Butler. For the genesis of his irritation it is necessary to go far back.

In 1882, a bill was offered in the New York State legislature to halt the manufacture of cigars in filthy city tenements. It was based on hygienic, rather than social, grounds. Assemblyman Roosevelt, as a member of the Cities Committee, investigated conditions and supported the measure. It was defeated that year, but in 1884 it became law. The inevitable court action followed, and Judge Robert Earl of the State Court of Appeals held the bill unconstitutional.

"It cannot be perceived," the court said, "how a cigar maker is to be improved in his health or his morals by forcing him from his home and its hallowed associations and beneficent influences."

This was not only nonsense; to Roosevelt it was an idiotic construction of the laws protecting property. "They knew legalism, but not life," he wrote of Judge Earl and his associates. "This decision completely blocked tenement-house reform legislation for a score of years and hampers it to this day." This was written in 1913, after Roosevelt had engaged in several combats with the courts.

Roosevelt's attitude toward the Supreme Court rested upon the logical position that it should not be immune to criticism. This might not always be just, "yet it is always a good thing that the possibility of it should exist." Forgetting his own extreme distaste for expressed disagreement with his own views, Roosevelt said that it was "astonishing how much any one can profit even by unjust criticism." He viewed the courts from two aspects—their relation to the law and their relation to Government. The second, to him, was far more important. The members of the Supreme Court, he said, should combine "the qualities of the great jurist and constructive statesman."

All this marked no departure from accepted views on

the relations of the three branches of the Government. The change, Roosevelt's desire to strengthen the executive at the expense of the judiciary, was gradual and clearly traceable to judicial decisions that interfered with Roosevelt's program. A liberal judge was one who affirmed the Roosevelt viewpoint. Hand in hand, obviously, went the President's increasing belief in the necessity for a strong Federal Government. He emphasized this in October 1906. He evolved the doctrine that "an inherent power [rests] in the Nation, outside of the enumerated powers conferred upon it by the Constitution, in all cases where the object involved was beyond the power of the several states." Narrow construction of the Constitution placed the Government "at a great disadvantage in the battle for industrial order."

5

It was inevitable that Roosevelt should weigh carefully his own appointments to the Supreme Court. In considering candidates for the judiciary, he told Cabot Lodge in 1906, "the *nominal* politics of the man has [*sic*] nothing to do with his actions on the bench. His *real* politics are all important." He desired, therefore, to name Justice Horace H. Lurton of Tennessee who was "right on the Negro question, right on the power of the Federal Government, right on the insular business, right about corporations, right about labor." It did not matter, he added, that Lurton was nominally a Democrat.

Roosevelt's belief that the Supreme Court should, as far as possible, reflect the convictions of the President had its inception in the attack on the Northern Securities merger. The decision in this case was a vital one. While argument was under way during the summer of 1902, the President was debating the appointment of Oliver Wendell Holmes, then chief justice of Massachusetts, to the Supreme Court. He told Lodge that he was definitely inclined to select Holmes, who had been a gallant soldier in the Civil War and whose character was above reproach. Moreover, his labor decisions constituted "a strong point in Judge Holmes' favor" for the very reason that they had been criticized by "the big railroad men and other members of the large corporations." He had been able to preserve "his sympathy for the class from which he has not drawn his clients":

In the ordinary and low sense which we attach to the words "partisan" and "politician," a judge of the Supreme Court should be neither. But in the higher sense he is not in my judgment fitted for the position unless he is a party man, a constructive statesman keeping in mind his relations with his fellow statesmen in other branches of the Government. The Supreme Court of the sixties was good exactly insofar as its members fitly represented the spirit of Lincoln.

This is true at the present day. Now I should like to know that Judge Holmes was in entire sympathy with our views, that is with your views and mine before I would feel justified in appointing him.

Judge Holmes, it appeared, qualified as a jurist who adequately reflected Roosevelt's views. He was appointed.

Meanwhile expensive attorneys wrangled and the Northern Securities case dragged on toward its conclusion. The lower court in St. Paul ruled in favor of the Government on April 9, 1903. On March 14, 1904, in a five to four decision, the Supreme Court held that the merger was in violation of the Sherman Act and ordered the company dissolved. For the first time the words "free competition" appeared in connection with the law which had originally referred to restraint of trade but not to competition.

"It seems hard," wrote Jim Hill, "that we should be compelled to fight for our lives against the political adventurers who have never done anything but pose and draw a salary."

These were harsh words, born of resentment, and were ill deserved. Yet with the passage of the years, expert opinion shifted to the belief that the Great Northern and the Northern Pacific railroads might well have been consolidated. In time it appeared that conflicting systems, and disastrous competition, could bring waste and destruction of railroad security values. Thus, by 1920, the trend was toward consolidation and adequate government regulation. In 1900 to 1904, it should be remembered, effective government regulation did not exist. Proposals to fix rates on any basis were viewed with horror. Proposals to do so by inquiry into the value of the railroad properties were dismissed as socialistic.

Curiously enough, Justice Holmes was one of the four members of the Supreme Court who dissented from the majority view and attempted to draw a line between restraint of competition and restraint of trade. Besides, he pointed out, the Sherman Act was a criminal statute and the decision should logically be followed by prosecution of Morgan, Harriman, Hill, Stillman, and their associates. No one, Roosevelt least of all, had any desire to start such prosecution. The purpose of the suit had been served. The Government now had power, in theory, to deal with the corporations dangerous to the public good. Besides, the 1904 campaign was approaching.

The dissenting opinion of Justice Holmes, one of the first in a long and distinguished series, caused rumors that Roosevelt was intensely annoyed. He had been sadly mistaken in the jurist selected because he was "in entire sympathy with our views." It was said that Justice Holmes, although he had previously called several times a week, had not been at the White House for some time. But if friction existed, there is no evidence of it among Roosevelt's papers; quite the contrary.

A misunderstanding would have been a source of mutual loss to these two Americans, so different and yet, each in his way, so charming. Holmes was already an adornment to the Supreme Court, a gentleman of culture and humor. On February 18, 1904, Cabot Lodge mailed to Roosevelt a newspaper clipping which announced that the Emperor of Korea, anxious to demonstrate his executive power, had abolished the Supreme Court of his country. "It makes suggestion of real value," noted Lodge. The President dispatched the item by messenger to Justice Holmes, having scrawled on the margin: "Respectfully referred to Mr. Justice Holmes, to read, mark, and return. The merit of the suggestion is obvious." Holmes promptly returned the communication, with his own notation:

As to the scurrilous suggestion of Cabot and Bill Bigelow [Sturgis Bigelow, of Boston, who had first discovered the clipping], I shall have to remind those gents that where the Chancellor is, there is the Court of Chancery, and that if I catch them in the New England circuit I will lay them by the heels if they do not keep civil tongues in their heads. The King, of course,— can do no wrong.

Chapter III

THE RIGHTS OF LABOR

❋

A storm was brewing in March, 1902, which was to add immeasurably to Roosevelt's stature and fame. The threat of a strike in the anthracite coal fields, with economic disaster and probable defeat for the Republican party in the Congressional elections that fall, was causing dissension in the ranks of the industrialists. They had been united in condemnation of the Northern Securities suit. This time, opposing the stupidities of the extreme conservatives, Roosevelt had as allies J. Pierpont Morgan, Elihu Root, Charles M. Schwab, and John D. Rockefeller, Jr.

Abuses in the coal fields had long been comparable to the horrors of slavery in the South. In a hundred dismal mining towns in Ohio, Illinois, Pennsylvania, and the other coal-producing states, the scaffold of the mine cast its shadow on despair. In 1899 there had been 358 fatal accidents; in 1901, although the number of men employed had increased only slightly, 441 men had been killed. This was before the day of workmen's compensation. The only recourse for death or injury was a long lawsuit with any possible damages fairly certain to go to attorneys.

The miners had struggled against their lot. Hope had come to them in 1885, when word drifted into the mining regions that the American Federation of Labor was being formed. But the Haymarket riots in Chicago caused bitter hostility toward labor and its leaders. They brought profound discouragement to a young miner named John Mitchell who was one day to be president of the United Mine Workers of America. He was to win the respect and friendship of Theodore Roosevelt.

By 1902 it was war. On one side was Mitchell. On the other, to select the most notorious of the mine operators, was George F. Baer of the Philadelphia and Reading Coal and Iron Company. It was Baer who growled that anthracite mining was "a business . . . not a religious, sentimental, or academic proposition," who knew that "God in his Infinite Wisdom has given control of the property interests of the country" to the right people. President Roosevelt, with Morgan and the rest behind him and with public opinion almost unanimously for the miners, played a dual role of arbitrator and judge.

Mitchell had become president of the United Mine Workers of America in 1899. The following summer he called the strike which made absurd the contentions of Republican orators that all was well in the best of all possible worlds. The men had received no increase in wages since 1880. They demanded ten per cent and also that they be paid on the basis of a 2,340 pound ton instead of a ton that ran from 2,700 to 4,000 pounds. Otherwise, they would strike. It was this disturbance which Mark Hanna settled by obtaining the ten per cent increase for the men.

The main grievances remained, however. The abuses of long hours of work for which the men were paid nothing, unfair prices at the company store, squalor and filth in the housing accommodations—all these remained. The miners had tasted blood in their 1900 victory, and in March, 1902, they asked for another wage increase, a shorter working day, and a minimum of fair play in the weighing of coal.

The conclusion is escapable that the arrogance of the operators caused the coal strike of 1902. In October, 1901, Mitchell went to New York City for a conference with E. B. Thomas of the Erie Coal Company and was denied a hearing. It was then that Hanna drew Morgan into the dispute. The financier saw Mitchell and said he would do "what was right" in the situation. He had great power over the railroads and their affiliated coal companies. But Morgan also listened to Baer and the other operators. He hesitated, and soon it was too late. The miners were angry because their overtures had been repulsed. The operators remembered the concessions made in 1900, and were determined that the politicians of the country should not again frighten them into weakness.

Mark Hanna labored incessantly, but Election Day was relatively remote as the strike grew imminent and he could not, as in 1900, point again to the perils of Bryanism, socialism, and ultimate government ownership of the mines. On March 18, 1902, the miners voted to strike on a date to be determined by their leaders. On March 22, Mitchell again sought peace. He telegraphed to Baer and asked whether the Philadelphia and Reading would join with the other coal companies in hearing the grievances of the men. They would not, Baer replied. When, in May, another appeal reached Baer, this time from Archbishop Ireland and Bishop Potter, he replied with his famous telegram pointing to the nonecclesiastical nature of the coal business.

The strike began on May 12, 1902, with 140,000 miners idle. On the whole, it was a peaceful war. The men refrained from violence and sabotage. It was not long before a singular group had rallied behind John Mitchell at his headquarters at Hazleton, Pennsylvania. One of them was John R. Commons, the economist. Henry Demarest Lloyd made frequent visits. It was known that Archbishop Ireland was in sympathy with the men, and a lesser churchman, Father J. J. Curran of Wilkes-Barre, Pennsylvania, offered what help lay in his power. It developed that he was able to do a great deal.

Whether it was the result of a trap laid for Baer is uncertain, but a Wilkes-Barre photographer named W. F. Clark addressed a letter to the head of the Philadelphia and Reading pointing out that it was his religious duty to end the strike. Baer replied on July 17, 1902:

I do not know who you are. I see that you are a religious man; but you are evidently biased in favor of the right of the working man to control a business in which he has no other interest than to secure fair wages for the work he does.

I beg of you not to be discouraged. The rights and interests of the laboring man will be protected and cared for—not by the labor agitators, but by the Christian men to whom God in his infinite wisdom has given the control of the property interests of this country.

Clark thoughtfully photographed this singular confession of faith and gave a copy to Father Curran. It was widely published, to the accompaniment of denunciation by the pulpit and the press. Mr. Baer was declared guilty of blasphemy as well as stupidity. The cause of the strikers was benefited accordingly.

2

The strike had reached serious enough proportions by June to cause appeals to Washington for action. On June 27, Roosevelt asked Attorney General Knox whether the coal and railroad companies, which had forced the strike, constituted a combination within the meaning of the Sherman Act. But Knox told the President that nothing could be done under that dubious statute.

Roosevelt delayed as long as possible. But during August, 1902, while he toured New England, reports came to him that the price of coal was rising rapidly. Cabot Lodge, whom he visited at Nahant, pointed to the probable political consequences. Then, on the morning of September 3, the President came perilously close to death in an accident. He had spent the previous night at the home of Governor Murray Crane of Massachusetts at Dalton, Massachusetts, and was being driven toward Pittsfield when his carriage was struck by a trolley car. William Craig, a secret service operative, was killed. The President was thrown clear of the barouche and, with Governor Crane, lay by the side of the road as members of the presidential party rushed up. He was not, it appeared, badly hurt. His face was bruised and he walked with a limp. But he insisted, with the determination to ignore physical disability which had become an obsession, on continuing his tour.

Still lame, Roosevelt left Washington again on September 5 for the convention of the Brotherhood of Locomotive Firemen at Chattanooga, Tennessee. On September 19, with the coal shortage becoming more acute, he started on a trip that was to have reached into the Far West. His leg grew much worse, however. In reality, the injury was extremely serious, although the facts were carefully kept from the public. Blood poisoning was threatened. The trip was halted at Indianapolis where, at a local hospital, an abscess was opened and the bone scraped. He was back in Washington on September 24.

"My leg was attended to just in time," he told Lodge, "as (in strict confidence) there had begun to be trouble with the bone."

It was well that the President had returned. Confined to a wheeled chair in the temporary executive mansion on Lafayette Place, being used because of extensive alterations at the White House, Roosevelt received alarming reports on the coal strike. From Lodge came grave warnings before the week was over.

The political consequences of inaction goaded Roosevelt to do what he could. The great obstacle, however, was the determination of the operators, he said, "to do away with what they regard as the damage done to them by submitting to interference for political reasons in 1900. From the outset they have said that they were never going to submit again to having their laborers given a triumph as Senator Hanna secured the triumph in 1900." Besides, Roosevelt pointed out, his own position was weak. He had granted no favors to the moneyed men of the nation, and how could he now make a "private or special appeal to them"?

"I am at my wits' end how to proceed," he complained. "We have no earthly responsibility for it," he lamented to Mark Hanna in a letter of September 27, 1902, "but the public at large will visit upon our heads responsibility for the shortage in coal."

Not very optimistically, the President summoned Matt Quay to Washington for consultation; the Pennsylvanian, if anyone, had the ear of the coal operators. He also consulted Elihu Root. On September 29, there was basis for faint hope in a letter from Mark Hanna, who had conferred with both J. P. Morgan and John Mitchell. Morgan, the Republican national chairman reported, had been inclined toward compromise with the strikers.

On the same day, Governor Crane of Massachusetts offered a plan. Both sides, he suggested, should be summoned to Washington immediately and the President, in their joint presence, might find a meeting ground for settlement. Roosevelt agreed to make the attempt. Telegrams were sent to the principals in the dispute naming October 3 as the day for a meeting at the temporary White House.

3

In front of No. 22 Lafayette Place, on the morning of October 3, 1902, congregated the groups that always appear when something of importance is going on. Most of them were the idle curious who fringe the outskirts of the locale where history is being made.

That morning, as for days, there had been little on the front pages except news of the anthracite strike. In New York City the schools had been closed because there was no coal. The price of the small stocks being hoarded in various yards had already risen to $30 and $35 a ton, and soon there would be none at any price. Those who had gathered early on Lafayette Place had watched important figures hurry inside; Attorney General Knox, Mitchell, George F. Baer, and other coal operators and union leaders. Beyond this, they saw little, although from across the street a small section of the conference room on the second floor was visible. There was an exciting moment when a wheeled chair flashed by, bearing a very vigorous invalid, who exhibited his teeth and gesticulated as he vanished. At 5 o'clock that afternoon it became known that the conference had failed.

The wall that obstructed the view of the curious on that October day still blocks the scene; only censored accounts of the wrangle have survived. That it was a bitter session, the air filled with invective, is apparent from the hints dropped by Roosevelt to his intimates and from the letters he wrote. Baer of the Philadelphia and Reading was the principal object of the President's wrath. It was this confidant of God, according to rumor, to whom Roosevelt referred when he told of one operator more offensive than the rest.

"If it wasn't for the high office I hold," he said, "I would have taken him by the seat of the breeches and the nape of the neck and chucked him out of that window."

Baer, the rest of the coal operators, the Attorney General, and Labor Commissioner Carroll D. Wright waited at one end of the large room just before 11 o'clock. At the other stood Mitchell of the United Mine Workers and two aides. A few seconds after the hour, the President wheeled himself in and started to speak. Had the adversaries now before him considered a third party to this dispute, the public? Roosevelt admitted that the Government had slight power to interfere, but "the terrible nature of the catastrophe impending, a winter fuel famine" had made obvious the need for peace. The meeting had not been called "for a discussion of your respective claims and positions. I appeal to your patriotism."

Mitchell, on behalf of the miners, denied responsibility for "this terrible state of affairs." The strikers were willing to have the President appoint a commission to pass on the issues. They would accept its decision as final, whatever the ruling. At this point, Roosevelt suggested a recess until 3 o'clock in the afternoon. But when Baer, spokesman for the operators, began his answer later in the day, all hope of a settlement vanished. He said angrily that thousands of men would be at work except for the "intimidation, violence and crime inaugurated" by the organization of which Mitchell was the chief. In contrast to the restrained and gentlemanly utterances of a labor leader who had started life as a breaker boy, the Philadelphia millionaire showed shocking absence of taste. Although the strike had been unusually peaceful, he accused the miners of sabotage and rebuked the President for "negotiating with the fomenters of anarchy and insolent defiance of law."

"We object," he remarked after the meeting, "to being called here to meet a criminal, even by the President of the United States."

Roosevelt alternated between anger and contempt. "The operators," he wrote to Mark Hanna that night, "assumed a fairly hopeless attitude." None of them "appeared to such advantage as Mitchell, whom most of them denounced with such violence and rancor that he did very well to keep his temper." At other times, Roosevelt added, the operators had attacked the Attorney General "for not having brought suit against the miners' union, as violating the Sherman anti-trust law."

The operators had indeed sacrificed the last remnants of public support. Senator Lodge wrote that his anger was so great that he dared not speak of the coal barons in public. Meanwhile the President was meditating a course of action having little justification in law. He was confident, however, that it would be heartily endorsed by the public. On October 8, he made a final appeal to Mitchell. If the men would return to work at once, he would appoint a commission and would do everything possible to effect a satisfactory settlement. Mitchell's answer, inevitably, was that his followers had already gone more than halfway.

4

On October 9, 1902, acting under orders from the President, Secretary of War Root addressed a letter to Pierpont Morgan. Since the failure of the conference a week before, the number of militiamen in the coal fields had been increased to 10,000. This had been done in answer to Baer's implied promise that the operators would produce coal if protection were given to men anxious to work in the mines. But this, Root told the financier, might not be the case. In that event, would it be practicable to have a commission "appointed by the President or by you" which would attempt a solution? Each coal company would be permitted to present its own evidence. The verdict would constitute a five-year agreement with the miners, who would return to their posts at once. Such a plan provided honest arbitration, but it avoided the necessity of "dealing with the mine workers' union."

Essentially, this plan did not differ from the proposal offered by Mitchell at the White House conference. If the operators had objected before, they would object now. At this stage, the President was acutely alarmed. There had been, he said, "ugly talk of a general sympathetic strike which, happening at the beginning of the winter, would have meant a crisis only less serious than the Civil War." Both sides in the controversy were unyielding. They were "apparently ignorant of the old common-law doctrine under which any peasant could take wood that was not his, if necessary for the preservation of life and health in winter weather."

Such was the threat which Root undoubtedly held over Morgan's head, for transmittal to the operators. As a matter of fact, no such common-law doctrine seems to exist. But it was to be very useful. The President saw himself *in loco* the peasant needing fuel and, with great secrecy, he made plans to take over the mines and operate them with soldiers. In his own words:

I notified Knox and Root that if the contingency arose where I had to take charge of the matter, as President on behalf of the Federal Government, I should not even ask their advice, but would proceed to take action which I outlined to them. I explained that I knew this would form an evil precedent, and that it was one that I would take most reluctantly.

The law on interference by the President, as distinct from this hastily evolved common-law aspect, was clear. He could not act unless requested by the governor of Pennsylvania or unless the situation in the coal fields had passed beyond control of the state authorities. Even then he could merely halt disorder and this, in itself, would produce no coal. Besides, there had been little or no disorder. These technical limitations Roosevelt brushed aside. The first step was to have Senator Quay instruct Governor Stone of Pennsylvania to request Federal assistance. "Then," wrote Roosevelt, "I would put in the army under the command of some first rate general. I would instruct him to dispossess the operators and run the mines as a receiver. I had to find a man who possessed the necessary good sense, judgment and nerve to act in such event. He was ready in the person of Maj.-Gen. J. M. Schofield."

Schofield was summoned to Washington on October 11, the day on which Root was impressing Morgan with the gravity of the situation. He saw the President on October 13. Roosevelt told the general, "a most respectable-looking old boy, with side-whiskers and a black skullcap," that he was to "act in a purely military capacity under me as Commander-in-Chief, paying no heed to any authority, judicial or otherwise, except mine." Schofield answered that he would open the mines and would run them despite interference by the strikers, the owners, the courts, or anyone else. Exactly how a military man and some troops were to dig much coal remains a mystery.

If Mr. Baer and his associated coal producers did not like this plan, with its horrid implications of socialism, they had only to accept the suggestion for arbitration. Ex-President Grover Cleveland, who had offered his assistance in the national emergency, would serve on President Roosevelt's arbitration commission. All this must have been outlined by Root on the morning of October 11 on the financier's yacht, the *Corsair*, anchored in the Hudson River. In the end, Morgan forced the operators to agree to arbitration. But they imposed foolish limitations regarding the personnel of the commission.

Obstacles still remained. Sunday, Monday, and Tuesday passed. Baer, having engaged a special train, hurried to New York to see Morgan. On October 13, 1902, came the first public indications of impending peace. The operators would consent to arbitration, but they would not allow Roosevelt freedom in the appointment of the commission. It must, they specified, consist of an army engineer, an expert mining engineer, a Federal judge from Pennsylvania, a man familiar with the business aspects of coal mining, and some one "of pronounced eminence as a sociologist." In other words, the operators demanded a commission weighted in their favor. They did not include a single representative of the strikers on the board that was to hand down an award, binding on both sides. Mitchell protested that this was grossly unfair.

It seemed, again, as though Schofield's gallant men would be forced to soil their uniforms by digging coal. Before giving the order to march on the mines, however, President Roosevelt dictated a letter to Morgan. With "a little ingenuity," he pointed out, it would be possible to appoint a board not unfair to either labor or capital and still remain within the limitations imposed by the operators. Could not the commission of five be expanded to one with seven members? In that event, he would name Judge George Gray of the United States Circuit Court, Labor Commissioner Wright, as the "eminent sociologist," Thomas H. Watkins, as the business expert, and either Professor Henry Smith Munroe of Columbia University or Edward W. Parker, editor of the *Engineering and Mining Record*. All these four, the President reminded Morgan, had been recommended by the operators. For the fifth member, he would select, in place of the suggested army engineer, ex-President Cleveland. The two added commissioners, who would more closely represent the strikers, would be Bishop John L. Spalding of Illinois and E. E. Clark, grand chief of the Order of Railway Conductors.

This letter to Morgan was not mailed, probably because it seemed wiser to have Secretary Root transmit the contents by telephone. Word came back, however, that the operators would not consent and that Bacon and Perkins of J. P. Morgan & Company had started for Washington. October 15 was the day that marked the crisis, and in the hours between the drafting of the communication to Morgan and 2:20 on the morning of the next day Roosevelt learned several surprising things about the wisdom of the American industrialist. Morgan, he told Lodge two days later, had been unable to "do much with those wooden-headed gentry and Bacon and Bob Perkins were literally almost crazy." They had brought word from New York that Roosevelt's plan for expanding the commission had been summarily rejected, nor would the operators consent to so dangerous a radical as Grover Cleveland.

Bacon, Perkins, and Roosevelt discussed possible solutions until almost midnight on October 15, with constant conversations by telephone with Morgan and the operators. The two representatives of the financier, Roosevelt recalled, "grew more and more hysterical, and not merely admitted but insisted that failure to agree would result in violence and possible social war." They could not, however, force the operators into line. At last, it dawned on the President "that the mighty brains of these captains of industry would rather have anarchy than tweedledum, but that if I would use the word tweedledee they would hail it as meaning peace":

> . . . it never occurred to me that the operators were willing to run all this risk on a mere point of foolish pride; but Bacon finally happened to mention that they would not object to any latitude I chose under the headings that they had given. I instantly said that I should appoint my labor man as the "eminent sociologist." To my intense relief, this utter absurdity was received with delight by Bacon and Perkins who said they were sure the operators would agree to it! Messrs. Morgan and Baer gave their consent by telephone and the thing was done.

After a minor point or two had been agreed upon, the commission was appointed. It consisted of Judge Gray, Parker, Watkins, Bishop Spalding, Commissioner Wright, and Brig. Gen. John M. Wilson. Spalding represented a last-minute concession. E. E. Clark, the seventh member, was added as the "eminent sociologist," although he actually was a labor leader. On March 22, 1903, the commission awarded a ten per cent wage increase, but denied recognition to the United Mine Workers. Certain other abuses were remedied, and the agreement was to last for three years.

Congress remained safely Republican in the elections the following month, and Roosevelt could assure himself that he had hewn a second plank for the platform on which he was to seek election in 1904. The first had been trust control. This was defense of the legitimate rights of labor. But even more important must have been the psychological effect of the triumph on Roosevelt himself. The last, lingering suspicions of the sapience of the American industrialist must have vanished during those hours on the night of October 15, 1902. Political expediency might, in the future, dictate caution, but the nation's business leaders were not, after all, dangerous foes.

For the balance of his first term, the President steered a safe course in matters pertaining to labor.

Chapter IV

THE BIG STICK

※

In 1896, Roosevelt praised the manner in which President Cleveland had been handling the dispute with Great Britain on the Venezuela boundary. "Primarily," he wrote, "our action is based on national self-interest. In other words, it is patriotic." He was police commissioner in New York City when this sentiment was expressed. Extraordinary changes altered the map of the world during the five years which passed before he became President. The ardent advocate of imperialism, Roosevelt faced problems and dangers resulting from it. The United States had become a world power.

To Roosevelt, the conduct of foreign affairs was essentially simple. The phrase first conceived to describe his attitude toward the New York Republican machine—"Speak softly and carry a big stick, you will go far"—became his slogan in dealing with the governments of Europe and South America. Right was right, and the United States defined and enforced the rules of the international game. Arbitration of disputes was laudable, except when America was a party to the issue. Peace was secondary to honor, and America defined honor. The Monroe Doctrine was the cornerstone of American diplomacy or belligerency; and before President Roosevelt had concluded his interpretations, it had been changed almost beyond recognition. The Roosevelt of 1901 to 1909 had more wisdom and discretion than the Roosevelt who had, in 1896, pronounced his theories on patriotism. Fundamentally, he had abandoned none of them.

There is delicious irony in the fact that this was the man who received the Nobel Peace Prize in 1906 for his skill and energy in ending the Russo-Japanese War. The countries of Europe, during Roosevelt's presidency, were far too concerned with the balance of power in the Balkans, in the Far East, and on the Continent itself, to have any stomach for war with the United States. It is idle to say that Roosevelt might have become involved in a long and costly struggle had circumstances been different. Had they been different, he might have been more conciliatory. On the one occasion when he believed war with a major power possible, with Japan between 1906 and 1908, he made valiant efforts to prevent it.

The innate provincialism of Roosevelt's early attitude toward Great Britain and Germany reflected the opinion of his day. Roosevelt, despite his friendship with Spring Rice, assured himself that he had no illusions about England. "On the whole," he remarked to Lodge in 1901, "I am friendly to England, [but] I do not at all believe in being over-effusive or forgetting that fundamentally we are two different nations." A few months earlier he had considered "a combination between Germany and England against the United States" as a possibility to be guarded against. In December, 1904, he wrote:

. . . the average Englishman is not a being whom I find congenial or with whom I care to associate. I wish him well, but I wish him well at a good distance from me. If we quit building our fleet, England's friendship would immediately cool.

Germany was considered actually dangerous, not only by Roosevelt but by Secretary of State Hay. She had been the one important neutral to exhibit overt hostility during the Spanish War, although the facts regarding the Manila Bay incident were probably exaggerated. The seizure of Kiaochau had been another source of alarm. In April, 1901, Hay had instructed the American chargé d'affaires at Berlin to investigate reports that the German Government contemplated the annexation, contrary to the Monroe Doctrine, of Margarita Island off the Venezuelan coast. Henry White, at the American embassy in London, was convinced that Germany had blocked the sale by Denmark of the Virgin Islands to the United States in 1902, and had designs of her own upon them.

The Kaiser appears to have been aware that harmony was in danger, but his endeavors to pour oil on the troubled waters of German-American friendship were not signally successful. In November, 1901, he had caused a medal to be conferred upon the President of the United States, and this inspired John Hay to amused contempt. The gift, he wrote, was worth about thirty-five cents and was of dubious artistic merit. Two additional gestures, the visit of Prince Henry early in 1902 and an invitation to have Alice

Roosevelt christen a yacht being built for the Kaiser in an American shipyard, seem to have been similarly fruitless. The prince was received with due ceremony, and the future Mrs. Longworth christened the yacht. Roosevelt's private letters, however, continued to reflect a decided irreverence toward the German royal family. Neither Mrs. Roosevelt nor himself "could be dragged to meet Prince Henry if it were not our official duty," he said. He appealed to John Hay, as arbiter in court etiquette, for advice on the state dinner to the Kaiser's brother:

. . . when we go into the dinner, how in the name of Heaven will we avoid hurting various Teuton susceptibilities? Will the Prince take Mrs. Roosevelt while I walk in solemn state by myself? How do we do it anyhow? I am quite clear that I ought not to walk in with my wife on one arm and the Prince somewhere alongside—but further than this I do not go.

As for the Kaiser's yacht, Roosevelt told Hay that the suggestion had been made that Alice prepare a brief speech for the christening. Her father, however, had hesitated. "The only motto sufficiently epigrammatic that came to my mind," he said, "was 'Damn the Dutch.'"

Against this background of distrust and suspicion must be viewed Roosevelt's handling of his first major problems in foreign affairs: the Venezuela debt friction, in which both Germany and England were involved, and the Alaska boundary dispute with Great Britain.

2

Cipriano Castro, an "unspeakably villainous little monkey" according to a subsequent characterization by Roosevelt, had achieved the presidency of Venezuela in 1899 by the traditional South American revolution. His rule, like the administrations of his predecessors, failed to bring an era of peace and prosperity, and by 1901 the foreign concessionaires were asking their governments for assistance in collecting the bills. Nationals of Germany and England seem to have been abused the most.

Nothing in the Monroe Doctrine, as it was universally understood in 1901, blocked the path of foreign nations to debt collection. "If any South American country misbehaves toward any European country," Vice-President Roosevelt wrote in July, "let the European country spank it." The chastisement, presumably, could inclue a blockade, the seizure of customs receipts to satisfy obligations, a bombardment of coast cities; in brief, any form of coercion or destruction. There was but one limitation. The United States could not permit a European country permanently to occupy new territory in Central or South America or in the Caribbean.

In an attempt to arrive at a conclusion of what really occured during 1901 and 1902 it will be simpler to limit the narrative to the actions of Great Britain and Germany and to ignore, for the moment, Roosevelt's own inaccurate and prejudiced version. The patience of these two powers had been strained by midsummer in 1901. In July, Germany offered to accept arbitration of her claims by the Hague Tribunal, but the self-confident Castro rashly rejected the offer. In December, Baron von Holleben, German ambassador to the United States, informed Secretary of State Hay that coercion against Venezuela might be undertaken. He specified that "the acquisition or permanent occupation of territory" would under no circumstances be considered by Germany. Mr. Hay quoted the President's message to Congress as indication that the United States had no objection to this program.

Great Britain, meanwhile, was nursing grievances which, she believed, were more serious than Germany's. In addition to owing money to her citizens, and refusing to pay, Venezuela had jeopardized British prestige by the seizure of ships flying the Union Jack. Her attitude changed later, but Germany was at first more inclined to conciliation than England. Thus it was that England stood by herself during the first half of 1902 in addressing several sharp notes to Castro.

By July of that year, joint irritation drew the two countries together. Count Metternich, German ambassador at London, informed Lord Lansdowne, the Foreign Secretary, that pressure upon Venezuela seemed to be the only solution. Would Great Britain consent to a blockade? On October 22, 1902, Lansdowne told Germany that England proposed to seize certain Venezuelan gunboats. A blockade, he added, might cause resentment on the part of "other powers," by which he probably meant the United States. Ultimately, both methods of chastisement were used. Final ultimatums were delivered on December 7, 1902. Four gunboats were captured by the allies and five ports were blockaded during the next four days. The approach of the German and English warships was enough to break Castro's spirit. When, on December 13, British guns bombarded Puerto Cabello because of a supposed insult to the flag, he scrambled to offer the arbitration he had once spurned.

What was Roosevelt doing, while these belligerent gestures were being carried out? Officially, he was doing little. Privately, through Speck von Sternberg, and through conversations with Holleben, he was expressing emphatic disapproval. If the formal diplomatic representations from Washington are examined without relation to the President's secret negotiations, however, it would appear that his subsequent version of what occurred was romantic to the point of absurdity. On December 5, two days prior to the ultimatums, the State Department expressed Roosevelt's hope of a peaceful settlement. Nothing came of this. On December 13, the State Department instructed its representatives at London and Berlin to transmit, "without comment," Castro's belated appeal for arbitration. On December 16, both England and Germany decided to accept arbitration, although with reservations as to certain of the claims against Castro. On the following day, just as acceptance of arbitration was being announced, the United States strongly recommended such action. In other words, Germany and Great Britain had agreed to arbitration before the American State Department had done anything except: first, send a mild suggestion that Roosevelt hoped for peace; second, transmit Castro's appeal "without comment."

Roosevelt's first accounts of the Venezuela episode were in perfect harmony with the facts as they appear in the documents. On April 2, 1903, he said that the sole interest of the United States had been to see that no territory was acquired. Both Great Britain and Germany had given assurances to that end. More than a decade passed. In 1915 William Roscoe Thayer was gathering data for his *Life and Letters of John Hay*. The World War had started. Roosevelt, like Thayer, was by that time ardently pro-Ally. Hay's biographer called on Roosevelt to say that he desired a true version of the Venezuela dispute of 1902 and remarked that any evidence of "German duplicity and evil plotting could not fail to help the American patriotic cause." The former President of the United States gave Thayer an account of German perfidy in 1902 that substantiated the current conception of the nature of the Hun.

In October, 1915, Thayer published his book. He said that Baron von Holleben had been summoned to the White House and had been told that Admiral Dewey, commanding a flotilla in Caribbean waters, would be ordered to sail unless Germany consented to arbitration within ten days. A week passed without acquiescence by the Kaiser. Then Roosevelt informed the German ambassador that thirty-six hours additional would be allowed before the sharpshooting gunners of Dewey aimed their weapons at the German gunboats off the Venezuelan coast. It was after this that Von Holleben, greatly agitated, announced that arbitration was acceptable to his country. This romantic story, obviously inaccurate in certain details, was promptly attacked by historians; by John Bassett Moore, among others. Challenged, Roosevelt put it in writing.

On August 21, 1916, he addressed a letter to Thayer giving further details. Germany, he wrote, was "the leader, the really formidable party in the transaction. England was merely following Germany's lead in a rather half-hearted fashion." This was the first error. England, as the official papers clearly show, was the aggressor. "I became convinced," Roosevelt continued, "that Germany intended to seize some Venezuelan harbor and turn it into a strongly fortified place of arms, on the model of Kiauchau." Perhaps he was, in fact, convinced of this. Why, then, did Roosevelt in April, 1903, state that both Germany and England had pledged nonaggrandizement? Other essential parts of the letter were:

For some time the usual methods of diplomatic intercourse were tried. Germany declined to agree to arbitrate. I finally decided that no useful purpose would be served by further delay, and I took action accordingly. I assembled our battle fleet, under Admiral Dewey, near Porto Rico, for "maneuvers," with instructions that the fleet should be kept in fighting trim. I told John Hay that I would now see the German Ambassador, myself, and that I intended to bring matters to an early conclusion.

I saw the Ambassador and asked him to inform his government that if no notification for arbitration came within a specified number of days I would be obliged to order Dewey to the Venezuelan coast, and asked him to look at the map, as a glance would show him that there was no spot in the world where Germany in the event of a conflict with the United States would be at a greater disadvantage than in the Caribbean Sea.

A few days later the Ambassador came to see me. I asked him if he had any answer to make from his government, and when he said no, I informed him that Dewey would be ordered to sail twenty-four hours in advance of the time I had set. He expressed deep apprehension. However, less than twenty-four hours before the time I had appointed for cabling the order to Dewey, the Embassy notified me that his Imperial Majesty, the German Emperor, had directed him to request me to undertake the arbitration myself.

It is difficult to separate the truth from the obvious impossibilities of this narrative. The most important flaw in the account is Roosevelt's theory that his threat forced the acceptance of arbitration by Germany. It will be recalled that arbitration was agreed to on December 16 and announced the following day. Until December 17, the United States, publicly, had not even recommended arbitration. When it did so, Germany had already given way.

Two explanations have been offered. The first is that Roosevelt, fired by the World War and his growing hatred of Germany, imagined the whole thing. The second is that a subsequent conversation with Sternberg, who was in Washington in February, 1903, became tangled in his recollection with earlier conferences with Holleben. Such a conversation did take place. Germany's earlier acceptance of arbitration had been with definite limitations. For a time, in late January and February, it seemed probable that the negotiations would be broken off. It is a matter of record that Roosevelt made inquiries in February regarding the strength of the German fleet off Venezuela. Moreover, the existing anti-German feeling in the United States had been further inflamed by bombardment of Maracaibo by a German gunboat in January. The British, having learned their lesson, had virtuously refrained from any part in this.

Roosevelt's private letters, however, invalidate both the theory that he had no conversation at all or merely one with Sternberg. Official documents can fall short of the truth just as a too dramatic memory can go beyond it. Exactly what occurred will, in all probability, never be known. In the Venezuela controversy, however, Roosevelt was acting as his own Secretary of State. His papers reveal that Sternberg had been in Washington during November also, as the Venezuelan crisis developed. He returned to Berlin and on December 15, 1902, was directed by his government "to submit the impressions of my visit."

Among the subjects discussed, he reported, had been Venezuela. Unfortunately, Sternberg did not give further details, but it seems wholly probable that he described Roosevelt's doubts regarding Germany's motives. At all events, Germany consented to arbitrate her claims on the following day. This, of course, is theory. That Roosevelt, however inaccurate his account of it, saw Holleben and made strong representations to Germany is demonstrable by a witness who was present. William Loeb, Roosevelt's private secretary, recalled two visits by the German ambassador to the White House during December, 1902, but believed it possible that only two or three days elapsed between them. He remembered saying to the President, following the first conversation:

"You gave that Dutchman something to think about. The trouble is [he] is so afraid of the Kaiser that I don't think he will give a correct picture of your attitude."

Long before the World War poisoned his mind against Germany, Roosevelt wrote letters that offer further substantiation. On August 9, 1903, he said that he had been "steadily engaged in teaching the Kaiser to 'shinny on his own side of the line.'" He told Spring Rice in November, 1905, that during the early part of his term he had felt that "the Germans had serious designs upon South America." "I finally told the German Ambassador," he wrote in June, 1906, "that the Kaiser ought to know that unless an agreement for arbitration was reached I would move Dewey's ships south." Other letters were to the same end; he had threatened Wilhelm.

The final scrap of evidence was an interview granted to the correspondent of the Newark *Evening News* by Admiral Dewey in March, 1903. The winter maneuvers, he said, had constituted "an object lesson to the Kaiser more than to any other person."

In all probability, Roosevelt hastened the acceptance of arbitration by Germany. Yet there is no possible doubt that he dramatized and heightened the part that he played. Arbitration would have come in any event. Germany and England both discovered that coercion of Venezuela had aroused alarm and irritation in the United States. The alliance with Germany had brought a storm of criticism in England. Each country was happy when an opportunity to end the ill-advised excursion came.

3

President Roosevelt's next excursion into foreign affairs related to the claims of Canada regarding the southern boundary of Alaska; Great Britain was his adversary. Interest in this question had been negligible until gold had been discovered in the Klondike in 1896. Then the small strip of land between the coast and British Columbia became exceedingly desirable. Alaska had been ceded to the United States by purchase from Russia, but a treaty between Great Britain and Russia in 1825 had fixed the boundary line with relation to Canada.

Canada's contention, after the gold strike, was that the

line was located behind the deep inlets in the jagged coast. This would have left her in possession of the heads, or harbors, of the inlets and given control of important passes to the Yukon River and the gold fields. The American position, of course, was that the strip began at the tips of the arms reaching into the sea and that the inlets were part of Alaska.

In its early stages the dispute was linked with other matters under consideration between the United States and Great Britain, among them the Newfoundland fisheries and revision of the Clayton-Bulwer Treaty. Great Britain, pointing to the fact that the United States had called for arbitration in the first Venezuela episode during the Cleveland Administration, suggested that all these matters be referred to an impartial tribunal. But Hay, with the backing of Lodge, declined to admit that concessions could be made on Alaska. The question was allowed to drift until 1902. Relations between the two countries had in the past been made none the happier by the extraordinary hostility toward Canada exhibited by American politicians.

If Lodge and Hay were opposed to arbitration in the Alaska matter, Roosevelt was even more emphatic in insisting that the United States, alone, would settle it. Characteristically, although he must have known that the possibility of conflict was grotesque, he made secret preparations for war. In July, 1902, Roosevelt told Hay that arbitration was out of the question, that the Canadian claim was "an outrage, pure and simple; to pay them anything would come dangerously near blackmail."

Had Roosevelt continued to oppose arbitration, the Alaska dispute would probably have dragged on for some time, but in the end would have been settled in favor of the United States. Instead, he permitted a treaty to be drafted in January, 1903, which provided for six "impartial jurists of repute," three to represent the United States and three, Great Britain and Canada. The tribunal would meet in London and would fix the line between Alaska and Canada. This treaty, and Roosevelt's conduct under it, placed the United States in a bad light throughout the world. If arbitration was out of the question, no reason for the treaty existed. For the "impartial jurists," the President selected the rabidly anti-English Cabot Lodge, Secretary of War Root, and George Turner, former Senator from Washington. Great Britain, however, chose Lord Alverstone, Chief Justice of England, Louis A. Jetté, Lieutenant Governor of Quebec, and A. B. Aylesworth, a Toronto attorney.

Roosevelt's appointments, wrote Henry White from London in April, 1903, had "caused a great deal of embarrassment; some dismay, as well as great surprise." Canada's protests to the home government had been violent and it was, White admitted, "difficult—not to say impossible—for the British Government to maintain that Cabot is 'an impartial jurist of repute' or that Root or Turner are impartial in the sense required by the treaty." Joseph Chamberlain, the British Colonial Secretary, had remarked that if the United States was so very certain that her position was right, and he conceded its strength, far greater confidence would have been inspired by "judges or lawyers not connected with the government."

In truth, Roosevelt's "impartial jurists" ill became a nation affecting to believe in arbitration. The President's attitude was similarly ungracious later in 1903. To reports that Great Britain might ask for postponement, he said that she "must be kept right up to the mark." He disliked "making any kind of a threat," but if England played "fast and loose," he would break off negotiations, send a special message to Congress, and "run the boundary as we deem it should be run"; in other words, offer an insult to British prestige which might have meant war had the issues been less absurd.

"You will, of course, impartially judge the questions that come before you for decision," began the contradictory instructions from the President to the members of the American commission. "In the principle involved there will, of course, be no compromise." By "principle," Roosevelt meant the boundary line itself. He was willing to award to Canada one or two of the uninhabited islands off the coast.

Certainly the evidence was overwhelmingly on the side of the American claims in Alaska. Even British maps, until the dispute arose, had substantiated them. The tribunal so decided at London on October 20, 1903. Two of the four islands were given to Canada as a consolation prize. The three American commissioners, naturally, voted in favor of the majority decision, while the two Canadians, Jetté and Aylesworth, declined to sign it. Lord Alverstone, by voting with the Americans, lived up to the obligations of his high judicial office. Bitterly criticized for his action, the Lord Chief Justice declared at a dinner in London:

If, when any kind of arbitration is set up they don't want a decision based on the law and the evidence, they must not put a British judge on the commission.

The result, said a delighted Roosevelt, "offered signal proof of the fairness and good-will with which two friendly nations can approach and determine issues."

4

When he became President, and appreciated the complexities of dealing with the quarrelsome and inefficient governments of the Caribbean and South America, Roosevelt abandoned his earlier lust for the acquisition of territory.

By 1901 the family of dependent nations was ample, even for a Chief Executive who believed in fecundity. It was in an endeavor to apply the Monroe Doctrine to this new world empire that Roosevelt so greatly expanded its meaning. The doctrine, as a matter of fact, had been violated quite openly by the annexation of the Philippine Islands; President Monroe, in his message to Congress on December 2, 1823, said that with "the existing colonies or dependencies of any European power we shall not interfere."

From the start of his first administration, Roosevelt denied that he had any desire to acquire territory. The Monroe Doctrine was equivalent, he wrote Sternberg on October 11, 1901, "to Open Door in South America." When, due to incessant revolutions and internal turmoil in Santo Domingo, the subject of intervention arose once more, the President insisted that he wanted to

do nothing but what a policeman has to do. As for annexing the island, I have about the same desire as a gorged boa constrictor might have to swallow a porcupine wrong-end-to.

The Venezuela trouble in 1902 marked Roosevelt's first amplification of the Monroe Doctrine. This was that the mere. threat of territorial aggrandizement by a European power was sufficient to justify intervention. Next came the theory that the smaller nations must not misbehave and thereby annoy Europe. "I think it will have a very healthy effect," he wrote regarding American intervention in September, 1904, Castro of Venezuela being again in trouble. "It will show these Dagos that they will have to behave decently." These charitable utterances, obviously, were private ones. Roosevelt's beliefs found formal and open expression in his famous Corollary of 1904, which declared, as the same idea was expressed on another occasion, that the nations of South America "will be happy if only they will be good." A kindly, if stern, Uncle Sam would then find chastisement unnecessary. This, it will be noted, differed radically from the earlier doctrine—if a South American country misbehaved toward Europe, "let the European country spank it."

Santo Domingo, otherwise unimportant in history, brought forth the Roosevelt Corollary. Dictatorships and revolution had reduced the island republic to bankruptcy by 1903. Foreign creditors had persuaded the Government to pledge part of the customs receipts to meet the obligations, but payments had been irregular and threats of intervention were constant. By 1904, the foreign debts totaled about $18,000,000, and in February Roosevelt heard of another revolution. He sent Admiral Dewey to see whether American interests were in danger.

The issue seemed clear to the President. Chastisement by a European power might result in territorial seizure and this would be contrary to the Monroe Doctrine. On May 20, 1904, Roosevelt addressed a letter to Secretary of War Root with the suggestion that it be read at a dinner in New York that night. The sole desire of the United States, this communication said, was

to see all neighboring countries stable, orderly, and prosperous. Any country whose people conduct themselves well can count upon our hearty friendliness. Brutal wrong-doing, or an impotence which results in a general loosening of the ties of civilized society, may finally require intervention by some civilized nation, and in the Western Hemisphere the United States cannot ignore this duty.

This amplification of the Monroe Doctrine was included in the message to Congress in December, 1904. The passage began with reiteration that the United States had no "land hunger" or considered anything save the welfare of her neighbors to the south. With only slight changes in phraseology, Roosevelt repeated the sentiments of the letter to Root. Interference would be a last resort and only because misdeeds had "invited foreign aggression to the detriment of the entire body of American nations."

In December, Roosevelt acted under the Corollary of 1904. Conditions had grown more acute. Commander A. C. Dillingham was detailed to Santo Domingo to assist the American minister, T. C. Dawson, in effecting an arrangement whereby the United States would supervise customs receipts. It was agreed that forty-five per cent of the total would go to the Dominican Government and the balance to reduce foreign debts. The United States Senate, jealous of its treaty-making rights, was highly irritated when it heard that this protocol with Santo Domingo had been drafted. A prolonged debate ended, despite a special message from Roosevelt, without ratification. The President, however, was more disgusted than dismayed. He was approaching the crest of his power. He ordered that American agents take charge of Dominican customs pending action by the Senate, and this was done. On March 23, 1905, Roosevelt confessed that he did not "much admire the Senate, because it is such a helpless body when efficient work for good is to be done." As for its treaty-making prerogatives:

The Senate is wholly incompetent to take such a part. After infinite thought and worry and labor I negotiated a treaty [with Santo Domingo] which would secure a really satisfactory settlement from every viewpoint. The result is that by a narrow margin we find ourselves without the necessary two-thirds vote. The Senate ought to feel that its action on the treaty-making power should be much like that of the President's veto; it should be rarely used.

The modus vivendi, as the President's extralegal device for bringing order in Santo Domingo was termed, was in operation for twenty-eight months and the results demonstrated Roosevelt's practicality, but not his reverence for the Constitution. It was, of course, an American suzerainty. At all events, the plan stabilized Santo Domingo's finances. The foreign debts were paid.

5

Two additional matters remained. The first was subjugation of the Philippine Islands. The second was Cuban independence, promised by the United States on the eve of the Spanish War.

A minority among the Filipinos had been reluctant to accept the rule of the United States even after the capture of their leader, Aguinaldo, in March, 1901. The guerrilla warfare continued, accompanied by the cruelties typical of such struggles. It is wholly probable that the American troops on the islands were guilty of atrocities. On the other hand, it should be recalled that they were fighting men inflamed by futile hopes of freedom and quite without knowledge of the limitations placed, in theory, on civilized warfare. President Roosevelt sympathized with his troops. He told the Grand Army of the Republic that they "fought under terrible difficulties and received terrible provocation from a very cruel and treacherous enemy." For "every guilty act committed by our troops," he said, "a hundred acts of far greater atrocity have been committed by the hostile natives."

"I have taken care," he confided to Von Sternberg, "that the army should understand that I thoroughly believe in severe methods when necessary, and am not in the least sensitive about killing any number of men if there is adequate reason. But I do not like torture or needless brutality."

This robust taste was not shared by the American people. Without Taft as civil governor of the Philippines, their protests might have been important politically. But Taft's appointment—by McKinley—had been a happy one. His sympathy for the small and puzzled brown men was as large as his huge body, and Taft won their confidence immediately. He was sent by Roosevelt to the Vatican in 1902 and settled the long-standing Filipino grievance of land ownership by Dominican and Franciscan friars. The purchase of their land by the United States went far toward bringing harmony on the islands. Roosevelt's advocacy of tariff reciprocity with the Philippines, although it was not approved by Congress until 1905 and even then for only sugar and tobacco, also hastened the day of tranquillity.

To its honor, the Roosevelt Administration resisted all pressure calling for repudiation of the agreement to grant independence to Cuba. Cuba occupied a peculiar position among the countries of the Caribbean. The United States, having brought about liberation from Spain, became her guardian. It was unthinkable, in view of Cuba's proximity to the Isthmus of Panama, for any foreign power to assume even temporary control of her affairs. The United States, therefore, insisted upon its own definition of independence.

This antedated Roosevelt as President. Brig. Gen. Leonard Wood had been appointed military governor in 1899 and American troops were withdrawn two years later. In May, 1902, Tomas Estrada Palma became President of the new republic. Meanwhile, the autonomy of Cuba had been the subject of conferences, and Secretary of War Root had suggested, in January, 1901, that the Constitution of Cuba contain certain vital clauses. It must permit intervention by the United States to maintain order. Cuba must not make treaties that granted special privileges to foreign countries or affected her independence. Naval stations must be offered to her benefactor. Other members of the McKinley Administration took part in drafting the restrictions, but such, in substance, was the proposal offered by Senator Orville H. Platt of Connecticut and called the Platt Amendment. The

Cuban Constitutional Convention realized that this was sovereignty of an abridged nature. Protests, however, were futile. In 1903 a treaty containing the Platt Amendment was signed by the two governments. That same year Cuba leased to the United States Guantanamo Bay and Bahia Hondo on the Cuban coast, for $2,000 a year.

Unquestionably, the Cubans consented to the Platt Amendment the more readily because of promises that commercial favors would be granted by the United States. In his first message to Congress, President Roosevelt said that "morality and national interest" called for reduced tariffs on imports from Cuba. An effective lobby organized by the beet sugar interests caused long delay, but Roosevelt continued to demand action on behalf of Cuba. At last, in December, 1903, reciprocity was authorized at a special session of Congress.

An unsuspected evil inherent in the Platt Amendment was that it constituted a safeguard for dictatorships in Cuba. The island was peaceful for several years, although complaints were frequent that prosperity had not been included among the blessings of freedom from Spain. In September, 1906, however, Roosevelt was compelled to make a public plea for order after charges had been circulated that President Palma had held himself in office through dishonest elections. Intervention, Roosevelt said, would be necessary if Cuba did not put down an incipient revolution. Then followed the familiar story. American troops were landed. Taft, by now Secretary of War, was hurried to Cuba to effect a compromise between the factions. The assignment proved extremely trying, but he had a measure of success. Yet it was not until 1909 that Cuba again assumed the sovereignty to which she was entitled as Queen of the Antilles. Although limited, it was better than none at all.

Roosevelt was still enforcing his Corollary of 1904. Perhaps, with the years, he began to regret the vigor of a Monroe Doctrine which insisted that righteousness justified might. The President had felt no hesitation regarding Venezuela; none regarding Santo Domingo. In 1903 he had "taken Panama," a phrase which crept into Roosevelt's speeches and writings to refute the legalistic justifications by Root and others. But when the insurrection in Cuba came, he moved with reluctance. In February, 1907, he appeared to regret that it had been necessary to interfere at all.

"I am doing my best," he said, "to persuade the Cubans that if only they will be good they will be happy; I am seeking the very minimum of interference necessary to make them good."

In 1906, Elihu Root, who had succeeded John Hay as Secretary of State, was dispatched on a tour of South America for the purpose of convincing the Latin-Americans that no menace to their rights lurked in the Monroe Doctrine. He was received with politeness, even with enthusiasm. But somehow salesmen from the countries of Europe obtained orders where American salesmen failed. The export trade with South America did not increase as it should have done.

The "Dagos" of Latin-America, as Roosevelt had referred to them in a less formal moment, continued to view the United States with distrust and alarm. The Monroe Doctrine, as amplified by Roosevelt, might classify them as the wards of Uncle Sam to be smiled upon when they behaved and punished when they erred. There was, however, no doctrine that compelled them to buy his goods. The loss of foreign trade is sometimes a penalty of imperialism.

Chapter V

SETTING FOR A MELODRAMA

The story of Panama is replete with heroes and villains. A canal was to be built which would fulfill a dream of centuries and connect the Atlantic and Pacific oceans. Every step toward realization, wrote Theodore Roosevelt, "was taken with the utmost care, was carried out with the highest, finest, and nicest standards of public and governmental ethics." M. Philippe Bunau-Varilla of Paris, who played an epic part, said that Reason struggled against Passion and finally triumphed in a mighty war for "Truth, Justice, and National Interest."

Self-hypnosis had again distorted Roosevelt's memory when he praised the ethics whereby the United States effected the preliminaries of the Panama Canal. His belief in the vital need for a canal dated from his first interest in foreign affairs and grew stronger in direct proportion to his imperialistic convictions.

His interest, like that of his fellow citizens, was greatly intensified by the hurried voyage of the U.S.S. *Oregon* around the Horn to join the fleet off Cuba in the Spanish

War. Until then a canal had been commendable, but now it was essential. Roosevelt, exiled from national affairs as governor of New York but nursing his hopes for greater glory, considered it in terms of national defense, not economic importance. He had opposed the first Hay-Pauncefote Treaty with Great Britain because it decreed that a canal built by the United States could not be fortified. This, Roosevelt declared, "strengthens against us every nation whose fleet is larger than ours." He objected equally to any provision that permitted foreign governments a voice in the control of the canal. This contravened the Monroe Doctrine. The Senate agreed with Roosevelt, although John Hay was resentful, and negotiations for the revised treaty were on the way to completion when McKinley died.

"I am entirely willing," Roosevelt wrote in July, 1901, "to guarantee neutrality to ships of commerce, [but] I insist that the canal be absolutely in our control in a military sense."

Such was the substance of the new treaty signed by Hay and Lord Pauncefote on November 18, 1901, and ratified four weeks later by the Senate. It must have gratified Roosevelt to know that the first important treaty negotiated while he was President terminated the provisions of the Clayton-Bulwer pact of 1850 whereby Great Britain and the United States agreed to joint control and nonfortification.

One fact became clear with the elevation of Roosevelt to the presidency. It would be an American canal or none. But as yet, Nicaragua was the favored route. In all of his references to a canal, Roosevelt either mentioned Nicaragua or did not specify a route. As far as Roosevelt was concerned, in the initial stages, Nicaragua would have been chosen and all the millions sunk by the bankrupt French company might have been lost forever. But there were others, a French adventurer-engineer and an American lawyer in particular, who saved $40,000,000 out of the wreckage. Claims of these two principals, Bunau-Varilla and William Nelson Cromwell of New York, offer a clue to an approximation of the truth. The former wrote a book, a charmingly Gallic book, in support of his contentions. The latter, submitting a bill for $800,000 for legal services, detailed to the French stockholders his labors in their behalf.

Bunau-Varilla, who lived to lose a leg at Verdun and to stump the boulevards of Paris with the rosette of the Legion of Honor in his buttonhole, had seen nearly all of the story of Panama, and had been part of a great deal. As a boy he had been inspired by the feat of Ferdinand de Lesseps in building the Suez Canal. He thrilled to the plans of this national hero to undertake another, this time at Panama, and in 1884 he asked for employment as an engineer on the isthmus.

Yellow fever and miscalculations as to cost soon brought failure. By 1889, $260,000,000 had been spent and the Universal Inter-Oceanic Canal Company, in which 600,000 French peasants and clerks had invested their life savings, went into bankruptcy. De Lesseps died in disgrace, while machinery in the jungles of Panama rusted in the tropical growth. Halfhearted attempts were made to revive the project. Bunau-Varilla, who at twenty-six had risen to become chief engineer of the original French company, hurriedly returned to France. The New Panama Canal Company was organized in 1894 to take over the assets and, ostensibly, to finish the work, but France had had more than enough of Panama. Capital could not be raised, and soon the only object of the new corporation was to sell its rights to the United States. For that purpose Cromwell was retained.

The prejudice against Panama had, however, extended across the Atlantic. In March, 1901, while Vice-President Roosevelt presided rather nervously over the deliberations of the Senate, there was a brief debate on the canal. Senator John T. Morgan of Alabama attacked the plan for a route through Panama. The project had been "gangrene with corruption from its beginning to its end." With indignation, Senator Morgan told of a proposal that the United States purchase the French rights, a proposal made in February, 1899, through Sullivan & Cromwell. This offer marked the first appearance of Cromwell. His lobby at Washington was to be active until, at last, a Nicaraguan canal had been rejected in favor of Panama.

In 1899, the clever lawyer prevented Senator Morgan from obtaining an endorsement of Nicaragua. In 1900 he made further progress. The Republican convention which nominated McKinley and Roosevelt at Philadelphia would almost certainly have gone on record for Nicaragua had it not been for the zealous attorney of the New Panama Canal Company. Mr. Cromwell told of his work when he filed a brief in support of his fee. "We renewed our arguments and objections; the platform was changed and the words 'an Isthmian Canal' were substituted for 'Nicaragua Canal.' This was the first occasion on which it was publicly recognized that a canal other than that of Nicaragua was possible." All this became known twelve years later, when the House

Foreign Affairs Committee started to dig back into musty records. It was then testified, also, that Mr. Cromwell had donated $60,000 to the Republican National Committee and had charged it, as a necessary expense, to the canal company.

Mr. Cromwell, however, did not labor alone. He had an ally, who was to become virtually a rival, in the person of M. Bunau-Varilla. That talented Frenchman had no illusions that the United States would be so naïve as to accept the first proposals of the New Panama Canal Company. The first task, he felt, was educational. He must break down the prejudice against Panama and point out that a route through Nicaragua was beset with peril. He prepared to come to the United States "to preach the Truth," he wrote. He was about to experience a series of fortunate events so remarkable that "they seem almost to belong to romance."

Roosevelt, a mere Vice-President, did not figure in the plans of either Cromwell or Bunau-Varilla.

2

While still in Paris, Bunau-Varilla had been introduced to two or three prominent residents of Cincinnati and so, after sailing in January, 1901, he made the Ohio city his first objective. There, he was given letters to Myron T. Herrick of Cleveland, a rising member of Senator Hanna's machine. He was promised an interview with Hanna himself. Good fortune attended him from the start. Bunau-Varilla began the preparation of a brochure which emphasized the advantages of Panama and pointed out that he had come to America "not as the representative of any private interest [but] to defend a grand and noble conception."

In March, he met Mark Hanna, expounded his views and was enchanted to hear McKinley's friend say: "You have convinced me." The following month he was received at the White House and received similar, if less definite, assurances from McKinley. Bunau-Varilla returned to France confident that the seeds of Truth which he had planted would grow into mighty trees.

The directors of the New Panama Canal Company were more concerned with money than with truth. In May, 1901, the Isthmian Canal Commission, appointed by McKinley to pass on the merits of the two routes, asked the French company to fix a price for its rights in Panama. In December of the same year, the commission reported in favor of Nicaragua. The rights of the French stockholders, the commis-

sion estimated, were certainly worth not more than $40,-
000,000.

The news dismayed Bunau-Varilla, who was still in Paris.
He had already been worried over the possible effect of
McKinley's assassination in September. Hanna had been
converted to Truth but the Ohio Senator might not now be
the impressive ally he had been before. Bunau-Varilla hurriedly conferred with M. Marius Bo, president of the New
Panama Canal Company. The time for evasions and bar-
gaining had passed, he told Bo. No longer could $60,000,-
000 or $70,000,000 be obtained. A price of $40,000,000
had been set by the Isthmian Canal Commission and this
was the last hope. On January 4, 1902, thus lashed by Bunau-Varilla, the alarmed directors reduced the price to $40,-
000,000. The price cut marked, it would seem, Roosevelt's
first recognition that Panama was a preferable route. "Originally I had been for Nicaragua," he said some years later.

Nicaragua still had its ardent advocates. The House had
already passed a bill declaring for this route, and the fight
now centered upon the Senate. Cromwell was busy in Washington. Bunau-Varilla once more sailed to continue his valiant work, to call upon Nature as his ally. She did not fail.
In the pamphlet he had written in March, 1901, he had
pointed to the dangers of volcanic eruptions in Nicaragua.
"Young nations," he wrote, "like to put on their coats of
arms what most symbolizes their moral domain or characterizes their soil. What have the Nicaraguans chosen to
characterize their coats of arms or their postage stamps?
Volcanoes!"

The winter of 1901-02 passed and spring came. Despite
the continued advocacy of Hanna and the probable preference of President Roosevelt, a defeat for Panama seemed
likely. How could the members of the Senate be made
really conscious of volcanoes? At this point Nature decreed
—"What an unexpected turn of the wheel of fortune!"
—the eruption of Mont Pelée on May 6, 1902, and the
destruction of St. Pierre in the Caribbean. Eight days later,
on the eve of the final debate in the Senate, Mt. Monotombo in Nicaragua itself providentially erupted as well.
Bunau-Varilla hastily called on the postage-stamp dealers
of Washington. This very volcano was engraved on the
stamps of the unfortunate republic:

I was lucky enough to find some ninety stamps, that is, one
for every Senator, showing a beautiful volcano belching forth in
magnificent eruption. I hastened to paste my precious stamps on
sheets of paper. Below the stamps were written the following

words which told the whole story: "An official witness of the volcanic activity of Nicaragua."

It is difficult to apportion the credit for the choice of Panama. Certainly Bunau-Varilla had performed miracles. Certainly a major share must go to Mark Hanna. The Ohio Senator arose in the Senate on June 5, 1902, and began the most important speech of his career. Hanna, unlike Roosevelt, was not interested primarily in national defense. He viewed the waterway in the light of its effect on commerce. It had been said that he would oppose a canal, because it might damage the transcontinental railroads which contributed so generously to Republican campaign chests. Instead, Hanna offered figures and maps and blueprints in behalf of Panama.

How much of the credit belongs to the comparatively secretive Cromwell? Undoubtedly he used what influence he possessed to sway the Senate and thereby obtain $40,-000,000 for his clients. His most important work was still to be done, however. The Spooner Act calling for Panama was passed, and signed by Roosevelt on June 25, 1902. Panama, said Congress, was to be the route if arrangements could be made with the Republic of Colombia within "a reasonable time." Otherwise, Nicaragua must be substituted.

3

With the passage of the Spooner Act, Roosevelt's period of inactivity ended. When, as the months passed, Colombia hesitated in accepting the proposals of the United States, the President became an ardent partisan of Panama. In this fact lay the hope of the conspirators.

There was no rest for Bunau-Varilla. The United States had been persuaded that Panama was superior, but would Colombia execute a satisfactory treaty? Otherwise, all was failure again. Indefatigable in energy, he was everywhere at once. He conferred with President Roosevelt, John Hay, and Cromwell. He sent lengthy telegrams, one of them costing the staggering total of $304.38, informing President Marroquin of Colombia that excessive greed was dangerous. The United States might be disgustingly wealthy, but an indemnity of $9,800,000 and annual payments of $250,-000 a year constituted the utmost that could be obtained in return for a concession to build the canal across Panama.

In January, 1909, Roosevelt said that "the vital work, getting Panama as an independent Republic on which all else hinged, was done by me without the aid and advice of anyone." This was not quite accurate, nor is it offered as evidence that Roosevelt actively fomented the Panama revolution in the fall of 1903. Its relevance here is merely to show that the diplomatic correspondence between the United States and Colombia in 1902 and 1903 reflected the views of Roosevelt. Never, perhaps, had there been a more unusual exchange of communications between sovereign powers technically at peace. The true story of Panama is an irrefutable answer to Roosevelt's repeated contention that his dealings with Colombia were honorable or justified by law.

In March, 1901, when the United States was criticized because the Senate had refused to ratify the first Hay-Pauncefote Treaty with Great Britain, Roosevelt insisted that

. . . no treaty is a treaty until the Senate has confirmed it. No question of good faith or bad faith in any way enters into confirming or rejecting a treaty. The question is purely one as to the wisdom or unwisdom of the action sought. Similarly, in my judgment, the nation has as a matter of course a right to abrogate a treaty in a solemn and official manner, for what she regards as a sufficient cause, just exactly as she has a right to declare war or exercise another power for sufficient cause.

But Roosevelt had one rule for treaty negotiations between first-class powers and quite another for negotiations between the United States and the "Dagos" of Latin-America. The Hay-Herran Treaty with Colombia was confirmed by the United States Senate on March 17, 1903. This was not, however, the agreement that Colombia had originally agreed to sign. In October and November, 1902, José Vincente Concha, Colombian minister to the United States, had addressed indignant notes to Hay regarding changes that impugned the sovereignty of his country. Then Concha left the United States in disgust and his chargé, Herran, carried on the work. Herran, too, objected, but he finally signed the draft on January 22, 1903. He did not do so until Hay, in a telegram to Bogotá on December 30, 1902, had frightened the Colombian Government into temporary acquiescence by stating that the Nicaraguan route would be substituted. On the one hand, President Marroquin of Colombia faced an obnoxious treaty which his representative in the United States had signed. On the other was the possibility that Panama, never pretending loyalty to the central government of Colombia, would secede unless an agreement for a canal was reached. Bunau-Varilla had been burning the telegraph wires to Bogotá with threats that exactly this would happen.

The Hay-Herran treaty provided that $10,000,000 in gold and an annual rental of $250,000 would be paid to Colombia by the United States. In return, a license to build the canal would be granted as well as control over a strip of land three miles on each side of the canal, but excluding the cities of Panama and Colón. All this, of course, had nothing to do with the $40,000,000 which the United States had agreed to pay to the stockholders of the old French company. Colombia gazed upon this pleasant sum with a greedy eye, and her greed was one source of the friction that followed.

It was not the only source. The treaty supposedly acknowledged the sovereignty of Colombia over the canal area, but stipulations had been inserted that no free people would willingly have accepted. The United States had inserted a remarkable provision that protected the clients of William Nelson Cromwell. It was agreed in the Hay-Herran pact that Colombia could not conduct independent negotiations with the New Panama Canal Company; in other words, demand a share in the $40,000,000. Another amendment to the original treaty established American courts in the canal zone.

Even Bunau-Varilla, who had no sympathy for Colombia, admitted that limitations upon her sovereignty constituted the fundamental basis of her opposition to the Hay-Herran Treaty. The dispatches of A. M. Beaupré, the American minister to Colombia, leave small doubt that such was the case. On April 15, 1903, he reported that the local newspapers were filled with "bitter hostility toward what they represent [as] the attempt of a stronger nation to take advantage of Colombia and rob her of one of the most valuable sources of wealth which the world contains. If the proposed convention were to be submitted to the free opinion of the people it would not pass."

But Roosevelt had no patience with such theoretical objections. His earlier views on the confirmation of treaties, as expressed regarding the Hay-Pauncefote agreement, underwent a radical change. Beaupré was instructed to inform the Bogotan Government that the United States would consider "any modification whatever of the terms of the treaty as practically a breach of faith on the part of the government of Colombia."

Roosevelt's bad temper is clearly evident in the letters exchanged with Hay. "Make it as strong as you can to Beaupré," he ordered on July 14, 1903. "Those contemptible little creatures in Bogotá ought to understand how much they are jeopardizing things and imperiling their own future." On August 17, he said that "we may have to give a lesson to those jack rabbits." On September 15, he referred to the Colombians as "foolish and homicidal corruptionists."

These judicial expressions were translated into the outward decorum of diplomacy by Mr. Hay, but the meaning of his dispatches was as plain, if less crudely set forth, as the President's private communications. The most extraordinary among them, since the United States and Colombia were at peace, was a message to Beaupré on June 9, 1903, to be communicated in substance to Colombia's Minister of Foreign Affairs. The United States felt that Colombia did not appreciate "the gravity of the situation," said Hay. She had initiated the canal negotiations. Her proposal had, "with slight modifications," been accepted by the United States. It was in "virtue of this agreement" that Congress had reversed its earlier judgment and "decided upon the Panama route." Delay in ratification or rejection of the treaty might compromise "the friendly understanding between the two countries [and] action might be taken by Congress next winter which every friend of Colombia would regret."

This communication, undoubtedly prepared with the advice and approval of Roosevelt, is notable for the number of misstatements it contains. First, the negotiations had not been initiated by Colombia but by the New Panama Canal Company, through Bunau-Varilla and Cromwell. Second, if the amendments to the treaty were "slight modifications," why did the United States insist upon their adoption? Third, the change from Nicaragua to Panama had been approved by Congress because of the activities of Bunau-Varilla and Cromwell, because of fear of volcanic disturbances, and because the Panama route appeared to be cheaper as long as the French rights could be bought for $40,000,000. Beaupré, of course, had no choice but to hand Hay's message to the Colombian Government and to report that it had "created a sensation." It was interpreted, the American minister telegraphed, "as a threat of retaliation" unless the treaty was ratified. Nevertheless, the Colombian Congress rejected the treaty on August 12, 1903, and it seemed as though the $40,000,000 so dear to the French stockholders had vanished once more.

What action that "every friend of Colombia would regret" was implied in the Roosevelt-Hay ultimatum? Was it merely the substitution of Nicaragua? Or did the President have some other plan in mind? The Colombian Government, uneasy over a possible revolution in Panama, attempted without success to learn what the hidden meaning, if any, was. Meanwhile, it is essential to examine the validity of Roosevelt's repeated contention that Colombia was interested only in obtaining additional money from the United States. It is true that outraged sovereignty was not the Latin-American republic's only grievance. On July 9, 1903, Beaupré telegraphed that the treaty would be ratified if the United States would increase its payment to $15,-000,000 and would require the French stockholders to surrender $15,000,000 out of the $40,000,000 to be paid for their rights. This fixes Colombia's honor at $20,000,000. It had also been intimated to Bunau-Varilla that an annuity of $600,000 from the United States was more suitable to the magnitude of the enterprise.

Roosevelt, as he worked himself into a rage at Colombia, distorted the facts. The Colombians were "entitled to precisely the amount of sympathy we extend to other inefficient bandits."

"We were," the President told Congress in December, 1903, "more than just in dealing with them. Our generosity was such as to make it a serious question whether we had not gone too far in their interest at the expense of our own . . . we yielded in all possible ways in drawing up the treaty."

Undoubtedly, Colombia sought more money, but who would be the actual victims? On August 12, 1903, the day on which Colombia rejected the Hay-Herran Treaty, Beaupré sent two messages to Congress and in neither of them was it suggested that the United States increase either the annuity or the outright payment. On the contrary, it is possible to show by quoting John Hay and Theodore Roosevelt that any additional sums were to be obtained from the $40,000,000 of the New Panama Canal Company. Who, actually, were the owners of the more or less worthless French stock for which this $40,000,000 was to be paid? Cromwell denied ownership, as did Bunau-Varilla. The sum was paid to J. P. Morgan & Company to be transmitted to the mysterious stockholders, but to this day their identity is unknown.

Colombia, because of the provisions of the Hay-Herran Treaty, could not strike a bargain with the French company. On May 30, 1903, Beaupré warned Cromwell that his clients would have to pay many millions of francs before ratification was possible. But when the American minister told Hay that a $10,000,000 payment to Colombia by the New Panama Canal Company would be sufficient, the Secretary of State answered that the United States could not "covenant with Colombia to impose new financial obligations on the canal company."

Roosevelt's letters offer further proof. "They are mad to get hold of the $40,000,000 of the Frenchmen," he wrote Hay on August 14, 1903, "and they want to make us a party to the gouge." In his final apologia, he wrote that the Colombians had "expected to get from us the $40,000,000 we were to pay the French."

To save the money of the unidentified stockholders, whose names he did not know, Roosevelt made ready to seize Panama. He was not deterred by possible bloodshed or by the fact that the United States would violate the fundamentals of international law. His program was formulated very quietly.

Chapter VI

I TOOK PANAMA

*

While Cromwell and Bunau-Varilla were busy with plans for a revolution in Panama in the summer and fall of 1903, President Roosevelt was giving consideration to a solution of his own. Virtuously, he "cast aside the proposition to foment the secession of Panama." The United States could not, "by such underhanded means," encourage a revolt against Colombia. The President admitted, however, in communicating these views to Dr. Albert Shaw on October 10, 1903, that he would "be delighted if Panama were an independent State." Roosevelt also told President Schurman of Cornell that "for me to announce my feelings would be taken as equivalent to an effort to incite an insurrection in Panama.

"If Congress will give me a certain amount of freedom and a certain amount of time," he added, "I believe I can do much better than by any action taken out of hand."

Three days before the United States Senate confirmed the Hay-Herran Treaty in March, 1903, Roosevelt prepared for possible trouble with Colombia. He ordered Secretary of

War Root to send two or three army officers "to map out and gather information concerning the coasts of those portions of South America which would be of especial interest in the event of any struggle in the Gulf of Mexico or the Caribbean Sea." Work on the canal might soon start and data on Venezuela, Colombia, and the Guianas would be valuable. The officers, he directed, should go in civilian dress.

These were merely precautionary measures. Roosevelt still counted upon ratification by Colombia. When the too generous offer of the United States was actually rejected, the President was unwilling to rely on the prospect of a revolution. This might fail, inasmuch as the United States could not openly assist in the plans. An alternative solution was transmitted to Roosevelt on August 15, 1903, three days after the rash action by Bogotá. Francis B. Loomis, First Assistant Secretary of State, forwarded a memorandum, drafted by John Bassett Moore of Columbia University, and said that it contained "strong and well supported suggestions which may be of very great importance." Roosevelt agreed as to their importance. Four days later, from Sagamore Hill, where he was resting from the heat of Washington, he sent the memorandum to John Hay. It was evident that some new plan for a canal across Panama was taking shape in Roosevelt's mind.

The possible solution by Dr. Moore vanished for some years and was a subject for speculation by historians. A copy is among the Roosevelt papers at the Library of Congress, however, and it is not difficult to understand why the President promptly sent it to his Secretary of State. Moore, already an authority on international law, had independently evolved a theory which fitted admirably into Roosevelt's views on Colombia and the canal. The United States, he wrote, "in undertaking to build the canal, does a work not only for itself but for the world." If, as expert opinion agreed, Panama was the best route, "it is the one that we should have. May Colombia be permitted to stand in the way?" Dr. Moore felt that it must not, and he offered an ingenious argument in support of his belief. He pointed to the Treaty of 1846 with New Granada, a country which became the Republic of Colombia in 1863, and its clause that "the right of way or transit across the Isthmus of Panama shall be free and open to the Government and citizens of the United States." This provision (Article XXXV of the Treaty of 1846) applied to "any modes of communication that now exist, or that may be hereafter constructed."

In return for this privilege, the memorandum continued, the United States guaranteed "the perfect neutrality of the isthmus, with the view that free transit from one to the other sea may not be interrupted or embarrassed in any future time, and guarantees, in the same manner, the rights of sovereignty and property which New Granada has and possesses over the said territory." The object in assuming this burden was to secure a canal, said Dr. Moore, and "in view of the fact that the United States has for more than fifty years secured to Colombia her sovereignty Colombia is not in a position to obstruct the building of the canal." As for technicalities or disagreement on the meaning of the treaty or international law, the memorandum said:

Once on the ground and duly installed, this Government would find no difficulty in meeting questions as they arose. The position of the United States is altogether different from that of private capitalists who, unless expressly exempted, are altogether subject to the local jurisdiction. The United States is not subject to such disabilities, and can take care of the future.

Obviously, the President was interested; a philosophy more Rooseveltian would be difficult to find. Unhampered by "such disabilities," a great deal could be accomplished by a courageous and impatient Chief Executive. Dr. Moore was invited to Oyster Bay to discuss "matters of foreign policy." The President told Hay that if, under the Treaty of 1846, "we have a color of right to start in and build a canal, my off-hand judgment would favor such proceeding." It may have been a rather dim color of right, but to Roosevelt it was sufficient. By September, 1903, he was intimating to Hay and to Taft that action would be taken in Panama without reference to the Bogotan Government. To a warning from Senator Hanna on October 4 that patience was essential, that ultimately an agreement with Colombia would be effected, Roosevelt expressed doubt that "the only virtue we need is patience":

This does not mean that we must necessarily go to Nicaragua. I feel we are certainly justified in morals, and therefore justified in law, in interfering summarily and saying that the canal is to be built and that they must not stop it.

All the while Bunau-Varilla and Cromwell were urging a policy of action. The Frenchman, hoping that his words would reach the President, wrote Dr. Moore on October 3, 1903, that Colombia sought a year's delay. This, he added craftily, would carry the situation close to Election Day in 1904 and would force Roosevelt "to come before the people without a solution of the canal problem." Cromwell, equally skillful in playing upon Roosevelt's ambitions, wrote that "this problem of the ages" had never been so near to solution. If lost, it would be lost "for centuries to come."

"Your virile and masterful policy," he said, "will prove the solution of this great problem."

The secession of Panama was to make it unnecessary to put in operation a plan based on Dr. Moore's memorandum. Roosevelt formulated it late in October in a rough draft of his message to Congress. Either Nicaragua should be substituted or "without any further parley with Colombia [we should] enter upon the completion of the canal which the French company has begun." The latter course "is the one demanded by the interest of this nation." In a private letter, Roosevelt described it more bluntly:

. . . if they had not revolted, I should have recommended to Congress to take possession of the Isthmus by force of arms; and I had actually written the first draft of my message to this effect.

2

Inciting the "most just and proper revolution," as Roosevelt described it, was a task that took all the skill of Bunau-Varilla, Cromwell, and the other conspirators. The faltering courage of Panamanian patriots had to be fortified by promises that the United States would, in spirit at least and probably actively, be behind them. Gold with which to bribe the Colombian troops had to be supplied. It was necessary to point out that the $10,000,000 to be paid by the United States would, in the event of independence, go to Panama and not to Colombia. This $10,000,000 could be spent as the sons of liberty saw fit.

In considering the relation of the United States to the revolution, and thereby the part played by Roosevelt, it is important to recall that Bunau-Varilla and Cromwell were men who commanded the ear of John Hay, of Senator Hanna, and of the President himself. So, during 1903, these two worked zealously and to great effect. Roosevelt did nothing to incite the revolution, perhaps, but he was extremely well informed regarding the plans.

The first hint regarding them came in June, 1903. Colombia had not yet acted on the Hay-Herran Treaty when a curiously prophetic item appeared in the New York *World*. A dispatch from Washington stated, without giving an authority, that President Roosevelt was determined to have the Panama route. But Washington had been informed that Colombia did not propose to ratify and had received the further information that "Panama stands ready to secede and enter into a canal treaty with the United States." The dispatch concluded with the news that on that day, June 13, 1903, William Nelson Cromwell had "a long conversation with the President." Subsequently, this aroused much interest and was offered as proof that Roosevelt had fomented the revolution. It eventually became known, however, that the dispatch had been inspired by a press agent for Cromwell and its purpose had been to frighten Colombia into signing the Hay-Herran agreement. The occurrence, together with a second visit by Cromwell to the White House on October 7, 1903, is of interest principally in connection with Roosevelt's ultimate insistence that

. . . no one connected with this government had any part in preparing, inciting or *encouraging* the revolution . . . no one had any previous knowledge . . . except such as was available to any person . . . who read the newspapers. I do not remember whether Mr. Cromwell was among my callers during the months immediately preceding the revolution. But if he was, I certainly did not discuss with him anything connected with the revolution. I do not remember his ever speaking to me about the revolution until after it occurred, and my understanding was, and is, that he had nothing to do with the revolutionary movement.

Surely Roosevelt was not as naïve as all that. It is inconceivable that a President so well informed on other subjects did not know about Cromwell's activities. A second source of information to which the general public had no access was Bunau-Varilla, who had again arrived from Paris in September, 1903. In recording with pride the means by which he brought independence to Panama, Bunau-Varilla enumerated conferences with Loomis, with Hay, and with the President. He saw Roosevelt on October 9 and predicted a revolution.

Roosevelt not only knew, in a general way, of the conspiracy; he was considering what action the United States would take when it came and whether, under the Treaty of 1846, Colombia could be prevented from putting down the rebellion. He even received memorandums from the State Department to the effect that Colombian officers and soldiers had not been paid for weeks, were close to starvation, and therefore open to bribery. Finally, he had confidential reports from two of the army officers who had been detailed to the South American coast and the Caribbean. Roosevelt admitted that Capt. Thomas B. Humphrey and

Lieut. Grayson M-P. Murphy had been to Panama—"on their own initiative (and without my knowledge)"—and had learned that a revolution would take place the end of October or early in November.

The youthful Lieutenant (later Colonel) Murphy, subsequently the head of Grayson M-P. Murphy & Company of Wall Street, recalled in 1930 a number of relevant facts. While the two officers were in Venezuela during July, 1903, Captain Humphrey received word from a friend in Washington that anything regarding Panama which could be learned would be of interest to the War Department. This was quite unofficial, but on the strength of it, Colonel Murphy remembered, they hurried to Panama, where they accumulated facts regarding the probable revolution. The prospects for Panamanian freedom looked so bright, indeed, that Humphrey and Murphy debated the financial wisdom of resigning their army commissions forthwith and assisting in its consummation. On returning to Washington in October, they considered a visit to J. P. Morgan & Company to ask financial assistance. They were prepared to supply the revolution if Morgan would agree to let them have $100,000 each as their share of the $10,000,000 that the United States would turn over to Panama.

On the night of October 16, however, the officers were summoned to the White House. President Roosevelt cautioned them to say nothing about seeing him, and questioned them exhaustively on the data they had obtained on the isthmus. They gathered from the conversation that Roosevelt intended some sort of action, but he said nothing to indicate that the Government was taking part in the revolution. Nor did he ask them when it would take place. After an hour, Murphy and Humphrey left, their dream of participation gone.

The plans of Cromwell and Bunau-Varilla, meanwhile, were making progress. The usefulness of the New York attorney lay partly in the fact that the Panama Railroad and Steamship Company was owned by his clients, the New Panama Canal Company. It had agents in Panama City and Colón who were to be very useful in hastening the day when, according to Roosevelt, "the people of Panama rose literally as one man" against the tyranny of Bogotá. During the summer of 1903 this rising tide of patriotism was barely discernible to the two major local conspirators.

One of the patriots was Dr. Manuel Amador de Guerrero, who had shortened his name to Manuel Amador and who was, by strange coincidence, physician to Mr. Cromwell's

226

Panama Railroad and Steamship Company. The railroad physician aspired to the status of the George Washington of the Republic of Panama, and he went to New York early in September, 1903, to determine whether funds and support were forthcoming.

But Cromwell, to whom Amador looked for aid, had grown somewhat cautious. A leak had developed and Herran, the Colombian chargé at Washington, had telegraphed his government on September 4, that the United States was undoubtedly in favor of a revolution. Amador encountered a distressing coolness when he called at the offices of Sullivan & Cromwell, and it was not until M. Bunau-Varilla arrived from France on September 23 that the prospects of assistance rose. Until then, the Frenchman had been carrying on negotiations from Paris. Now, he established himself in Room 1162 of the old Waldorf-Astoria Hotel, a room, he wrote, which "deserves to be considered as the cradle of the Panama Republic." The hotel and the shrine unfortunately gave way to the Empire State Building. Having seen Roosevelt on October 9 and finding encouragement, although no pledge was given, in the attitude of the President, Bunau-Varilla called upon John Hay. The Secretary of State, Bunau-Varilla recalled, said that "we shall not be caught napping; orders have been given to naval forces in the Pacific to sail toward the isthmus." This was precisely what Bunau-Varilla wanted to hear. He returned, greatly encouraged, to Room 1162.

On October 14, Dr. Amador presented himself at the Waldorf. He received full instructions. Bunau-Varilla would supply $100,000 for the preliminary expenses of a revolution to be staged on November 3, 1903—Election Day in the United States. Amador was handed a draft of Panama's new constitution, a secret code whereby the rebels could communicate with the cradle of their liberty, a proclamation of independence, and, most important of all, a message to be sent as soon as Panama was free. This message was an appeal to Bunau-Varilla to become, though a citizen of France, first Panamanian minister to the United States.

"Nothing remains but to make the model of the flag," said Bunau-Varilla as he ushered Amador out of Room 1162. "I am going tomorrow to join my family. I shall find the agile and discreet fingers that will make a new flag."

On the following day, a Sunday, Mme. Bunau-Varilla, the Betsy Ross of Panama, secreted herself and stitched "the flag of liberation." It was, her husband felt as he gazed on its folds, a fitting emblem; very much like that of the United

States, but with yellow instead of white for the background and with two suns in place of stars. He later recalled with irritation that the ungrateful Panamanians ultimately changed the design.

3

It is lamentable that Roosevelt, whose sense of humor and love for the dramatic would have been gratified, was denied detailed knowledge of these preparations. While Bunau-Varilla waited at the Waldorf, while Cromwell left for Paris to be near his clients, lesser conspirators were busy in mosquito-infested Panama. Amador arrived at Colón on October 27, 1903, and was greeted at the wharf by H. G. Prescott, another employee of the Panama Railroad and Steamship Company. The patriots met that night and soon were expressing disgust at the meager assurances brought back by Amador. Why had he not obtained a secret treaty of defense signed by Hay?

This reasonable sentiment was echoed by others. To make matters worse, word came that Colombian troops had been dispatched to reinforce the garrison on the isthmus. Depressed and alarmed, Amador cabled Bunau-Varilla on October 28, that the Bogotan forces would arrive at Colón on November 2 or 3. If the revolution was to have a chance of success, an American warship must be rushed to the scene. Bunau-Varilla felt, in view of knowledge acquired from the newspapers and by discreet inquiries, that the role of prophet was safe. He telegraphed Amador that one warship would arrive at Colón, on the Atlantic side, within two days. Within four days, two other American vessels would drop anchor at Panama on the Pacific side.

His cable gave heart to the conspirators and they set November 4 as the date of the blow for liberty. Señorita Maria Amelia de la Ossa, a lady engaged to be married to the brother of Prescott of the railroad company, was commissioned to design a new flag. J. Gabriel Duqué, owner of the Panama *Star and Herald*, was placed in charge of 287 members of the fire brigade at Panama City and drilled them for battle. Three hundred section hands of the Panama Railroad were mustered into service at Colón.

The strategy of the revolution was not complicated. General Huertas, in command of the Colombian troops at Panama City, was to be commander in chief. His men were to be bribed for $50 a head. An arrangement was effected whereby José Domingo de Obaldia, governor of Panama, would consent to friendly arrest early on November 4; he was very close to the revolutionists and was living in Amador's house. To prevent the possibility that the troops bound for Colón could cross the isthmus, it was arranged that all rolling stock on the railroad would be sent to Panama City. This detail was the work of Col. J. R. Shaler, superintendent of the Panama Railroad.

Behind all this, in influence and in power, was the United States. Roosevelt insisted, probably truthfully, that he had no idea what assurances might have been given by Bunau-Varilla to the revolutionists. He was "a very able fellow, and it was his business to find out what our government would do. I have no doubt that he was able to make a very shrewd guess, and to advise his people accordingly." In other words, by November 1, 1903, the plans had progressed so far that no need existed for further encouragement.

The decision of the conspirators to delay the revolution until November 4 was very nearly fatal to the cause of liberty. The U.S.S. *Nashville* arrived at Colón at 6:30 o'clock on the evening of November 2. That same day the Navy Department sent instructions to Commander John Hubbard of the *Nashville* and to the commanding officers of the other vessels steaming toward Panama. They were directed to "maintain free and uninterrupted transit" on the isthmus. But Hubbard's cable had not arrived. He saw no disturbance nor any basis for action in the uncontested landing at midnight on November 2 of 500 Colombian soldiers from the gunboat *Cartagena*. On the morning of November 3 all remained quiet, and he cabled Washington to that effect.

On hearing that the Bogotan warriors had arrived, and that only the narrow isthmus stood between them and the patriotic revolutionists, Dr. Amador and his associates at Panama City were again plunged into gloom. This time Señora Maria de la Ora de Amador (de Guerrero), the leader's wife, buoyed their courage. It was too late to retreat, said the future First Lady of Panama. Their plans had been carried so far that retreat was impossible. In this crisis, Cromwell's men saved the day. Generals Tovar and Amaya of Colombia were greeted at 8 o'clock that morning in Colón by Shaler, the Panama Railroad superintendent. He exuded cordiality, and he led them with appropriate flourishes to a special train consisting of a single car attached to the locomotive. The troops would follow at 1 o'clock that day, the superintendent explained, when the Colombian generals asked why they were being shipped to Panama City by themselves. Then, as they still hesitated, Shaler pulled the bell cord, hopped off, and waved a genial farewell as the train rolled out. In due time it arrived on the other side of the isthmus, where Tovar and Amaya received a reception worthy of their high rank. Governor Obaldia, a member of the reception committee, was at the station to meet them, but he said nothing about the revolution shortly to take place.

Amador, his courage fortified by desperation, had decided to strike. Shaler telegraphed that the troops would not be transported. When Colonel Torres, the commanding officer at Colón, demanded a train, the bluff and hearty railroad superintendent said that this was impossible unless the fares of the troops were paid in advance. When Torres protested that his superior officers had all the money, $65,000 conveniently borrowed from the collectors of customs at Barranquilla and Cartagena, Shaler said that he was damned well desolated, but what could he do? If only Governor Obaldia were present, he could sign authorizations in lieu of cash. But the governor was at Panama City and, as Shaler was well aware but kept to himself, was hand in hand with the rebels. Thus it was Shaler, in the employ of Cromwell's clients, who saved the day. No train was supplied. Tovar and Amaya, being elaborately entertained at the Government House in Panama City, grew slightly uneasy as the afternoon wore away and their soldiers did not appear.

A final change in plans by the excitable revolutionists scheduled the revolution for 8 o'clock that night, November 3, during a band concert on the plaza. Generals Tovar and Amaya were to be invited to the musical feast and then arrested. The rebellion, however, got out of hand. At about 5 o'clock the fire brigade began the distribution of weapons to the crowds in the streets. The two generals were escorted to police headquarters while a great crowd assembled, shouting *"Viva el Itmo libre!" "Vive Huertas!" "Viva el Presidente Amador!"* and shot off their guns, to the extreme peril of spectators. The hour of freedom was precisely 5:49 P.M. on November 3, 1903.

On the following morning Dr. Amador, soon to be President of Panama, directed that the troops which had taken part in the revolt be drawn up at the barracks. Somehow during the night funds had been obtained; according to one rumor by backing a mule cart up to the subtreasury in the city.

"The world is astounded at our heroism!" said Amador. "Yesterday we were but the slaves of Colombia; today we are free. President Roosevelt has made good. Long live the Republic of Panama! Long live President Roosevelt!"

Then the president-elect suggested that each of the heroes be given the $50 in gold which had been pledged. It was done, amid further cheers for America and Roosevelt. Later that day a demonstration was held in the plaza of Panama City. Huertas was carried aloft on an ornate chair, while the American consul, Ehrman, walked on one side with an American flag and Amador strutted on the other with the new emblem of Panama. The parade wound up at the Century Hotel, where Huertas was nearly drowned as bottle after bottle of champagne was poured over the warrior's head. Nor did his countrymen deny to Huertas more substantial rewards. He was immediately paid $30,000 in silver and later received $50,000 additional in gold. Most of the junior officers received $10,000 each.

At Colón on November 4, while these jollifications went on across the isthmus, there was a moment of gravity. It was, however, as brief as the interval in Panama on the evening before when a Colombian gunboat had tossed a shell or two into the town and had killed a Chinaman. Colonel Torres was still outraged because he had been denied transportation to Panama City. He announced that he would kill every American in Colón unless his generals were released. Thereupon Commander Hubbard, no longer in doubt as to his function, landed some marines and announced that the troops could not, in any event, use the railroad. Torres calmed down. He assured Hubbard of his deep friendship for the United States and on November 5, in return for $8,000 advanced by Shaler, he consented to withdraw with his men. They sailed on the S.S. *Orinoco* as Shaler, always gallant, sent aboard two cases of champagne. On November 6, the Panamanian flag was raised at Colón.

4

All this excess of patriotism must not obscure the real reasons for the Panama revolution—to preserve untouched the $40,000,000 of the New Panama Canal Company and to accelerate the construction of the canal across the isthmus. President Roosevelt was notified that freedom had been finally and definitely accomplished. He thereupon acted with haste that was indecent, not to say unwise. Hay instructed the American consul at Panama City to recognize the *de facto* government. Identical instructions were sent to Beaupré at Bogotá and to Malmross at Colón. On November 10 Amador and Frederico Boyd were en route to the United States to sign a treaty.

Bunau-Varilla, actually a realist despite the romantic flavor of his writings, did not propose to wait for the arrival of the two Panamanians. The possibility loomed that the new republic, like Colombia, might grow dissatisfied with $10,000,000 and demand part of the $40,000,000 to be paid to the French stockholders. Bunau-Varilla did not intend to have all his labors thus undone, and he persuaded Roosevelt to receive him, as the minister from Panama, on November 13. The treaty was signed on November 17 by Hay and Bunau-Varilla. Amador, if he had any hope of raising the price, arrived too late.

Roosevelt's defense, as submitted in a message to Congress on January 4, 1904, and repeated on many subsequent occasions, was based, in essence, on the Treaty of 1846. Nothing could "be more erroneous," he said, than the interpretation that this agreement merely protected Colombia from revolution. The basic purpose had been to "assure the dedication of the isthmus to free and unobstructed interoceanic transit, the consummation of which would be found in an interoceanic canal." The President then cited precedents to show that on many occasions the United States had intervened to preserve free transit, "with or without Colombia's consent." A more careful search of the precedents, or a more honest one, would have demonstrated to Roosevelt that, with one exception, American troops had been used on the isthmus only to put down revolts at the request of Colombia. The exception had been followed by a prompt apology offered through the State Department.

In June, 1904, as Elihu Root prepared his summary of administration accomplishments for the 1904 convention, Roosevelt instructed him to tell about "Panama in all its details." The following year he declared that the United States had shown "a spirit not merely of justice but of generosity in its dealings with Colombia." These convictions of righteousness in "the most important action I took in foreign affairs" never deserted him. Pride in his achievement caused him to make indiscreet statements, however. On June 19, 1908, he referred to "taking Panama" in a letter to Sir George Trevelyan. Finally, on March 23, 1911, Roosevelt made the address at the University of California which was to cost his country $25,000,000. He said:

I am interested in the Panama Canal because I started it. If I had followed conventional, conservative methods, I should have submitted a dignified state paper to the Congress and the debate would have been going on yet, but I took the canal zone and let Congress debate, and while the debate goes on the canal does also.

This public confession gave new impetus to Colombia's efforts, carried on since 1904, to obtain redress for her grievance. Even Roosevelt, by suggesting that Panama turn over to Colombia for ten years her annuity of $250,000, tacitly admitted some basis for her resentment. Roosevelt would tolerate no frank admission, however, that he had been wrong. Halfhearted attempts to appease Colombia were made during the Taft Administration. Then Wilson became President and a treaty was drafted which offered an apology and $25,000,000 to Colombia. Roosevelt, of course, was furious.

Roosevelt's friends in the Senate, among them Cabot Lodge, blocked confirmation that year. The World War postponed further consideration until Roosevelt was dead and the Harding Administration came into being in 1921. Now, new and all-persuasive influences were demanding conciliation of Colombia. In the final debate on an indemnity in April, 1921, Senator Lodge spoke at length of his reverence for the memory of Theodore Roosevelt, who had been his closest friend. It was unthinkable that he would act counter to the wishes of that friend. The treaty under consideration, he said, was not the one to which Roosevelt had objected so violently, which he had branded as countenancing blackmail. The "amount of the indemnity," said Lodge suavely, "carried no admission as to wrong-doing of any kind, but was simply a question of the amount to be paid in consideration of the recognition by Colombia of the independence of Panama."

This was an obvious absurdity. Why should the United States, innocent of wrongdoing, turn over $25,000,000 to the Bogotan "corruptionists"? When, in history, had this country paid millions to persuade one Latin-American country that the independence of another should be recognized? Other reasons lay beneath the speech of the Senator from Massachusetts, and Lodge soon revealed them. The treaty would "promote our commerce; our exports have been falling off," he said. But even this was not the specific reason; it was a generality. The reason was oil. Its spokesman was Albert B. Fall, the Fall who was "a faithless public servant." Senator Lodge told of valuable oil concessions that might otherwise be awarded to British interests. Colombia was inclined to discriminate against the United States in accepting bids, but the $25,000,000 would result in a treaty of "amity and commerce" that would "improve our opportunities of making secure these concessions."

Payment was a fitting climax to the negotiations for Panama conducted "in accordance with the highest principles of national, international, and private morality." In none of Roosevelt's innumerable comments on the treaty had he differentiated between payments of the $25,000,000 and the apology:

> Either there is or there is not warrant for paying this enormous sum or for making the apology. The payment can only be justified upon the ground that this nation has played the part of a thief, or of a receiver of stolen goods.

5

Who got the $40,000,000 paid by the United States? "Doubtless in Paris, and perhaps to a lesser degree in New York," Roosevelt admitted, "there were speculators who bought and sold in the stock market." But although, on December 10, 1908, the President wrote Philander Knox that "Mr. Cromwell has sent on to me the complete list of the stockholders of the Panama Canal Companies," no such list has ever been made public nor is there a trace of it among the papers at the Library of Congress.

The original De Lesseps Company went into bankruptcy in 1889 and with the crash vanished the savings of 600,000 French citizens. The New Panama Canal Company, also French, was then organized and ultimately, with the assistance of Bunau-Varilla and Cromwell, accomplished the revolution and the sale to the United States. There was also a third company, regarding which little is known: the Panama Canal Company of America. This was organized in New Jersey on December 27, 1899, for the ostensible purpose of exchanging its securities for those of the New Panama Canal Company. Its capital was $30,000,000. The incorporators were clerks in Cromwell's law office and among those supposedly interested were August Belmont, Kuhn, Loeb & Company, and Levi P. Morton. About $5,000,000 of the stock was subscribed. This, of course, was before Roosevelt had become an enthusiastic partisan of Panama.

On February 27, 1906, Cromwell was summoned by the Senate Committee on Inter-Oceanic Canals, of which Morgan of Alabama, the bitter opponent of the Panama route, was chairman. The attorney could not recall, he said, a contract between himself and the New Panama Canal Company, although he freely admitted his activities as counsel. Then Morgan produced an agreement dated November 21, 1899, in which Cromwell was empowered to form a syndicate for the "Americanization" of the canal. Cromwell, however, declined to testify regarding it. The document, he said, was merely "a power of attorney to me to accomplish broad plans. It never matured into anything and it is obsolete."

"Whatever was done was done," he told the Senate Committee.

"Your case of lockjaw," said the angry Senator Morgan, when Cromwell persisted in his refusal to testify, "seems to be getting worse. It is the most extraordinary case I have ever encountered."

No information was obtained from Cromwell and insinuations continued, particularly by Democrats seeking political capital, that evil disposition had been made of the $40,000,000. In February, 1904, Senator Edward W. Carmack of Tennessee said that the peasants and shopkeepers of France received only $24,000,000, while Bunau-Varilla and his associates retained the $16,000,000 balance. Marse Henry Watterson exploded with an editorial saying that there had been "nothing so good since the Crédit Mobilier. A more palpable confidence game, a greater robbery, was never perpetrated upon a people's treasure house."

Colonel Watterson's criticism followed the action of President Roosevelt in prosecuting the New York *World* and the Indianapolis *News* for criminal libel in December, 1908. It was an occasion on which Roosevelt lost his head completely and on which he met defeat. On October 3, 1908, the *World* published an article stating, in brief, that unnamed persons were attempting to blackmail William Nelson Cromwell in connection with the sale in 1904 of the French canal properties to the United States. A complaint had been filed by Cromwell which set forth that Douglas Robinson, brother-in-law of the President, Charles P. Taft, brother of the Republican presidential nominee, and Cromwell would be accused of participation in a syndicate which had taken over the French rights. Bunau-Varilla was also to be included among those who had been "able to reap a rich profit."

A later edition, also of October 3, 1908, contained a statement dictated by Cromwell denying that he, or any associate, had profited from the Panama transaction. He said that the money had been paid by the United States, through its bankers, to the Bank of France and there placed to the credit of the old and the new French companies. The *World* was careful to point out that no evidence existed to show any connection on the part of Robinson or Taft. The blackmail proceedings were dropped. Mr. Taft denied the imputation that he had been associated with any syndicate. The *World,* as did every one else, accepted his denial.

But the incident revived interest in the canal. A presidential campaign was under way and the *World* was opposing the election of Roosevelt's candidate, Taft. Prior to Election Day, it published six articles recalling the revolution and the payment of the $40,000,000 by the United States, and these implied that a syndicate of Americans had obtained part of the $40,000,000. Anti-Roosevelt papers reprinted them and on November 2, 1909, the Indianapolis *News* asked editorially where the $40,000,000 had actually gone. This was the day before the balloting. It was supposed to have reduced the small margin by which Taft carried Indiana and to have been responsible for a Democratic victory in the state elections.

Roosevelt was violently angry over these articles. In a private letter on October 30, 1908, he said that the charges were absurd, that "we paid the money to the liquidators appointed by the French government. Not a cent was reserved or sent back for the use of anyone here." The President took no public action until after Taft had been safely elected. On December 1, 1908, he attacked the Indianapolis *News* for its editorial of November 2:

. . . the most minute official knowledge, every important step, and every important document have been made public in communications to the Congress and through the daily press. The fact has been officially published again and again that the Government paid forty million dollars, and that it paid this forty million dollars direct to the French Government. The United States Government has not the slightest knowledge as to the particular individuals among whom the French Government distributed the sum. That was the business of the French Government. So far as I know there was no syndicate; there certainly was no syndicate in the United States that to my knowledge had any dealings with the Government, directly or indirectly.

The balance of the President's statement denied that Douglas Robinson or Charles P. Taft could have been connected with the Panama negotiations. It concluded with a bitter attack on newspapers in general and the Indianapolis *News* in particular. The New York *World,* which had started the trouble, was not mentioned by name.

That newspaper promptly assumed full responsibility. On

December 8 it charged that Roosevelt had been guilty of untruth when he said that the money had been paid directly to the French Government. It had been paid to J. P. Morgan & Company for transmittal, as Cromwell had testified in 1906. The President had issued a statement "full of flagrant untruths, reeking with misstatement, challenging line by line the testimony of his associate, Cromwell, and the official record."

Roosevelt struck back. "I do not know anything about the law of criminal libel," he wrote on December 9, 1908, to Henry L. Stimson, United States Attorney for New York, "but I should dearly like to have it invoked against Pulitzer, of the *World*. Would you have his various utterances for the last three or four months looked up?"

This was followed by a curious document, a special message to Congress on December 15, 1908, which constituted an attack on Delavan Smith, editor of the *News,* and Pulitzer. The statements of these editors, Roosevelt said, were "a libel upon the United States Government." It was the duty of the Government to see that Pulitzer, the real offender, was prosecuted. President then quoted a statement by Cromwell that 226,296 claims had been paid by the French liquidator and that all records were available at the Paris offices of the New Panama Canal Company.

The national Government had no definite powers regarding libel. It was a matter for the various states. But indictments were sought against the Indianapolis *News,* the *World,* their editors and owners, under an act passed in 1898 to "Protect the Harbor Defenses and Fortifications Constructed or Used by the United States from Malicious Injury, and for Other Purposes." This was a fantastic application of a statute which had been derived from a long-forgotten law of similar purpose passed in 1825. Indictments were returned on the theory that copies of the two newspapers containing aspersions on Roosevelt and the Government had been circulated on government property in the District of Columbia and in New York City. Stimson, to his probable regret, went ahead with the prosecutions, but United States Attorney Joseph B. Kealing of Indianapolis, a Roosevelt appointee, resigned rather than undertake so strained an interpretation of the law. Ultimately, United States District Judge Anderson decided against Roosevelt's theory of the law and his opinion contained a significant statement:

There are many very peculiar circumstances about this Panama Canal business. There were a number of people who thought there was something not just exactly right about that transaction, and I will say for myself that I have a curiosity to know what the real truth was. The man who knew all about it—I think that is the proper way to speak of Mr. Cromwell—stood upon his privilege as an attorney and refused to answer.

While preparations were made for the trial of the *World*, that newspaper attempted to learn in Paris the identity of the stockholders and was informed by its investigators that no records, as claimed by Roosevelt and Cromwell, existed. Nor has this author, over a quarter of a century, ever been told about them. In view of the issue of free speech that Roosevelt had raised, the *World* was obliged to fight the case on the law. A victory for the Government would have meant the death of an independent press in the United States. The *World's* position was upheld by unanimous decision of the United States Supreme Court.

"It would be impossible," said Chief Justice White on January 3, 1911, "to sustain this prosecution without overthrowing the very state law by the authority of which the prosecution can alone be maintained."

In other words, Roosevelt and Taft and Robinson had their remedy in the libel statutes of the states. None of the three chose to demand such prosecution, nor did any start suit for damages under the civil laws. Cromwell, too, was silent. He was permitted to give $5,000 to the Republican campaign in 1904. But Taft, four years later, was apprehensive over the wisdom of accepting $50,000 more.

"If I were in your place," Roosevelt wrote, "I would accept that contribution of Cromwell's with real gratitude."

Chapter VII

TRIMMING SAIL

✳

In April, 1903, passing through Des Moines, Iowa, on a tour that extended to the Pacific coast, Roosevelt was received with great enthusiasm. He had made many speeches on the journey, partly in support of his legislative program and partly to make more certain the presidential nomination in 1904. At Des Moines the crowds pressed about the rear platform of his special train. The President seemed exhilarated and happy. But as the train left he grew morose. All this meant nothing, he said to a member of his party—nothing personal. The cheers would have been as loud for any other President. The homage had been for the office, not for the man.

He was frank and honest about wanting the nomination. But his alarmed imagination led him into strange forebodings. The next January he told his oldest son that Hanna would probably seize the prize for himself.

Roosevelt was grossly unfair to the Ohio leader, and his gloom had very little real foundation. The congressional elections of 1902 had been encouraging. Party friction in New York State was merely a successful attempt by Benjamin B. Odell to depose Tom Platt as the Republican leader. Reason did exist, however, for a degree of apprehension regarding Odell. This leader's reputation had been tarnished by accusations that he held stock in a grocery concern which had sold supplies to state institutions. Roosevelt was familiar with the charges and was concerned over their possible accuracy, but as 1904 approached he felt that Odell's backing was vital. Rather impetuously, he invited him to the White House and then expressed to Murray Crane and Elihu Root regret that he had done so.

"What shall I talk to him about?" he asked, but Mr. Root smiled inscrutably and edged toward the door of the presidential study.

"I've an appointment, Mr. President," said the Secretary of War, looking at his watch. "I'd suggest you talk about groceries."

The lot of a presidential aspirant, when he is in the White House already and is seeking a second term, is not a happy one. The President must serve two masters. He must convince the voters that their rights and desires are paramount. He must reassure potential campaign contributors that his program does not threaten business unrest. Early in 1903, with Election Day still distant enough to make it feasible, Roosevelt continued to press his trust-control measures. He was tortured by pondering their political effect, but—to his credit—he went on.

No important opposition to the first railroad legislation of Roosevelt's administration existed. The Elkins Law, which forbade rebating, was framed with the consent of the operators. It was, in fact, a railroad bill. The attitude of business toward the President's specifications for his new Department of Commerce and Labor was far different. It had no objection to a Federal commission that would issue polite statements and disseminate statistics on industrial conditions. The hostility was due to Roosevelt's plan for a Bureau of Corporations, to be established in the department. A statement from the White House on January 6, 1903, made the significance of this all too obvious. The bureau was to "investigate the operations and conduct of interstate corporations." This alarmed the alert industrialists.

An organized opposition was apparent as Congress prepared to debate the bill in January, 1903, and Roosevelt attacked it. He told the Washington correspondents that the Department of Commerce and Labor act must contain provision for a Bureau of Corporations with full investigatory powers. Unless the Fifty-seventh Congress, going out of existence in a month, provided it, he would call a special session. This was a conventional threat; the President went much further. He cautioned the newspapermen that they must not reveal the source of their information, but authorized them to state that six members of the Senate had received telegrams from John D. Rockefeller urging that no antitrust legislation be enacted. Roosevelt said that he did not know the exact wording of these messages; it had been substantially as follows:

We are opposed to any anti-trust legislation. Our counsel, Mr. ——, will see you. It must be stopped.

The storm was immediate, and as satisfactory as Roosevelt could have wished. After the first day, it was impossible to maintain the fiction that he had not been quoted. It did not matter that no Senator could be located who had received this or any other message from Rockefeller or that, to Uncle Joe Cannon, the incident represented the mendacity to which Roosevelt would stoop in his crusade for righteousness. The Speaker of the House insisted that "the Rockefeller telegrams originated in the brain of the President."

"I got the bill through by publishing those telegrams and concentrating the public attention on the bill," said Roosevelt subsequently, and he did. The House collapsed and passed the measure, with all of the administration amendments, on February 10, by 251 to 10. The Senate rushed it through on the following day.

Technically, Roosevelt had not told the whole truth when he instructed the correspondents to state, "on high authority," that Rockefeller had been sending telegrams. Mr. Hearst's New York *American* offered the first proof, however, that his charges were substantially correct. It published a telegram from Archbold of Standard Oil to Senator

Matt Quay of Pennsylvania, dated February 6, 1903, which protested against "vexatious interference with the industrial life of the country." No telegram had been signed by Rockefeller himself, but Archbold was his man. The President, in using Rockefeller's name, had demonstrated again his sound grasp of public psychology. Archbold's name meant very little; Rockefeller personified the evil of the trusts.

Having won his victory for the people, Roosevelt did a characteristic thing. George B. Cortelyou, his private secretary, became Secretary of the Department of Commerce and Labor. James R. Garfield, a young man rapidly rising in the President's favor, was appointed Commissioner of the Bureau of Corporations. But the investigations and inquisitions so feared by business did not begin until after Election Day. At first, it was a very inoffensive body.

2

The perplexities which faced Roosevelt as he planned for 1904 must, at times, have seemed overwhelming. There was still the tariff, which McKinley had promised to revise. It was a dangerous issue and Roosevelt convinced himself that it was "one of expediency and not of morality. I doubt whether it would be best to make a reduction in the year preceding a Presidential election." He decided to let it alone. Similarly distasteful was currency reform. Speaker Cannon was pained to learn that "figures, statistics, schedules, all those things meant nothing" to the President. Beyond vague recommendations in his messages to Congress, Roosevelt avoided currency reform also.

Innumerable minor worries added to the pessimism which gripped the President regarding 1904. Under the administration of Henry C. Payne, whom he had appointed Postmaster General, had come to light long-standing frauds perpetrated by high officials of the Post Office Department. By October, 1903, twenty-nine individuals had been indicted, and Roosevelt was forced to announce that Perry Heath, secretary of the Republican National Committee, would be among the officials "prosecuted with all the vigor and resourcefulness of the government." At first hesitant, Roosevelt finally acted decisively in the postal frauds by appointing Charles J. Bonaparte as a special prosecutor. It was, however, an unfortunate affair; it placed the administration on the defensive when voicing the necessary demands for honesty in government.

Another vexation was the case of William A. Miller, who

was removed in May, 1903, from his civil service position under the Public Printer because he had been expelled from the International Brotherhood of Bookbinders. Roosevelt upheld the Civil Service Commission's ruling that this was not a valid reason for dismissal from the government service, and so was denounced as an enemy of organized labor. Still another, and in this instance Roosevelt's part was less creditable, arose when the Grand Army of the Republic demanded more liberal pension payments. Roosevelt surrendered. By executive order, he established pensions for all veterans, disabled or not, between 62 and 70 years old. The cost was about $5,000,000 a year.

No doubt can exist that Theodore Roosevelt, as the 1904 convention drew near, was playing politics in his own behalf. Expediency dictated certain of his appointments. One was James S. Clarkson of Iowa, whom Roosevelt, as Civil Service Commissioner, had scathingly denounced as a foe of the merit system. This Clarkson was; yet on April 17, 1902, the President chose him for surveyor of customs in New York.

"In politics," Roosevelt apologized privately, "we have to do a great many things that we ought not to do."

The function of Clarkson was to solidify Roosevelt sentiment among Negro Republicans in the South. This was a weak spot in the Roosevelt machine in 1902, for Mark Hanna still controlled the majority of these delegates. Through Clarkson, the President attested his opposition to the proposal to give to white Republicans the control of their party in Southern areas.

Roosevelt's tour across the country, undertaken to place his views before the people, began on April 1 and lasted until June 5, 1903. This, too, had its own special problems; a hunt in Colorado was to be one of the features of the trip. The President, always aware of possible public disapproval or mirth, did not propose to appear ridiculous. "I cannot afford to make a failure of it," he wrote four months before he started. "The knowledge of the way the amiable non-hunting public looks at a failure to get game makes me feel that I would like what our Southern friends call 'sure enough' information." In March, he asked whether it "would be possible to have the mountain lion region located in advance."

Even when an election did not confront him, Roosevelt was nervously anxious to appear in the best light as a hunter. Another expedition was organized for 1905, this time a bear hunt. It was essential, the President told a friend,

that the first bear must fall to my rifle. This sounds selfish, but you know the kind of talk there will be in the newspapers about such a hunt, and if I go it must be a success, and the success must come to me.

Custom frowned upon extensive campaigning by a President seeking re-election. In 1904, Roosevelt would be forced to remain rather inactive while his foes went forth to battle. It was for this reason that the trip in 1903 seemed so essential. The cheers and the crowds were fuel for his exuberance, and no less so were the occasional incidents that were irresistibly humorous. At Butte, Montana, he arrived to find a bitter quarrel in progress between two wings of the local Republican organization. Both demanded the honor and prestige of entertaining the President, and Roosevelt finally brought peace by arranging that one faction would manage the parade in the afternoon and the other a banquet at night. The mayor of Butte presided at the dinner.

. . . the Mayor led me in or, to speak more accurately, tucked me under one arm and lifted me partially off the ground so that I felt like one of those limp dolls with dangling legs carried around by small children. As soon as we got in the banquet hall and sat at the head of the table, the Mayor hammered lustily with the handle of his knife and announced, "Waiter, bring on the feed!" Then, in a spirit of pure kindliness, he added, "Waiter, pull up the shades and let the people see the President eat!" But to this I objected.

3

During the course of his coast-to-coast trip, Roosevelt had been able to outmaneuver Mark Hanna and to obtain the Republican national chairman's endorsement for the 1904 nomination. This was a source of gratification to the President, and he convinced himself that his conduct had been entirely ethical. Politically, it was a master stroke.

To Roosevelt, seeking a term in his "own right," the Ohio Senator was an ogre. Actually, Hanna had done nothing, since September, 1901, to thwart Roosevelt's hopes. He might have done a great deal. On the contrary, he assisted in the coal strike, in the Panama Canal matter, in irrigation and conservation legislation. He had even favored the creation of the Department of Commerce and Labor.

But Roosevelt, who preferred to personify the forces of evil if possible, made Mark Hanna the personification of the unrighteous elements which sought to reject him for 1904. He ignored Hanna's growing cordiality and the fact that the stubby little national chairman had swiftly revised his earlier belief that Roosevelt was wild and reckless. The President could think only of Hanna's refusal, in 1901, to pledge his support for 1904. Soon he became the center of a conspiracy on the part of the criminal rich.

Politics is fundamentally a hysterical calling. Roosevelt's fears, then, are understandable, even if without basis. Hanna repeatedly denied that he was a candidate for the nomination. He happened to be sincere, but he paid the penalty for the traditional hypocrisy of politicians. Conspirators were actually at work, but not precisely as Roosevelt believed. One of them was Senator Foraker, Hanna's unfriendly Ohio colleague, whom Roosevelt was soon to cast into oblivion. Foraker had ambitions; when he shaved he saw a face that would grace the White House in 1908. But he first had to replace Mark Hanna as the Republican leader of Ohio. On May 23, 1903, he summoned the correspondents to his Washington office. He mentioned obscure dispatches a week earlier stating that the Ohio state convention, due to meet in June, would decline to endorse Roosevelt. Foraker then issued a clever statement. Since the "issue is raised, it would be a mistake not to endorse him. I know little about the controversy in Ohio, but it is well-defined. It was precipitated by the friends of Senator Hanna."

This seemed innocuous, but it was not. Foraker, thereby, had vaulted lightly to a front seat in the Roosevelt bandwagon. Thereby his rival, Mark Hanna, had been left in the uncomfortable predicament of standing on the pavement while the wagon rumbled on to probable glory. Hanna had to say something, and he said the wrong thing. To an Associated Press correspondent, also on May 23, he denied that he had "anything to do with raising the question." Foraker had a right to make any endorsement he wished, but he thought it improper for the Ohio state convention, meeting in 1903, to assume the prerogatives of the national convention of 1904. The national chairman said that he was opposed to the adoption of a Roosevelt endorsement, but this was not due to any "personal desires or ambitions of my own." He was speaking as the head of the national committee.

At the same time, Hanna telegraphed to Roosevelt, who

was at Seattle, Washington, that the issue had "been forced upon me in a way which makes it necessary for me to oppose such a resolution. When you know all the facts, I am sure you will approve my course." This was a veiled reference to Foraker. Roosevelt, Hanna may have assumed, was familiar with Foraker's aspirations regarding the Ohio leadership and would understand Hanna's embarrassment. If he did, the President was singularly unkind. On May 25, at Walla-Walla, he said:

I have not asked any man for his support. I have had nothing whatever to do with raising the issue as to my endorsement. Sooner or later it was bound to arise, and, inasmuch as it has now arisen, of course those who favor my administration and nomination will endorse them, and those who do not will oppose them.

All this was not quite fair. The President did not make public the telegram of explanation he had received from Hanna. His challenge was based only on· the clumsily expressed statement that the Senator had given to the Associated Press. Roosevelt made it appear that Hanna was planning to oppose his nomination. The result, as the President must have foreseen, was humiliation for the national chairman. Hanna had no other course but retreat. On May 26, he telegraphed that he would not oppose action for Roosevelt by the Ohio state convention.

"This wordy city," murmured John Hay, "poisons men, who might be friends, against each other."

Happily, Roosevelt and Hanna came together again before the end. Hanna was sixty-six years old, and in poor health. On February 9, he fell seriously ill and physicians hurried in and out of the old Arlington Hotel where he lay. It became known that the national chairman had typhoid fever. "You and I are on the home stretch," he said weakly to Mrs. Hanna on February 8. He died on February 15, 1904. Had Roosevelt been faintly ashamed? He made, at all events, atonement at the end. They had exchanged brief notes, and Hanna was touched.

"May you soon be with us again, old fellow, as strong and as vigorous as ever," the President wrote on February 5. On the day after his death, Roosevelt penned an obituary:

Hanna's death is very sad. No man had larger traits. I think that not merely I but the whole party and the whole country have reason to be grateful to him for the way, after I came into office, he resolutely declined to be drawn into the position which a smaller man of meaner cast would have taken; that is, the position of antagonizing public policies if I was identified with them.

4

The nomination of Roosevelt had been a moral certainty since the start of 1903. After the victory over Hanna in May and finally, of course, when the Senator died, even a pessimistic President could find little cause for gloom. A week or so later, Cabot Lodge was able to relay information that J. P. Morgan and other supposedly hostile financiers would surely swing to his support.

Roosevelt had done his share to obtain their benedictions. He had softened his expressions of wrath regarding greedy corporations. He offered to appoint Frick of the United States Steel Corporation to the Isthmian Canal Commission. He submitted a draft of his third annual message to James Stillman, president of the National City Bank, and promised to make changes in the passages referring to the currency question. He even invited Morgan himself to the White House.

"I should like very much to see you to talk over certain financial matters," he wrote him on October 8, 1903.

The Standard Oil Company was the one outcast. This worried the officials of that corporation a good deal; Roosevelt would almost certainly be in the White House until 1909. They communicated again with the faithful Congressman Sibley, who told Archbold that Roosevelt believed Standard Oil antagonistic toward him. On the contrary, said Archbold, "I have always been an admirer of President Roosevelt and have read every book he ever wrote, and have them, in the best bindings, in my library." This gave Sibley an idea. He knew the weakness of all authors to flattery. He would mention Archbold's literary acumen to Roosevelt, he said, and would ask for an audience for the Standard Oil official.

"The 'book business' fetched down the game at the very first shot," he wrote in jubilation to Archbold on January 6, 1904. "You had better read, at least, the titles of those volumes to refresh your memory before you come over."

The President, however, was less gullible than Mr. Sibley believed. He contrived to keep separate his roles of President and author. Soon after Election Day the Bureau of Corporations awoke into life and began its investigation of the petroleum industry.

"Darkest Abyssinia," testified the outraged Archbold, "never saw anything like the course of treatment we received at the hands of the administration following Mr. Roosevelt's election in 1904."

Roosevelt's third message to Congress, on December 7, 1903, is further evidence of the caution that marked the precampaign months. American prosperity was painted in brilliant hues. The President told of the "sane and conservative lines" on which all legislation affecting business had been framed. He warned that organized labor would be held just as strictly to the law as capital. He avoided a definite statement on currency.

"The President," said the *Wall Street Journal* on December 8, 1903, "makes clear that his policy, neither in intention or fact, is directed against wealth. We admire the courage and strength of the President."

A shade inopportunely, in view of the campaign, the Supreme Court upheld the Government in the Northern Securities suit on March 14, 1904. From the angle of popular approval, the decision was an asset. But when the New York *World* declared that Roosevelt would be loved "for the enemies he has made," the administration forces must have been slightly worried. These "enemies" would soon be called upon to supply the funds for a Republican victory. In 1896 and 1900 they had answered in generous measure the appeals from Mark Hanna.

5

A successor to Mark Hanna as national chairman had to be selected, and Roosevelt proposed to do it himself. Matt Quay of Pennsylvania had passed to his reward in May, 1904. With Penrose, Quay had controlled Pennsylvania absolutely, and it was this, rather than personal grief, which caused Roosevelt to pay tribute to him as "my staunch and loyal friend." The message gave rise to rumors, however, that Penrose would manage Roosevelt's campaign. The rumors were without foundation. It soon became known that the new national chairman would be George B. Cortelyou, Secretary of the Department of Commerce and Labor.

"The man who was to run this campaign had to be a man of my type," Roosevelt later explained.

That Roosevelt could insist upon Cortelyou was an indication of his hold upon the Republican party. To the Old Guard, their ranks thinned by the deaths of Hanna and Quay, the appointment was a blow. The New York *Times* sarcastically echoed their views when it said editorially on May 28, 1904, that "we doubt whether Mr. Cortelyou is sufficiently imposing to work a trust magnate up to the contribution pitch." This was a glaring underestimate of Cortelyou's ability.

The President gave minute attention to preparation for the Chicago convention. Root was to be temporary chairman and make the keynote address. Roosevelt directed him to emphasize "Panama in all its details," the Northern Securities suit, Cuban reciprocity, the Alaska boundary, Cuban independence, the administration of the Philippines, the army and navy, irrigation and forestry, the Department of Commerce and Labor, the Open Door in China, the "Venezuelan business," and the administration's "striking enforcement of the Monroe Doctrine." But the tariff, he added, required careful thought:

> I do not want to promise the impossible, and I have to recognize a tendency in the majority to "stand pat," while in a large and fervent minority there is a growing insistence upon a reduction of duties.

It was a dull convention. Roosevelt was unanimously chosen on June 23. On the same day Charles W. Fairbanks of Indiana was nominated for Vice-President, not because anybody wanted him, particularly, but because, as Roosevelt told Dr. Butler of Columbia, "who in the name of Heaven else is there?"

The platform adopted at Chicago was the usual specious broadside, which praised the Republican party for its defense of the gold standard, and which again neglected to mention the fight that Grover Cleveland had made for sound currency. It gave the impression that the Spanish War had been fought by Republicans alone. It told of the administration's record on trust control, army reorganization, and all other matters that would redound to the welfare of America. The Republican party was the guardian of prosperity. The tariff policy of the Democrats would bring disaster. It was not an inspiring document, but it was Roosevelt's own.

The Democrats, meeting at St. Louis and remembering Bryan with pain, bowed to conservatism with an obeisance almost as profound as that of their rivals. Alton B. Parker, presiding judge of the New York Court of Appeals, was chosen on July 9. He was a gentleman of substance and intelligence. But the nomination for Vice-President was one of the strangest in the history of political parties. Henry G.

Davis of West Virginia, who was eighty-two years old, was selected in the apparent belief that he would make a large campaign contribution. He did not even do that. The Democratic platform called for gradual revision downward in tariff schedules. It asked for added powers for the Interstate Commerce Commission. It said nothing at all about the gold standard, and this alarmed August Belmont and Thomas Fortune Ryan, who were almost the only sources for Democratic campaign funds. The result was a telegram from Parker to the convention in which he said that the gold standard was "firmly and irrevocably established," that he would "act accordingly."

The nomination of Parker was based on the theory that the financiers of the nation would swing toward him and away from the potentially dangerous, if momentarily cautious, Roosevelt. It was a false assumption. "We are going to support Roosevelt emphatically," was the announcement from J. Ogden Armour of the Chicago packers. "I hope Roosevelt will win," said Andrew Carnegie. "I am convinced that Republican rule is best for the country."

6

Roosevelt, being President, could not go on the stump. Judge Parker, whose only chance of victory lay in a vigorous attack, would have preferred to issue judicial statements from his home. The result was a campaign as dull as the national conventions that preceded it. Then, a New York newspaper owner injected life, and lethargy vanished. On October 1, Joseph Pulitzer published an editorial over his name in the New York *World*. Eight columns long, it said that the Bureau of Corporations had been in existence for 583 days and had done nothing. Why had the President placed Mr. Cortelyou, who was head of the department in which the bureau operated, in the post of national chairman? Did not the corporations

that are pouring money into your campaign chests assume that they are buying protection? It makes little difference how guarded or explicit Mr. Cortelyou's promises may be. Supposing, Mr. President, even at this late day, you were to give the country a little of that real publicity you once favored by telling it— 1, how much has the beef trust contributed to Mr. Cortelyou? 2, how much has the paper trust contributed to Mr. Cortelyou? 3, how much has the coal trust contributed to Mr. Cortelyou? 4, how much has the sugar trust contributed to Mr. Cortelyou? 5, how much has the oil trust contributed to Mr. Cortelyou? 6, how much has the tobacco trust contributed to Mr. Cortelyou? 7, how much has the steel trust contributed to Mr. Cortelyou? 8, how much have the national banks contributed to Mr. Cortelyou? 9, how much has the insurance trust contributed to Mr. Cortelyou? 10, how much have the six great railroads contributed to Mr. Cortelyou?

For three weeks Parker said nothing, and Roosevelt was equally silent. On October 22, 1904, Daniel S. Lamont, Secretary of the Treasury under Cleveland, called on the Democratic candidate. "It is all underwritten and there is no show for you," he said, and described a conference in New York City at which a group of financiers had agreed that Roosevelt's election was essential. They would supply the money. This information goaded Parker into tardy action. On October 24, he incorporated part of the *World's* indictment in a speech. He had worked himself up to attacking "Cortelyouism" by the night of October 31. On the following day, he repeated the questions compiled by Pulitzer, but on November 3 he made a serious error. He described the corporation donations as "blackmail" and intimated that they were made in return for silence regarding damaging facts gathered by the Bureau of Corporations. This gave Roosevelt an opportunity to reply. He denied the less demonstrable accusation that money had been extorted, not the charge that corporations had given large sums:

That contributions have been made is not the question at issue. Mr. Parker's accusations against Mr. Cortelyou and me are monstrous. If true they would brand both of us forever with infamy; and inasmuch as they are false, heavy must be the condemnation of the man making them. The assertion that Mr. Cortelyou had any knowledge, gained while in an official position, whereby he was enabled to secure and did secure any contributions from any corporation is a falsehood. The assertion that there has been any blackmail, direct or indirect, by Mr. Cortelyou or by me is a falsehood. The assertion that there has been made any pledge or promise or that there has been any understanding as to future immunities or benefits, in recognition of any contribution from any source is a wicked falsehood.

The retort thundered through the land; Parker had no further ammunition. On November 8, Roosevelt won overwhelmingly. Even Missouri went into the Republican column, and Parker carried no state outside of the Solid South. Roosevelt had 336 electoral votes to 140 for Parker, and a popular majority of 2,540,067. In his ecstasy of joy that night, he issued a statement that was to cause him poignant regret in the years to come:

On the 4th of March next I shall have served three and a half years and this constitutes my first term. The wise custom which limits the President to two terms regards the substance and not the form; and under no circumstances will I be a candidate for or accept another nomination.

Either Roosevelt closed his eyes to the facts deliberately, or elaborate precautions were taken to keep him in ignorance of the forces that worked for his election in 1904. The evidence indicates that his knowledge was slight. The "course followed," he insisted in March, 1906, had been "in every respect right." The President obviously realized that the big corporations were contributing. He contented himself, at first, with assurances from Cortelyou that "I would be elected without a promise or a pledge of any kind, expressed or implied, to any corporation or individual." On October 26, the President instructed his national chairman to return, if the donation had already been made, a rumored gift of $100,000 from Standard Oil. He reiterated this on the following day.

Those were halcyon days for a campaign manager. No law required him to report on contributions. No law forbade corporations to give as much as they pleased. It was the invariable custom to burn all ledgers or records. The first hint of what really happened in 1904 came a year later when Charles Evans Hughes, in his life insurance investigations in New York, discovered that the New York Life had contributed $48,000 to the Republican National Committee. Contributions of about the same amount had come from the Mutual and the Equitable companies. On April 2, 1907, a few more facts leaked out. E. H. Harriman said he had donated $50,000 and had collected $200,000 more.

The full extent of the corporation donations did not become known until 1912. The Progressive campaign was at its height; Roosevelt faced the enmity of the regular Republicans as well as of the Democrats. Cornelius N. Bliss, who had been treasurer of the Republican National Committee in 1904, was dead. But a Senate committee questioned nearly everyone else. It became known that seventy-two and a half per cent of the $2,195,000 collected had come from corporations. Mr. Morgan testified that he had given $150,000 in cash. Edward T. Stotesbury, whose Philadelphia bank was associated with Morgan's, had collected $165,795.50.

When Cortelyou was summoned by the committee, he had only the vaguest recollections regarding 1904. He had never heard of a contribution from Harriman. It had been reported to him that James Hazen Hyde of the Equitable gave something. He knew nothing but rumors with respect to Standard Oil. He did not remember the banks in which the funds were deposited, and said that Bliss had destroyed the accounts. He could not recall whether Morgan or Frick gave anything, but he remembered $10,000 from Carnegie. His assurance to Roosevelt that no pledges had been given in return for cash had been made, Cortelyou admitted, when he had not seen the committee's books. Bliss had never reported to him on the donors.

The testimony before the Clapp Committee was endless. Among the many star witnesses before the Senate committee in 1912 was Archbold, and his testimony made it clear that he had done much more than familiarize himself with Roosevelt's writings. On October 25, 1904, when rumors were current of Standard Oil interest in the campaign, a statement was issued by S. C. T. Dodd, of counsel. It was not true, this said, that the company was interested in "any business not directly related with and necessary to the petroleum trade"; nor had "Mr. John D. Rockefeller or any other officer taken part in securing the nomination of any of the candidates for office."

If one may classify politics as a business directly related to the petroleum trade, which it was, the first part of this statement was true. So was the second, in so far as nominations were concerned. Mr. Archbold, testifying in August, 1912, said that a total of $125,000 had been given to the Republican National Committee in 1904 "in currency" on behalf of the Standard Oil Company. He swore that the money had been solicited by Treasurer Bliss. He had understood that Roosevelt knew all about it. But the President had not, in fact, been informed. His first knowledge that his order against Standard Oil money had been disobeyed came in September, 1908. After Archbold had testified, Roosevelt quoted an interview Bliss had given in 1911 pointing out that "his [Roosevelt's] orders were ignored, as this was something about which I brooked no interference." Campaign managers, and particularly campaign treasurers, have often found it wise to guard their candidate from the true facts of party finances.

Chapter VIII

THE IMPERIAL YEARS BEGIN

✳

On the afternoon of March 3, 1905, Roosevelt did not conceal his impatience that the inaugural ceremony was still almost twenty-four hours distant. The President was extremely happy, and orders were issued that everyone who called was to be shown into his study without delay. So the day wore on, with a bouncing, effusive Chief Executive slapping his visitors on the back. To one or two, who were his close friends, Roosevelt is supposed to have declared:

"Tomorrow I shall come into my office in my own right. Then watch out for me!"

It is really unimportant whether he made such a statement; it represented his viewpoint accurately. Soon after Election Day, suspicion had dawned that Roosevelt had no scruples against biting the plump hands which had fed him during the campaign. The end of 1904 had brought signs of a new independence. Roosevelt's public utterances were less cautious. It was rumored that the Bureau of Corporations would start innumerable investigations. Even the tariff might be revised.

Business breathed more easily, however, when Roosevelt's annual message was read to Congress on December 6, 1904. It decided that nothing in the message was particularly dangerous. In retrospect, the optimism seems hardly justified. The hints that labor was entitled to certain rights were exceedingly pallid. But the men of vision who guided the nation's industries failed to note Roosevelt's growing conviction of the necessity for Federal action to regulate corporations, his insistence that it was "an absurdity to expect to eliminate the abuses by state action." Regarding railroad regulation, he said that he did not favor fixing of rates, but he added the disquieting phrase that this was his opinion "at present." He referred to the possibility of workmen's compensation laws and of the need for eliminating child labor abuses; two reforms that were to be bitterly opposed by associations of manufacturers. He asked Congress to consider supervision of insurance transactions. He recommended "a law against bribery and corruption in Federal elections," a law that was to make campaign contributions from friendly corporations far more difficult.

The fourth annual message did not, it is true, specifically urge all these reforms, nor were all of them new. But questions were again raised which well-bred people preferred to ignore. Then, in January, 1905, the President addressed a dinner of the Union League Club in Philadelphia. The beginning of Roosevelt's speech was innocuous, a tribute to the principles of Abraham Lincoln, but he thereupon departed from reassuring platitudes:

> . . . the great development of industrialism means that there must be an increase in the supervision exercised by the Government over business-enterprise. Such men as the members of this club should lead in the effort to secure proper supervision. Neither this people nor any other free people will permanently tolerate the use of the vast power conferred by vast wealth without lodging somewhere in the Government the still higher power of seeing that this power is used for and not against the interests of the people as a whole.

President Roosevelt said the business of the country was now carried on "in a way of which the founders of our Constitution could by no possibility have had any idea." Then came the threat that an amendment to the Constitution would have to be passed if the courts ruled against Federal regulation of corporations. As for the railroads, "this control must come through the National Government." Doubtless it would be abused, "but this is only another way of saying that any governmental power, from taxation down, can and will be abused if the wrong men get control of it."

Less than two months had passed since the annual message had been read to Congress and had been received with calm. This was different. That night in Chicago the speech was praised as "perfectly sound" by William Jennings Bryan, the specter whose presence in politics was anathema to Union League Club members everywhere.

Just what some of them were thinking was revealed in a letter from the observant Sibley of Pennsylvania to Archbold on March 7, 1905. It expressed alarm over the situation at Washington; Mr. Sibley warned that there was to be an extra session of Congress the following October at which tariff revision and other obnoxious measures would be taken up. All in touch with conditions at Washington agreed that the thing to do was "to start a backfire." He offered a constructive plan:

An efficient literary bureau is needed, not for a day but [for] permanent and healthy control of the *Associated Press and other kindred avenues.* It will cost money, but it will be the cheapest in the end and can be made self supporting. No man values public opinion or fears it as much as Theodore Roosevelt. No man seeks popularity as much as he. Mild reproof or criticism of his policy would nearly paralyze him. Today he hears only the cries of the rabble and thinks it is public sentiment.

2

Four years previously, when Roosevelt had become Vice-President, the weather forecaster at Washington had promised that Mr. McKinley would enjoy the finest weather "ever experienced at the inauguration of a President." Unhappily for his optimism, rain fell throughout the ceremonies and the day was raw and cold. Consequently, in 1905 the forecaster was cautious. The outlook was for either "clear or cloudy weather." The rain gods were appeased at this concession to their power, so March 4 dawned fair, with Washington in a high state of excitement.

Roosevelt was loyal to his own. Eight years before, the Rough Riders had followed him up Kettle Hill. They had helped him blaze trails leading first to the governorship of New York and then, with the aid of fate, to the White House. Naturally, then, the Rough Riders supplied the principal motif at the inauguration in 1905. They made the streets echo with their yippings, roped an occasional Negro with their lariats as they thundered over the asphalt, and with great self-control kept their revolvers in their holsters.

In 1901, Roosevelt had been the center of attention and, although a mere Vice-President, had crowded McKinley from the role he properly should have played. In 1905, it was again a one-man performance, with the Rough Riders as exuberant supernumeraries. Somehow Roosevelt could abandon dignity on certain occasions and yet avoid being grotesque. On March 4, 1905, it seemed entirely appropriate for him to stand up in his carriage as it moved toward the Capitol. People expected him to be very red in the face, to shout above the turmoil that the detachment of Rough Riders was to be placed immediately beside him in the procession. They would have been disappointed had he failed to wave enthusiastically as the carriages passed between cheering thousands in the streets.

Roosevelt could be dignified enough when the moment

came for dignity. He took the office of President very seriously and was quick to resent the most unintentional indication of disrespect. The pedantic Cabot Lodge had labored with the President over his inaugural address and had finally given his approval. He had suggested "a few verbal changes because in such utterance every word is worth pondering."

The words Roosevelt had written with such care were swept away on the cool March breeze over the heads of thousands who had come to see, not to hear. They were simple and dignified words, without sensationalism and without merit enough to make them remembered ten days after they had been spoken. The President stepped out from the Rough Rider guard of honor at his back, looked down; and in front of his eyes swam the words, "Be ye doers." The oath of office was taken. He began to speak.

First he gave thanks "to the Giver of Good" for the blessings that had come to a new country. "It would be our own fault if we failed," he said. The success that had already come "should cause in us no feeling of vainglory. We have duties to others and duties to ourselves; and we can shirk neither." Then Roosevelt expressed his conception of an ideal from which, as President, he sometimes departed but to which he sincerely subscribed. It was his better self who spoke:

Toward all other nations, large and small, our attitude must be one of cordial and sincere friendship. We must show not only in our words but in our deeds that we are earnestly desirous of securing their good will by acting toward them in a spirit of just and generous recognition of their rights. But justice and generosity in a nation, as in an individual, count most when shown not by the weak but by the strong.

Before the President had finished speaking, the crowds in the Capitol plaza had started to hurry for points of vantage from which to watch the second act of the show staged every four years. This was the parade, and once more Roosevelt played the part which best suited the popular imagination. Reserve disappeared as the parade began in the afternoon. He watched with eager glee as the marchers appeared. First there was a detachment of Puerto Rican and Filipino troops, brought to Washington for the ceremonies, and the President called out that they hardly looked to be the victims of imperialism, as his critics had charged. "See the slaves rejoicing in their shackles!" he cried.

The President was alternately amused and delighted. He made no effort to suppress his grins as the nonmilitary marshals, wearing top hats and frock coats, rode nervously past on livery-stable hacks. The day was Roosevelt's day. He had been a hero, and now he was an elected President. He was a young man—not yet forty-seven years old—to hold the highest office in the land. He was young and bubbling, and when a band swung by to "There'll Be a Hot Time in the Old Town Tonight," he was on his feet once more. He had heard the melody many times around bivouacs in Cuban jungles. The President had heard it rendered, with variations, by German bands during campaign tours in small Minnesota towns. Perspiring bandmasters in the Bad Lands rehearsed their amateur musicians in its cadences, and the song had reverberated among the buttes and arroyos of the prairies.

But music and cheers did not reach the recesses of the Capitol where, until noon on March 4, 1905, the Senate was busy wrecking the President's legislative program.

3

"I am having my own troubles here," Roosevelt had complained to Spring Rice, "and there are several eminent statesmen at the other end of Pennsylvania Avenue whom I would gladly lend to the Russian government, if they care to expend them as bodyguards for Grand Dukes wherever there was a likelihood of dynamite bombs being exploded."

It had been a lame-duck Congress, to be replaced in December, 1905, by the members elected in the Roosevelt landslide in November, 1904. Its conduct during the closing days of the session made Roosevelt's homicidal yearnings understandable, although he had expected nothing better. As adjournment drew near, it was apparent that his annual message in December, his address to the Union League Club, and the numerous private appeals he had made, were all futile. Speaker Cannon had remarked at the start of the session that Congress would "pass the appropriation bills and mark time," and this it had done. Congress disregarded pleas for economy—which Roosevelt, to be sure, never took seriously himself—and the appropriations were likely to result in an increased deficit at the end of the fiscal year. The President did, however, receive authorization for the two new battleships needed for the continued strengthening of the fleet.

The Senate of the Fifty-eighth Congress went out in defiance. Its members would have been wiser had they spent more of their time circulating among the crowds on the streets and in the hotel lobbies. The Old Guard was marked for death, but no murmurings of the whirlwind penetrated the walls where it sat and monotonously, as bill after bill was called up for vote, smothered the Roosevelt program.

In actual fact, Roosevelt was not too far ahead of the Old Guard which had momentarily wrecked his program. Nor was there, in 1905, any outward and easily discerned manifestation of public discontent. On the contrary, the Republican party had every reason for arrogant confidence. In the Fifty-ninth Congress there would be ample Republican majorities. In 1905 the United States was heady with the wine of prosperity and the prophets proclaimed, as prophets always do, that this blessing would last forever. Even the farmers were happy, for their crops had a market value of $3,000,000,000 and their orders for machinery were elating the directors of the International Harvester Company in Chicago. In science, there had been definite advances. During 1904, vessels throughout the world were installing the new wireless device. The Wright brothers had raised their flimsy kite from the ground in December, 1903.

Sudden prosperity is never wholly healthy, however, and Roosevelt, although fundamentally conservative and in sympathy with the aspirations of the nation's industrialists, knew more about certain hidden forces than did his enemies. He did not yearn, in 1905, for a new economic order. He wanted to preserve the old. By January, 1906, he was writing that there "had been an era of overconfidence and speculation. Sooner or later we shall undoubtedly have reaction." He became increasingly nervous as the muckrakers of 1905 and 1906—Upton Sinclair, Ida Tarbell, Lincoln Steffens, and the rest—began their exposures. Roosevelt thought they could "do nothing effective" because they lacked intelligence. Some were "Socialists, some are merely lurid sensationalists; but they are all building up a revolutionary feeling." As early as February, 1905, Roosevelt felt "that the growth of the Socialistic party in this country" was "far more ominous than any populist or similar movement in the past."

The Old Guard, representing the industrialists and the financiers, and Roosevelt desired the same end—the preservation of the status quo. Their paths diverged because the Old Guard had no apprehensions and no fears; in smug complacency it was satisfied merely to let things drift. The

President, so often torn by anxiety for the future, was led to radicalism by his desire to perpetuate the existing order. Specifically, he was led to adopt a considerable part of the program of William Jennings Bryan and the Democratic party.

"Somehow or other," he wrote Sir George Trevelyan, the historian, on March 9, 1905, "we shall have to work out methods of controlling the big corporations without paralyzing the energies of the business community."

He was to accomplish a good deal, with the aid of once-hated Bryanism, toward that end. Had the Old Guard learned, missing all else, that Roosevelt had public confidence behind him, that his imperial years lay just ahead, there might have been no Progressive party in 1912. Taft would have been re-elected in all probability, and Woodrow Wilson might never have guided the nation through its years of peril, a task for which T.R. and the Republican party believed themselves far better qualified.

4

The spiritual union with Bryan, which Roosevelt never acknowledged, was a subject for comment at the beginning of 1905. Both the President and his former foe attended the Gridiron Dinner in Washington that January, and during the course of the evening the toastmatser suggested that a debate might be arranged between them.

"What's the use?" called out a member of the club from one of the tables. "They're both on the same side."

Ultimately Bryan arose to speak and said he had seen the President abstract plank after plank from the Democratic platform. But Roosevelt was equal to the occasion. He pointed out, with entire accuracy, that the good things in the platform were useless in Mr. Bryan's possession, since he would never be in a position to put them into effect.

Roosevelt was curiously intolerant toward the Commoner, considering the political ideas he borrowed. He said in 1906 that Bryan was "a kindly, well-meaning soul, but cheap and shallow." He had all the vices of Thomas Jefferson, "and Jefferson's nervous fear of doing anything that may seem to be unpopular with the rank and file of the people." This harshness was born of apprehension on Roosevelt's part that Bryan might still come into power. This dreadful possibility was to return, but in 1905 no apparent reason for it existed and the President could afford to be magnanimous even to the point of receiving Bryan at the White House on January 21, 1905. The Democratic leader said, as he left, that they had discussed many things, that it had "been a pleasure to commend his attitude."

Bryan's approval of Roosevelt had antedated the Union League Club speech at Philadelphia. On January 11, 1905, he addressed the General Assembly of Indiana and promised that he would "recommend the defeat of every Democrat who stands for renomination if he opposes President Roosevelt's efforts to regulate the railroads." As preparations were made, that summer, for the fight over railroad legislation there came still another pledge of support.

"The Democrats," Bryan assured Roosevelt solemnly, "are citizens first and Democrats afterwards. Stand by your guns."

Without Democratic support and the assistance of the insurgent group in his own party, Roosevelt would never have effected as much of his program as he did. He was to follow, more or less consistently, the policy of recoiling in horror from the radical ideas of the Democrats, then adopting them with slight modifications, and finally condemning, as obstructionists, those who opposed his adaptations or called them dangerous. By 1912, when Roosevelt found himself standing at Armageddon, an idea or two from the Socialist portfolio had crept quietly in among the sound, sane, and conservative principles which Theodore Roosevelt had made his own.

No political crystal gazing could discern with accuracy the personal strength that Roosevelt was to win during 1905 and 1906, the years that were the pinnacle of his career. John Morley, who said that Roosevelt was "an interesting combination of St. Vitus and St. Paul," was quick to explain that this had not been said in disparagement.

"Do you know the two most wonderful things I have seen in your country?" he added. "Niagara Falls and the President of the United States, both great wonders of nature!"

He was more in the public eye, not merely in the United States but in the whole world, than any other man. Emperors sought his advice and kings obeyed his will. Hardly a European power refrained, at one time or another during those years, from attempts to obtain his backing. He disabused the American businessman of his conviction that divine right had passed from the throne to the counting room. His popularity survived a panic, business depression, and unemployment. Then he made the incredible error of dictating the choice of a successor in the White House. The Roosevelt flame burned low, then bright, then dim once more. It finally went out; while the Princeton professor, whom he hated more than he had ever hated any man, watched with calm, cold malice as it vanished.

Perhaps the flame had never burned so brightly as toward the close of 1905. In the fall of that year Roosevelt went on a long tour through the South. He praised the Confederacy, where once he had damned its leaders as traitors. The thousands who had come to cheer the President remained to cheer Roosevelt, and the correspondent of the Washington *Star*, who was on the journey, telegraphed in amazement of gossip at Richmond that Roosevelt might be nominated for President in 1908 on the Democratic ticket. Sentimentality over Roosevelt's Southern lineage, which had been mentioned in most of his speeches, was partly responsible:

> Wherever the President's visit is discussed you will hear men who believed in and fought for the Confederate cause speak of him with the affection of a comrade. One would suppose that the President himself fired the last two shots from the *Alabama* instead of his uncle. Mr. Roosevelt's relationship with a Confederate officer is accepted as practically equal with having fought for the cause himself.

The article, if he read it, must have entertained Marse Henry Watterson of the Louisville *Courier-Journal*, who was devoted to Theodore Roosevelt and wrote editorials questioning his sanity.

Chapter IX

IMPERIAL YEARS

The old sets could not yet be discarded as the inauguration was being held in 1905. Roosevelt was not finished with his role as the Conscience of Big Business and he was still to chastise the railroads and the Standard Oil Company. A vaster stage was being prepared, however. The President had already appeared on it, in a minor skit or two. This was his first full-length drama. Against such varied backgrounds as the Russo-Japanese War and turbulent

Morocco, he would now tread the boards with Wilhelm II, with Edward VII, with Czar Nicholas; and with premiers, foreign ministers, and diplomats. He was to hear, only half recognizing it, the march of the armies that nine years later would engage in the most terrible of wars until another Roosevelt would command a second one.

Roosevelt was not fully aware of all the forces behind the tangled diplomacy of Europe and the Far East. At times he undoubtedly jeopardized the safety of his own country. The extraordinary thing, however, is that he did so well. His motive was not primarily altruistic. He viewed the United States, with intelligence, as no longer isolated but a member of the family of nations. America's future would be profoundly affected were either Russia or Japan to become the undisputed master of the Pacific. And because the fate of the Far East rested with Europe, the destiny of the United States was concerned, too, with the relative strength of Germany, France, Russia, and England.

Behind the ornate phrases of statesmanship lie facts. As yet there has been no war over the polar regions, although their potential for danger has been vastly heightened by the age of flight. If Korea and Manchuria had been wildernesses, they would have constituted no menace to peace. But Germany, Russia, France, and England were watching their commercial possibilities; this was the fact behind the diplomacy and the fighting. The United States, too, had become interested in this trade. In brief, the United States demanded in China the Open Door—a fair field and no favor for all those who come to China to trade. Secretary of State Hay had so notified the powers of Europe in September 1899.

Roosevelt, as President, inherited the Open Door policy, but he had long pondered the relation of the United States to the Far East. Japan was the country which first alarmed him. His apprehension in 1897 that Hawaii would be seized will be recalled. Before long, however, Russia became the more dangerous enemy in his mind—he wished that Japan held Korea, to check the Czar. Thus early in Roosevelt's public career is seen the germ of the policy he ultimately followed.

For half a century, the basic policy of both Continental and British powers had been to pay debts, make concessions, and discharge obligations to neighboring nations in Europe by drawing demand notes on the foreign offices of the independent states of the Far East. Unhappy China, being weak, saw England, Germany, France, and Russia keep peace among themselves by bland agreements for the partition of her territory. They were contented enough. But Russia, which had merely "leased" Port Arthur, wanted more, a great deal more, and her ambitions clashed with those of Japan.

The Open Door had been accepted by all the powers concerned. Mr. Hay stated that the United States did not object to domination in Manchuria by any one power as long as our commerical interests were protected. Vice-President Roosevelt had again received a warning, in March, 1901, from Admiral Mahan. Neither the United States nor England, the admiral said, could halt the advance of Russia in China save through their navies. But if "the sea powers will require of China liberty of entrance for European *thought* as well as European commerce, China will be saved."

This confirmed Roosevelt's own convictions. But American public opinion was "dull on the subject of China." As the friction between Russia and Japan grew more acute and as war seemed possible, Mahan's advice must have lingered in his mind. He became President, and a dozen projects of the first importance occupied his time. In June, 1903, however, he expressed his anxiety over the Open Door in Manchuria.

"I do not intend to give way and I am year by year growing more confident that the country would back me in going to an extreme," he told Hay in July, 1903.

On February 8, 1904, the Japanese attacked the Russian fleet off Port Arthur without waiting for a declaration of war, as almost four decades later she would attack at Pearl Harbor. Two days later, in a letter to his oldest son, Roosevelt revealed that he had actually contemplated war with Russia and was well pleased that the Japanese torpedo boats had won a victory.

It has certainly opened most disastrously for the Russians, and their supine carelessness is well-nigh incredible. For several years Russia has behaved very badly in the Far East, her attitude toward all nations, including us, but especially toward Japan, being grossly overbearing. We had no sufficient cause for war with her. Yet I was apprehensive lest if she at the outset whipped Japan on the sea she might assume a position well-nigh intolerable toward us.

The President continued to find ground for satisfaction in the amazing victories of the Japanese forces which were "playing our game." "I think the Japanese will whip them handsomely," he wrote Hay. They were consistently doing so. Port Arthur fell in January, 1905. The great naval victory that May virtually ended the war. In the interim, Roosevelt was characteristically providing for the possibility that this country would go to the aid of Japan. Dispute had arisen over contraband on neutral ships, as such disputes invariably arise. If Russia seized an American vessel, the President said in a confidential note to the Secretary of State, his inclination was "to move our Asiatic Squadron northward with the intention of having our squadron bottle up the Vladivostok fleet." He ordered the Bureau of Navigation to make plans for such an emergency.

He was to shine, instead, as a man of peace. It was gratifying, but much less enjoyable.

2

The torpedo boats of Japan would not have attacked the Russian fleet on February 8, 1904, had it not been for the benevolent neutrality of the United States and for the alliance between England and Japan. The United States, Great Britain, and Japan had been enjoying a monopoly of foreign trade in Manchuria and so the obstructionist tactics of the Slavs principally injured these countries and gave them a common purpose. Protests had been made at various times; notably by Hay to Count Cassini, the Russian ambassador, in February, 1902. They had been unavailing.

The moral issues so dear to Roosevelt's heart in any problem must be discounted. Russia desired Manchurian commerce. Japan wished to control Korea. On January 30, 1902, a treaty between Japan and England was signed. This provided that Japan should have a free hand in the event of a war with Russia. If some other power, meaning France or Germany, came to Russia's assistance, Great Britain would throw the might of her navy into the balance for Japan. The treaty disclaimed aggression in Korea, but it tacitly acknowledged the pre-eminence of Japan in that tottering empire. Soon this was to be openly acknowledged by Great Britain. Soon Roosevelt, much less openly, was to go as far as a President of the United States could in negotiating a secret treaty with Japan which granted the same sphere of influence. Russia, with reason, saw Japan, the United States, and England in an alliance against her in the Far East.

This country was not really an ally, of course. The

American people may have had a sentimental sympathy toward Japan, a small nation attacking the giant Russian bear, but war in her behalf was unthinkable. Roosevelt had to be cautious in taking action very similar to that of Great Britain. The President could make no treaty with a foreign power. No draft was valid until the Senate had confirmed it. But as soon as the Russo-Japanese War began, Roosevelt confided to Spring Rice in July, 1905, he had "notified Germany and France in the most polite and discreet fashion that in the event of a combination against Japan I should promptly side with Japan and proceed to whatever length was necessary in her behalf."

If Russia had cause for apprehension so had the German Kaiser. His fears were to reach an acute stage when England and France quietly agreed in 1904 to the elimination of German interests in Morocco. They were to increase with the years. Wilhelm undoubtedly influenced the Czar in the Manchurian policy that led to the war. Among the strange contradictions of this involved period nothing is more curious than the Kaiser's attitude toward Russia. On the one hand, he indulged in purple dreams with "Nicky" and hoped for a coalition in which the Admiral of the Atlantic, as he styled himself, would work with the Admiral of the Pacific, as he christened the Czar, for the peace of mankind. For this purpose, he hoped that Nicky would win. On the other, however, he pondered the alliance between Russia and France. Nicky must not be too strong. A weakened Russia would minimize another danger to German safety, the Franco-Russian menace in Europe. Of the Kaiser's dream that Russia and Germany would form an alliance of their own, Roosevelt appears to have been unaware.

The seas through which Roosevelt steered were made perilous by the crosscurrents of which he knew very little. While the President of the United States, by inference, was conceding the rights of Japan in Korea, the Kaiser was expressing to the Czar his conviction that the Korean Empire, and also Manchuria, were properly the subject of Russian influence. Roosevelt was saved from possible disaster by his distrust of the Kaiser and by his irritation toward Russia. Specifically, he was prevented from accepting a proposal offered by Wilhelm.

This was extended immediately after Russo-Japanese hostilities had started in February, 1904, and it clearly demonstrated Germany's sympathy with Russia. Wilhelm suggested that the United States notify the various powers that the neutrality of China be respected, but he added the limitation that this should be "outside the sphere of military operations." Since the fighting was in Manchuria, that region could be dealt with as Russia saw fit when the war had ended. Apparently it was Hay, always suspicious of Germany, who realized the significance of the proposal. On February 16, 1904, Roosevelt wrote to Root:

Yes, it was on the suggestion of "Bill the Kaiser" that we sent out the note on the neutrality of China. But the insertion of the word, "entity," was ours. His suggestion was that he wanted us to guarantee the integrity of China south of the Great Wall which would have left Russia free to gobble up what she wanted. We changed the proposal by striking out the limitation, and Germany cheerfully acceded!

One purpose of the Kaiser was achieved. He partly, although not entirely, convinced Roosevelt that his intentions were for peace. There are indications, indeed, that through Von Sternberg Roosevelt was being swung further toward Germany's side as 1905 approached. The German ambassador had been able earlier to transmit to his imperial master encouraging reports of conversations at the White House.

"Should the President be re-elected," Specky reported, "he would like to go hand in hand with Germany in Eastern Asia." On another occasion he quoted Roosevelt as saying that "the only man I understand and who understands me is the Kaiser."

These reports greatly heartened the German Emperor, who had also been assured by Count von Bülow that "the President is a great admirer of Your Majesty and would like to rule the world hand in hand with Your Majesty, regarding himself as something in the nature of an American counterpart to Your Majesty."

Wilhelm, no doubt, placed rather too much faith in these less than accurate reports of Roosevelt's warmth. Four years later, the President compared himself and Wilhelm:

He is, of course, very jumpy and nervous and often does things which seem jumpy. But most people say that about me, whereas I never act except upon the most careful deliberation. I do admire him, very much as I would a grizzly bear.

3

If two thoughts in the back of Roosevelt's mind are recalled, his efforts to end the Russo-Japanese War will be most clearly understood. The first was his conviction that the safety of American interests in the Far East rested upon a balance of power between Russia and Japan. The second was his belief that of the two powers Russia was the more dangerous. His first thoughts of peace were by no means those of an impartial mediator. In July, 1904, he confided to Hay that the United States might be "of genuine service, if Japan wins out, in preventing interference to rob her of the fruits of her victory."

Japan amazed the world by her military and naval prowess. In January, 1905, Port Arthur fell and this was followed by the victory at Mukden. The last hope of Russia was her navy, and Roosevelt now began to wonder whether things had not gone too far. He was afraid that Japan might get "puffed up with pride and turn against us." "The Japanese have treated us well," he wrote on March 9, 1905. "What they will do to us hereafter, when intoxicated by their victory over Russia, is another question." The President then started active negotiations for peace and learned, to his distress and surprise, that Great Britain would do little to persuade her Japanese ally to consent to mediation.

The groundwork was being prepared in December, 1904. John Hay's health was failing; the assistance of the Secretary of State would not be available. The first essential, Roosevelt believed, was lines of communication through which he could deal with the governments of Europe and also with Russia and Japan. On the whole, Roosevelt was fortunate in having excellent channels through which to transmit his views. He felt he could trust Von Sternberg, the German ambassador, implicitly. Jules Jusserand, the new ambassador from France, was rapidly winning a place in Roosevelt's confidence equal to those of Von Sternberg and Spring Rice. Lloyd C. Griscom, the American minister to Japan, was a diplomat of discernment and experience. On the other hand, Roosevelt had developed a violent prejudice against Sir Mortimer Durand, the British ambassador, which appears to have had slight basis. He distrusted, and with reason, Count Cassini. The President's first task was to correct these defects.

"Unfortunately," he wrote Springy, "there is no one in your Embassy here to whom I can speak with even reasonable fullness. I wish to Heaven you would come over, if only for a week or two."

Spring Rice was reluctant to undertake the mission,

since it would reflect upon Durand, whom he liked and respected. On January 13, 1905, however, Roosevelt wrote Hay that Spring Rice was coming and wanted to stay with Henry Adams, his old friend.

The other break in the line of communications was Russia. On December 26, 1904, the President notified George von L. Meyer, who had been a class ahead of him at Harvard and was now ambassador to Italy, that he would be transferred to St. Petersburg, where "I want some work done." He would be able to confer with Spring Rice who was attached to the British embassy at the Russian capital and from whom, Roosevelt added, "I have gained better information than from any of our own people abroad, save only Harry White."

Some time in January President Roosevelt intimated through these emissaries, that he was ready to extend his good offices. At about this same time, T.R. said, he had "privately and unofficially advised" the Czar to sue for peace. Meyer made a trip to Berlin and received fresh assurance from the Kaiser that he still opposed the partition of China. He conferred with Spring Rice at St. Petersburg and learned that France, Russia's ally, believed it futile for the war to go on. On April 13, 1905, Meyer described to Roosevelt an audience with the Czar and that monarch's evasive reaction to a message from the United States offering to serve as the agent of peace.

It was obvious at Washington that the time for negotiations had not arrived. Russia was pinning her last hope on the navy. Japan saw further military glory and a cash indemnity ahead. In April, 1905, Roosevelt departed on a hunting trip in the West, explaining he had "left Taft sitting on the lid," as Acting Secretary of State, and that everything would be taken care of.

4

"I do not much admire the Senate," the President had complained in connection with his Santo Domingo treaty, "because it is such a helpless body when efficient work for good is to be done."

In his activities as mediator between Russia and Japan, Roosevelt had no such embarrassing handicap. "On all of these matters," he told his daughter Alice, referring to the peace endeavors, "I have had to proceed without any advice or help." The President did not lack either courage or initiative, perhaps because he did not appreciate the degree to which he might involve the United States in the affairs of Europe. While Roosevelt was hunting in Colorado, Premier Théophile Delcassé of France had been discussing the possibility of peace with the Japanese minister to Paris, Monotno. On April 18, 1905, Acting Secretary of State Taft communicated to Roosevelt Delcassé's belief that the war would end if Japan would abandon her demands for an indemnity from Russia. In this instance, Japan replied that the terms had best be discussed by the two belligerents without interference, but disavowed any "intention to close the door to friendly offices exerted purely for the purpose of bringing the belligerents together."

Roosevelt replied that he agreed with this view, and several additional messages were exchanged between Japan's representative and the President before he returned to Washington. To the President's suggestion for an interview between Cassini and Takahira, the Japanese minister to the United States, however, the response was negative. In a dispatch on May 2, 1905, Takahira said that in his opinion an indemnity from Russia, while justified, could not be collected without prolonging the war, a course that would probably cost more than the indemnity would be worth. The significance of these communications lies in the fact that Roosevelt, by obvious choice of Japan, was to be the mediator. The preference of the Japanese is understandable. The German Kaiser, naturally, also preferred to have Roosevelt serve as mediator. France was Germany's enemy, a dangerous one, with the Moroccan crisis arising.

The attempts to end the war prior to the naval battle on May 27, 1905, failed. Roosevelt, however, had formulated what he believed to be fair terms. They offer further evidence of the President's partiality toward Japan. That country was to be given a protectorate over Korea, "which has shown its utter unability to stand by itself." It should succeed to Russia's rights (the leasehold) in and around Port Arthur. It should agree to restore Manchuria to China. Between February and July, 1905, Roosevelt went to the very threshold of a secret agreement with Japan for the absorption of Korea. "Cassini is now having a fit," the President wrote Hay on May 6, "about Taft stopping at Japan on his way to the Philippines." The Secretary of War left Washington, ostensibly to use his influence and sunny nature to iron out some difficulties in the Philippine Islands. On July 29, an extraordinary cablegram was received at Washington from Taft, a cable that would have caused a sensation and doubtless ended the efforts toward peace had it become public. On July 27, 1905, Taft had seen Count Katsura, the Japanese Premier. He reported their conversation in detail.

Regarding the Philippine Islands, Count Katsura said, his country had no aspirations; the talk in America of a yellow peril was absurd. The purpose of Japan was peace in the Far East and the best way in which this could be achieved was through an understanding among Japan, Great Britain, and the United States. Mr. Taft reported Katsura's realization that an actual alliance was not possible, but he thought that "an alliance in practice if not in name" might be arranged. Roosevelt's emissary replied that it would be "difficult, indeed impossible" to do this without the consent of the Senate. Taft assured the Japanese Prime Minister, however, that the United States agreed in policy with Great Britain and Japan.

Then Count Katsura brought up the subject of Korea. This, he told Taft, had been the cause of the war. Left to her own devices, the Korean Empire would certainly become involved in agreements and treaties with other powers and all the complications would be repeated. It was essential to Japan that this be avoided. Mr. Taft saw the justice in these views. He suggested, and felt confident that President Roosevelt would agree, a suzerainty over Korea whereby Japanese troops would be placed in Korea and all treaties with other powers would be subject to her veto. All this is not at all irrelevant to that distant day when American soldiers would be fighting in Korea.

The Katsura interview was not casually arranged on the spur of the moment. Roosevelt had ordered Taft to stop off in Japan. "Your conversation with Count Katsura," the President cabled to Taft, "absolutely correct in every respect. Wish you would state to Katsura that I confirm every word you have said."

"No wonder you are happy!" Roosevelt wrote Baron Kentaro Kaneko, a journalist-diplomat, on May 31, 1905. "Neither Trafalgar nor the defeat of the Spanish armada was as complete—as overwhelming." He referred to the victory of the Japanese fleet four days earlier. Events began to move more swiftly. On the same day, May 31, the Japanese ambassador transmitted a message received from his government. This set forth that the naval victory no longer made it possible for Russia to win. Japan still believed that the peace negotiations should be conducted exclusively between the belligerents, but the "friendly assistance of a neutral" was needed to bring them together. Minister Takahira was directed to tell Roosevelt of the hope of Japan that "of his own motion and initiative" he would invite Russia and Japan to consider peace.

The conception of offering, at the suggestion of Japan, to negotiate on "his own initiative" amused the President. Count Cassini had also called at the White House and had again been told that, in the opinion of the President, Russia's cause was hopeless. In St. Petersburg, Ambassador Meyer was attempting to gain an audience with the Czar, at Roosevelt's suggestion. He reported by cable on June 7, 1905, that if Roosevelt desired to "act on his own initiative" in persuading Japan, Russia would consent to peace negotiations. Nothing was to be made public until both countries had agreed.

This, of course, was a result of the President's maneuvering; Meyer, at Roosevelt's directions, had suggested just this to the Russian ruler. He said nothing about the request already received from Japan, on May 31, for overtures to Russia. It is not remarkable that Roosevelt was alternately amused and irritated: "the more I see of the Czar, the Kaiser and the Mikado, the better I am content with democracy." When it was all over, he confided to Jusserand:

Dealing with senators is at times excellent training for the temper, but upon my word dealing with these peace envoys has been an even tougher job. To be polite and sympathetic and patient in explaining for the hundredth time something perfectly obvious, when I really want to give utterance to whoops of rage and jump up and knock their heads together—well, all I can hope is that the self-repression will be ultimately good for my character.

The chief obstacle, after both nations had apparently consented to a peace conference early in June, was the threat that Japan would insist upon an indemnity. On June 19, Roosevelt wrote Meyer at St. Petersburg that Russia might as well face an indemnity because she had been defeated. On the other hand, he did not wish to see Russia driven from the Pacific and "I will do my best to persuade Japan to be moderate." One possibility was to persuade Great Britain to bring pressure upon her ally but this, as publication of the British documents in 1928 revealed, met with slight sympathy.

"In my opinion," Roosevelt wrote, "every true friend of Japan should tell it that the opinion of the civilized world will not support it in continuing the war merely for the purpose of extorting money from Russia."

The President's troubles had not ended after a conference at Portsmouth, New Hampshire, had been agreed upon. On August 5, 1905, in an impressive ceremony on board the U.S.S. *Mayflower* off Oyster Bay, Long Island, Baron Komura and Minister Takahira, the representatives of Japan, faced Baron Rosen and Count Witte of Russia. They shook hands urbanely. They were presented to the President of the United States and retired to a buffet luncheon in the cabin of Commander Cameron Winslow.

When the sessions at Portsmouth got under way on August 9, the hostility soon became apparent. Curiously, as the argument continued, American public opinion shifted to Russia. Roosevelt had been right; Japan's demand for an indemnity proved highly unpopular. The Russians, moreover, were far more adroit in handling the newspaper correspondents who covered the deliberations. On July 29, Roosevelt felt that failure was probable, that neither side would give in and that the war would go on. After prolonged discussion, two points remained. The first was the transfer of the island of Sakhalin, off Siberia, to Japan. The second was the indemnity. Again, Ambassador Meyer carried messages from Roosevelt to the Czar. Again, the German Kaiser urged peace. On August 29 it seemed as though the conference would break up. The President had suggested, as a compromise, that half of the island be given to Japan. Rather unexpectedly, at the session that day, Komura agreed to the compromise. Count Witte and Baron Rosen passed from the conference hall to be faced by excited crowds. Did they have to pay indemnity?

"Not a sou," they answered.

Roosevelt was inclined to think that the Japanese had given up more than was necessary. However, "I think the peace is just to Russia and Japan."

"You have established a record," congratulated Henry Adams, from Paris, "as the best herder of Emperors since Napoleon."

5

Behind the Russo-Japanese War was a related situation even more dangerous to the peace of Europe. Roosevelt was exceedingly proud of the part he played in preventing, as he believed, the partition of Morocco. He felt, with some accuracy, that he had assisted in halting the outbreak, in 1905 or 1906, of a conflict in which all the powers of Europe might have been involved. He did not know that new wounds would soon be festering as a result of the agreement that gave France virtual control of Morocco. If the President of the United States was the spiritual ally of Japan in the events which led to Portsmouth, he was the ally of France in the negotiations before and during the Algeciras Conference. Through France, he was the ally of Great Britain. Through Great Britain, soon to conclude a treaty of amity and defense with the Czar, he was the ally of Russia. It is not remarkable that Roosevelt was irritated when statements were made that he was under the domination of the Kaiser. The President was not aware of it, but he forged a link or two in the chain that finally bound the German Empire, which finally forced her excitable ruler toward his policy of *Schrecklicheit.*

President Roosevelt, although not directly, had enjoyed one fleeting contact with the Moroccan Government. On the outskirts of Tangier was a villa called the Place of Nightingales where lived an American citizen of wealth, Ion Perdicaris, a gentleman of sixty years or so who dabbled in painting. In the household with him was a Mr. Varley, his stepson, who was a British citizen, Mrs. Varley, and Mrs. Perdicaris. They were sipping their heavy black Turkish coffee in the gardens on the evening of May 18, 1904, when some brigands in the band of the picturesque chieftain, Raisuli, swept down from the hills and carried off Messrs. Perdicaris and Varley. It appeared that Raisuli was having a personal controversy with the Sultan and used this method to show his defiance. Sir Arthur Nicolson, the British minister, was notified. Cable messages sped to the State Department at Washington.

The two men were in no danger. Raisuli was, reported Perdicaris, "the most interesting and kindly-hearted, intelligent gentleman it has been my good fortune to have known . . . it is impossible not to like the man." Meanwhile the chieftain's demands on the Moorish Sultan had been satisfied and it was clear that Perdicaris would be released. But Roosevelt seized the occasion to stir the lethargic Republican National Convention, then in session at Chicago, into life with a message, actually written by John Hay, to the United States consul general at Tangier. It was read to the delegates on June 33, and brought forth the expected cheers.

"We want either Perdicaris alive or Raisuli dead," said this historic message.

So another phrase was added to Roosevelt's many, and the fact that Hay had been the author was quite forgotten. Perdicaris was released, according to the arrangements already made.

Unless it persuaded Roosevelt that the Moroccans, like Central Americans, were miserable little brigands and entitled to no consideration, the incident has no bearing on the crisis of 1905 and 1906. It was merely added proof that the Sultan could not preserve order. The clue to the Moroccan situation lies in the mazes of European diplomacy. In 1899 Great Britain had considered a secret agreement with Germany for the division of Morocco. But as in 1901, when Germany might have achieved a defensive alliance with Great Britain and let the golden moment slip by, this time Von Bülow hesitated and so lost. All that Germany desired in Morocco, said Wilhelm II, in March, 1904, was a fair chance to trade. But meanwhile Lord Lansdowne and Paul Cambon, the French ambassador at London, were holding the "conversations" that led to the Anglo-French treaty signed on April 8 of that year. This provided, in substance, that France would not interfere in Egypt if Great Britain allowed France a free hand in Morocco. The public portions of the document gave the impression that this applied to Morocco, as it then existed, that it portended no disturbance of the status quo. Secret articles, however, provided for eventual partition and in October, 1904, by means of an equally secret treaty between France and Spain, their boundaries were defined. If the Kaiser realized what had occurred, as eventually he did if not at the moment, he must have seen that new alliances were forming. These were to be carried further, very much further, before an inconspicuous assassin murdered a grand duke at Sarajevo ten years later.

The agreement between France and England had two results. First, German prestige in Morocco suffered. Second, the Sultan felt that he had been betrayed and insisted to his shoddy court that the Kaiser was his one true friend. The German Chancellor waited for a year in the expectation that he would be informed regarding the treaty, and perhaps permitted to share in its benefits. He then persuaded his monarch to visit Tangier, which the Kaiser did much against his will on March 31, 1905. "It was to please you," he wrote Von Bülow, "for the sake of the Fatherland, that I landed, mounted a strange horse and might have come within a hair of losing my life." His speech started vibrations among the raw nerves of European diplomats. He considered the Sultan an independent sovereign, he said. This was accepted as a challenge to French supremacy in Morocco and as an attempt to shatter the newborn Anglo-French cordiality. It is now agreed, on the contrary, that the Kaiser was deeply disturbed by the effect of his Tangier utterance. He saw vanishing forever his dream of a majestic alliance among Germany, Russia, France, Austria, and Italy, with himself as a new and holier emperor who would preserve the peace of the world. His first plan for counteracting the evil which had been done was to enlist the services of Roosevelt, with whom he had been in correspondence relative to the Russo-Japanese War.

An appeal from the Kaiser reached the President on March 6, 1905, through Speck von Sternberg. The Kaiser asked that Roosevelt join him in informing the Sultan that he must stand for the Open Door in Morocco, that the United States and Germany would support him in opposition to any nation (France) that might seek exclusive control:

On the following day he [Von Sternberg] submitted to me a memorandum stating that the Emperor regarded France and Spain as "a political entity" who wished to divide up Morocco between themselves and debar her markets to the rest of the world . . . on April 5, he maintained that England and France were allies.

For the United States to combine with Germany against France in Morocco was patently absurd, and Roosevelt so viewed it. His answer was that he could not interfere because the interests of this country were slight. Three weeks later, the Kaiser made his Tangier speech and the President saw only the outward explosiveness of this. On April 2, 1905, he wrote John Hay that the hostility between England and Germany was "as funny a case as I have ever seen of mutual distrust and fear bringing two peoples to the verge of war." On April 8, crossing Texas on his way to the bear hunt in Colorado, Roosevelt wrote to Taft:

I wish to Heaven our excellent friend, the Kaiser, was not so jumpy and did not have so many pipe dreams. Tell Speck that I shall wait until I get home before I try to discuss it with him.

Roosevelt's participation in the Moroccan question had two aspects: first, the suggestion of the Kaiser for an international tribunal to settle the matter, and second, the

Algeciras Conference itself. "His Awfulness," as John Hay referred to the German monarch, was not wholly sincere with Roosevelt. His insistence upon territorial integrity for Morocco was not quite honest; what he wanted was Roosevelt's assistance in extracting the chestnut of German prestige from the fire of European diplomatic maneuverings. On May 31, 1905, again through Specky, the Kaiser impressed upon Roosevelt the relationship between this problem and the Far East. Virtuous Germany, interested only in her right to trade in Morocco on a fair basis, was being seduced by suggestions that France would agree to give her a slice of the Land of the Umbrella in return for acquiescence in Russia's freedom in Manchuria. Germany had sternly refused. Her fine sense of honor made war with France a distinct possibility.

Roosevelt groped in the fog of American diplomatic inadequacies. The United States had no agents in Europe, conveniently light of finger, who could lift from embassy pouches papers that shed illumination on the secret activities of foreign ministers and kings. The President was guided by counselors who were hardly impartial; Jules Jusserand of France, Spring Rice, and Speck von Sternberg. In the matter of Morocco, no less than in that of the Russo-Japanese War, Roosevelt was his own State Department.

Von Bülow, because of dispatches from Von Sternberg, decided that Roosevelt was "now convinced of the sincerity of German policy." He brought forward an idea that might save German prestige: an international conference on Morocco. He used the most effective of all arguments, that England and France, if the power of Germany were diminished, would surely partition China. Would Roosevelt, a message on April 13 from the Kaiser suggested, express to Great Britain a "confidential hint" as to his attitude regarding such a conference? In part, but only in part, the efforts of Von Bülow were successful. The President returned from his hunt on May 11, and two days later Von Sternberg quoted him as saying:

I feel very indignant at the attitude of England in the Conference question, especially when there are voices to be heard in France favoring the Conference idea. It seems as if England in Morocco wants to dispose as it sees fit of the rights of others. I emphatically wish to see an improvement in the relations between Germany and England.

Such, at least, was Specky's version of Roosevelt's reaction. The influence of Jusserand, who refrained from mentioning the secret treaty between his country and England, is clearly perceptible in the President's private letters, however. Roosevelt was irritated by England, particularly by the unfortunate Sir Mortimer Durand, her ambassador. On the other hand, "I desired to do anything I legitimately could for France because I thought her in this instance to be right," he wrote in his interminable letter to Whitelaw Reid a year later. "I had not at any time credited the three powers [England, France and Italy] with having made the several propositions they were alleged by the German Government to have made." In other words, ignorant of the real relations of France and England, the President was also unaware that Italy had been given a free hand in Tripoli in return for consent to the division of Morocco.

The phrase "France was right on this issue" appears several times in the Reid letter setting forth Roosevelt's version of the situation. No possible doubt exists that he had complete confidence in the French ambassador's judgment and integrity. Reluctant to interfere, believing that the United States had no real basis for doing so, he felt that a war between France and Germany should be prevented. Through Jusserand, he informed the French Government that it would be wise to "avoid a war if it could be done by adopting a course which would save the Emperor's self-esteem." In the same communication, the President said that in the event of war, English assistance would be of slight value to France, since invasion by land would be faced. He repeated that he would, if necessary, "take very strong grounds against any attitude of Germany which seemed to me unjust and unfair."

Roosevelt's intervention, it would seem, had not proceeded exactly as the Kaiser had hoped. But the Sultan's request for a conference, made at Germany's suggestion, had one important result. Théophile Delcassé, France's Foreign Minister, was placed in the position of having brought his country close to war because of imperialistic designs in Morocco. M. Rouvier, the Prime Minister, secretly made inquiries and learned that the hostility in Germany would be lessened if France would agree to drop Delcassé and would consent to a conference of powers on Morocco. On June 6, 1905, Delcassé resigned. "Voices are now heard," said the Kaiser to Roosevelt on June 11, "which consider a conference as the safest way to clear a situation created by the reckless statesmanship of M. Delcassé." On June 25, France agreed to the conference and Roosevelt, in accordance with his custom which clouded the real facts of his attitude toward the German Kaiser, sent a fulsome message to Wilhelm congratulating him upon this "genuine triumph for the Emperor's diplomacy."

Before the conference assembled at Algeciras, the Russo-Japanese War had been concluded by the Peace of Portsmouth. The Kaiser had failed, in the famous meeting at Björkö on July 25, 1905, to effect an alliance between Russia and Germany. He was to have few allies when discussion of the Moroccan question began on January 16, 1906. Again, Roosevelt's influence was on the side of France. In England, the Conservative government had fallen, but Sir Edward Grey, the new Foreign Secretary, was as ardently pro-French as Lansdowne had been. After all, Edward VII was still King. He had spent much of his youth on the Riviera. It was largely the King's influence which had brought about Anglo-French cordiality.

Not only was England secretly allied with France for the partition of Morocco, but she did everything possible to defeat the purposes of Germany at the conference. Spring Rice, at St. Petersburg, was informed by Grey that "His Majesty's Government would agree to any solution which is acceptable to France." It was not true, Grey told Count Metternich, the German ambassador, that England was "more French than the French," but on February 20, 1906, Great Britain's Foreign Secretary drafted a memorandum:

If there is war between France and Germany it will be very difficult for us to keep out of it. The *Entente* and still more the constant and emphatic demonstrations of affection (official, naval, political, commercial, municipal and the Press) have created in France a belief that we should support her in war. If this expectation is disappointed, France will never forgive us . . . we should be left without a friend and without power of making a friend.

But war, added Sir Edward, as though talking to himself, "is horrible." If Germany would recognize French claims in Morocco, could not "a port or coaling station be awarded her" in return for peace? So much for England's basic attitude on partition.

Two main issues were to be treated at Algeciras. The first was the organization of an international bank for financial reforms. This presented no great difficulty. The obstacle that seemed at first insuperable was whether France and Spain were to have exclusive control of the policing of the important ports of Morocco. It was the claim of Germany that this meant control by France and the loss of German trade. That it was not an unreasonable apprehension may be seen by a conversation in which Sir Charles Hardinge, British ambassador to Russia, discussed the Moorish police with M. Paul Cambon, French ambassador at London. Sir Charles recalled:

> I was surprised at his alluding to three arms [at Tangier] and asked what he meant. He said infantry, cavalry and artillery! . . . who has ever heard of police with artillery? I told him he had better keep that idea dark as the Germans had already said that the French intended to get hold of the Moorish army.

It was "kept dark." France, with the aid of England, insisted upon sharing with Spain alone the responsibility for order in Morocco. The Kaiser countered with a proposal which Roosevelt believed, not without reason, to mean "the partition of Morocco . . . the very reverse of what she was claiming to desire." Germany's alternative was that the powers organize the police in various parts of Morocco, and that a port be given each. If this was not acceptable, she would consent to control by Switzerland, Holland, or Sweden. A third possibility was organization of the police by the Sultan with volunteer officers selected from among the smaller powers. This Roosevelt rejected. As a compromise he said that the police might consist of Moors, but that French and Spanish officers would be in control.

In the end, curiously enough, Roosevelt was instrumental in forcing Germany to recede even further than Sir Arthur Nicolson and Sir Edward Grey thought necessary. Austria, at the suggestion of the Kaiser, specified that France should command the police in four ports on the Moroccan coast and Spain in three. At Casablanca, where Germany's interests were paramount, the Dutch or Swiss could select the highest police officer, and this official was to be inspector general of the police in all the other ports. "The Germans have been wonderfully conciliatory," wrote Nicolson on March 8, 1905. Two days later, Grey notified Nicolson that "Germany has conceded the substance and it would be a great pity if France sacrificed the substance to the shadow."

It was not, however, the Open Door, and Roosevelt did not know that the powers of Europe really cared not a farthing for this principle. Again, Roosevelt publicly congratulated the Kaiser and Germany for what he believed to be the happy outcome of the Algeciras Conference. It is doubtful whether the result was as salutary as it then seemed. To England and France it was, of course, a victory. War would then have been peculiarly awkward, since Russia, France's ally, lay helpless from the effects of internal disorder and the struggle with Japan. England had made, of course, no preparations for war. The German army was at a high point of efficiency.

The outbreak was delayed, not halted. The sores remained. The people of Germany were to listen more cordially than ever to the demands of Von Tirpitz for a mighty navy. Dapper German guardsmen were to drink to *Der Tag* with greater enthusiasm. The conclusion is inescapable that Wilhelm II did not want war in 1906. But the policy of encirclement was to continue and to grow more energetic with the years. Very soon, the pretenses were abandoned. France took over Morocco. Two World Wars came in the decades ahead. In the uneasy peace which followed the second, France's leaders pondered, as riots spread in North Africa, the wisdom of ever having acquired Morocco at all.

Chapter X

THE JAPANESE MENACE

Theodore Roosevelt's jingoism faded when the responsibility for war became his own. When, in the fall of 1906, the yellow peril appeared over the horizon of the Far East, the President made energetic efforts to conciliate Japan. He was filled with wrath toward American and Japanese jingoes in the last three years of his administration. He had been disturbed by the Pacific coast anti-Japanese agitation since June of 1905, when he had been apprehensive that it would block his efforts to end the Russo-Japanese War. The attitude in California was "as foolish as if conceived by the mind of a Hottentot."

Japanese hostility toward the United States developed before the California trouble became acute. It is unjust that Roosevelt, whose friendship for Japan had been profound, should have been criticized in 1905 for his part in settling the Russo-Japanese War. It is now agreed, although the facts were not clear at the time, that Japan had been worn to exhaustion by the struggle and grasped the opportunity when the chance of peace came. Her financial situation was desperate. She had destroyed the Russian navy, but the overwhelming manpower of her foe must in the end have thrown Japan back. When at the Portsmouth Peace Conference, however, Roosevelt induced the Japanese delegates to forgo an indemnity, the impression was given that Japan had been denied what was rightfully hers. Angry murmurings arose from Tokyo and Yokohama.

The terms of the Portsmouth Peace constituted the first cause of friction between the United States and Japan. During the first week of September, 1905, anti-American riots broke out in Tokyo. Roosevelt still admired the Japanese, however. He believed "their advent into the circle of great civilized powers is a good thing." There would probably be no trouble if the United States treated Japan "with real courtesy and friendliness."

This was to prove difficult, in view of the conduct of California whose sins against Japan were laid at the door of the Federal Government. Still another cause of hard feeling arose before the difficulties on the Pacific coast drew the two countries, as Roosevelt and many others believed, perilously close to war. This was during the summer of 1906. The United States had been annoyed for some years by poachers who killed seals on the Pribilof Islands of Alaska. On July 16 and 17, 1906, crews from Japanese vessels raided the islands and were beaten off by a United States patrol; five of the Japanese were killed. Roosevelt caused representations to be made to Japan and prompt admission came that the United States had been wholly in the right. But the indignation among fervent patriots in Japan was heightened. Then, in October, came the ruling by the school board of San Francisco that Japanese were to be excluded from the schools. Vigorous protests from Japan declared this in violation of the Treaty of 1894, and Roosevelt's displeasure was directed against both California and Japan. The former, he thought, had acted rudely and in violation of national treaty-making powers. He announced that troops would be used, if necessary, to bring California to terms. Precisely what he proposed to do with them is not clear. The President believed, in late 1906 and in 1907, that war was possible, even probable. He dispatched the battle fleet on its voyage around the world to prove that Uncle Sam was still virile. Privately, he worried over an "inordinate love of ease and of pleasure" among his countrymen.

Meanwhile, particularly in California where Hearst made the most of it, the tom-toms of war began to beat. It was whispered that Japan enjoyed great strength because of her alliance with England and was ready for war. Soon there were riots against inoffensive Japanese shop-keepers in San Francisco. The alarm would have approached abject terror had the people of California been permitted to see the confidential letters reaching the desk of Theodore Roosevelt from various personages in Europe. Publication of these letters might well have precipitated a struggle with Japan long, long before 1941. Inflammatory statements in certain of the documents might have drawn Great Britain, Germany, Russia, and France into the hostilities.

2

The President's office in the White House, like the inner offices of all heads of governments, is the center of a great web. On its threads travel reports and rumors that are carefully kept from the light of day. They tell of conversations with this premier and communications addressed to that monarch. Often they relay scraps picked up at some foreign court or indiscretions uttered around a dinner table as the liqueurs are passed. During 1907 and 1908, Roosevelt was warned by the German Kaiser that war with Japan was certain. T.R. told Root that France, Germany, and England believed that war would come and that the United States would lose. From numerous sources the President received descriptions of hostile statements made by influential Japanese. The President showed these dispatches to one or two close advisers, but he saw to it that they did not fall into the hands of Congress and, on the whole, he kept his head very well indeed.

Among the reports was one from Maj. Gen. J. F. Bell, chief of staff of the United States Army. General Bell's report was based on hearsay, but so were most of the others. He had received a letter, he wrote Roosevelt on July 17, 1907, from a retired American army officer then living in St. Petersburg. This officer, although not present, had been told of a dinner at which a normally taciturn Japanese diplomat had partaken of a glass or two of champagne and had unburdened himself regarding the aspirations of his country. She was, he said, anxious to be friendly with

Europe. She no longer feared Russia. Why, then, was she hastening to build guns and ships? He was said to have continued:

Gentlemen, you hear it said that Japan will take the Philippine Islands when she desires it and is ready. *She is ready now*, and to take the Sandwich Islands as well. But do you imagine *that* will satisfy us?

General Bell, in transmitting this excited declaration of an unnamed Japanese in his cups, said he had "not the slightest doubt but that these thoughts have occurred to mighty nearly every Jap official, either high or low, now in existence."

A second report came from Berlin. The Associated Press correspondent said that he had talked with Capt. Philip Dumas, British naval attaché at Berlin, early in July, 1907. Captain Dumas had recently been in London and there had heard members of the British Admiralty express the opinion that Japan's chance of victory in a war with the United States was about five to four. That such a war would come, he was certain. Elmer Roberts, the Associated Press man, then called on Baron F. von Holstein of the German foreign service, who had given great weight to the views of Dumas. But he saw England as the villain in the plot; she had renewed her alliance with Japan and was scheming for the economic extermination of Germany. Von Holstein insisted that Great Britain was systematically warning Russia of the probability of another war with Japan. Russia had no stomach for a second fight and the English hoped, said Von Holstein, to win her gratitude and support by restraining Japan.

On July 19, 1907, Ambassador von Sternberg amplified the German theory that England was a troublemaker. He quoted from a letter received on the previous day from Von Holstein, a letter intended for the President's ear. Von Holstein had said that the British King was "trying everywhere a system of bluff." He added that British diplomats

who stand in closest proximity to the King are at present using their efforts to create anxiety in the United States for a sudden attack by Japan in consequence of the troubles in California. A British official has been constantly at work to impress on American journalists the dangers of a war with Japan. England is using Japan as her bogey so as to appear the savior of the threatened powers.

By passing this on, Von Sternberg revealed that he was less of a friend than he pretended. The sinister rumors continued throughout 1907. In November, Charlemagne Tower, American ambassador to Germany, described a conversation with an important German, whom he did not name, but whose opinions were "unquestionably" those of the Kaiser. This German had told Tower that "the Japanese are arming to the teeth," that they planned to seize the Philippine Islands and to strike at the Panama Canal. On December 19, 1907, the then Capt. William S. Sims reported to the President that three battleships were being constructed in England ostensibly for Brazil. In design, however, the vessels were exactly like others being built for Japan. Was it possible that they actually were for Japan?

The most remarkable of all the alarmist reports that came to Roosevelt, however, was the result of an interview between the Kaiser and the American ambassador to Germany. This took place on January 27, 1908, and Mr. Tower hastened to transmit an account of the conversation to his President. It was for Roosevelt alone, Wilhelm had warned, and not for the American Government itself. The Kaiser said:

Tell him that I have just had a report of one of my men who has just come back from Mexico where I sent him orders to travel through the country and give an account of what he saw. He tells me that Mexico is filled with Japanese. They have gone there in large numbers of late, and are distributing themselves throughout the country as laborers and farmhands. My man's attention was attracted toward them during his journey by the fact, among other things, that many of them had brass buttons on their coats. There is no doubt that they are soldiers.

The historical significance of all these reports and rumors depends on two facts. How imminent was war between Japan and the United States in 1907-09? Second, just what credence did Roosevelt place in this mass of gossip and incendiary statements?

As to the first, there is nothing whatever to support the theories advanced by Von Holstein and others that Great Britain was spreading apprehensions regarding war with Japan. Japan was her ally; such propaganda was definitely harmful to Japan's commerce and to her reputation. England, moreover, had more to lose than to gain from any struggle between America and Japan, and no one could tell when the circulation of such alarms would lead to actual war.

The rumors of war were vastly exaggerated. Any attempt to arrive at the truth in this confused situation must be based on recognition of the fear then enfolding Europe, fear of a war in which every nation might be embroiled. England, by the end of 1907, had made herself fairly secure. But what of Germany? The Kaiser's efforts to negotiate a treaty with Czar Nicholas had failed. Wilhelm, too, was thinking of the day when war might come. He saw Germany, allied only with weak Austria and fickle Italy, as far less powerful than her enemies. Fear sat beside him and a delusion that England was the archconspirator who sought to strangle the Fatherland. On the one hand, perhaps, the hope of a humbled Japan—defeated in a struggle with the United States—created the conviction that such a war was probable. On the other, his hatred of England led the Emperor to see specters that existed only in fantasy.

Just how alarmed Wilhelm was during 1908 became evident when an American journalist, William Bayard Hale, obtained an interview, which was never published. Roosevelt, however, was informed of what the Kaiser had said.

"He expressed himself," the President told Root, "with extreme bitterness about England and said that very shortly Germany would have to go to war with her. He said that within a year or two we, the Americans, would certainly have to fight the Japanese."

The President missed the point of the interview quite completely. He saw not a frightened monarch, but one who was indulging "in red dreams of glory." Abler historians than Roosevelt were to make the same mistake.

3

The second point, the credence Roosevelt placed in the reports of Japanese hostility during 1907-08, is best judged in connection with the friction in California. Hostility arose when Japan began to look toward the West for room to expand. Her people had been unwilling to settle in Manchuria and Korea; economic conditions there were worse than in Japan. But Japanese could greatly improve their status by living in the United States. They could do this and still accept very much lower wages than Americans were accustomed to receive.

By 1906 about 75,000 Japanese were in the United States, and residents of California, where most of them settled, became irritated over their crowding into the schools. In October, 1906, the San Francisco school board ordered Japanese students to attend Oriental schools established for them, together with Chinese and Koreans. Roosevelt promptly pointed to the Treaty of 1894, containing a "most favored nation" clause in which the Japanese were guaranteed all the rights, save naturalization alone, enjoyed by other peoples. He said that "Japanese soldiers and sailors have shown themselves equal in combat to any of whom history makes note," a truly Rooseveltian qualification for citizenship, and he recommended a law permitting naturalization of Japanese.

Thus, in his annual message to Congress, Roosevelt demanded that California withdraw from her position and declared that "all of the forces, military and civil, of the United States" would be used to protect the rights of the Japanese. It did not, however, prove feasible for Roosevelt to declare war on California, and the resentment toward the Japanese continued. The President did succeed in frightening the Californians. A delegation headed by Mayor Schmitz of San Francisco, the picturesque executive who had once been a bassoon player and who was even then under indictment for graft, was received at the White House on February 9, 1907. Roosevelt, after pledging them to secrecy, said that war was probable and promised that he would force Congress to pass a bill barring Japanese laborers seeking to enter the United States by way of Hawaii, Mexico, Canada, and the Canal Zone. In return, San Francisco was to remove the educational restrictions. This was a compromise, a means of getting around the Treaty of 1894. By exchange of memorandums between Secretary of State Root and Minister Takahira, Japan agreed to restrict emigration to those countries. Skilled and educated Japanese were to be admitted as usual. It was hoped that the flood of cheap labor would be halted. Like most compromises, the "Gentlemen's Agreement" failed to work. In June, 1907, there were riots against Japanese restaurant keepers in San Francisco, the resentment in Japan reached new heights, and the first of the alarming confidential reports soon reached the White House. By July, Roosevelt's plan to send the fleet on its voyage had been drafted.

"I am more concerned over the Japanese situation than almost any other," he wrote to Root from Oyster Bay on July 13, 1907. "Thank Heaven we have the navy in good shape."

A full eighteen months prior to this time, Roosevelt had been debating in his own mind the probability of war with Japan. In January, 1906, he had written Maj. Gen. Leonard Wood that Japan had no immediate intention of moving against the United States and that no attack on the Philippine Islands would come "for a decade or two." A year later, the California school question having arisen, he was less confident; but it is impossible to judge with entire accuracy just what Roosevelt was thinking at this time. In October, 1906, he was using the Japanese scare to convince Senator Eugene Hale, chairman of the Senate Naval Affairs Committee, that the navy must be kept at a high point of efficiency because "the Japanese are proud, sensitive, warlike, and flushed with the glory of their recent triumph." War, he said, was not improbable. This, to a degree, was propaganda.

The President's private letter files reveal, however, a period of genuine alarm when the anti-Japanese feeling continued in the face of the Gentlemen's Agreement. On June 22, 1907, he received from Secretary of War Taft a detailed report on the proper steps for defense of the Philippine Islands, Hawaii, Guam, and the Pacific coast. On July 6, 1907, Roosevelt transmitted in code to General Wood, who was in command on the islands, directions for holding the Philippines against a Japanese attack. A week later, in a letter to Root, he expressed concern over "disquieting statistics of the Japanese arrivals in the United States for the fiscal year just closed." It was plain that the Japanese were violating their agreement; "we shall have to urge most strongly the need of restricting the total number of passports if we are not to have trouble."

The only real discouragement experienced by the President was over the lack of public interest in strengthening the navy. This found expression in August, 1907, in a letter to Secretary Taft in which Roosevelt, for the moment, considered a policy that he would have condemned as abject cowardice had someone else offered it. This was to abandon the Philippine Islands. He wrote:

The Philippine Islands form our heel of Achilles. They are all that makes the present situation with Japan dangerous. I think that in some way and with some phraseology that you think wise you should state to them that if they handle themselves wisely in their legislative assembly we shall at the earliest possible moment give them a nearly complete independence. I think that to have some pretty clear avowal of our intention not to permanently [sic] keep them and to give them independence would remove a temptation from Japan's way and would render our task easier.

The President's pessimism did not last. Taft left quietly on a journey which again took him to Tokyo and Yokohama. The exact truth is that the Secretary of War was not easily frightened. He declined to make any statement about independence for the Philippines. Roosevelt was greatly reassured by Taft's report in October, 1907, that "the Japanese government is most anxious to avoid war," that the finances of the country made war almost impossible.

Before the inflammatory messages came from Wilhelm, the fleet had started on its voyage. Roosevelt was able to view with complacency "the Imperial pipe dream forwarded through Ambassador Tower."

4

The world voyage of the battle fleet, "the most important service that I rendered to peace," was the direct result of the Japanese trouble. In January, 1907, Captain Mahan warned the President against the danger of dividing the fleet. He viewed with dismay, Mahan wrote, a report that four battleships were to be sent to the Pacific coast. What could these four do against Japan? In case of a war with some European power, the four would be needed in the Atlantic.

A united battle fleet became a cornerstone of Roosevelt's naval policy, and plans for a trip to the Far East were considered with this view. Aside from the tactical value to the navy, there were two other reasons for the trip. The first was to impress Japan with the might of the United States. The second was to spread propaganda for naval increases. "Before matters become more strained," Roosevelt wrote Cabot Lodge on July 10, 1907, "we had better make it evident that when it comes to visiting our own coasts on the Pacific or Atlantic and assembling the fleet in our own waters, we cannot submit to any outside protests or interference." Count Aoki and Admiral Yamamoto both called at Oyster Bay two days later to protest against the California discriminations and "I talked freely of the intended trip of the battleship fleet through the Pacific." The President told Henry White, on July 30, 1907, that he was anxious to have the Japanese know of his friendly attitude, "but I am none the less anxious that they should realize that I am not afraid of them."

Word that the fleet actually was to sail aroused a degree of public opposition, on the ground that war would probably result and this, as opposition always did, cemented Roosevelt's intention to have the voyage made. When Senator Hale of the Committee of Naval Affairs announced that the fleet could not go because Congress would not supply the money, Roosevelt retorted that funds already existed to carry them as far as the Pacific coast and the ships could remain there as far as he was concerned. The money was promptly supplied.

The fleet steamed out of Hampton Roads on December 16, 1907, with a very proud President watching the column from the deck of the *Mayflower*. "Proceed to duty assigned" was the brief message from the President's yacht which started the squadron moving. They disappeared into the mist and for the next fortnight military and naval experts argued the probability of a clash with Japan. The President instructed his naval commanders to prepare for the worst, to be ready for any emergency. He added, however, that he was quite certain no hostility would be shown.

The progress of the squadron was watched with interest throughout the world. In 1910, while in Europe, Roosevelt was told by Admiral von Tirpitz that all the German naval experts had felt certain Japan would launch an attack. This was two years later. Looking back, Roosevelt saw indications of Japanese pugnacity that were not apparent to him at the time. Perhaps, as in the case of the Venezuela trouble at the start of his years as President, he was again dramatizing a situation in which he had played a leading part.

"I had," he wrote Sir George Trevelyan, "become uncomfortably conscious of a very, very slight undertone of veiled truculence in their communications and I finally made up my mind that they thought I was afraid of them . . . it was time for a show down."

Japan was far too wise to precipitate a war at this time, even had she desired one. Instead, her Government extended an invitation, which Roosevelt could not decline, to have the fleet visit her shores. The ships arrived on October 18, 1908, and three days of Oriental hospitality followed, with the dove of peace fluttering serenely over the scene. Astute Japanese merchants seized the opportunity to drum up a little trade among the wealthy United States sailors. Advertisements urged that they provide themselves with Mitsukoshi washing powder and "rid yourselves of the seven blemishes on the way home." The Diamaru Drygoods Company published a drawing of Uncle Sam bowing before a pretty girl with a dove on her finger; an Oriental representation of the Flowery Kingdom.

"Ah! Madame Rising Sun," Uncle Sam was saying. "Ain't that lovely? We Puritans like it, you know."

With dispatches from the seven seas describing the world voyage, the navy was very much in the public mind during

1908 and Roosevelt lost no time in pressing upon Congress his demand for four new battleships. In the end only two battleships were authorized. But that Roosevelt was the winner in the skirmish, that he had expected nothing better, is shown in a letter to Henry White:

"I knew I would not get two and have those two hurried up unless I made a violent fight for four."

Roosevelt delayed, rather than settled, the problem of the status of Japanese in California. By January, 1909, the fires of discord blazed again. Pressure from Washington this time blocked passage of a bill which would have kept Orientals from owning land. The issue, however, was as vexing as ever during the Wilson Administration; in May, 1913, the Alien Landholding Bill became law. Roosevelt had returned to relatively private life, but he consented to telegraph a protest to Gov. Hiram Johnson of California. It was a question that only the Federal Government could decide, he said. California should ask for relief at Washington. Regarding President Wilson's failure to halt the embattled Californians, Roosevelt remarked that "the attitude of President Wilson and Mr. Bryan has been hopelessly weak." He contrasted this attitude with his own position in 1907 and 1908. The Democratic President should have adhered rigidly to the Rooseveltian precedents then established. But the assassination at Sarajevo a year later relegated the Japanese question, for the time being, to an obscure place in international affairs.

Chapter XI

MALEFACTORS OF GREAT WEALTH

"I do not like the social conditions at present," Roosevelt complained to Taft in March, 1906. "The dull, purblind folly of the very rich men; their greed and arrogance and the corruption in business and politics, have tended to produce a very unhealthy condition of excitement and irritation in the popular mind, which shows itself in the great increase in the socialistic propaganda." The President deplored the "swollen and monstrous fortunes" of the day.

The domestic policies of Roosevelt in his second term were largely a result of these apprehensions. He was nervously anxious to cure the evils that existed; perhaps Roosevelt's genius lay in the fact that he realized their existence. The assets that gave him power were his gifts as a politician and his flair for arousing public interest. The liabilities that held him back were his sparsity of knowledge on economics, which approached ignorance, and his alliance with the Republican party.

Always in the back of T.R.'s mind, also, was the fear that if he went too far or too fast he faced the peril of business unrest. A panic might mean the defeat of his party. This was the worst of all possible dangers, for Roosevelt sincerely believed that the Democratic party was far less talented than his own in the science of government. To subject the United States to the risk of Democratic rule was close to treason.

Roosevelt had often compromised, but hitherto his own political fortunes had been responsible. A higher expediency moved him in 1905 and 1906, and the first issue on which he surrendered was tariff revision. On April 4, 1903, Roosevelt spoke on this troublesome issue at Minneapolis and his address, which avoided any positive recommendations, contained a phrase or two that had a familiar sound. When David B. Hill, the New York State Democratic leader, pointed to a deadly parallel in sections of Roosevelt's speech and an address by Elihu Root in October of the previous year, the President confessed:

Alas! Hill has proved that I plagiarized from you. The worst of it is that I did, you know! I am now busy looking through your last tariff speech with the firm intention of plagiarizing from it, too.

If he did, he took the precaution of changing the phraseology instead of again repeating Root word for word. But no suggestion for downward revision came from the White House. The 1904 campaign was approaching and, as Uncle Joe Cannon remarked, "no matter how much of an improvement the new tariff may be, it almost always results in losing the election." But after Roosevelt's victory even Root thought that the party could not successfully go before the voters in 1908 unless some action toward revision had been taken.

Roosevelt, however, remained dubious. "It is not an issue," he said, upon which I should have any business to break with my party." His message to Congress on December 6, 1904, did not mention the tariff, and all the rumors about changes to be made by the "friends of protection" came to nothing. It was Speaker Cannon whose influence predominated.

"Whence comes this so-called demand for tariff tinkering?" Uncle Joe demanded in November, 1905. "Aren't all our fellows happy?"

By 1906, Roosevelt had concentrated on other matters.

"I believe that the tariff must be revised," he told Jacob Riis in April, "but of course I am up to my ears in all the fighting that I can well undertake at the moment."

Before long, however, he was wavering again; "If I were the legislative as well as the executive branch I would revise the tariff right away," he said in August. Again, Uncle Joe forced his views upon the White House. From his home in Danville, Illinois, he wrote that a "promise now to revise would bring us defeat" in the approaching congressional election. Roosevelt's fears that, on the other hand, failure to make this pledge would result in a Democratic victory were not realized. On February 28, 1907, the President admitted that the Speaker of the House had been right all along:

For the last two years I have accepted your view as to just what we should say on the tariff—or rather as to what we should not say—and I am satisfied that it was wiser than the course I had intended to follow.

2

In selecting regulation of the railroads as an issue on which he was willing to fight, Roosevelt demonstrated his grasp of popular prejudices and popular limitations. "We *must* have legislation," he wrote in January, 1905. "On the interstate commerce business, which I regard as a matter of principle, I shall fight."

Hostility toward the railroads had been increasing since 1900. At first, until well past the middle of the century, the railroads basked in the sunlight of public approval. The new civilization they were to bring had seemed very fair indeed and legislatures and municipal governments bid against each other in offering inducements to the promoters building the new lines. Even during the era of expansion in 1880 to 1890, however, it appeared that evils had arisen. The word "rebates" came to have a sinister meaning to the farmer and the workingman. It appeared that the railroads had been cutting their rates in order to strengthen powerful shippers at the expense of weaker competitors.

Since there were certain to be numerous weak men who

suffered at the expense of each beneficiary, the building of the strong became a cause for denunciation. The railroads were soon as weary of rebating as the shipper who had been discriminated against. They learned, unfortunately too late, that an industry to which they had given rate concessions, and which had flourished, soon demanded further reductions. The Standard Oil Company went so far as to insist that a surtax be added to the tariffs imposed on its competitors. Out of these evils grew the Interstate Commerce Act of 1887, an ineffective measure. Insufferable delays followed the promulgation of its orders against secret rebates.

In his first message to Congress, President Roosevelt pointed to defects in the act of 1887 and recommended changes that would bring fair rates to all shippers. But this was when Roosevelt was exceedingly cautious; he hurriedly added that the railroads were "the arteries through which the commerical life blood of this nation flows." He left the details to Congress, and nothing was done. By 1903, the railroads were again suffering from the demands made by large shippers, and they cordially endorsed amendments to the 1887 law sponsored by Senator Elkins of West Virginia. The important point to be remembered in judging Roosevelt's railroad regulation fight was that this bill did not relate to the main problem. It was not even a preliminary skirmish in the main struggle for railroad rates that would be fair and reasonable.

Hill of the Great Northern made this clear in January, 1905. "Every railroad would be happy to have rebates abolished and the law against them enforced," he said. But government regulation of rates was far different. "Competition," he insisted, "is the test which proves the survival of the fittest. The laws of trade are as certain as the laws of gravity."

The impression has been given that President Roosevelt's message to Congress in December, 1904, recommended a law giving power to fix rates to the Interstate Commerce Commission. This was not the case at all. He told Congress that "I am of the opinion that at present it would be undesirable, if it were not impracticable, finally to clothe the commission with general authority to fix rates." The commission should, however, have power, "where a given rate has been challenged and after full hearing found to be unreasonable, to decide what shall be a reasonable rate to take its place." This was to go into effect at once, subject to "judicial review." The distinction is important because Roosevelt, after venturing somewhat further during one of the most bitter debates in congressional history, ultimately accepted as a compromise the Hepburn Bill providing virtually his December, 1904, specifications. It was in the Union League Club address at Philadelphia on January 30, 1905, that the President called for control over rates by "some tribunal."

Real rate control was sheer socialism, obviously. In May, 1904, President Butler of Columbia University warned Roosevelt that Governor Robert M. LaFollette of Wisconsin, whose reverberations against the corrupt alliance of business and politics had been echoing through the country, was a fanatic, and dangerous to Republican success in 1904. "I agree with you . . . you read LaFollette exactly right," answered Roosevelt. On June 5, 1908, he wrote to Lincoln Steffens:

. . . you contend that Taft and I are good people of limited vision who fight against specific evils with no idea of fighting against a fundamental evil; whereas LaFollette is engaged in a fight against *the* "fundamental" evil. LaFollette has been three years in the Senate. His "plan" consists of a string of platitudes and to adopt it wouldn't mean anything.

LaFollette, however, was not in the Senate when the rate fight started in 1905. His revelations in Wisconsin, combined with rising freight rates since 1900, caused the more liberal House of Representatives to pass a bill, the Townsend-Esch measure, by which the Interstate Commerce Commission could declare a freight or passenger rate unjust and could fix a substitute, which would go into effect in thirty days. Appeal could be taken to the courts. No action was taken by the Senate, however, and as he drafted his message for 1905, the President approached, although he did not fully accept it, the principle of blanket rate-fixing. By November, he was sponsoring a bill that would grant authority to the Interstate Commerce Commission to specify maximum rates.

"The railroads have been crazy in their hostility," he wrote.

"The most pressing need," the President said in his message on December 5, 1905, "is the enactment into law of some scheme to secure to the Government such supervision and regulation of rates as shall summarily and effectively prevent the imposition of unjust or unreasonable rates." This was definitely more affirmative language than had appeared in his earlier messages. The advance in Roosevelt's position was clear. Even more indicative of the President's growing radicalism was his specification that there should be full publicity of all accounts of the common carriers. It caused additional apprehension in the breasts of the railroad men and their bankers, for they saw in it a threat of future action that could be defined, again, only as socialism—an impartial valuation of the railroad properties and the fixing of rates on the basis of a fair return on capital invested. Roosevelt did not touch on this in his message but he added, characteristically:

"We desire to set up a moral standard."

3

Both sides prepared for the battle during 1905. The railroads did so by flooding the newspapers of the country with propaganda. Nor was Roosevelt idle. He took action of his own to portray the corporations, in general, and the railroads, in particular, in dark tones before the country. The Elkins amendments, besides stiffening the penalties for rebating, provided that the shippers who received the concessions were culpable along with the railroads. On December 11, 1905, Attorney General William H. Moody gave instructions that prosecutions were to be started by the Federal authorities of all jurisdictions. Two days later, the Chicago grand jury returned an indictment which charged that the Chicago & Alton, and various of its officers, had given rebates to certain packing concerns. Eight additional indictments were returned in Chicago on December 14, the Great Northern being among the latest defendants. On December 15, a Federal grand jury in Kansas City accused such eminent Republican campaign contributors as the Armour Packing Company, Swift & Company, the Cudahy Packing Company, and Nelson Morris & Company, as well as the Burlington, the St. Paul, and the Chicago & Alton railroads, of having received or granted freight rebates.

Further animosity toward the corporate interests had been aroused during the past few years by the muckrakers, those industrious and honest writers whose exposures sometimes disturbed Roosevelt as much as they disturbed the respectables. On March 4, 1906, while the debate on railroad regulation was in progress in the Senate, the President made public the official report of his Bureau of Corporations on Standard Oil.

"The report shows," said Roosevelt, transmitting it to Congress, "that the Standard Oil Company has benefited enormously up almost to the present moment by secret rates. This benefit amounts to at least three-quarters of a million a year." Roosevelt added that Standard Oil was not the only corporation thus profiting. An investigation under way "as to shipments by the sugar trust over the trunk lines out of New York City tends to show that the sugar trust rarely, if ever, pays the lawful rate for transportation."

It was to be a gaudy battle, this debate in which "liar," "unqualified falsehood," "betrayal," "surrender," and "chief cuckoos of the White House" were among the words and phrases scribbled by hurrying stenographers as they recorded for history the barrage of oratory. Representative Peter Hepburn of Iowa offered the President's bill, which provided substantially his plan for railroad regulation contained in his message in December. It was promptly passed by the House by the large majority of 346 to 7.

Opposition so strong that defeat of the Hepburn Bill seemed probable was at once apparent in the Senate. On February 12, 1906, Senator Lodge made a long, scholarly address in which he said that more stringent penalties against rebating were doubtless needed as well as publicity for railroad earnings. But freight rates, on the whole, were not excessive. This defiance on the part of Roosevelt's closest friend naturally started rumors of a break in the harmony that had lasted for so many years. But the President, in a letter to Lyman Abbott, conceded Lodge's sincerity. It was not the only desertion; Senator Knox of Pennsylvania opposed the measure also. On February 18, 1906, he introduced an amendment providing for liberal court review of decisions in rate cases.

The leaders of the opposition were Senator Aldrich, the Republican party whip, Foraker, and Elkins. Elkins was chairman of the Senate Committee on Interstate Commerce. It was Aldrich and Elkins, apparently, who evolved what appeared to be an exceedingly clever scheme to embarass Roosevelt. First, Elkins declined to sponsor the bill, although as the Republican chairman of a Senate committee this would be his usual course in relation to an administration measure. Then Aldrich, who also was a member of the Interstate Commerce Committee, secured adoption of a resolution that placed Senator Tillman of South Carolina, the famous "Pitchfork Ben" Tillman, in charge of Roosevelt's bill. This was on February 23.

"I regarded the action as simply childish," Roosevelt said, on the Aldrich-Elkins maneuver, but it seriously jeopardized hope of success. Tillman was an ardent supporter of

Roosevelt's rate bill, but how could he confer with the President? How could the President summon, at the peril of a rebuke, the leader of the opposition? He went so far as to intimate that he believed the once despicable Tillman to be a great and good man, after all. It was said that the White House latchstring had been hastily hung out for his benefit.

The final debate in the Senate was whether rates were to be regulated by the executive branch or by the judiciary. It is not difficult to understand why Roosevelt energetically supported the former theory, but it was on this point that he compromised, a compromise that brought heated charges of falsehood and bad faith. Late in March a solution was offered for the awkward situation of having a Democrat, who was also personally antagonistic to Roosevelt, in charge of the President's bill. A personal conference was not possible, but former Senator William E. Chandler of New Hampshire, holding a lame-duck appointive post at the capital, could serve as intermediary. On March 31, 1906, the President requested Chandler to call at the White House. An amusing, almost an idiotic, series of visits followed. Chandler hurried from the White House to the office of Pitchfork Ben and quoted Roosevelt as saying that Senators Knox, Spooner, and Foraker were attempting to defeat the bill. On April 1, Tillman shared this information with his colleague, Senator Joseph W. Bailey of Texas, and then Chandler brought word from the White House that there should be no difficulty about an agreement on the Hepburn amendments. The liaison activities continued until April 15, when Chandler, Bailey, and Tillman had a conference with Moody, Roosevelt's Attorney General. The result of this was the drafting of an amendment that gave to the courts limited powers in passing on the rates fixed by the Interstate Commerce Commission.

Such, at least, was the story told by Senator Tillman when he spoke in high indignation on May 12, 1906, and charged the President with breaking faith. Meanwhile, as soon became evident and as Roosevelt's letters prove, the President had been negotiating with the conservative group. On April 12, he had written to Senator Allison of Iowa that he opposed an amendment providing interference with the commission by the injunction method. On the following day, he wrote that he was not certain that the Constitution would permit such an amendment because it limited the power of the courts. On May 5, he announced that he would accept—not the Tillman amendment drafted by his own Attorney General—but an amendment written by Senator Allison. It permitted the rates to be set aside by injunction proceedings and it represented victory, of a sort, for the railroad senators.

Thereupon Tillman exploded in the Senate that Roosevelt had made derogatory remarks regarding members of his own party. When the South Carolinian finished, Cabot Lodge presented a message from the President who, said the Massachusetts Senator, had declared the accusation "a deliberate and unqualified falsehood." The quarrel, as Roosevelt's usually did, became even more violent before it ended. Articles appeared in the Chicago *Tribune* and the New York *Tribune* in which it was said that the President had been forced to desert Tillman because of the defection of his colleague, Senator Bailey. Undoubtedly these articles were inspired by the White House. They were written, said Bailey in the speech in which he, in turn, defended himself, by correspondents who were the "two chief cuckoos" of the administration. The statement that he had abandoned Tillman was "an unqualified, a deliberate and malicious lie." Five years later President Taft, talking to Archie Butt, recalled that Roosevelt had occasionally "left his old friends," but soon returned to the fold:

. . . when he would get into hot water, he would send for the conservative members of the Cabinet and depend upon us to get him out of it. How well I remembered the time he was pressing his rate bill.

In all probability, despite his denials, Roosevelt had used derogatory terms in talking about the opponents of his bill. It was his invariable custom to do so. "It's only *a* railroad law you want; not to cut the railroads out of the government," accused Lincoln Steffens, and to this Roosevelt agreed. Such was his policy. Such, as he saw it, was the path of progress.

For all its defects, the Hepburn Act of 1906 was a step forward and without Roosevelt the Senate would never have passed the bill, as it did on March 18, 1906, by a vote of 71 to 3. The Interstate Commerce Commission now had jurisdiction over pipelines, express and Pullman operation, refrigeration, storage, and all the other aspects covered by the general term, transportation. The rate-making powers of the commission had been strengthened, although the courts were given more jurisdiction than Roosevelt desired. Honest accounting, now obligatory because the Government could examine the books of the railroads just as it could investigate the books of national banks, made for honesty of freight tariffs.

But the plea of LaFollette, that fair rates could not possibly be determined unless the property of the carriers had first been evaluated, had no effect for a good many years to come; not until Aldrich and Spooner and Allison and Lodge had seen their party wrecked by the upheaval of 1912. On May 8, 1907, Roosevelt confessed in a letter to Beveridge of Indiana that "events have moved so fast in the valuation business that I think it is impossible to avoid taking a conservative ground in its favor." He had already ordered the Interstate Commerce Commission to study the matter. On May 30, at Indianapolis, the President said that the I.C.C. should undertake valuation of the roads, but he urged this in the name of "real conservatism." He said that it would guard the carriers against "inadequate and unjust rates." In his final message to Congress of December, 1908, Roosevelt called for "complete control over the issue of securities as well as over the raising or lowering of rates." But he was soon to leave the White House. It was President Taft, whom T.R. would fight in 1912 on the ground of his conservatism, who finally got a fairly good railroad law.

4

The 1904 to 1909 years were busy years. The Russo-Japanese War, the Algeciras Conference, the possible menace of Japan, railroad regulation, the tariff; all these problems, technical and involved as they were, did not occupy fully the energies of the extraordinary personality in the White House. The very fact that Roosevelt groped for remedies that would benefit everyone made their solution almost impossible.

The victory of the Government in the Northern Securities case had made valid again the provisions, whatever they may have been worth, of the Sherman Anti-Trust Law. In Roosevelt's mind this was not adequate protection against corporate power and on this, as much as on any issue, he worried his advisers. On December 24, 1904, as Roosevelt gave consideration to his trust-control program, Elihu Root begged him not to be precipitate regarding a proposal for Federal licensing of corporations. "It was Bryan's," he wrote, "and I think involves evils far greater than its benefits."

But the President was far wiser, politically, than Root on this occasion at least. In his message to Congress in December, 1905, he said that the corporations engaged in interstate business were "subjects without a sovereign," and that it might be essential to amend the Constitution to provide adequate control. A year later he mentioned a national license law as a possible solution. In 1907, he definitely advocated such a statute.

"This is not advocating centralization," he said, "it is merely looking facts in the face."

But Roosevelt was again ahead of his time and it was impossible, even for him, to engage in battles comparable to the one on railroad rates on all these issues. Partly because the Government was handicapped by the law and thwarted by clever attorneys employed by the trusts, partly because Roosevelt was so busy on other matters, rather little was accomplished in actual prosecutions or in the dissolution of illegal combinations. Suits were instituted against the tobacco and packing trusts. But it was not until the Taft Administration that the Standard Oil Company and the American Tobacco Company were ordered to dissolve. It was not until Woodrow Wilson came into power that the Clayton Act, an extension of trust control, became law. Roosevelt's title as "Trust Buster" was an exaggeration. He started only twenty-five proceedings leading to indictments under the Sherman Act, while Taft began forty-five. The significance of Roosevelt's corporation activities lay in what he said rather than what he did. Even the spectacular fine of $29,000,000 assessed by Federal Judge Kenesaw Mountain Landis on April 13, 1907, against the Standard Oil Company of Indiana came to nothing. The higher courts set aside the penalty, and the Standard Oil Company paid nothing.

Even the muckrakers, who had brought into the light so many of the evils on which Roosevelt acted, were to learn, in pained surprise, that he endorsed their exposés with distinct reservations. In 1901, although he said nothing publicly, he expressed doubt that the indictment of Frank Norris against the Southern Pacific Railroad in California was accurate. On March 17, 1906, when Speaker Cannon was the host at a dinner to the Gridiron Club, the President deprecated, quoting from *Pilgrim's Progress*, the man who fixed his mind only on things that were vile and debasing, on filth alone.

But one muckraker—the term was original with Roosevelt—inspired the President to another brisk fight with Congress. On March 9, 1906, Roosevelt wrote Upton Sinclair, whose *The Jungle* had recently been published, that "I shall read it with interest," although Commissioner of Corporations Garfield believed the conclusions regarding the Chicago packing houses "too pessimistic." At the same time he directed Secretary of Agriculture Wilson to appoint an investigator who would confer with Sinclair and begin an inquiry. Two examiners were appointed, James Bronson Reynolds and Charles P. Neill, and their disclosures moved the President to horrified action. Beveridge of Indiana introduced a bill permitting effective inspection of the packing houses on May 22, 1906, and it passed the Senate three days later. Then it slumbered in the lower house.

The packers, who once had so gladly supported Roosevelt for office, continued to exert pressure against passage of the bill, and he struck at them on June 4, 1906, by making public a report compiled by Reynolds and Neill. It was a loathsome document. It told of filth, disease, and gross carelessness in the packing houses. Tuberculosis was prevalent among the workers. Old bits of rope had been discovered in chopped meat about to be placed in cans. The buildings in which the work was done were dark, damp, and badly ventilated.

The folly of the packers was endless. Thomas E. Wilson, of the Nelson Morris Company, said that his plant was "as clean as any kitchen." He was confident that Reynolds and Neill, being men "of fine sensibilities," had been shocked into gross inaccuracies by the mere sight of blood. Then the President let it be known that this was only a "preliminary report," and that additional facts might be published unless the packers told their agents in the House that the bill should be passed. At the same time it appeared probable that the export trade in American meat would suffer. This economic argument, added to Roosevelt's threats of additional exposures, brought passage of the inspection bill on July 1, 1906.

The reform is illustrative of the degree to which the innovations for which Roosevelt received credit were suggested by others. Another instance was the battle for pure food. In 1883, Dr. Harvey Washington Wiley had been appointed chief chemist of the Department of Agriculture. By 1902 his "poison squad" of twelve young assistants was permitting experiments in the effect of adulterated foods and drugs to be made upon it. Unfortunately, Dr. Wiley and the President irritated each other. The pure-food enthusiast felt that Roosevelt did not accord sufficiently firm support to those who enforced the law and that too much credit for its passage had been given to the White House. On his part, the President believed that Dr. Wiley was a fanatic; but "I have such confidence in his integrity and zeal that I am anxious to back him up to the limit of my power wherever I can be sure that doing so won't do damage instead of good."

A degree of justice undoubtedly lay in the position of each. Roosevelt was not bashful in taking credit to which his title was clouded. Dr. Wiley was probably overeager. Certainly the Pure Food Bill would not have been passed on June 23, 1906, had not Roosevelt recommended some such law in December, 1905.

Another aspect of his program for the suppression of socialistic unrest remained: protection for labor against the excessive use of the injunction. "If the attitude of the New York *Sun* toward labor becomes the attitude of the Republican Party," he told Knox just after Election Day in 1904, "we shall some day go down before a radical and extreme democracy with a crash, which will be disastrous to the nation. We must not only do justice, but be able to show that we are doing justice."

In 1905, in addition to suggesting employers' liability for the District of Columbia and an investigation of child labor, Roosevelt raised the question of limiting the power of the courts in defeating the aspirations of labor by means of the injunction. In May, 1906, he said that he opposed having "any operation of the law turn into an engine of oppression against the wage worker." In his message to Congress, the President pointed to "grave abuses" possible because of this weapon in the hands of capital.

5

Roosevelt's passionate interest in the national forests, in reclamation of arid Western lands by irrigation, in conservation of water power and other natural resources, may well be considered as part of his campaign against the malefactors of great wealth. There can be little controversy regarding Roosevelt's contribution to the cause of conservation, although he was faintly jealous of credit given to Senator Francis G. Newlands of Nevada, a Democrat. It is probable, too, that Roosevelt minimized the contribution of Senator Hanna, who had first become interested in irrigation in 1897. On all these important matters, however, there is credit enough for all.

The preservation of the forests and the irrigation of desert lands were part of the heritage of Roosevelt's own years in the West. His opposition to exploitation of water power was based on the conception, novel in that day, that this was the property of the people and should redound to their benefit. In 1903, when the Fifty-seventh Congress passed a bill awarding to one N. J. Thompson the right to build a dam and construct a power station at Muscle Shoals, Alabama—thus ancient are the issues of American politics—the President vetoed the bill.

Roosevelt told the story of conservation, competently and without the distortions that sometimes marked his writings, in his autobiography. The influence of Gifford Pinchot, which started when Roosevelt was governor, was the dominant one in the great and significant changes whereby the forests were placed under adequate supervision. The Newlands Act, passed in 1902 with Roosevelt's energetic assistance, provided within four years the irrigation of some 3,000,000 acres, and engineering projects nearly as great as the Panama Canal.

Chapter XII

THE WICKED SPECULATORS

❋

During the summer of 1905, Dr. Butler of Columbia University was granted an audience by the German Kaiser. They discussed various problems relating to their two countries, among them finance. Who, asked Wilhelm II, managed government financial matters in the United States?

"God," answered Dr. Butler.

The inference, obviously, was that no one, not even J. P. Morgan, had shown competence in dealing with this aspect of government. Some years later, Professor J. Laurence Laughlin, who had attempted to instill some knowledge of economics into Theodore Roosevelt at Harvard in the '80's, called at the *Outlook* office where the ex-President was an associate editor. Dr. Laughlin was anxious to obtain Roosevelt's support in a movement for banking reform, but his former student said that his knowledge of finance was largely limited to arguments against free silver: ". . . when it comes to finance or compound differentials," he said, "I'm all up in the air."

This being so, it was unfortunate that Roosevelt was in the White House during a period when the attitude of the public toward a national monetary system was beginning to change. The Republican leaders of 1896 to 1900 thought that the problem had been settled when gold became the indisputable basis of currency. Gold afforded protection for the nation's financial institutions and for the man of wealth, or so it was believed. The new conception, which called for an elastic currency, demanded protection against panics for men of moderate means and wealth alike. There is a vital difference between this philosophy, which the most conservative economists endorsed in theory during the pioneer work that led to the Federal Reserve Act, and the agitation for free silver. In 1896, the gains of the masses would have been at the expense of the few.

If, as Roosevelt believed, the Government must protect its citizens from extortion by industrial monopoly and from unfair railroad rates, it was logical to extend this protection to financial matters. This, however, was an issue on which Roosevelt was not qualified for leadership. Nor was Secretary of the Treasury Leslie M. Shaw, of Iowa, of much assistance. His retirement was permitted and George B. Cortelyou, Secretary of Commerce and Labor, took his place.

During flutterings of the financial seismograph at various times between 1901 and 1907, Roosevelt's inclination was to blame, not without reason, the nation's financiers. In August, 1903, when the tremors became acute, he said that they were "due chiefly, almost solely, to the speculation, the watering of stock on a giant scale, in which Pierpont Morgan and so many of his kind have indulged during the last few years." This was true enough but the President was a shade ungracious in so expressing himself again in January, 1908. Morgan, James Stillman, and their associates had acted *in loco Dei* during the crisis in October of the year before.

Currency reform, although vaguely recommended by the President in his messages to Congress, continued to drift. In December, 1906, Roosevelt said that to leave the law unchanged meant "the liability of a business disaster." Then the President offered for the attention of Congress a plan for additional elasticity. National banks might issue notes which would be taxed out of existence as soon as the emergency passed. But Roosevelt made no fight for it, as for railroad regulation. The Fifty-ninth Congress, before it adjourned in March, 1907, passed a palliative which permitted the Secretary of the Treasury to deposit customs receipts in the national banks instead of leaving them in the national treasury.

The financial interests, naturally enough, did not share Roosevelt's belief that undue speculation was the basis of the unrest. They said, on the contrary, that the President's crusades against business had undermined public confidence. So carefully edited a journal as the New York *Times* carried a dispatch from Washington which said that Roosevelt intended to "break" Harriman, that the Harriman railroad lines would be declared in restraint of trade, and somehow dissolved. Not long afterward, Roosevelt had his famous, and all too public, quarrel with E. H. Harriman, a controversy that reflected discredit on both men.

The accusation that the President had undermined public confidence in railroad securities, and thereby in industrial issues, was emphasized during January, 1907, and this worried Roosevelt. "If trouble comes from having the light turned on," he said, "remember that it is not really due to the light but to the misconduct which is exposed." On the same day, however, he directed Chairman Martin A. Knapp of the Interstate Commerce Commission to "lay greater emphasis upon the administrative side. You should stop the *evils* in advance." After flurries in December, the stock market steadied somewhat in the early part of 1907. Then came a sharp break on March 4, and Harriman, who had been in Washington to confer with Roosevelt, said that cooperation between the Government and the railroads was essential. On March 14, Union Pacific dropped twenty-five points, Reading slipped from 115 to 91, and Great Northern from 143 to 132.

"I would hate to tell you," said Harriman, seen by reporters, "to whom I think you ought to go for an explanation of all this."

Meanwhile efforts had been made to heal the breach between Roosevelt and the railroad men. On March 1, Morgan was secretly at the White House and urged that the President confer with them. This was followed by demands that some statement from the White House be made to restore public confidence. "I have been much inclined to yield," Roosevelt said, "but when I wrote out my speech I was simply repeating what I had already said. I do not like to seem to talk just for the effect upon the stock market."

The conference with the railroad men did not take place, largely because the crisis was momentarily averted. As the apprehensions of a more severe storm continued, Roosevelt decided to speak. On May 30, at Indianapolis, he disavowed any belief that the railroads were overcapitalized. By August the situation was again grave. Credit was difficult to obtain. Even the City of New York had been unable to find a market for its bonds. Several big failures occurred and others were rumored. Roosevelt was deluged with requests that he take some action, but he still felt that his critics were in the wrong. On August 12, from Oyster Bay, he protested to his first wife's kinsman, Major Henry Lee Higginson, that most of the letters he was getting struck "the same note of lunacy":

Now, my dear Major I do not understand some of the points you make. You say that the verdict against the Standard Oil Company has done great damage, and you advise me to let the public know that the prosecutions will not be pushed. I am sure you will understand how difficult it would be for me to make such an announcement and defend it against any reasoning man the moment the panic in Wall Street (or the flurry in Wall Street) was over. I have tried my best not to rake up any old offenses; but I cannot grant an illegal immunity. If we have to proceed against anyone it is because he has sinned against the light.

On August 20 he declared, as so many politicians were to insist twenty-two years later when another panic came, that the economic unrest had been world-wide. Roosevelt, however, said even more: ". . . certain malefactors of great wealth," he added, and intimated they were stinging from the just chastisement of a righteous Government, might have combined "to bring about as much financial stress as possible in order to secure a reversal of that policy."

Clearly, Roosevelt was preparing to abandon the wicked speculators to a just fate. When the storm broke he was hunting bear in the Louisiana brakes, but he returned to Washington in time to be badly frightened and to forget his declaration to Major Higginson that no pledges of immunity could be given.

2

J. Pierpont Morgan sat among the lay delegates to the General Convention of the Protestant Episcopal Church and thought, perhaps, of spiritual things. The bishops, the vicars, the clergymen, and the curates who had come to Richmond, Virginia, in October, 1907, may have stolen a glance or two in the direction of Mr. Morgan. They saw telegrams brought to him, as he was dining at his hotel, and watched him stare stolidly into space after he had read them. When the convention had adjourned, Bishop Lawrence of Massachusetts, who kept a finger on the pulse of lay affairs, noted in his diary an incident or two that had interested him on the final day, Saturday, October 19:

As I was going out of the door to the House of Bishops on Saturday morning, Mr. Morgan called me into his room and said,

"Bishop, I am going back to New York on the noon train." I said, "Why do you do that?" He answered, "They are in trouble in New York. They do not know what to do, and I don't know what to do, but I am going back." I replied, "Why do you go back at noon? Why not the early evening train tonight: we will all pack up and go with you." It was done, and though we went up by the evening train there was no suggestion of care or anxiety on his part . . . he was in the best of spirits.

Sunday morning as we ran into Jersey City, we went into Mr. Morgan's car for some bread and coffee before arrival, and found him sitting at the table with a tumbler turned upside down in each hand, singing lustily some tune which no one could recognize.

Reason enough existed for the banker's return. During the week of October 6 to 13, new lows had been recorded on the New York Stock Exchange. Monday, October 14, brought further uneasiness. Certain securities controlled by F. Augustus Heintz, president of the Mercantile National Bank, had been fluctuating like the temperature of a patient in whose body a virulent fever burned. Then came rumors that the Mercantile Bank was, in the ominous Wall Street phrase, "in trouble." United Copper, a Heintz stock, crashed from 53 to 10. At midnight on Wednesday, Heintz announced his resignation as president of the Mercantile Bank. On Thursday, October 17, the stock exchange firm of Otto Heintz & Company was suspended from trading, and a savings bank in far-off Butte, Montana, closed its doors.

These disturbing events had, presumably, been described in the telegrams received by Morgan at Richmond. On Sunday afternoon, October 20, the members of the New York Clearing House Committee called in the waiting reporters and said that the Mercantile and other banks touched by rumors were solvent. The nefarious interests represented by Heintz and Charles W. Morse had withdrawn. New officers had been elected. The public must have confidence that all was fundamentally sound. But on Monday, October 21, 1907, another wave of pessimism swept New York City and spread, by telegraph, to the rest of the country. Now the Knickerbocker Trust Company, which had recently opened magnificent new offices on Fifth Avenue, was the subject of rumor. No word came from Roosevelt, hunting the elusive bear of Louisiana.

That afternoon, although the morning papers had been optimistic, the National Bank of Commerce notified the Knickerbocker Trust that its checks would not be honored. From meetings in the financial section and at Sherry's restaurant that night, spread word that the Knickerbocker could not meet its obligations on Tuesday. Again, officials attempted to stop the probable run by issuing reassuring statements, by insisting that $8,000,000 in cash lay in the vaults. They were without effect. When the doors opened at nine o'clock on Tuesday morning, long lines had already formed. Every check presented was cashed, but several hundred men and women were still waiting at three o'clock.

As the depositors clamored for their money on Tuesday, Secretary of the Treasury Cortelyou took a train for New York City and arrived in the afternoon. He went at once to the Manhattan Hotel, where Morgan was closeted with Stillman, George F. Baker, George W. Perkins, and other financiers. Cortelyou gave assurance, as he subsequently testified, that the Treasury Department would help "in every possible and feasible way." On that night, in effect, the financial machinery of the United States Government was turned over to Morgan, whom Roosevelt had so recently described as an unhealthy influence. In so far as his letters show, the President took no part in the arrangement. He was returning from the bear hunt.

Morgan would not save the Knickerbocker Trust. "I can't go on being everybody's goat," he is supposed to have said. Its cash was exhausted at noon on Wednesday, October 23. All day mobs besieged the Trust Company of America and other banks, but there were no additional failures. Cortelyou established offices in the Sub-Treasury building, not far from Morgan's offices. There was another conference at the Hotel Manhattan that night, and the Secretary of the Treasury agreed to place $25,000,000 in government funds in the national banks. At the same time, Cortelyou pointed out that most of the rumors had been "unfounded" and most of the anxiety "unreasoning." Roosevelt had reached Washington on Wednesday afternoon.

"I have had a delightful time," he said. "I am extremely gratified that I got a bear."

The banking situation had improved somewhat on October 24, but it was an agonizing day on the stock exchange. At two o'clock, call money rose to one hundred per cent. Stocks were dumped at any price. Then, mysteriously, call money suddenly dropped to ten per cent and the situation had been relieved. Cortelyou notified the White House next day that conditions were still grave, but that the crisis would be over if the obstacles of the forthcoming twenty-four hours could be surmounted.

On October 25, Roosevelt drafted a communication to

reassure the country and gave Cortelyou authority to make it public. It appeared on the front pages of all the papers on Sunday; a somewhat premature message of congratulation to the Secretary of the Treasury and also to "those influential and splendid business men who have acted with such wisdom and public spirit."

Trouble was still ahead, but at this point it is relevant to examine subsequent charges that the $25,000,000 tendered by Cortelyou went to the relief of stock exchange houses on Thursday afternoon and not to the banks. Three trust companies, in addition to the Knickerbocker, and one national bank in New York failed during the panic of 1907. Five years passed before light was thrown on the activities behind the scenes. In 1912, Ransom H. Thomas, president of the stock exchange in 1907, testified that on October 24, 1907, he had waited for twenty minutes in Morgan's office and had then been told to hurry back to the stock exchange and announce that $25,000,000 would be supplied. He did not know where the money had come from, but in two or three minutes the national banks were again lending in the call market and the rate dropped from one hundred per cent to ten per cent.

On June 13, 1912, Cortelyou told the "Money Trust" investigators that he had not differentiated "the stock market from the community generally"; he had deposited the $25,000,000 for "the relief of the community generally." He could recall few of the details regarding the conferences with Morgan. He did not remember whether the call money situation had been discussed. He did not know which banks received the $25,000,000. He assumed that "considerable of the money" had been used to relieve the stock market.

3

Whatever the actual disposition of the $25,000,000, it had effected only temporary relief. "I have confidence in the banks," said Archbishop Farley at a special mass for businessmen in New York on Sunday, October 27. But on Monday call money fluctuated between twelve and seventy-five per cent and on Tuesday a large stock exchange house was suspended. The extreme shortage of currency continued. As October ended, disquieting trends were seen in runs on savings banks in various parts of the country and in announcement by the Santa Fe Railroad that a $7,000,000 improvement on its lines had been postponed.

Morgan no longer sang lustily and balanced tumblers on

each hand; he was more grim. He sat, on Saturday and Sunday nights, October 27 and 28, in a small room adjoining the magnificent library in his home on Madison Avenue and played "patience" while he smoked large black cigars. From time to time he would emerge from his solitary card game to reject some proposal that had been drafted by lesser financiers. On Sunday night scores of men passed in and out, among them Elbert H. Gary of United States Steel. They hurried past the newspaper reporters who clustered around them as they left, but it became known that the chief subject under discussion was the Tennessee Coal and Iron Company, whose stock had been pledged against loans by numerous brokerage houses and was now in disfavor. It was rumored that Moore & Schley, one large firm, held $5,000,000 of this stock as collateral and might crash on Monday; it was acknowledged that if this occurred the whole flimsy structure euphemized as High Finance would come tumbling down. Mr. Morgan had helped to build the structure; he did not want this to happen. Some one suggested that the United States Steel Corporation, formed in the days of McKinley prosperity, might purchase the Tennessee Coal and Iron Company for $45,000,000 and thereby validate its securities.

Events moved swiftly that Sunday night. At ten o'clock, William Loeb, secretary to President Roosevelt, was called to the telephone at Washington by Judge Gary. Could he, accompanied by Henry C. Frick, have an appointment with the President at the earliest possible moment the following morning? At about the same time, orders were telephoned to the chief dispatcher of the Pennsylvania Railroad in New Jersey. A special train was to be made up at once, merely a locomotive and a Pullman. Between ten o'clock and midnight signalmen on the right of way to Washington received instructions which told of the one-car special that would flash by in the night. Just after midnight Gary and Frick slipped from the Morgan mansion and hurried to the train.

It reached Washington in the early morning, but at eight o'clock the two emissaries could restrain themselves no longer and started for the White House, where, an hour later, they were received by Loeb. The President's secretary said that it was quite impossible for them to see Roosevelt until ten o'clock, but they explained the gravity of their mission and soon the President appeared, having interrupted his breakfast.

Gary, as he later testified, explained the altruistic nature of his mission. He also told of the necessity for haste; it was vital to telephone news of the outcome before the exchange opened in New York at ten o'clock. The President, however, felt that wisdom required some consultation. Attorney General Bonaparte was not in Washington and Secretary of State Root was summoned. Gary then said that the United States Steel Corporation had an opportunity to acquire control of the Tennessee Coal and Iron Company at a "price somewhat in excess of its true value." Did the President object? If the deal went through, would the Steel Corporation be prosecuted under the Sherman Act?

"I do not believe," Gary quoted Roosevelt as replying, "that anyone could justly criticize me for saying that I would not feel like objecting to the purchase under the circumstances."

Meanwhile, at his home in New York, Morgan retired at five o'clock in the morning for a few hours of sleep. At 8:30 he breakfasted and waited for a telephone call from Washington. At the Morgan offices on Wall Street, George W. Perkins held the end of a telephone wire connected with the White House and at 9:55, he heard Gary's voice bearing the glad tidings. The President would not interfere and word to this effect was transmitted to the stock exchange, where it was received with the proper bullish sentiment.

As to the conversation between Gary and Roosevelt on the morning of November 4, there is no essential disagreement. Mr. Root confirmed Mr. Gary's recollection. As soon as Gary and Frick left, the President dictated one of his characteristic "posterity" letters in which he said:

Judge E. H. Gary and Mr. H. C. Frick on behalf of the Steel Corporation have just called upon me. They state that there is a certain business firm (the name of which I have not been told, but which is of real importance in New York business circles), which will undoubtedly fail this week if help is not given. Among its assets are a majority of the securities of the Tennessee Coal and Iron Company. Application has been urgently made to the Steel Corporation to purchase this stock as the only means of avoiding a failure. Judge Gary and Mr. Frick informed me that as a mere business transaction they do not care to purchase the stock, because but little benefit will come to the Steel Corporation. They further informed me that the acquisition of the property in question will not raise it [their proportion of steel properties] above sixty per cent. I answered that, while of course I could not advise them to take the action proposed, I felt it no public duty of mine to interpose any objections.

"It was necessary for me to decide on the instant, before the Stock Exchange opened," Roosevelt testified in 1911, "for the situation in New York was such that any hour might be vital." He added that he had been under the impression the action was necessary to "save one big trust company." No names had been mentioned, however, "and I thought it just as well that I should not ask."

4

Soon it was declared that Roosevelt had been grievously misled by the representatives of the Steel Corporation, a charge that Mr. Gary repudiated on, as he said, the obvious grounds that "everyone connected with the United States Steel Corporation cares more for his conduct and reputation and his character than [for] making or losing a few dollars." Perhaps Gary and his associates, like Roosevelt, saw their own motives hallowed by the passage of time. At all events, they became indignant when it was intimated that an enormously valuable property, available at a bargain, had been in their minds. The evidence, even portions of their own testimony, refutes them, however.

Certainly the President had been misled when he was told that "a certain business concern" would fail. This was not a trust company. It was the brokerage house of Moore & Schley. At the first Congressional investigation into the negotiations, held in 1908, Grant B. Schley said that outright sale of the Tennessee Coal and Iron Company had not been essential, that his firm would have been able to weather the storm if five or six million dollars in "real money" had been forthcoming. Three years later Gary reluctantly admitted as much. He was asked whether Moore & Schley would not have been saved had the Steel Corporation merely made a loan of its bonds to the brokerage house.

"I should think so," he said.

Nor was the United States Steel Corporation quite so reluctant to take over the Tennessee Coal and Iron Company as the President was informed. Its sixth annual report pointed, not without satisfaction, to the deal as one that "promises benefit to the corporation. The Tennessee property is very valuable. Its mineral resources are large." John Moody, the financial expert, said that the price of $45,000,000 paid for the property made it "the best bargain the Steel Corporation or any other concern or individual ever made in the purchase of a piece of property."

The coal and iron ore owned by the T.C. and I. in Alabama, Tennessee, and Georgia had, at a "very conservative estimate," a potential value of "hardly less than $1,000,000,000." Even Judge Gary, testifying before the House Ways and Means Committee on the tariff in 1908, said that a valuation of $200,000,000 on the property, even one of two or three times that sum, "is not very much too high."

In short, Gary and Frick had used the panic to put across a very shrewd deal.

Roosevelt never lost confidence, however, that his action had been wise and necessary. "The results," he insisted in 1911, "were beneficial from every standpoint. I would have shown myself a timid and unworthy public officer if I had not acted as I did. I never had any doubt of the wisdom of my action—not for a moment."

The truth is that Roosevelt was a badly frightened Chief Executive toward the end of 1907, and saw himself ending his term "under a more or less dark cloud of obloquy." On August 22, 1907, he directed Attorney General Bonaparte that no suit was to be filed against the International Harvester Company, for the present. This was not, as Roosevelt's adversaries in the Progressive campaign in 1912 were to point out, because any secret arrangement had been made with George W. Perkins of the Harvester Trust. It was because Roosevelt was deeply alarmed. On November 4, 1907, when the financial situation appeared most grave, inspired dispatches from Washington stated that an investigation into the steel trust being undertaken by the Bureau of Corporations would undoubtedly result in a friendly verdict. It was the Taft Administration that sought to dissolve the United States Steel Corporation, in October, 1911, and the attempt failed. The United States Supreme Court held that the purchase of the Tennessee Coal and Iron Company had not created a monopoly within the meaning of the Sherman Act.

Roosevelt soon recovered from his alarm.

Chapter XIII

SUBSTANTIAL JUSTICE

❈

Q. How did you know that substantial justice was done?

Mr. Roosevelt. Because I did it, because I was doing my best.

Q. You mean to say that when you do a thing thereby substantial justice is done?

Mr. Roosevelt. I do. When I do a thing I do it so as to do substantial justice. I mean just that.

So Roosevelt testified under oath in 1915. It was the essence of his philosophy, the conviction of righteousness that strengthened him in his moments of inner doubt. Justice was an essential part of righteousness. And yet there were men and women who went to their graves convinced that they had been grievously wronged by T.R. A lieutenant general of the army, whose bravery had helped to win the Civil War, encountered the presidential wrath and retired with his record tarnished. A railroad magnate was publicly branded an undesirable citizen. A remarkably unimportant ambassador, Bellamy Storer, was dismissed. A regiment of Negro soldiers, probably the victims of a conspiracy, learned that "substantial justice" did not include the constitutional provision that men are innocent until proved guilty beyond a reasonable doubt.

Lieut. Gen. Nelson A. Miles had suffered Roosevelt's displeasure, although unaware of it, during the Spanish War. The colonel of the Rough Riders noted in his diary, when giving vent to his disgust over the blunders of the High Command, that General Miles was "merely a brave peacock." He felt that Miles was one of those responsible for the disorder which attended the comic-opera war.

The general made a grave mistake in June, 1901, when he publicly intimated that Roosevelt, then Vice-President, had not been at San Juan Hill at all; perhaps a fact far better left unsaid.

"What a scoundrelly hypocrite the man is!" exclaimed Roosevelt. "At a dinner of Seawanaka Club he toasted me as the 'bravest of the brave' at Santiago."

But this was forgiven when Roosevelt entered the White House and sought, on all sides, harmony for his first troublesome days. The President rode one of General Miles's horses pending arrival of his own from Oyster Bay. He even invited the "brave peacock" to accompany him on a ride.

Roosevelt did not have to wait long to find an outlet for his suppressed irritation, however. During 1901 a Naval Court of Inquiry had been investigating the conduct of Rear Admirals William T. Sampson and Winfield S. Schley at the Battle of Santiago. The court, Admiral Dewey excepting, held that Schley had been guilty of errors in judgment in maneuvering the fleet prior to June 1, 1898. The trial created undue excitement and the verdict, in December, 1901, merely strengthened the convictions of Schley's partisans that he had been wronged. Thereupon, General Miles blundered into this hornet's nest. "I am willing to take the judgment of Admiral Dewey in the matter," he said on December 16, 1901. "I have no sympathy with the efforts that have been made to destroy the honor of an officer under such circumstances."

Admiral Dewey, being a member of the Court of Inquiry, was entitled to his dissenting opinion. General Miles, in no way concerned with the Sampson-Schley matter, had no right to say anything. He did not know that indiscretions were dangerous unless they were in harmony with some prejudice held by the President. Miles, on the contrary, expressed an opposite opinion; Roosevelt was to endorse the finding of the Court of Inquiry. The first official thunderbolt that struck the general of the armies was hurled by Secretary of War Root. His statement had been "subversive of discipline. It would not be tolerated in a subaltern and it will not be tolerated in any officer of whatever rank." By "direction of the President," said Root, the general's conduct had been judged "liable to censure, which I now express."

The distress of Miles was pitiful. He was growing old; behind him stretched an unstained record in the Civil War and in Indian campaigning. He hurried to the office of the Secretary of War and then to the White House in an effort to save himself. It was without avail, but as a result of the interview at the White House public attention shifted from Sampson and Schley to Roosevelt and Miles. The excitement reached such proportions that the President was apprehensive over its political effect on the Grand Army of the Republic. Unfortunately, no authentic account of the conference is available.

The White House interview was on December 21. According to the New York *Herald*, "President Roosevelt, in a voice loud enough to be heard all over the room, told General Miles that he had committed a breach of military discipline. He spoke with great sharpness and General Miles left the room in confusion." Within a week, this version had been embroidered to one in which the President shook his finger in the general's face. The ultimate exaggeration was that Roosevelt had shrieked, "I'll show you I've got teeth! I've got teeth and you shall feel them!"

That the bitterness came to the surface, and was exhibited in the presence of others, is confirmed by the President's official biographer, who gives no authority, however, for his account. This version was that Miles had demanded an immediate interview to protest against the reprimand. Roosevelt, greeting visitors in the reception room, instructed the general to wait until he had finished. Miles, however, persisted and the President said:

"I wish to show you courtesy, but your conduct has been not merely silly but insubordinate and unmilitary. You deserve a severe reprimand."

The *Army and Navy Register* openly defended General Miles. It said, with some truth, that the views expressed on the Sampson-Schley affair had not justified "the severity—not to say the brutality" of the reprimand imposed. In the public rebuke at the White House, the President had "offended the amenities of official and unofficial intercourse." Then it added a phrase that must have sent Roosevelt's anger to white heat: General Miles had been entitled to consideration at the hands of "a man of no military experience, a younger man, as yet hardly trained in the responsibilities and tribulations of his high office."

Miles further offended by commenting on the perfectly obvious atrocities of the American troops in the Philippine campaign. During 1902, the President apparently debated the wisdom of forcing the retirement of the general, but was dissuaded because of the certain political effect.

"We are a queer, emotional, hysterical people on occasions," he confided to Cabot Lodge.

2

In December, 1906, Edward H. Harriman gave bristling answers to the Interstate Commerce Commission. He said that he would take over the Santa Fe, if the law would permit, and also the Northern Pacific and the Great Northern.

"And your power," he was asked, "would gradually increase so that you might spread not only over the Pacific Coast, but over the Atlantic Coast?"

"Yes," answered Harriman.

Here was another rival to the power of Government and a clash with its champion, Roosevelt, became inevitable because Harriman, too, had no misgivings as to the righteousness of his cause. The enmity which would develop was in sharp contrast to the earlier friendship of Roosevelt and Harriman, although in 1903 T.R. had privately wondered whether the railroad magnate was "entirely straightforward." In April, 1899, from Albany, the governor of New York had written of "a most enjoyable dinner, for which I am greatly your debtor." As late as January, 1905, they were still corresponding amicably, and the President was gratified that Harriman wished to have his picture painted and hung in the Capitol at Albany.

The open break did not occur until April, 1907, and then it was bitter enough to reveal the antagonism that had smoldered for at least four years. If Harriman had kept to his last, the quarrel might have been avoided. He was not, however, satisfied with power in the financial and railroad world. He wanted political power as well, and by 1904 was looking upon himself, with some reason, as the actual boss of the New York Republican machine.

Harriman's ultimate undoing was not solely the work of Roosevelt. The Hughes insurance investigations, September to December, 1905, revealed his affiliation with the Equitable Life Assurance Society and he suffered, although his responsibility was slight, for the misdeeds of that company. On his part, Harriman viewed askance the fight being waged by the President for regulation of railroad rates. He felt that Roosevelt was betraying the interests that had accomplished his election in 1904. In December, 1905, he wrote a letter to Sidney Webster, a friend, and did not dream that fifteen months later a discharged employee would sell it to the New York *World* for $150.

As he wrote the famous Webster letter, Harriman's opinion of his own political gifts was at a low ebb. "I am quite sure I have none," he said, and insisted that any prominence in politics at the moment was

entirely due to President Roosevelt because of my taking an active part in the autumn of 1904 at his request. About a week before Election in the autumn of 1904, when it looked certain that the state ticket would go Democratic, and was doubtful as to Roosevelt, himself, the President sent me a request to go to

Washington to confer upon the political conditions in New York State. I complied and he told me that he understood the campaign could not be carried on without sufficient money, and asked me if I would help them in raising the necessary funds.

Harriman said he had informed Roosevelt that difficulties in the state campaign were due to unwillingness on the part of certain leaders to support Depew for another term in the Senate. If Depew could "be taken care of in some other way" the party would again present a united front. Roosevelt, he wrote, then agreed to name Depew as ambassador to France. Harriman subscribed $50,000 of his own and brought in an additional $200,000. He had no doubt that the contributions had been reported to Roosevelt, and was shocked to learn after the election that Depew would not be sent to France, after all.

"Where do I stand?" he asked Webster.

He was standing, Harriman learned when the letter was published on April 2, 1907, in an uncomfortable spot. Between December, 1905, and April, 1907, the friction with Roosevelt had become acute. On the afternoon of April 2, 1907, Roosevelt joyfully summoned the Washington correspondents and tore apart the latest foe of righteousness. He produced from his files one of those letters justifying his conduct and confounding his adversaries. It was dated October 6, 1906, and was addressed to Representative James S. Sherman of New York, then chairman of the Republican Congressional Campaign Committee. It told about a conversation between Roosevelt and Sherman that had taken place the same day. The Congressman had described a recent visit to Harriman's office to ask for another campaign contribution. The railroad man had expressed indignation. Roosevelt's "posterity" letter continued:

. . . you asked him if he thought it was well to see Hearstism and the like triumphant over the Republican Party. You inform me that he told you that he did not care in the least, because those people were crooks and he could buy them; that whenever he wanted legislation from a State Legislature he could buy it; that he "could buy Congress," and that if necessary he "could buy the judiciary." This shows a cynicism and deep-seated corruption which make the man uttering such sentiments at least as undesirable a citizen as Debs, or Moyer, or Haywood.

As for the statement by Harriman that the President had asked him to raise $250,000 and had promised to appoint Depew, Roosevelt called this "a deliberate and willful untruth—by rights it should be characterized by an **even shorter** and more ugly word. I never requested Mr.

Harriman to raise a dollar for the Presidential campaign of 1904." Their letters on the campaign related exclusively to the gubernatorial contest in New York, a contest in which Harriman had been "greatly interested because he regarded the attack as being an attack on him and Governor Odell." Roosevelt then quoted letters passing between himself and Harriman as proof that the visit to Washington in October, 1904, was at the initiative of Harriman, because of his concern over the state election.

This was not quite the truth, and Roosevelt was not above distorting the evidence to prove his point. The letters to Sherman gave the impression that the Roosevelt-Harriman correspondence relative to 1904 did not begin until September of that year. After attending the national convention, where he voted for Roosevelt's nomination, Harriman went abroad. For some reason a letter from the President, dated June 29, 1904, was not forwarded: "As soon as you get home, I shall want to see you. The fight will doubtless be hot then."

Roosevelt refrained from making this letter public, because it revealed his desire to see Harriman. He mentioned, but did not quote, Harriman's reply on September 20 stating that he would come to Washington at any time. The next letter, from Roosevelt to Harriman, was on October 10, 1904:

When you wrote me before, I did not feel the situation was such that I was warranted in asking you to take the trouble to come down, but in view of the trouble over the ticket in New York, I should much like to have a few words with you.

This was proof that in the Webster letter Harriman had told the truth when he said that "the President sent me a request to go to Washington to confer upon the political conditions in New York State." Roosevelt must have known this. At all events, he struck out the first phrase of this letter when he made it public; it now gave the impression that the President was merely consenting to see the railroad man, at his own request.

After all, it was a fine distinction. The state and national campaigns were really inseparable. At no time, despite Roosevelt's loud assertions, had Harriman claimed that the $250,000 was to be spent elsewhere than in New York. The controversy was unfortunate because it heightened the public distrust and aggravated the unrest that culminated in the panic of 1907. It was unfortunate for Roosevelt because he carelessly included, in the long communication to Sherman, his phrase, "You and I are practical men," from one of the letters to Harriman. Taken with its context, the phrase had no sinister meaning, but Roosevelt's enemies used it to show that he had some secret arrangement with Harriman. It was the kind of indiscretion of which political adversaries dream.

3

On November 20, 1906, word reached the White House that the members of Congress had received an extremely interesting pamphlet from Bellamy Storer, who in March, 1906, had been ordered by Roosevelt to resign as United States ambassador to Austria-Hungary. The President, having obtained a copy, read it with blended amusement and chagrin. He was aware that the document would certainly be made public. He addressed a lengthy communication to Secretary of War Root. This was put aside while the explosion was awaited.

Roosevelt was not kept long in suspense. Senator Shelby M. Cullom considerately left the Storer pamphlet on his desk after intimating to two newspaper correspondents that no inquiry would be made if it disappeared during his absence. It was published on December 8, 1906, and confirmed rumors current the previous March that Storer and his wife, Maria Longworth Storer, had informed the Vatican that the President of the United States would be gratified by the elevation of Archbishop Ireland of St. Paul, Minnesota, to the rank of cardinal. In quoting letters that had passed between Roosevelt and the Storers, the pamphlet accused the President of dealing lightly with the truth.

This was, perhaps, Roosevelt's most amusing public row. Certain facts were conceded. The President had known the Storers since the days when he was Civil Service Commissioner. They had intervened with McKinley to bring about his appointment as Assistant Secretary of the Navy. Storer had been a member of Congress from Ohio and, under McKinley, minister to Belgium and to Spain. Maria Longworth Storer's nephew, Nicholas Longworth, was the husband of Alice Roosevelt. Thus the controversy, spread across the front pages for an edified public, had all the pleasant aspects of a family quarrel.

Long before the public excitement, as far back as January, 1902, Roosevelt had become apprehensive regarding letters he had exchanged with "Dear Maria." Would

Storer, he wrote, "ask Maria if there is any letter of mine to her in the hands of anyone else?" Rumors were current that Cardinal Mariano Rampolla at the Vatican had one:

I care very little, as far as I am personally concerned, for what I write I stand by, but it is obviously not wise on general principles that any letter of mine should be in the hands of anyone to whom it was not addressed, at this time.

The phrase "at this time" was the crux of the situation. Roosevelt was now President of the United States. In March, 1899, while Roosevelt was governor of New York, Storer had suggested that Archbishop Ireland was a churchman whose views were those of the Republican administration. Should he become a cardinal, the effect would be excellent, particularly in the Philippine Islands, where the friars had endangered relations between the United States and the Vatican. Would Roosevelt speak to McKinley?

"I wrote to the President [McKinley]," Roosevelt promptly replied. "I absolutely agree with you as to Archbishop Ireland."

On March 27, 1899, in answer to a request from Mrs. Storer, Roosevelt said that "I have written to the President stating my belief that it would be a most fortunate thing for this country if Archbishop Ireland could be made a Cardinal. While I would not like to have this letter published, you are welcome to show it to anyone you see fit."

President McKinley, however, recognized the danger in interfering in a matter that concerned the Vatican alone. When Roosevelt urged again in June that he express some sentiment to Rome in behalf of Ireland, the President declined. "I guess your position is the correct one," Roosevelt admitted.

Mrs. Storer went on with her proselyting. In October, 1902, President Roosevelt appointed Storer ambassador to Austria, and in the summer of 1903 a conversation may or may not have occurred at Oyster Bay. Archbishop Ireland was again the subject.

"The President said to me," asserted Storer in his pamphlet, "that if I went to Rome he would like to have me see the Pope and say to him in person that the Archbishop was his friend, and that he would be pleased to hear that he had received the honor of promotion to the cardinalate."

In December, 1903, Storer called on Pope Pius X and delivered this supposed message. A newspaper correspondent at Rome heard of it, and cable dispatches to the United States said that Roosevelt was seeking to influence the Vatican in behalf of Ireland. The result was unfortunate. Roosevelt directed Storer to be more careful.

The question is directly one of the veracity of Roosevelt, the Storers, and Ireland himself. Any final judgment among the three is difficult. Roosevelt denied that he had sent any message to the Pope. He had entertained the Storers at his home in 1903. He had probably again expressed cordial sentiments toward Ireland. Further than that, he had not gone. This version is borne out by Roosevelt's private letters before and after the disputed conversation. In March, 1903, he wrote that he would "simply have laughed at any suggestion" that he should interfere in the matter. But Archbishop Ireland also wrote Mrs. Storer that "the President told me that he had commissioned Mr. Storer to speak at the Vatican."

Undoubtedly there was a degree of misunderstanding. Yet in the case of the Storers, "substantial justice" was exact justice, even generosity. Roosevelt forgave the indiscretions of 1903. In July of 1904 he felt that Mrs. Storer was "an awful trial. I wish to Heaven she would either quit her professional sectarian business or get Bellamy to leave public life!" Her efforts continued, while the Vatican exhibited increasing reluctance to elevate Ireland, and the climax was delayed until December, 1905. Then the President ordered Mrs. Storer to refrain from further activities, to give him assurances to this effect in writing, to realize that the only alternative was for Bellamy to retire as ambassador. Hurt and indignant, apparently believing himself in the right, Storer declined to answer this letter. His removal followed.

Most of all this, and a good many irrelevant details as well, were spread broadcast by the Storer pamphlet and Roosevelt's letter to Root. A newspaper correspondent was with the President as he drafted this document; just then Lodge dropped in and expressed regret that it had to be made public.

"It is too bad," agreed Roosevelt, his eye running over some of the letters. He was silent a moment, and then he grinned. "But some of it is delicious," he shouted.

4

And now the unhappy Negro regiment in Texas: Fort Brown was located on the banks of the Rio Grande on the outskirts of Brownsville, Texas. On or about August 1, three companies of the Twenty-fifth United States Infantry, colored, arrived at the army post, and were greeted with conspicuous lack of enthusiasm by the citizens of Brownsville, who, conscious of their white supremacy, resented the presence of Negroes in uniform. Between August 1 and August 12, one or two disturbing incidents took place. One Tate, an inspector of customs, found it necessary to strike a trooper on the head with a revolver because he had not, with sufficient alacrity, moved out of the path. A Mrs. Evans told an excited story of a tall Negro soldier, whom she could not identify, who seized her as she stood in front of her home, threw her to the ground, and then was frightened away. This occurred some time on the early evening of August 12.

On the following day excitement ran high in Brownsville. Protests had already been forwarded to Washington regarding the presence of the troops. That night, August 13, Maj. Charles W. Penrose, commanding, took the precaution of restricting his men to quarters. It was a dark night, without a moon. At approximately ten minutes past midnight the garrison was aroused by the sound of firing, which seemed to be coming from beyond a brick wall at the north side of the post. The order for the men to fall in, with their arms, was given, and the company lines were formed as rapidly as possible. By that time, it was estimated, about a hundred shots had been fired. The roll was called and all men were present except two in C Company who had been permitted to leave Fort Brown on pass earlier in the evening. Thereupon Captain Lyon, commanding D Company, was detailed to go into Brownsville to look for these men. He returned, a horrified officer, with the mayor of Brownsville, who said that one civilian had been killed and a police officer wounded in an assault upon the city perpetrated by the soldiers of the Twenty-fifth. Major Penrose, incredible, protested that this could hardly be the case. His men had all reported present save the two on leave.

That night the men were kept in formation for about three hours. Then additional sentries were posted. At daylight next morning, all the rifles were inspected and were found to be clean, a fact accepted as additional proof of the innocence of the Negro troops because it was difficult, if not impossible, to clean rifles thoroughly by artificial light. But at this point the mayor, a Dr. Comb, appeared at the post with a number of empty cartridge cases and a few unfired shells which, he said, had been found in the streets. Penrose was dismayed. He was heartbroken when a group of citizens called shortly afterward to say that reliable witnesses had seen ten or fifteen Negro soldiers advancing northward along a street called Cowen Alley, discharging their Springfields. Major Penrose admitted that the discharged shells were identical to those supplied by the ordnance. He felt convinced that his men must be guilty; somehow they had stolen out and returned in time for the roll call.

Official machinery was set in motion. Penrose forwarded a report on August 15, 1906, in which he conceded that certain of his men, whom he could not name, must be guilty. Thereupon Maj. August P. Blocksom of the Inspector General's Department went to Brownsville. He heard of the prejudice against the Negro troops. But from the witnesses brought forward by the mayor he concluded there was no doubt that the raiders were soldiers. Nor was there doubt in his mind, he added, that the raid was "preconcerted," that many of the men must have known of the plan.

Probably because he feared its possible effect on the Negro vote in the 1906 Congressional campaign, the President withheld action until November 5, 1906. He then ordered the men of the three companies dishonorably discharged from the service. About 160 were affected, and these included men who had been in the army for fifteen years, six Medal of Honor soldiers, thirteen soldiers holding certificates of merit for bravery. The order meant that these men would forfeit their pensions, could not be admitted to soldiers' homes and would, in some cases, be destitute.

The drastic punishment caused adverse editorial comment, but it was Senator Foraker of Ohio who made a major issue of the Brownsville affair. Roosevelt may have been correct in his belief that Foraker, who had opposed railway regulation and who had presidential aspirations for 1908, was motivated by political considerations. When Congress convened in December, 1906, Foraker offered a resolution calling for investigation and this brought, on December 19, a bristling message from the President. It was based on the investigation by the Inspector General's staff. It was far more positive than the official reports of the guilt of the men.

The Blocksom report, the President said, was supported by "the testimony of scores of witnesses" and established the facts "beyond chance of successful contradiction."

Roosevelt referred to "the atrocious conduct of the troops" who "in lawless and murderous spirit" had attacked the citizens of Brownsville. He even described how they "leaped over the walls from the barracks and hurried through the town, shot at whomever they saw moving, shot into houses where they saw lights." The "evidence of many witnesses was conclusive that the raiders were Negro soldiers. The shattered bullets, shells and clips of the Government rifles, which were found on the ground, are merely corroborative." The "act was one of horrible atrocity unparalleled for infamy in the annals of the United States Army." As to knowledge of the outrage being shared by all the soldiers, Roosevelt ignored the fact that no evidence to this effect had been found. There could, he said, "be no doubt whatever that many were necessarily privy, after if not before the attack, to the conduct of those who took part in this murderous riot." Roosevelt then denied, truthfully, that his action had in any way been based upon the fact that these were Negro soldiers.

Foraker, in the Senate on December 20, effectively demolished this message from Roosevelt. Instead of "scores of eye-witnesses," only eight had made any claim to Major Blocksom that they had seen the riot. Despite his earlier positive assertions, Roosevelt must have agreed that the evidence was insufficient. He sent an Assistant Attorney General to Brownsville for further investigation and on January 14, 1907, transmitted another message to the Senate. This time, he did not mention "scores of witnesses"; the President specified fourteen. He added that if any of the men dismissed could thereafter prove his innocence, he would be reinstated but "upon any such man [is] the burden of thus clearing himself."

"The President does not propose to retreat from his position," remarked Secretary of War Taft. He was to worry a good deal about the Negro vote when he ran for the presidency.

Foraker continued to collect evidence for the defense throughout 1907 and presented it to the Senatorial committee, but in March, 1908, a majority report upheld the action of the President. In his most important speech, on April 14, 1908, the Ohio Senator analyzed the dissenting minority opinion and demonstrated his unusual talents as an attorney. He had previously impugned the testimony of the witnesses who declared that they had seen the Negro soldiers in the raid; now he went to the heart of the matter. He offered impressive facts in support of the theory, dismissed by Roosevelt as absurd, that the shooting had been the work of residents of Brownsville who then placed the blame on the Twenty-fifth Infantry.

The most damaging evidence against the men consisted of the shells found in the street on the morning of August 14. These had been fired from army rifles. They had been fired, tests had demonstrated, from rifles belonging to B Company of the Twenty-fifth Infantry. Foraker admitted this, and his fellow senators listened in fascination as he proceeded with an air of triumph. The shells, he continued, had been fired from these rifles—but not on the night of August 13-14. He described, in support of the theory he was to advance, a peculiar double indentation on the head of each shell. He then told of target practice held when the regiment had first arrived at Brownsville. At that time, the guns had been heavily coated with the grease in which they had been packed, and action had been slow. It had often been necessary to reinsert a shell that had failed to explode when the pin had sluggishly struck it. This, he said, accounted for the double indentation. In Foraker's opinion, it proved the innocence of the Negro soldiers.

The shells found in the streets of Brownsville had been located within an area of about ten inches, and the Ohio Senator asked whether shells ejected from rifles during hurried shooting by excited, rioting men would fall within so limited an area. He recalled once again the fact that all of the troopers had been in their places immediately after the shooting, and that at daylight their rifles had been inspected and found clean. What, then, had happened? Foraker pointed out that for weeks a box of empty rifle shells had been standing on the porch of B Company's barracks, having been brought in from the rifle range. He charged that a group of Brownsville men had shot up the town and had scattered the shells, previously taken from the barracks, as evidence that the despised Negroes had been guilty of an atrocious crime.

"I am absolutely convinced," wrote President Schurman of Cornell University to Foraker after reading the speech, "that the President has made a terrible mistake."

Perhaps Roosevelt, at heart, also felt that he had made a mistake. During the rest of 1908 he spent $15,000 in government funds seeking additional evidence. On December 14, 1908, he sent still another message, a far less categorical message, to Congress describing the result of his investigation. He withdrew from his position that all the men must be barred forever from the army. He said that the investigation fixed "with tolerable definiteness" the guilty members. The rest had doubtless been intimidated into silence and the Secretary of War should be given power to reinstate them if convinced of their innocence.

Roosevelt's action in reopening the case was the worst of his blunders. Foraker, by 1908, was twice as bitter as before. Roosevelt had attacked him in connection with Standard Oil. His presidential aspirations had ended, and he was to retire to private life under a cloud. On January 12, 1909, Foraker arose to say his last word on the Brownsville matter. According to Roosevelt's investigation, former Private Boyd Conyers of B Company had admitted the leadership in the riot. He had so told William Lawson, a Negro detective. Herbert J. Browne, another detective engaged by the War Department, had also interviewed Conyers and corroborated the testimony of Lawson. Conyers had been located at Monroe, Georgia. Foraker set forth these allegations and then read into the record an affidavit from Sheriff E. C. Arnold of Monroe in whose presence Trooper Conyers had been questioned by Detective Browne:

We kept Conyers under most severe cross-examination, but without getting any information. He positively denied that he knew anything to tell.

I desire to state that the report of Mr. Herbert J. Browne in this matter, insofar as the same relates to these conversations with Boyd Conyers, is not true. To the contrary, and I say it under the most solemn oath, it is the most absolutely false, the most willful misrepresentation of the truth and the most shameful perversion of what really did take place that I have ever seen over the signature of any person. I was both shocked and horrified when I read it.

Within a few weeks, Roosevelt went out of office. Innumerable hearings were conducted by the War Department, and a few of the troopers were reinstated. The whole Brownsville matter is another of the incidents that Roosevelt omitted from his biography, perhaps as conclusive evidence as any regarding his real reaction toward it. On the other hand, he insisted almost until he died that he had done, at the least, substantial justice.

Chapter XIV

HANDING DOWN THE LAW

*

"I think you are right," admitted Roosevelt to Lawrence Abbott in July, 1907, regarding the bad judgment that had led him into the onslaught against nature-fakers:

This is another way of saying that a President ought not to go into anything outside of his work as President. But it is rather a hard proposition to live up to.

To Roosevelt, seething with ideas on every imaginable subject, it was an utterly impossible proposition. Few of his opinions languished, unknown, in dark chambers of his mind. He shot forth ideas on morals, literature, and art; on marriage, divorce, birth control, football, Joseph Conrad, Charles Dickens, simplified spelling, a more artistic coinage, and nature-faking. He reveled in the controversies that his words inspired, and when the weight of opinion was too heavily against him he retreated, not by public admission of guilt, but by an outburst on some other subject. All this may explain why, everything considered, Roosevelt was the happiest President, with the possible exception of a distant kinsman with the same last name, ever to dwell in the White House.

Defeats, inevitable when he rode with his spear against some windmill that whirled too rapidly, did not disturb him unduly. One such defeat was his advocacy of simplified spelling. It was Roosevelt's friend Brander Matthews of Columbia University who involved him in the ill-advised attempt to eliminate some of the more obvious English spelling absurdities by presidential edict. Andrew Carnegie had provided an endowment for the Spelling Reform Association, in which Matthews was a leading spirit.

On June 25, 1906, the Spelling Reform Association issued a circular suggesting a number of moderate changes, and on August 22 Roosevelt informed Matthews that the Public Printer had been instructed to follow the new circular and that "Mr. Loeb, himself an advanced spelling reformer, will hereafter see that the President, in his correspondence, spells the way you say he ought to!"

The newspapers could not have treated the subject in greater detail had Roosevelt directed all the members of the Senate to wear long beards. Elaborate forecasts were made of the future spelling in presidential papers. This was good-natured fun and Roosevelt enjoyed it as much as did his critics. The suggested changes had actually been quite mild. Many of them were already established, and the most radical was the omission of the final "ed" on such words as "dropped" and "chased," making them "dropt" and "chast." Other revisions that attracted attention were "thru" for "through" and "thoroly" for "thoroughly."

Simplified spelling was not an issue on which Roosevelt proposed to wage energetic battle. The President deserted the cause when it became apparent in December that Congress, in none too friendly a frame of mind on other matters, was to make simplified spelling a subject for serious debate. Roosevelt announced that if Congress officially disapproved of simplified spelling he would withdraw his order to the Public Printer. After a debate in which Congressional wits made the most of their opportunity, this was done.

"I could not by fighting have kept the new spelling in," the President told Matthews, "and it was infinitely worse to go into an undignified contest when I was beaten. But I am mighty glad I did the thing anyhow. In my own correspondence I shall continue to use the new spelling."

In September Roosevelt was watching a naval review off Oyster Bay from the deck of the *Mayflower,* when a launch marked "Pres Bot" chugged ostentatiously by. The President waved his hat, and laughed with delight.

"Reformed spelling!" he shouted across the water. "A most delicate compliment; a most delicate compliment!"

2

Soon after 1900 innumerable books were published attributing unsuspected qualities to the fauna of North America. The imaginative naturalists who wrote these books did not bother to point out that the episodes they described were, in the majority of cases, pure fiction. Foxes, it was related, had lured dogs over railroad trestles just in time to be caught by thundering trains. Woodcocks had fashioned splints out of mud for their broken limbs.

These fantasies irritated Roosevelt, who had enjoyed the Uncle Remus stories of Joel Chandler Harris because they were honestly offered as fiction. They also irritated his friend John Burroughs. By 1903, Burroughs had attacked the pseudo-naturalists in an article, "Real and Sham Natural History," and Roosevelt expressed keen approbation. The President, in fact, was envious. He would have enjoyed the task of demolishing the myth creators himself but felt, with unusual self-restraint, that he could not engage in a public quarrel while President. The impulse soon overwhelmed him, however.

Coincident with the public rebuke by Burroughs, a new newspaper correspondent arrived at Washington, Edward B. Clark of the Chicago *Evening Post*. He became one of Roosevelt's favorites, because he had once written a monograph on the "prothonotary warbler," and frequently accompanied the President on rambles through the woods. On these, Roosevelt reiterated his wrath against the inaccurate naturalists. One evening in the spring of 1907, Clark was with the President in his study when the subject again arose and this time he suggested that Roosevelt allow his ideas to be incorporated in an interview. Consent was given. It was an energetic condemnation, but not enough so for the President, who added several hundred words to a first draft by Clark. Then it was dispatched to *Everybody's Magazine*, which published the article in its June, 1907, issue.

It began with a prefatory note by Dr. C. Hart Merriam, chief of the United States Biological Survey, that "Theodore Roosevelt is the world's authority on big game mammals in North America." Roosevelt said that he did not believe that "some of these men who are writing nature stories and putting the 'truth' prominently in their prefaces know the heart of the wild things." It was "an outrage" to place such books in the hands of children in the guise of truth. He criticized a tale by Jack London as "the very sublimity of absurdity." He declared that "William J. Long is perhaps the worst of the offenders." One of his books abounded in "the wildest improbabilities and a few mathematical impossibilities. Mr. Long must produce eye-witnesses and affidavits." He upbraided the author for stating that the incidents in the book were based on fact.

Mr. Long, a Congregational clergyman, had won a wide following for his rather gentle tales of life in the woods, but he demonstrated that he had qualities as a fighter also. The President, he said, had used his high position "to attack a man of whose spirit he knows nothing; his article [is] not only venomous but cowardly." Long then closeted himself with the President's many works on hunting and wild life. Rather effectively, he seized upon Roosevelt's phrase that the criticized naturalists did not know "the heart of the wild things." He said that Roosevelt's acquaintance with the heart of wild things was limited to using it as a target. As for eyewitnesses, it was easier for Roosevelt to supply these, "for he goes into the wilderness with dogs, horses, guides, followers, men servants, reporters and cameramen," whereas "I go alone into the woods . . . never killing unless I need food." He drew up an impressive indictment; that Roosevelt's devotion to animal life had been subordinated to his enthusiasm for killing.

3

When he dealt with subjects that concerned pure morals—marriage and divorce, birth control, child-training—T.R. was on safer ground. Yet he faced backward, nor forward, on the purely moral issues. Like other self-confident extroverts, for instance, he had long believed that Chaucer was rather indecent.

On feminism and the rights of women, so dependent upon voluntary motherhood and intelligent divorce legislation, Roosevelt had once held radical opinions however. His senior dissertation at Harvard in June, 1880, had been on "The Practicability of Equalizing Men and Women Before the Law." He wrote that obstacles stood in the way, but "in an ideally perfect state strict justice would at once place both sexes on an equality." The youthful Roosevelt did not ignore the difficulties, the chief of which was physical inferiority. "As long as the world continues in its present state, just so long will women be continually subjected to abuse, owing to their weekness [sic]," he wrote.

. . . even as the world now is, it is not only feasible but advisable to make women equal to men before the law. A son should have no more right to any inheritance than a daughter. The man should have no more right over the person or property of his wife than she has over the person or property of her husband. I would have the world "obey" used not more by the wife than the husband.

Can this have been the voice of the vanished Alice Lee, who seemed to be so womanly, so innocent of wielding a quiet lance for her sex? Roosevelt was in love with her at the time, and was seeing her constantly. They were to be married within four months. But that was long ago; no one exhumed this confession of faith written in 1880, or confronted Roosevelt with it. He never became a champion of equal rights, although he halfheartedly supported the movement from time to time. But two decades later he sincerely deplored the "terrible punishment" exacted from sinning women compared with men.

For the genesis of Roosevelt's subsequent convictions regarding large families, virile men, and womanly women, it is necessary to go back to the days of his jingoism; when Spain had been conquered, when a new world in the Pacific had been opened. He was lamenting to Spring Rice the decadence of the Anglo-Saxon races. He said that among all the evils in America the worst was "the diminishing birth rate among the old native American stock." He began to express pleasure when, on campaign tours, virtuously potent fathers and correspondingly withered mothers appeared at railroad stations with incredible numbers of children stumbling after them.

"Did I write you of my delight," he asked Lodge in September, 1899, "at meeting one Hiram Tower, his wife and his seventeen children?"

It was logical that Roosevelt should at this time draw a distinction between the training of girls and boys. Let the girl, he said, be "wise, with a well-trained mind, thoroughly awake to all that is going on in the world." Let the boy be brought up "to use his fighting instincts on the side of righteousness . . . punish anything like cowardice." His favorite aphorism, offered to untold numbers of dazzled small boys, was "Don't flinch, don't foul, hit the line hard!"

"I am the father of three boys," he said, " [and] if I thought any one of them would weigh a possible broken bone against the glory of being chosen to play on Harvard's football team I would disinherit him."

Roosevelt's attacks on birth control started while he was President. In February, 1903, anyone who disliked having children was "a criminal against the race . . . the object of contemptuous abhorrence by healthy people." This swiftly brought him to the position that only the exceptional mother could have interests outside the paramount ones of her home. Yet he admitted that "intellectual, cultivated" girls made better wives and mothers. Roosevelt's final position was taken in 1911, when he was associated with the *Outlook*. It was not, said Roosevelt, true that the large family brought a decrease in the health of its members. On the contrary, "when quantity falls off, thanks to willful sterility, the quality will go down too." At this time, obviously, Roosevelt was not recommending from twelve to seventeen children. He was attacking the childless marriage, and the marriage with but one or two children. This, he said, was "willful sterility"; "more debasing than ordinary vice."

Emotional condemnation of birth control, in which Roosevelt rejected the more modern and more rational view of the marriage relationship, had clouded his earlier and more intelligent convictions regarding the intellectual capacities of women. He was similarly heated concerning lax divorce laws. In December, 1906, addressing Congress, the President recommended "that the whole question of marriage and divorce should be relegated to the authority" of the Federal Government. He recognized that an amendment to the Constitution would have to be passed for this purpose but "when home ties are loosened, when men and women cease to regard a worthy family life as the life best worth living; then evil days for the commonwealth are at hand."

4

Authors found in the Roosevelt years a golden era. If they wrote wholesomely, they were invited to the White House, and dispatches from the capital told of presidential endorsements. Their royalties increased. If they wrote realistically, particularly about sex, word was circulated that Roosevelt had disapproved, that he considered them foul-minded. Their royalties increased even more.

Roosevelt was an omnivorous reader. He had the type of mind that could assimilate the printed page in gargantuan gulps, and he was able to retain the major part of his hasty literary meals. But he was far from an objective critic. Books, plays, poems, philosophical essays—all were judged in the light of his own stern moral code. Emile Zola, he told Owen Wister, had readers because "he says things out loud that the great writers from Greece down to the present have mostly passed over in silence. Conscientious descriptions of the unspeakable, do not constitute an interpretation of life, but merely disgust all readers not afflicted with the hysteria of bad taste."

Tolstoy, condemned with equal vigor, had "preached against war as against marriage." He was guilty of a "fantastic theory of race annihilation by abstention from marriage." T.R. would no more read Rabelais, he told T.R. Jr., than "examine a gold chain encrusted in the filth of a pigpen." Charles Dickens, who had undoubtedly caricatured America in *Martin Chuzzlewit,* was a man without

understanding of what the word gentleman meant and no appreciation of hospitality or good treatment. Naturally he would condemn all America because he did not have the soul to see what America was really doing.

Nor could Roosevelt divorce the personal life of an artist from his art. The smugly moral United States, so very close in its outlook to the outlook of Theodore Roosevelt, had affected pious horror over the visit of Maxim Gorki, accompanied by a woman who was not, in law, his wife. Gorki was declined accommodations at hotels. Editors wrote scathing denunciations. It did not matter to them, or to Roosevelt, that Gorki's wife had been hopelessly insane for years and that Russian law prevented a divorce, that the woman who was his mistress was superior, gentle, a lady. He was curtly refused an audience at the White House.

"If they treated Theodore as they deal with certain composite substances in chemistry," remarked Owen Wister to Mrs. Roosevelt at about this time, "and melted him down, it's not a statesman that they'd find, or a hunter, or a historian, or a naturalist; they'd find a preacher militant."

And Mrs. Roosevelt, who had listened to the preparation of so many Rooseveltian sermons, and softened the anger of a few of them, appeared to agree.

Yet Roosevelt was not merely a destructive critic. "I have enjoyed your poems so much, especially *The Children of the Night,*" he wrote to Edwin Arlington Robinson on March 27, 1905. "Will you permit me to ask what you are doing and how you are getting along?" This letter, on the heavy stationery of the White House, reached the poet, then almost unknown, at a time when his fortunes were precarious. He was attempting to write advertising in Boston. He was without funds, his literary work was being carried on under the handicap of poverty.

Apparently, Lyman Abbott of the *Outlook* heard that the President had enjoyed *The Children of the Night* and suggested that Roosevelt write a review of the collection. This was done; it appeared in the *Outlook* in August, 1905. There was, said Roosevelt, "an undoubted touch of genius" in Robinson's poems, ". . . just a little of the light that never was on land or sea."

Before writing this appreciation, Roosevelt had been making arrangements to the end that Robinson would have opportunity, at least, to demonstrate his ability for sustained flight. "Perhaps I could give him some position in the Government service," he pondered. On May 12, 1905, he notified Robinson:

I think I can appoint you after July 1 to a $2,000 position as special agent of the Treasury, say in New York, although possibly in Boston. It will give you plenty of time to do your outside work. That you will perform your duties in the position, I am sure.

This was a novel exercise of presidential patronage. The poet accepted the offer in the spirit in which it was made, and rarely went to his office at the Custom House in New York. Perhaps history will judge this to have been one of Roosevelt's major appointments.

Chapter XV

END OF THE REIGN

✳

The administration, said Roosevelt in September, 1906, when Speaker Cannon was running for re-election to Congress, "has had no stouter friend than the Speaker of the House. He is a patriotic American. He is for every man, rich or poor, capitalist or labor man, so long as he is a decent American." A fortnight earlier, the President had written to Uncle Joe:

. . . you need never waste your time in thinking that I will give so much as a second thought to any kind of a story in the remotest degree reflecting on you. You have done your part up to the handle. More power to your elbow!

Before the end of 1908, however, this hypocritical cordiality had vanished. Too long had the proud head of Congress bowed to the imperial will in the White House. The memory of frequent defeats rankled, and the revolt began in 1907. Speaker Cannon became a general of the rebel forces. The President was no longer the potent influence he had been, for the simple reason that he would go out of office on March 5, 1909; it had been a grave mistake to announce in 1904 that he would never again be a candidate for the presidential nomination. The President was facing an unpleasant fact—that power was slipping from his grasp.

Theodore Roosevelt, as the day of abdication rushed toward him all too swiftly, was not yet fifty years old. He had been the youngest President; he was far too young to retire to slippered ease. "When you see me quoted in the press as welcoming the rest I will have take no stock in it," he told William Jennings Bryan in May, 1908. "I like my job. The burdens will be laid aside with a good deal of regret."

The irritation of Congress was not, however, based solely on resentment toward Rooseveltian victories of the past. It was also due to apprehension over 1908; depression had followed the panic. Roosevelt's federalism was another factor. This had been increasing with the years and was to be emphasized in his forthcoming messages. In June, 1907, the President said that "most great civilized countries have an income tax and an inheritance tax. In my judgment both should be part of our system of federal taxation."

2

The hostility toward Roosevelt was not limited to the legislative branch. He denied that the courts were exempt from criticism, and the judiciary shuddered at this blasphemy. At Vicksburg, Mississippi, in October, 1907, he dared to recommend that the Constitution be interpreted with liberality:

. . . while I agree heartily that the Constitution of the United States represents a fixed series of principles, yet I hold that it must be interpreted not as a strait-jacket, not as laying the hand of death upon our development, but as an instrument designed for the life and healthy growth of the Nation. Sometimes executive and legislative officers are under temptation to yield too much to an improper public clamor. The temptation to the judge—the long term appointive or elective judge—is often just the reverse.

Two events in 1908, invalidation by the Supreme Court of the Employers' Liability Act of 1906 and reversal of the Landis fine against the Standard Oil Company of Indiana, strengthened Roosevelt's conviction, of long standing, that the courts were an obstacle to progress; again, there is an obvious parallel with Franklin Roosevelt. On January 31, 1908, T.R. addressed a remarkable message to Congress. Many of its recommendations were balanced by his customary qualifications. But there were phrases that stood out, startling and vehement phrases, and newspaper editors hurriedly crowded them into headlines.

First, the President recommended revision and then reenactment of the liability law, which had applied to all common carriers, so that the Supreme Court's objection would be met. The Court had ruled that the Federal Government could pass such a law for interstate carriers only. Then Roosevelt called for workmen's compensation for all government employees, and expressed the hope that the "same broad principle" would be made applicable "to all private employees." His next point was further emphasis upon the abuse of injunctions in labor disputes.

This was the first of the statements which distressed the respectables. The President also paid his respects to the business leaders who had been attacking his attempts to enforce the law. He said that "corporation lawyers" were often successful in blocking endeavors to that end, and yet "the Federal Government does scourge sin; it does bid sinners fear; for it has put behind the bars with impartial severity the powerful financier, the powerful politician, the rich land thief, the rich contractor—all, no matter how high their station, against whom criminal misdeeds can be proved." At this point, Roosevelt came to the heart of his policy. It was "the moral regeneration of the business world." He expressed his contempt for those who would hesitate because

it will "hurt business." The "business" which is hurt by the movement for honesty is the kind of business which, in the long run, it pays the country to have hurt. It is the kind of business which has tended to make the very name "high finance" a term of scandal. I do not for a moment believe that the actions of this administration have brought on business distress; it is due to the speculative folly and flagrant dishonesty of a few men of great wealth.

"I don't believe it," was the bland retort from Joseph H. Choate. Thus was one old supporter alienated. The President's message caused, too, a break between Nicholas Murray Butler and Roosevelt, although their friendship and their political relations went back for twenty years at least. They exchanged letters, and then were silent. Dr. Butler wrote:

Of all your real friends perhaps I, alone, am fond enough of you to tell you what a painful impression has been made on the public mind by your special message sent to the Congress on Friday of last week. No other expression of any kind has reached me. I am besought on every hand to know whether I, as a friend whom you trust and who has no ulterior end to serve, cannot in some way bring you to see what damage has been done both to your own reputation and to the Presidency itself by the message. You may imagine that the task is anything but a grateful one.

337

The feeling of sorrow and regret is due in part to the fact that you as President have descended into the arena of ordinary newspaper and hustings debate, in order to attack those individuals and institutions that you do not like or that have attacked and criticized you. If you will read this message over quietly, you will see how lacking it is in the dignity, in the restraint, and in the freedom from epithet which ought to characterize so important a state paper.

My honest opinion is that so far as the message has had any purely political effect, it is to bring Mr. Bryan measurably nearer the White House than he has ever been before.

President Roosevelt replied:

My luke-warm friends [have been] upset . . . [my] real supporters have hailed it as they have no other speech or action of mine for a long time. To me, your regret is incomprehensible. To me, it seems that I have the right to the fullest and heartiest support of every good man whose eyes are not blinded by unhappy surroundings, and who has in him a single trace of the fervor for righteousness and decency without which goodness tends to be an empty sham. If your soul does not rise up against corruption in politics and in business, why, then, naturally you are not in sympathy with me.

So began the rupture which later separated Roosevelt from Root and Cabot Lodge also. At the end of February the President informed his son Archie that his mother had recently been riding a new mare and had, "because, at the moment she was angry with President Butler," named the horse "Nicoletta." Thus passed Nicholas Miraculous from the Roosevelt years.

However radical in theory, the President's criticisms of the courts were mild enough in phraseology until the summer of 1908. On July 22, however, the Circuit Court of Appeals in Illinois invalidated the $29,000,000 oil fine. On the following day, Roosevelt announced that the Government would again prosecute Standard Oil for accepting railroad rebates, that "there is absolutely no question as to the guilt of the defendant nor of the exceptionally grave character of the offense," that "the President would consider it a great miscarriage of justice if, through any technicality of any kind, the defendant escapes punishment which would unquestionably have been meted out to any weaker defendant guilty of such offense. The President will do anything in his power to bring the offenders to justice."

"There is altogether too much power in the bench," was Roosevelt's final word on the Standard Oil decision.

The Congress that convened in December, 1907, was virtually Roosevelt's last. The short session to meet after Election Day in 1908 would pay even less attention to the President's recommendations. Currency reform, made imperative by the panic, was the chief issue, and Speaker Cannon was the undisputed leader of the House. His attitude toward the President was made clear in his statement that there had been "several incidents in the last few years" which had shaken business confidence; the worst of them had been the Standard Oil fine. Roosevelt's annual message was a less important state paper than the blast against business corruption. Its principal weakness was the absence of definite ideas on the troublesome financial question.

The session was marked by a deluge of messages from the White House: demands for improvement of inland waterways, labor reforms, insistence that the menace of Japan made four new battleships necessary, peremptory requests that Congress take action on postal savings banks, extension of Interstate Commerce Commission authority, limitation of the injunction, publicity on campaign contributions. Toward the end of May, 1908, as Congress prepared to adjourn so that its members could hurry to their home districts for the coming campaign, the friction between the executive and the legislative branches was obvious. Only two battleships had been authorized. The legislation against injunction abuses, for postal savings, for campaign publicity, for the Interstate Commerce Commission, had been killed. The Aldrich-Vreeland Act, providing additional currency elasticity, but of a very limited nature, had been passed. The liability laws requested by Roosevelt had also been enacted. But the majority of Roosevelt's twenty messages had been futile.

Any remnants of harmony were abandoned after the President's message had been read to the houses of Congress on December 8, 1908. In repeating his criticism of the courts, the President characterized as "a very slovenly piece of work" the liability law which had been held unconstitutional. This was interpreted as disparagement of a coordinate branch of the Government, and there was additional basis for Congressional indignation in Roosevelt's remarks regarding the secret service. The 1908 session had restricted the operations of the service to detection of counterfeiting and to protection of the President. Regarding this change, the President said:

> . . . this amendment has been of benefit only, and could be of benefit only, to the criminal classes. The chief argument in favor of the provision was that the Congressmen did not themselves wish to be investigated by Secret Service men. Very little of such investigation has been done in the past; but I do not believe that it is in the public interest to protect criminals in any branch of the public service.

Plans to rebuke the Chief Executive for this culminating insult began to take shape at once. Back of the anger lay suspicion that the President was using the secret service to obtain interesting data when the gentlemen of Congress trod, heavily and rashly, the Primrose Path. Wild rumors had been circulated the previous April and May of a Secret Service system similar to that of the hated Black Cabinet of St. Petersburg. It was said that palaces of sin had been watched by the presidential sleuths. The purpose of the White House was to confront Congressmen opposing the Roosevelt program with damaging evidence and thereby win their support. Roosevelt's private letters offer no substantiation whatever of these theories, but in Washington, the current opinion was that the President received confidential reports from the secret service.

Roosevelt's message of December 8, 1908, was followed by a conference in Speaker Cannon's office and by the appointment of a committee of investigation. On December 11, Representative James B. Perkins of Rochester, New York, said that the dignity of Congress "should be properly maintained, the statements made by the President of the United States cannot be lightly disregarded." On December 16, the guns of the Senate bombardment opened. Senator Aldrich himself drafted a resolution of condemnation and inquiry. On December 19, even Cabot Lodge turned against his friend in the White House. The journal of the previous day's Senate session was being read, when a clerk from the White House appeared with a presidential message. According to custom, it was suggested that the proceedings be interrupted to receive the message, but the Senator from Massachusetts jumped to his feet.

"I object," he said. "Let the reading of the journal go on."

Ultimately the Senate adjourned without taking notice of the communication from the White House. It was a studied rebuke.

The resolution of the House had called upon Roosevelt to

present proof of any wrongdoing on the part of its members. He replied on January 4, 1909, in a manner that further aggravated the hostility. He denied any intention of shadowing the members of Congress, but he reiterated his contention that restriction of secret service operations was a boon to the criminal class. On the following day, in a letter to Senator Eugene Hale, the President attacked his old enemy, Senator Tillman of South Carolina. As "illustrating in striking fashion" the usefulness of detectives and investigators, Roosevelt offered evidence that the South Carolinian had abused his franking privilege.

Three days later the House of Representatives voted to reject the message of January 4, 1909, on the ground that it lacked due respect. Party lines were wholly ignored in the vote of 212 to 35; an act of Congressional chastisement that no President since Andrew Jackson had suffered. This spelled final defeat for Roosevelt's program, which, in its more important aspects, would have been rejected in any event. Yet the very recklessness of his language advanced the day when workmen's compensation, the inheritance tax, valuation of railroad properties, and the rest of the reforms were adopted.

Undoubtedly, Theodore Roosevelt would have been happier but for the limitations imposed by the Constitution and by Congress. He saw so many evils, and evolved so many cures.

4

The end of the reign would not have been complete had there not been at least a minor controversy with some foreign monarch, and the opportunity for this arose when that most intriguing adversary, the German Kaiser, objected to an ambassador whom Roosevelt proposed to dispatch to Berlin. It was one thing for Theodore Roosevelt to apply pressure upon the British and German Foreign Offices to have Cecil Spring Rice and Speck von Sternberg detailed to Washington. It was quite another to have Wilhelm II object to a Roosevelt ambassador to Germany.

On November 8, 1907, the State Department announced the selection of David Jayne Hill, then American minister at the Hague and a diplomat of distinction, as the new emissary to Germany. Charlemagne Tower, the retiring incumbent, had been extremely popular with the German monarch, perhaps because he so faithfully relayed to Washington the Kaiser's frequent alarms and apprehensions regarding Japan. For the same reason, he was rather less popular with the other members of the diplomatic corps in Berlin, who, in the words of Spring Rice, may have resented "the Kaiser's violent love-making to Tower."

No reason existed to suppose, however, that Wilhelm would object to the successor who would replace the Kaiser's American friend; Tower had asked to be relieved. On March 16, 1908, however, the ambassador wrote, directly to Roosevelt, regarding a conversation on the previous day:

> . . . the Emperor expressed with much earnestness the hope that you will not appoint Mr. David J. Hill. The Emperor said: "He is not the sort of man we ought to have here and I do not want him. My brother, Prince Henry, knew this Mr. Hill in America, and he tells me that he will not do at all for Germany; all my reports from the Hague are unfavorable."

A visitor in Berlin at the time was Lloyd Griscom, American ambassador to Rome, and to him, also, the Kaiser described his regret that Hill, *"einer ganz kleiner Mann,"* had been selected. Griscom reported at length to Roosevelt. He quoted Wilhelm further:

> "We have now a little rosebud of friendship which is sprouting but requires the most careful nursing. It would really be a most serious thing for me, and I believe for the United States, if we allow it to die. I am convinced that our plant will wither and our whole structure fall to the ground if a man of the type of Mr. Hill is sent here; try to give your President an idea of what a great position your Embassy has here in Berlin today. I am determined that it shall not be lost if I can help it."

The "little rosebud of friendship" was in danger of a severe frost, however, when the attitude of the Kaiser toward Hill became public. On March 25, 1908, Secretary of State Root expressed surprise; the German Foreign Office had, on November 6, 1907, acquiesced in his appointment. On March 26, 1908, the newspapers carried a dispatch from Berlin that Dr. Hill was not acceptable.

The resulting public comment, fired by the presumption of the German Government in attempting to interfere with appointments by the President of the United States, caused annoyance and alarm in Berlin. Ambassador Tower cabled on March 29 that the German Foreign Office had again overruled its impetuous monarch, that the Kaiser, who was in Venice at the moment, had "confirmed fully his conversation to me," but that the Foreign Office asked that "the Emperor's message to the President, conveyed through Griscom and from me, may be treated as never having been sent." On the following day, Mr. Tower had "the honor to announce that Mr. Hill will be welcomed in Berlin."

Someone had to be sacrificed so that an explanation could be offered to the public. The evidence is clear that Roosevelt decided to sacrifice Tower. After all, he was merely an ambassador; the Kaiser was a monarch. It was revealed at Washington that the White House was irritated, that Mr. Tower had talked too much in Berlin. Roosevelt convinced himself that the American ambassador's "usefulness at Berlin is ended." His resignation was formally requested, as of June 1, instead of in the late summer.

Again, what were the facts? Rumors reached Washington of a dinner in Berlin on March 13 at which the Kaiser had lightly expressed regret that Hill was to be the new ambassador. On April 4, in a letter of rebuke, Roosevelt told Tower that the leak had been at the American embassy in Berlin, that he was responsible for it, for the "mischief caused by the affair." This was based, considering the effect of the President's action on Tower's reputation, on sparse evidence. At least one of the newspaper accounts of the opposition toward Hill came not from Tower, but from the State Department at Washington. It was perfectly clear that someone had talked regarding a confidential cable dispatched by Tower on March 21. Roosevelt himself, in a lengthy letter to the Kaiser, admitted he was not certain whether the information had come from the American embassy. Bishop, the President's official and considerate biographer, was careful to delete the admission when he quoted this letter from Roosevelt to Wilhelm.

"I am the American in this case," Tower wrote, in a moving letter to the President, "appealing to my own Chief of State, whose interests I safeguard and represent,—that whatever telegrams may have been sent you from German sources in this matter, *there can be no mistake or misunderstanding* as to the conversation with the Emperor. I have been accustomed to talk with him; he speaks English as well as I do. I regret the publicity of the affair, for which I am, however, not responsible."

To this plea, the President was silent. The "little rosebud of friendship" was nurtured. Suave letters passed between the President and the Kaiser: ". . . if I had only been notified privately that you preferred some one else, I should have at once made the change," said Roosevelt on April 4. "[I] feel that you were wise in having your Government state that there was no objection to Hill's appointment." "I need not assure you that Mr. Hill will meet with a sympathetic reception, he will be most welcome," answered Wilhelm.

The end of the reign included one other presidential action related, if less directly, to foreign affairs. In March, 1908, Roosevelt confided that President Pardo of Peru had

sent me a florid South American telegram about our Navy visiting Peru. I never saw it. Adee, in the State Department, prepared one of the usual fatuous answers, into which he unwarily put the statement that I extended to him all good wishes from "me and my people." Jaded, overworked Root signed my name and sent it off. Thereupon all the New York papers had hysteria over this, as showing marked imperialistic and megalomaniac tendencies. Of course I could not possibly explain because to do so meant that poor President Pardo would have had his feelings deeply hurt by learning that I had never seen his telegram or my answer.

Thereupon orders were given that only the President was to sign his name. In December of that year, Roosevelt's growing impatience with the "fatuous" nature of diplomatic correspondence found expression in a sharp letter to the State Department. The specific annoyance was the use of "Your Excellency" during a White House reception to the Chinese ambassador. "Any title is silly when given the President," Roosevelt scolded. "This title is rather unusually silly." Even more irritating, however, was the address of welcome which some official of the State Department had written for Roosevelt's use at the ceremony:

I do not object to the utter fatuity of the ordinary addresses made to me by, and by me to, the representatives of foreign governments when they deliver their credentials or say good-by. The occasion is merely formal and the absurd speeches are simply rather elaborate ways of saying good-by. It seems to me that some form could be devised, just as we use special forms in the absurd and fatuous letters I write to Emperors, Apostolic Kings [sic], Presidents, and the like—those in which I address them as "Great and Good Friend," and sign myself "Your good friend." These letters are meaningless, but they strike me as absurd and fatuous only when I congratulate the sovereigns on the birth of babies with eighteen or twenty names, to people of whose very existence I have never heard; or condole with them on the deaths of unknown individuals.

But on a serious occasion, as in the present instance where a statesman of high rank has come here on a mission which may possess real importance, then there should be some kind of effort to write a speech that shall be simple and that shall say something, or, if this is deemed inexpedient, that shall not at least be of a fatuity so great that it is humiliating to read it. It should be reasonably grammatical, and should not be wholly meaningless. In the draft of the letter handed me, for instance, I am made to say of the letter I receive: "I accept it with quite exceptional sentiments as a message of especial friendship." The next sentence goes on: "I receive it with the more profound sentiments in that you bring it now no less from the Emperor." What in Heaven's Name did the composer of this epistle mean by "quite exceptional sentiments"? Can he not write ordinary English? Politeness is necessary, but gushing and obviously insincere and untruthful compliments merely make both sides ridiculous; and are underbred in addition.

5

On October 28, 1904, the President's birthday, Elihu Root had scribbled a note of congratulation that Roosevelt had reached "the respectable age of forty-six."

"You have made a very good start in life," he said, "and your friends have great hopes for you when you grow up."

This was Roosevelt's tragedy, for he had just turned fifty when the end of the reign arrived. Politics was his true profession; and he had held the most exalted office in the realm of American politics. Wisdom, experience, and precedent— all of them dictated that he lay down the scepter. Roosevelt's intelligence, as distinct from his emotions, made him well aware that only trouble would follow any other course. What, however, was he to do? Becoming the ostensible head, the window dressing for some vast corporation, was quite unthinkable. He did not really enjoy writing. He might have found satisfaction in teaching, but no offer came. Certainly, as a professor of American history, he would have stimulated his classes.

One position, opportunely open, might have pleased Roosevelt. On October 26, 1908, President Eliot of Harvard resigned. It was natural that Roosevelt should be considered as Eliot's successor. He was a Harvard man. He was far more of a scholar, despite the prejudices which clouded his historical writings, than most of the men who had been in the White House. William James, who had once taught Roosevelt the undergraduate, felt that the President was, in many ways, qualified to fill the place of Eliot. But Henry Lee Higginson, an Overseer, was doubtful:

I do not believe that he could give up the very large field in which he has lived and be happy in a quiet, studious atmosphere of Yankee scholars. Next, we need a man of judgment, and is judgment to be found coupled with such enormous energy?

It was just as well that the post was not offered to Roosevelt. The role of Overseer, to which Roosevelt had been elevated in 1895, was actually as close an approach to the cloister of the academic as was safe.

"I felt," he told Owen Wister, after one meeting, "like a bull-dog who had strayed into a symposium of perfectly clean, white, Persian cats."

The problem of an occupation for ex-Presidents of the United States is always acute, and was unusually so in Roosevelt's case. In May, 1906, Dr. Butler had suggested that he become a candidate for the Senate, and thereby provide "on March 4, 1909, the unprecedented and dramatic spectacle of the outgoing President taking the oath of office as Senator before proceeding with his successor to the east front of the Capitol to hear the inaugural address." "Offhand," answered the President, "I can only say that I should be greatly pleased by what you propose." But what would the attitude of Platt and Odell be? Nothing came of it, nor of a proposition to become mayor of New York.

By the summer of 1908, Roosevelt had already decided upon the only possible use of his talents. He told his friend and admirer, Lyman Abbott, that he would write twelve articles a year for the *Outlook,* the weekly journal of opinion which then most closely reflected his political beliefs. For this he was to be paid $12,000 a year. First, however, he would spend a year hunting in Africa, not only for the sake of the sport, but because he was anxious to leave Taft unhampered in his arduous task of beginning an administration. One other outlet remained: there might be another war. Roosevelt, considering this possibility, added quickly that he hoped against it. But if there was a war and he was still "physically fit," he would "certainly try to raise a brigade, and if possible a division, of cavalry." Lacking this, he would devote his time to "fighting for political, social and industrial reforms."

War did come again, but it was grim and businesslike and dirty, and the college professor who had become President of the United States told Roosevelt that he could not go, that his services were not needed. Strife remained, of course, while Roosevelt lived, and swirled about him like fog before a wind. But the Roosevelt years were really ending as March, 1909, drew close. They had been exciting years, and colorful. The world had been peopled with villains and with saints. It had been a time for brave men to exhibit the "cardinal virtues" and to smite the unrighteous. It had all been a little naïve and romantic and in many ways quite splendid. But this was the end. There was a hint of it, faint and imperceptible, when the fleet returned from its voyage around the globe and President Roosevelt welcomed it on February 22, 1909, at Hampton Roads, Virginia. The ships were still white as they steamed, a seven-mile line, past the *Mayflower* and crashed out the presidential salute. Soon they dropped anchor, and barges were darting toward the President's yacht. The higher officers were presented to their commander in chief.

After the Roosevelt years came reality, and the hint of the future lay in an order transmitted to the fleet that night. The brilliant white, the gilt, and the brass that had been its dress were to be changed to gray and gunmetal. These ships were engines of destruction, not pretty playthings.

The formalities of the Taft inauguration remained, but in reality the Roosevelt Administration ended on March 1, 1909. That day, at noon, a luncheon was tendered to the "Tennis Cabinet." Among the thirty-one guests were cabinet members, ambassadors, and jurists. But also there were Bill Sewall, who had been with Roosevelt in Maine and in the Bad Lands, Jack Abernathy, who had astonished him by catching wolves with his bare hands, and Seth Bullock, United States marshal of Oklahoma. Roosevelt told them that, nominally, his guests were present as members of the "Tennis Cabinet." Actually, they were there because "you are the men with whom I have worked while I have been President. No Administration has ever had finer or more loyal service. The credit has come to me, to the chief of the Administration. I greet you for yourselves. I greet you still more as symbolizing others." The President's words were commonplace enough, but emotion was close to the surface as he spoke, and many of his guests wept openly.

6

"If you don't mind," Henry Adams had written on February 10, 1909, in answer to some invitation from the White House, "I think I would rather come, with just ourselves to look at for the last":

After this spring, Andrew Jackson and I will be the solitary monuments of the Square, and he will have to drop in to cheer me up. I don't find the prospect amusing. Andrew may be as handsome as you, but he is not as good company at dinner. I feel no disposition to celebrate the occasion in crowds, and still less to see others do it, so, if you please, I will play cheerful as well as I can, on the 2nd at dinner.

Presumably Adams crossed from Lafayette Square to the White House on the evening of March 2. He came again on the final day.

"I shall miss you very much," he said, and shook hands. It was strange that Henry Adams, so aloof and so removed, should have been the one to voice, at the last, a sentiment so nearly universal in Washington.

BOOK III

BOOK III

Chapter I

THE FIRST ERROR

※

In 1836, after Andrew Jackson had enjoyed the fruits of the presidency for eight years, he chose Martin Van Buren as his heir in the White House and the Jacksonians obediently brought about his nomination. Theodore Roosevelt, as a historian, frowned upon this incident in his country's past. In 1887 Roosevelt wrote:

Van Buren was the first product of what are now called "machine politics" put into the Presidential chair. The people at large would never have thought of him for President of their own accord; but he had become Jackson's political legatee.

No parallel is exact, even mathematically. The quotation can best be classified, perhaps, as another example of the peril that lies in combining historical writing and a political career. In 1908, Roosevelt brought about the nomination of Taft, not with any ulterior purpose but because he wished to have his righteous program continued. The fact remains, however, that Taft would almost certainly not have been nominated had it not been that he was Roosevelt's political legatee. It is also clear, although he denied it, that the President used the weapon of patronage upon officeholders. Thereby, Taft delegations to the Republican National Convention were elected. In denying the improper use of his appointive power, Roosevelt drew one of his finest distinctions:

I appointed no man for the purpose of creating Taft sentiment; but I have appointed men in recognition of the Taft sentiment already in existence.

The boom for William Howard Taft was not started by that amiable gentleman himself. This is demonstrated by his correspondence with Roosevelt. Mrs. Taft wanted him to be President. He had been mentioned as a possible successor to Roosevelt in 1905, just as any prominent member of an administration is certain to be discussed under similar circumstances. Early in 1906, another opportunity came for appointment to the Supreme Court, and on March 14, 1906, Taft wrote to Roosevelt that he did not share the latter's belief that he himself might be President. He preferred, some day, to go on the bench. At the moment, however, he felt that he must continue his work as Secretary of War. Ever since his period as governor of the Philippines, Taft had been deeply concerned with the destiny of those islands. As Secretary of War, this problem was under his jurisdiction.

There can be no possible doubt as to Taft's sincerity. His wife, however, desired him to decline the Supreme Court for less altruistic reasons. She called on President Roosevelt on the day of Taft's letter, March 14. On the following day, Roosevelt told Taft of "a half-hour's talk with your dear wife." Were the decision his, he added, "[I] would as a matter of course accept the three years of service in the War Department and then abide the fall of the dice as to whether I became President."

The President concluded by remarking that Secretary of State Root would be "at least as good a President as you or I," but he would be difficult to elect. This, obviously, was a reference to Root's former activities as counsel for the large corporations.

During 1906 and through most of 1907, reports were constant that the President planned to retract his declaration of 1904 that he would not again be a candidate.

"I may possibly be shirking a duty," a worried Roosevelt admitted. At the same time rumors spread that Taft was to receive the presidential blessing. In his letters, Roosevelt revealed his preference for the Secretary of War. On April 10, 1907, Congressman Nicholas Longworth announced that he favored Taft. The President's son-in-law explained that he spoke for himself alone, however. In July, the President confided that he desired Taft rather than Hughes.

"I believe," he told Longworth, "that the Taft business is getting along all right."

This was good will, rather than political support. If it was interpreted as more, it was because Roosevelt sincerely wished Taft well and did so very audibly. He told the candidate whom he would in due course support that when traveling it was wise to stay at hotels instead of in private homes "and give everybody a fair show at you."

The President's belief that the national convention in June, 1908, might suddenly stampede toward him was not without foundation. Despite the financial depression, he was as strong as he had been in 1904. His onslaughts upon the railroads, his quarrel with Harriman, the increasing asperity of his relations with Congress; all these gave new depth to his portrait as defender of the people, the foe of Wall Street, the chastiser of the wealthy malefactors. Even the fact that, in 1904, he had permitted Harriman to raise money for the campaign did not damage him. He swiftly countered by circulating, with the aid of his newspaper friends, vague but lurid stories of a $5,000,000 fund being raised by the reactionaries of his party to defeat any liberal candidate for the 1908 nomination. Senator Penrose of Pennsylvania was offered as the villain of this plot.

2

On December 20, 1907, Taft returned from his trip around the world. He found that the march of political events had been swift. On December 11, Roosevelt had again repeated his statement that he would not accept a nomination. A few days later the President's secretary, William Loeb, confronted Roosevelt at breakfast. Unless the President sponsored some candidate, Loeb pointed out, the political atmosphere would be filled with rumors. It would be said that Roosevelt had a candidate, but could not effect his selection, that he was secretly plotting for another term and would seize the opportunity when the convention became deadlocked. The only solution was to have a candidate of his own.

Yes, T.R. agreed, Loeb was right. But it was a difficult situation. Taft wanted the nomination. Roosevelt then instructed Loeb to see Taft, to tell him that he was the heir apparent. The whole strength of the administration would be behind him. The public would be permitted to know. He had obviously quite forgotten that less than a half a year earlier he had said he would take no part in Taft's nomination.

No doubt exists that Roosevelt followed traditional methods in working for Taft's nomination. Opposition to his candidacy came from two sources, aside from the mere ambitions of his rivals. Labor was not too friendly. The Negro voters were angry because, as Secretary of War, he had followed Roosevelt's instructions in the Brownsville affair. In using the power of the Federal machine, Roosevelt merely did what every other President had done and would do. By June, 1908, one hundred and twenty-five Federal officeholders had been chosen as delegates to the convention and of these ninety-seven were for Taft. In the southern states, where presidential patronage is particularly strong, the Taft forces controlled nearly all the delegates. This was established custom.

The President was still nervous, as the opening session at Chicago drew near, lest he should be nominated. It was, he told Kermit, to be a "hair-trigger convention." His own nomination, not that of his candidate, would be certain if anything "like a mass-meeting of Republicans were assembled." But this was machine politics. More than half of the delegates were "under solemn pledge to Taft" and his nomination should not be difficult unless his "foolish opponents are able to hold up the nomination until after the first ballot." In that event, the President added in somewhat mock alarm, "there is a chance of a stampede for me. If it really gets under way nothing that I could do would stop it."

But this disaster was avoided. The gathering was, beyond doubt, among the strangest of conventions. Roosevelt the politician used the G.O.P. organization to crush Roosevelt the popular hero. He dictated the platform. He wrote a letter, to be circulated if an emergency arose, demanding that the Taft delegates stand firm until the end. Actually the situation was far from desperate. On June 18, Taft's name was placed in nomination and, back in Washington, Mrs. Taft waited anxiously while the cheers continued.

"I want it to last more than forty-nine minutes," she said. "I want to get even for the scare that Roosevelt cheer of forty-nine minutes gave me yesterday."

Her husband was nominated on the first ballot, however, and T.R. extravagantly declared that nowhere in the whole country could be found a man "so well fitted to be President":

He is not only absolutely fearless, absolutely disinterested and upright. He would be as emphatically President of the plain people as Lincoln, yet not Lincoln himself would be freer from the taint of demagogy, the least tendency to arouse, or appeal to, class hatred of any kind.

3

Roosevelt had chosen the party nominee and forced his selection. It was, then, his duty to insure a victory for Taft, who did not, he deplored, arouse much enthusiasm. He proceeded with accustomed energy to infuse his own tempestuous methods into the lethargic candidate. Meanwhile the Democrats had turned in fatalistic hopelessness back to Bryan. He was nominated for a third and final time; a candidate with much of his ammunition gone because the income tax, inheritance tax, and vigorous corporation control had become Roosevelt doctrine. It was difficult for Bryan to trumpet their virtues when Roosevelt had already toured the land in their behalf.

Taft would have preferred a dignified and restrained campaign. He even contemplated the possibility of refraining from the usual tours and receiving delegations at his Cincinnati home. He faced, however, a deluge of letters and suggestions from Roosevelt.

All too many problems faced Taft. At Virginia Hot Springs, where he had retired to prepare his address of acceptance, he found discord among the party workers, new apprehensions over the attitude of organized labor, and continued hostility from Negro leaders. He believed in conciliation, whereas Roosevelt felt that drastic action to discipline the unruly should be taken. On July 15, Roosevelt wrote him:

Poor old boy! Of course you are not enjoying the campaign. I wish you had some of my bad temper! If you would care to come here and spend a day or two with me in going over your speech and letter, I would get Root to come down and go over the matter with you.

During July, the letters from Roosevelt to Taft came daily. Decline to bow to the extreme prohibitionists, the President directed on July 16. By September, the President was concerned over the fact that Taft was being criticized for playing the aristocratic game of golf:

The folly of mankind is difficult to fathom; it would seem incredible that anyone would care one way or the other about your playing golf, but I have received literally hundreds of letters from the West protesting about it. It is just like my tennis; I never let any friends advertise my tennis, and never let a photograph of me in tennis costume appear.

More grave than these details of election to public office in a pure democracy was a total lack of public interest in the campaign. Roosevelt could not resist pondering the activity that would have marked the canvass had he, not Taft, been the candidate. Roosevelt begged him to strike:

Hit them hard, old man! Let the audience see you smile always, because I feel that your nature shines out so transparently when you do smile—you big, generous, high-minded fellow. Moreover let them realize the truth, which is that for all your gentleness and kindliness and generous good nature there never existed a man who was a better fighter when the need arose.

On September 17, 1908, speaking at Columbus, Ohio, in support of his curious Independence Party, William Randolph Hearst read to a fascinated audience the letters that had passed between Senator Foraker and John D. Archbold of the Standard Oil Company. This was a sensation that Roosevelt could not ignore. He did not yet know that Standard Oil had contributed heavily to his own campaign in 1904. He did know that Foraker had been his bitter enemy in the fight for railroad regulation and in the Brownsville matter. On September 19, 1908, he telegraphed Taft that, in view of the disclosures,

if I were running for President, I should decline to appear upon the platform with Foraker. I would like to see you in the strongest and most emphatic way do what I should do in your place— make a fight openly on the ground that you stood before the people for the triumph over the forces which were typified by the purchase of a United States Senator to do the will of the Standard Oil Company.

Taft replied that he had never intended to speak from the same platform with Foraker, but this assurance was not vigorous enough for the President. He wished that "Taft would put more energy and fight into the matter."

He ought to throw Foraker over with a bump. I have decided to put a little vim into the campaign by making a publication of my own.

On September 21, 1908, Roosevelt issued a statement pointing out that the Republican candidate had been urged to support Foraker for the Senate in return for the nomination for the presidency. As far back as July 20, 1907, Taft had declined to enter into such an agreement. The Hearst disclosures had also connected C. N. Haskell, treasurer of the Democratic National Committee, with Standard Oil, and the President insisted that Taft was the only hope of those who opposed the entry of corrupt business into the Government. From that moment on, there was no restraint in Roosevelt's participation. He addressed open letters to Bryan condemning Haskell, who had meanwhile resigned from the Democratic National Committee. He again denied that he had, in 1904, requested E. H. Harriman to raise $250,000 for the presidential campaign. He defended Taft's record on labor and pointed to the pro-labor attitude of his own administration. Mr. Taft, during the uproar, became relatively inconspicuous.

The President's pugnacious virtue was more than a little false. When Taft recoiled from a $50,000 campaign donation from Cromwell, of Panama Canal notoriety, T.R. told his "deal old trump" that he was "oversensitive."

Perhaps there had been grounds for Roosevelt's anxiety regarding the outcome. On November 3, Taft was elected by a popular majority of 1,269,606 over Bryan, but this was not quite half the Republican lead in 1904. Unmistakable signs of unrest might have been seen, had any one bothered to look, in the statistics of this election. Since 1896, the Republican party had been in undisputed control of the nation. But now the pendulum was swinging back. Within two years, the House of Representatives would be Democratic by a large majority.

4

That Roosevelt and Taft began to draw apart immediately after Election Day in 1908 has been reiterated so many times that the theory has been accepted as fact. It is quite unsupported by evidence. Roosevelt would have preferred to have the President-elect retain certain members of his Cabinet. These men were his close friends, and it was inevitable that he should be pleased when Taft first intimated that he would do so. His disappointment when other men were chosen was natural. But Roosevelt, at that time, found no fault with his successor. "Taft is going about this thing just as I would do," he said late in January, 1909. They had conferred on the matter of the Cabinet late in December or early in January and Roosevelt had not asked for the retention of a single member of his official family.

"Ha! Ha! *You* are making up your Cabinet," Roosevelt jeered in a letter on December 31, 1908. "*I* in a lighthearted way have spent the morning testing the rifles for my African trip. Life has compensations!"

But there were many people in Washington who were really bitter. They felt, quite illogically, that Taft was somehow guilty of displacing Roosevelt and open to censure because of it. They said that Taft had shown ingratitude and had written, soon after his election, that Roosevelt had been the greatest influence toward his victory "except my brother Charley." This was a perversion of a remark Taft actually made, in a letter to Roosevelt; that "you and my brother Charley made that [nomination and election] possible." The difference is, while slight, significant. Taft gave Roosevelt the bulk of the credit. In June, 1909, he was careful to impress Archie Butt with this fact.

"I think your inaugural is simply fine!" the President wrote to his successor on March 1. Their relations on the final day were wholly cordial, while during the preceding week Taft had written:

People have attempted to represent that you and I were in some way at odds during this last three months whereas you and I know that there has not been the slightest difference between us. With love and affection, my dear Theodore.

Chapter II

AMONG THE KINGS

*

Tom Platt of New York, no longer an influence in politics, must have been gratified when asked, in March, 1909, for his opinion on the future of Theodore Roosevelt. So much had happened, and all the while Platt had grown smaller while the stature of Roosevelt had increased. A touch of malice is discernible in Platt's answer:

There are a great many people who do not think Mr. Roosevelt will ever return from Africa alive. Many who have undertaken the same trip have been stricken by disease or killed by accident. He is taking a long chance.

Those who were closest to Roosevelt and who loved him, however, could not suppress moments of anxiety as they contemplated the journey into Africa. He was not as strong —so his premature death finally proved—as his vitality seemed to indicate. A touch of Cuban fever was still in his blood. He was totaly blind in one eye and the sight of the other was imperfect. Although only fifty years old, he was considerably overweight. He was, in fact, in exactly the condition of so many men of middle age—a little soft, and wholly unwilling to admit that the time had come for comparative nonactivity. Roosevelt's friends well knew his disregard for danger. They did not see how a Rooseveltian attitude of not flinching was going to safeguard him from fever or the bite of the tsetse fly. One of those who worried was Cecil Spring Rice, but Roosevelt laughed at his apprehensions:

Oh! You beloved Mrs. Gummidge! I laughed until I almost cried over your sending her [Mrs. Roosevelt] the pamphlet upon the "sleeping sickness," and explaining in your letter that it was perfectly possible that I would not die of that, because (in the event of my not previously being eaten by a lion or crocodile, or killed by an infuriated elephant or buffalo) malarial fever or a tribe of enraged savages might take me off before the sleeping sickness got at me!

The scientific aspects of the trip had been provided by arrangements with the Smithsonian Institution at Washington to send taxidermists along, and to take care of the trophies when Roosevelt returned. This, he admitted, had been a great relief to Mrs. Roosevelt, who "felt that she would have to move out of the house if I began to fill it full of queer antelopes, stuffed elephants and the like." Roosevelt, repeating his precaution of the Spanish War, ordered nine pairs of eyeglasses for the excursion into darkest Africa. Arrangements were also made for publication of his experiences. He was deluged with offers from publishers. He finally accepted $50,000 from *Scribner's Magazine*.

"President Roosevelt is coming out as a penny-a-liner," remarked King Edward to Spring Rice. "That is a great pity." It was an unjust criticism. Roosevelt was far from wealthy; he had rejected an offer of $100,000 from *Collier's Weekly* because he felt that his story should appear in the more dignified medium.

With his son Kermit and the other members of his party, Roosevelt sailed from Hoboken on March 23, 1909. Before the steamer left, the ex-President had shaken hands with five or six hundred people. He stood on the bridge, wearing the greatcoat of a colonel of the Rough Riders, with the braid of his rank on the sleeves. Among the visitors at the pier had been Captain Archie Butt, now aide to President Taft. He brought a letter and a parting gift from the White House. He returned to Washington on the midnight train and told Taft that Roosevelt had sent his affectionate regards.

This was another year of pleasant adolescence. Roosevelt was again to face danger, and to jot down lengthy Latin names of the specimens obtained. It was almost as if time had turned back forty years to the days when he had been a juvenile, but ardent, naturalist. Roosevelt told the story of his hunt, and told it extremely well, in articles written for *Scribner's* and in the subsequent book, *African Game Trails*. He found, in the jungles and waste spaces of Africa, much the same thrill that he had first experienced in the Bad Lands of the Dakotas.

The party steamed down the White Nile in March, 1910, and the expedition disbanded at Khartum on March 14. Roosevelt had been ill for only five days during the eleven months, and then from the fever contracted at Santiago. The colonel listed 296 specimens shot during the hunt. He was indignant when he learned a year later that the Smithsonian Institution intended to mount and exhibit only fifty of the best of his trophies.

"These specimens," Roosevelt protested, "which are now lying in the National Museum were brought here for the American people. They should be mounted and placed on exhibition immediately."

2

Before leaving the White House, President Roosevelt had been invited to give the Romanes Lecture at Oxford. This was followed by invitations to speak in Germany, France, and Norway, and his hope, whether sincere or not, that he might retire to private life, was not realized. In 1910, even more, perhaps, than when he was in the White House, Roosevelt was a world figure. This was partly because, as President, he had taken an active, sometimes a dramatic, part in European affairs. It was because as cowboy, Rough Rider, and hunter he seemed, to the people of Europe, to typify the slightly mad national characteristics of the republic across the sea. A chief subject of discussion in many a royal drawing room was this ex-President of the United States. Did he actually carry a Big Stick with him? Was he, perhaps, that American phenomenon, a two-gun man?

Roosevelt, as he paused at Khartum, where Mrs. Roosevelt joined him, grew absorbed by the problem of English rule in the Sudan and Egypt. Still an ardent imperialist, he saw a parallel to American colonial difficulties in the Pacific. The English residents found Roosevelt a sympathetic listener when they said that the nationalist sentiment was a menace to the future of Egypt. If only he would speak in their behalf, his words would aid their cause in England. It must have taken very little urging to convince Roosevelt that the duty of an imperialist was the same abroad as at home. He was quite willing to warn the natives that loyalty to the British was in their best interest, that English rule "in the Sudan was really the rule of civilization." He declared, two days after arriving at Khartum, that it was "incumbent on every decent citizen of the Sudan to uphold the present order of things; to see that there is no relapse; to see that the reign of peace and justice continues."

His remarks, Roosevelt observed, "caused an outburst of anger and criticism among the Egyptian Nationalists, the anti-English and fanatically Moslem party." He went on to Cairo, where, although at first requested to avoid the subject because of the delicate situation, he denounced the assassination of the Egyptian Prime Minister. The final reference to this subject was in London on May 31, 1910. This was the occasion of the impressive ceremony attendant upon Roosevelt's election as Freeman of the City of London at the Guildhall. Roosevelt said that he would not make an "extended address of mere thanks"; he preferred to speak

on matters of real concern as to which I happen to possess some first-hand knowledge. I speak as an outsider. I advise you only in accordance with the principles on which I have myself acted as American President in dealing with the Philippines.

In Egypt you are not only the guardians of your own interests; you are also the guardians of the interests of civilization. Now, either you have the right to be in Egypt or you have not; either it is or it is not your duty to establish and to keep order. If you feel that you have not the right to be in Egypt, then, by all means get out of Egypt. If, as I hope, you feel that your duty to civilized mankind and your fealty to your own great traditions alike bid you to stay, then make the fact and the name agree and show that you are ready to meet in very deed the responsibility which is yours.

This was strong language from an outsider. The London *Star* said that "Mr. Roosevelt should learn that he is not exempt from the customs of civilized nations," while the *Standard* called his address "a social crime not far from a sacrilege." But in general, England agreed that Roosevelt had voiced sentiments as correct as they were obvious.

3

The cavalry charge, the lion hunt, the presidency of the United States: these events in the perfect life as visualized by the American small boy had already been experienced by Roosevelt. Now came the fight with the Pope. "At

Rome I had an elegant row," he told Lodge. The representative of Pius X, he exploded, had "made a proposition that a Tammany Boodle Alderman would have been ashamed to make."

Before crossing the Mediterranean and continuing to Rome, Roosevelt had been informed of probable complications in connection with an audience with the Pope. The Holy Father, it appeared, was in a somewhat excitable state because of the activities of a group of American Methodist missionaries who had chosen to proselyte their faith on the unsympathetic soil of the Imperial City. One of the Methodists, as Roosevelt later described the situation, was a particularly offensive fellow who hoped to win converts by referring to Pius as "the whore of Babylon."

Religious prejudice had no place in Roosevelt's nature. Intolerance toward the Catholic Church had nothing whatever to do with Roosevelt's quarrel with the Pope. At Cairo, he received word from Merry del Val, the Papal Secretary of State, regarding an audience with Pope Pius. Del Val offered a singular suggestion: the former President of the United States would be welcomed at the Vatican only on condition that he agreed to see nothing of the offensive Methodists.

Roosevelt replied that it would be "a real pleasure to be presented to the Holy Father." The right of Pope Pius "to receive or not to receive whomsoever he chooses for any reason that seems good to him" was unquestioned. On the other hand, "I must decline to make any stipulations which limit my freedom of conduct."

The folly of the Vatican gives weight to Roosevelt's description of the Pope as a "worthy, narrowly limited parish priest; completely under the control of Merry del Val." The answer to Roosevelt's dignified communication was word that he could not be received save under agreement that he would not see the Methodists. The absurd situation was further aggravated by newspaper publicity as Roosevelt stopped in Naples on April 3. It was then that Del Val made the suggestion which Roosevelt fittingly classified as that of a Tammany alderman. He said that the former President of the United States might secretly agree not to visit the Methodists while announcing publicly that no such concession had been made. This proposal Roosevelt scornfully rejected; he did not see Pope Pius while in Rome.

Meanwhile, a reception had been arranged for the Methodist missionaries. But one of them, doubtless the zealot who had been viciously attacking the Pope, issued a statement criticizing the Vatican. Thereupon, with praiseworthy impartiality toward troublesome Christians of whatever faith, Roosevelt canceled the reception.

The whirl through Europe was now in full progress. T.R. was having a magnificent time, his doubts regarding the manner in which a former President of the United States should conduct himself on such a tour having been dissolved by the simple expedient of being perfectly natural, quite himself, and wholly charming. When disputes arose, as in Italy, regarding the exact status of an ex-President and his precedence at state functions, Roosevelt exhibited both common sense and good taste:

I was purely a private citizen. [I said] that at any function, formal or informal, I should be perfectly happy to walk or sit or stand anywhere, and below any one, just as the local people desired—or not to appear at all, unless they expressly wished it. I added that I was really speaking less in a spirit of humility than of pride. To me there is something fine in the American theory that a private citizen can be chosen to occupy a position as great as that of the mightiest monarch and then leave it as an unpensioned private citizen, who goes back into the ranks of his fellow-citizens with entire self-respect, claiming nothing save what on his own individual merits he is entitled to receive.

Roosevelt was interested, but not dazzled by the monarchs. He was tossed by almost uncontrollable glee as he observed the peculiarities of their personalities and life. He wrote:

I thoroughly liked and respected almost all the various kings and queens that I met; they struck me as serious people devoted to their people and anxious to justify their own positions by the way they did their duty. Of course, as was to be expected, they were like other human beings in that the average among them was not very high as regards intellect and force. Apparently what is needed is that [a king] shall be a kind of sublimated American Vice-president.

If any of the lesser monarchs were amused by Roosevelt, and it is far more probable that they admired him excessively, their amusement was mild compared to his own: ". . . delightful people," was his verdict on the King and Queen of Italy. But he had been surprised, at the royal banquet, to have an attendant return his hat when he arrived at the palace:

When I was brought up to the Queen to take her in to dinner, I again thought it was time for me to get rid of my hat. But not a bit of it! I found that I was expected to walk in with the

Queen on my arm, and my hat in the other hand—a piece of etiquette which reminded me of nothing with which I was previously acquainted except a Jewish wedding on the East Side of New York.

In Austria-Hungary, the aging Emperor Joseph was their host at a banquet at Schönbrunn. In conversing with him, Roosevelt used French, which "I speak with daring fluency." He found the Emperor a pleasant although not "a very able man," but at the royal banquet the Emperor and all the Austrian guests had one horrid habit. The finger-bowls were brought on, each with a small tumbler of water in the middle; and the Emperor and all the others proceeded to rinse their mouths and then empty them into the finger-bowls.

The journey continued to Paris and thence to Brussels. On the following day, Queen Wilhelmina was their host at Het Loo in Holland. They passed through Denmark into Norway; then they crossed into Germany, for the most intriguing monarch of all: Kaiser Wilhelm.

A degree of friction preceded the visit to Berlin. "I have just been administering private discipline to the Pope and the Kaiser, on questions of ethics and etiquette respectively," he informed Lodge, from Cairo. This was a reference to Wilhelm's failure to include Mrs. Roosevelt in an invitation to stay at the castle. On the day of their arrival, the Kaiser and Von Bethmann-Hollweg entertained at lunch at the Neus Palais at Potsdam. On the following day, the Kaiser put on his most impressive exhibition; military maneuvers.

"Roosevelt, my friend," said the Kaiser, surrounded by the members of his High Command, "I wish to welcome you in the presence of my Guards; I ask you to remember that you are the only private citizen who has ever joined the Emperor in reviewing the troops of Germany."

Roosevelt and the Kaiser, astride magnificent chargers, watched the troops file by for five hours. The Kaiser "talked steadily," the ex-President recalled; a remark which must have delighted those of his friends who had found it difficult to stem the torrent of Rooseveltian conversation. It appears to have been a mutually pleasing occasion, for the German monarch was in one of his happier moods. He had a photographer on hand to take pictures while the maneuvers were in progress, and he sent a set of the prints to Roosevelt's hotel. On the backs of them, the Kaiser had scribbled inscriptions and these, his guest felt, demonstrated "a real sense of humor." One of the photographs showed Roosevelt and Wilhelm, on their horses, talking earnestly. On this the Kaiser wrote: "The Colonel of the Rough Riders instructing the German Emperor in field tactics." On another his note was: "When we shake hands we shake the world."

Roosevelt treasured these mementos, which were carefully mounted between two sheets of glass so that both sides were visible. He often showed them to visitors at Oyster Bay and told, with particular satisfaction, of efforts made by the German Foreign Office to prevent this further indiscretion on the Kaiser's part. Before Roosevelt left Berlin, a messenger appeared to ask whether Roosevelt would be so gracious as to return them.

"Oh, no," Roosevelt answered. "His Majesty, the Kaiser, gave the photographs to me and I propose to retain them."

4

Roosevelt's personality, rather than his speeches, caused the intense interest in his European tour. Aside from his remarks on the duty of Great Britain in Egypt and suggestions for a world association of nations for peace, his public addresses were commonplace. The first formal speech was at the Sorbonne on April 23, 1910. But the speech itself was one he might have made at home; it was a dissertation on the moralities.

The most important of the addresses, in Roosevelt's mind at least, was the Romanes Lecture at Oxford on June 7. The invitation to deliver this lecture had been tendered by Lord Curzon, the chancellor of Oxford, in August, 1908, and had been promptly accepted by President Roosevelt. The subject chosen was "Biological Analogies in History," and he gave a great deal of time and thought to preparation. It was supposed to be exceedingly profound and Roosevelt, although he prided himself on familiarity with both science and history, was nervous. He consequently sent a draft to his friend, Henry Fairfield Osborn of the Museum of Natural History. Subsequently, Dr. Osborn recalled:

In a relatively short time I received the manuscript. It was full of analogies between the extinct animal and the kingdoms and principalities in the human world, in which he compared one moribund government in Europe to the *megatherium*, and another that ceased to progress about three centuries ago to the *glyptodon*. I drew heavy pencil lines across these pages with the word "omit" in the margin and wrote: "I have left out certain passages that are likely to bring on war between the United States and the governments referred to."

Thus expurgated, the address was given after Lord Curzon had introduced Roosevelt and had recited a rather mediocre couplet of his own composition:

> Before whose coming comets took to flight,
> And all the Nile's seven mouths turned pale in fright.

The lecture may have been a little dull, but Oxford and the rest of England took this buoyant American to their hearts, and under the spell of this affection vanished a degree of Roosevelt's Anglophobia. Some years later, Dr. Osborn met the Archbishop of York in London and the conversation turned to the Romanes Lecture.

"In the way of grading which we have at Oxford," said His Grace, "we agreed to mark the lecture 'Beta Minus,' but the lecturer 'Alpha Plus.' While we felt that the lecture was not a very great contribution to science, we were sure that the lecturer was a very great man."

The archbishop also recalled that, after the lecture, Roosevelt had asked for his opinion of it. When this was cordial, but qualified, Oxford's guest said that it would have been "a great deal stronger had not one of my scientific friends in America blue penciled the best part of it."

It is not to be wondered that the first-rate Englishman, looking at Roosevelt, discovered a bond. He hunted and rode horseback. He was opinionated. He believed in imperialism and in the virtues of the more provincial patriotism. He had the faculty, also possessed by the English despite theories to the contrary, of laughing at himself. Roosevelt had been delighted by a cartoon in *Punch* that greeted his arrival. It showed the lions of Trafalgar Square being guarded by a bobby and a placard reading, "These lions are not to be shot."

5

King Edward VII, although he felt that Roosevelt had been undignified in accepting $50,000 from *Scribner's Magazine,* sincerely admired the former President: ". . . such a brave man, fought like a tiger," he had once remarked to Spring Rice, referring to the Spanish War. "I hope to meet and talk with him," the King said when he heard that Roosevelt was to visit England. But on May 6, 1910, while the American was in Norway, the King died. President Taft asked Roosevelt to attend the state funeral as the representative of the United States.

To say that Roosevelt enjoyed this function more than any other in Europe is to attribute to him no callousness. Edward had been a good king and was sincerely mourned by his subjects. But a state funeral, with monarchs from the entire civilized world in attendance, was a pageant rather than an occasion for lamentation. It had its pathetic aspects, such as the moment when the King's small terrier trotted mournfully after the hearse, but otherwise it was merely a parade marching in slow tempo.

Roosevelt had been in London for several days. On the afternoon of May 19, he attended a tea at the home of Whitelaw Reid, American ambassador to Great Britain. The ex-President was in high spirits. Some time during the afternoon he drew aside Mrs. William Hooper, the wife of a Harvard classmate, and whispered with obvious pleasure, "I'm going to a wake tonight. I'm going to a wake." The ambassador, overhearing, was scandalized and hurried Roosevelt off to rest before dinner. His apprehensions regarding the ex-President's conduct at the banquet being given that night to the visiting monarchs by King George had been preceded by other worries. Mr. Reid heard rumors that the former President had in his trunks the Rough Rider uniform he had worn at San Juan Hill and/or Kettle Hill. It was said that he might insist on wearing this in order to ride, on a stately charger, with the nine kings who would be in the parade. In civilian dress, he would be required to sit in a carriage.

The ambassador was quite wrong if he believed that Roosevelt would violate the proprieties on such an occasion. He was correct when he felt that the representative of the United States would, had the circumstances permitted, have greatly preferred to wear a uniform. Except for a veto by Mrs. Roosevelt, he might have taken on the European trip the dress uniform of a colonel of cavalry, a gaudy affair with innumerable yards of gold lace. In September, 1908, while discussing his forthcoming journey, the President told Archie Butt that he would not wear knickerbockers and silk stockings at court functions. When Butt said, probably in fun, that he was entitled to the uniform of a cavalry colonel, Roosevelt announced that he would order one and wear it with patent-leather boots.

"Theodore," protested Mrs. Roosevelt, "I would never wear a uniform that I had not worn in the service; if you insist upon doing this I will have a *vivandière's* costume made and follow you throughout Europe."

The plan was dropped. Reid's alarm, then, was without real basis. The ex-President attended the banquet at Buckingham Palace on the night of May 19 in civilian evening dress and wore the same clothes for the funeral on the following morning. He needed no uniform to be the center of attention at the dinner. Most of the visiting monarchs, who included the Kaiser, had already seen him. The rest were anxious to meet the famous American. Henry White watched with amusement as the crowned heads clustered about him. "Oh, I would never have taken that step at all if I had been in your place, your Majesty," he said to one attentive king. To another, "That is *just* what I would have done."

"The kings have been fairly scrambling for a share in his conversation," reported White to his wife in a letter written that same night.

Roosevelt had a superb time. King George, as host, sat in the center at one side of the large banquet table. Wilhelm was opposite him. Roosevelt was seated between Prince Henry of Prussia and a vague Teuton noble called the Prince of Cumberland. "Everyone went to the table with his face wreathed and distorted into grief," said Roosevelt when he described the scene to Taft on his return home.

Before the first course was over, we had all forgotten the real cause of our presence in London. I have never attended a more hilarious banquet in my life. I never saw quite so many knights. I had them on every side. They ran one or two false ones on me, and each had some special story of sorrow to pour into my ear. Finally, when I met a little bewizened person known as the King of Greece, he fairly wept out his troubles to me. He insisted I must make a speech on the subject of Crete.

"You know that Europe is acting abominably toward Crete," he tearfully said.

"I cannot discuss Crete even with you," I said.

"You must mention Crete in some of your speeches," he at last yelped.

Finally I simply walked away from him while he was pitifully muttering and spluttering Crete to me.

Roosevelt was amused by this minor potentate, by the inclination of the German Kaiser to dominate his fellow monarchs. Evidently, he told George Trevelyan, Wilhelm "liked to drill them." He did, however, find Alfonso of Spain wholly satisfactory. But when the Czar of Bulgaria, an object of suspicion generally because he had assumed this august title, began to tell Roosevelt of his problems, Emperor Wilhelm interfered.

"That man is entirely unworthy of your acquaintance," he said loudly. "I should not spend any more time talking to him. He is a poor creature."

Roosevelt, the banquet over at midnight, hurried to tell his family about its amusing details. He was to find equal entertainment at the funeral the following morning. On the previous evening, at dinner, M. Pichon, the French Minister of Foreign Affairs, had with indignation insisted that the representatives of the world's two great republics were being slighted by the bevy of monarchs. Had not the American ex-President noticed that his coachman had worn a mere black coat while the coachmen of all the other official mourners had been in scarlet?

I told him that I had not noticed, but I would not have cared if ours had been green and yellow. My French, while fluent, is never very clear, and it took me another half hour to get it out of his mind that I was not protesting because my livery was not green and yellow. He wanted me to enter a protest with him and I declined to do so and finally sidetracked him.

At eight o'clock next morning, the only guest who was not gorgeously uniformed, Roosevelt again presented himself at Buckingham Palace. The infuriated Pichon again leaped at him, this time with protests that their carriage was by no means ornate enough, that further insult had been heaped upon them by placing a somewhat obscure Persian Prince in the same coach. Again, Roosevelt declined to disrupt the proceedings by filing an objection:

. . . when the Persian prince was put into our carriage I laughed until I almost cried. I saw Pichon leap into the carriage, and I naturally thought it was for fear I would take the right-hand seat. But it was not so. He hauled me in after him, giving me the seat of honor. He really thought the poor little Persian would take possession of the back seat. Nothing was further from his mind. He was frightened to death and looked as if he would rather die than enter the carriage at all. He did not dare look at Pichon and apologized to me when he had to address some remark to one of us.

Pichon's final protest came when their carriage, eighth in the line on the drive to Windsor Castle, was placed behind that of Portugal's representatives. "For heaven's sake be quiet," Roosevelt begged. "This is a funeral and we are in deep grief for a great and good friend. Wait until another king dies and settle it beforehand."

If Roosevelt, as the procession moved through London, was struggling to suppress his mirth, he was very successful. Sir Arthur Conan Doyle, engaged by the London *Daily Mail* to describe the historic occasion, saw the "strong profile of the great American, set like granite as he leans back in his carriage." Sir Arthur was mistaken in thinking that this was the outward mark of sorrow.

Chapter III

RETURN TRIUMPHANT

At times, despite the cheers of the populace and the eager hospitality of the reigning monarchs, Roosevelt was not completely happy as he moved through Europe. Taft, who was to have been "the greatest President, bar only Washington and Lincoln," had become involved in controversies that caused forebodings in the heart of his predecessor. T.R. well knew, although it would soon be convenient, if also cruel, to ignore them, the complications that Taft was facing.

The national capital, while Roosevelt was in Africa, was in political turmoil. Two controversies, in particular, were to be used as ammunition against Taft when the break leading to the Bull Moose movement finally came. The first was the removal of Chief Forester Gifford Pinchot by Taft; in doing which the unhappy President had no other choice. The second was the struggle of insurgents in the House to clip the autocratic wings of Speaker Cannon. Taft's action in selecting his own Cabinet and in declining to continue Henry White as ambassador to France were not issues until Roosevelt's anger distorted his memory. Roosevelt told Lodge in July, 1909, that he was "pleased but not surprised" to hear that Taft's official family was doing well. He was disappointed that White was not to be retained at Paris; Taft had assured him that this would be done. But Roosevelt admitted that Taft's pledge had been only "an expression of 'present intention,' and he was always at liberty to change his mind."

The dismissal of Pinchot was far different. Gifford Pinchot was a passionate follower of Roosevelt. He had been the real pioneer and a dominant influence in the conservation program which Roosevelt had made his own. The Pinchot-Ballinger controversy is historically unimportant; any objective reading of the evidence is convincing proof that Taft and Ballinger were right and their critics quite wrong. Briefly: Richard A. Ballinger of Seattle, Washington, had been chosen by Taft as Secretary of the Interior. Although he replaced James R. Garfield, another of Roosevelt's younger followers, Ballinger wore the Roosevelt mantle. He had been Commissioner of the General Land Office in the Roosevelt Administration. But within six months after Taft's inauguration, Ballinger was involved in a dispute with the very excitable and unreliable Louis Glavis, chief of a field division in Alaska. In August, 1909, Glavis told Pinchot that Ballinger had violated the principles of conservation by restoring to public entry valuable power sites. He later made a complaint to Taft to the same effect.

Taft, however, upheld Ballinger and ordered the dismissal of Glavis. Pinchot's entry into the controversy was ill-advised. While Congress was considering an investigation of the Department of the Interior, the Chief Forester wrote to Senator Dolliver of Iowa praising Glavis as a "defender of the people's interests." Taft, he said, had been mistaken. In January, 1910, Pinchot made matters worse by saying that the issue was conservation versus the spoliation of natural resources; it was, in fact, nothing of the kind. Reluctantly, because he knew of the probable reaction of Roosevelt, Taft dismissed Pinchot. He did this only after Elihu Root, now Senator from New York, told him that "there is one thing for you to do, and that you must do at once."

Roosevelt, with his rigid jealousy regarding the power of the executive, could not have consistently tolerated an appeal from a subordinate to the legislative branch of the Government. Pinchot, by his letter to the Iowa Senator, had been guilty of just such an appeal. The Chief Forester then hurried across the Atlantic to meet Roosevelt on the White Nile, while Lodge appealed to his friend not to give the impression that he was "upholding Pinchot against the administration." Roosevelt, however, could not refuse to see this faithful follower. He groped for excuses for Pinchot, and praised his work, but he was forced to admit that the letter to Dolliver should never have been written. "I am not yet sure whether Taft could have followed any course save the one he did," Roosevelt told Lodge in April, 1910. But other factors were to confuse T.R.'s original reactions.

2

Of far greater significance politically was the revolt in the House of Representatives against the dictatorship of Uncle Joe Cannon. It is strange that this, of all possible issues, should have been one of the conflicts between Taft and Roosevelt. The struggle against Cannon was taking shape in 1908. This, therefore, was a major issue on which Taft could not avoid taking a stand. "I feel just as you do about Cannon," Roosevelt had written during the campaign. "He is our burden and the ideal result would be to have a Republican Congress with a majority so small" that his re-election as Speaker would not be possible. The subject was again discussed just after Election Day. Should the President-elect use his influence to defeat Cannon? Roosevelt answered:

If it is evident that four-fifths of the Republicans want Cannon I do not believe it would be well to have him in the position of the sullen and hostile floor-leader bound to bring your administration to grief, even tho you were able to put someone else in as Speaker.

By personal example of his predecessor and by specific advice, then, Taft was called upon to support Cannon. No wonder the President's corpulence exuded irritation, not geniality, when men said that Roosevelt would have hurled Uncle Joe into an oblivion as black as the cigars that he smoked. Those who said this, protested Taft, did not know Roosevelt nor his manner of working: ". . . it was Roosevelt who persuaded me to hold up until I could count the votes whereby I could defeat him. The first message I got from Roosevelt was to make peace with Uncle Joe."

Elevated to the presidency against his better judgment, it was Taft's tragedy that the solid virtues which were his were ineffective against the winds that struck him. Taft had integrity. He had honesty. He needed finesse and skill, and these he did not have.

"There is no use trying to be William Howard Taft with Roosevelt's ways," he said pathetically, ". . . our ways are different."

And so they were. Men had not criticized when Roosevelt, at the beginning, had cautiously crept along the middle of the road. But they expected Taft to go on from the point where Roosevelt stopped and they forgot, or deliberately ignored, the fact that the ex-President who was their hero had accomplished little or nothing as his administration ended.

So the President would not take part when the insurgents in the House attacked Cannon during the special session which was called for tariff revision in March, 1909, but lost their main point: to have the Speaker deprived of the right to appoint committees. The battle started again on March 16, 1910. George W. Norris of Nebraska, then a member of the House, offered a resolution which called for a Rules Committee, important because of its control over legislation, on which the Speaker would not sit. Uncle Joe lost the fight, but when he proposed to declare the chair of Speaker vacant, sentiment came to his rescue. Uncle Joe was saved, but he was no longer the Czar. The victory did not increase Taft's prestige, for he had thrown in his lot with Cannon.

Finally, the tariff. This was the issue which Roosevelt had called one of expediency and not morals and therefore to be shunned. This he had done. The 1908 Republican platform, however, had promised downward revision and Taft suffered from the honest, if quaint, illusion that platform pledges had to be redeemed. He met the usual fate of a President who is not a leader. The Payne-Aldrich Bill was a compromise, drawn after interminable debate, to still the cries of special interests seeking higher, not lower, tariff levies. The average rates were above those of the existing law. The reductions were on insignificant items. But Taft signed it and, in an incredible blunder, declared at Winona, Minnesota:

On the whole I am bound to say that I think the Payne-Aldrich bill is the best tariff bill that the Republican Party has ever passed.

"I dictated that speech to a stenographer on the cars between two stations," Taft subsequently confessed, "and glanced through it only enough to straighten out the grammar. The comparative would have been a better description than the superlative."

The tariff bill widened the breach in the party. It now seemed possible that the rule of the Republican party, unbroken since 1896, would be shattered by the election of a Democratic Congress in the fall of 1910. All the while, headlines from Europe proclaimed the greatness of Theodore Roosevelt, who was about to return, like Cincinnatus, to the scene of strife. To question the sincerity of Roosevelt's reluctance to enter the fight is to attribute to him craft and guile that he did not possess. How, he demanded in April, 1910, could he help the situation? Taft was entitled to the benefit of every doubt. No, Roosevelt begged, he would not take part again. "I most emphatically desire that I shall not be put in the position of having to run for the Presidency, staggering under a load which I cannot carry; my present feeling is that Taft should be the next nominee." Alas for 1912! But Lodge was insistent that Roosevelt aid the party in the approaching Congressional fight. Defeat was fairly certain, but Roosevelt must show that he wished the party well.

Roosevelt prepared to return in May, 1910. "Ugh! I do dread getting back to America and having to plunge into this cauldron of politics," he told Lodge. The prospect must have seemed even more dismal when he received, just before sailing from Southampton, a rather touching letter from the President of the United States:

I have had a hard time—I do not know that I have had harder luck than other Presidents, but I do know that thus far I have succeeded far less than have others. I have been conscientiously trying to carry out your policies but my method of doing so has not worked smoothly. The tariff bill was in my judgment a good bill and a real downward revision, not as radical a change as I favored, but still a change for the better. The revenues from it have been remarkable. But it did not cut low enough the rate on print paper and so we have had a hostile press, whether Republican or Democratic.

President Taft analyzed at length the failures and achievements of the past fifteen months. A tax on corporations had "moderated the enthusiasm of many business men for the administration." But the President believed that it constituted a valuable source of revenue and would provide, in addition, "a useful means of discovering and supervising the affairs of our corporations." In other words, it was a step toward the publicity of corporate earnings and capitalization so often recommended by Roosevelt. Taft then said that Arizona and New Mexico would be admitted as states, also a Roosevelt policy. The "chief conservation measure" would become law. A postal savings bill would probably pass. The proposal to limit the use of injunctions in labor disputes might have to be put over until the short session, but "we shall succeed in securing a commission to recommend a proper employers' liability law." Taft continued:

The Pinchot-Ballinger controversy has given me a great deal of pain and suffering, but I am not going to say a word to you on that subject. You will have to look into that wholly by yourself without influence by the parties if you would find the truth.

But T.R., as the immediate future proved, would listen only to Pinchot and his friends.

The pleas from Taft, the defendant, were not without corroboration. In the fulminations of 1911 and 1912 it was forgotten that many a good word was spoken for President Taft at the end of the Congressional session in 1910. "The fighting Taft—that's a new conception," wrote Charles Willis Thompson, one of Roosevelt's closest friends among the correspondents. Sometimes, his "jaw sets in grimness and [his] blue eye flashes fire." As for his subservience to Cannon and Aldrich, Thompson pointed out that Taft's ability to work with these leaders had been responsible for the success of his program.

Recognition of the commendation won by Taft in June, 1910, in which even the *Outlook*, ardently Rooseveltian as that journal had become, joined, is essential to an understanding of the causes which led to the ultimate rupture. The break was based on personalities, not on issues.

3

Roosevelt, out of office, typified an ideal. Taft, in office, was imperfect reality. Once again the tide had turned against the bosses. Once again the people had wearied of the alliance between business and politics. Their cry was for justice: for control by the people of their courts, for protection of the lowly. The cry, vague and inarticulate, was for the iridescent dream of a social democracy, and somehow Roosevelt, out of office, personified the dream.

Unbelievable, in a day when receptions are for bathing beauties, and generals, is the greeting that Roosevelt received in New York upon his return from Europe. It was an organized greeting, of course, but the skeptic will search in vain for evidence that it had been planned by the enemies of Taft or that political maneuvering was behind it. He was not due until June 18, 1910, but by May 25 the details had been arranged. A special medal had been struck. United States senators, representatives, governors, and mayors had been invited and an enclosure, where 2,500 of these dignitaries would be sequestered from the common herd, had been provided at the pier.

All this made the difficult task of President Taft no easier.

Archie Butt, torn by devotion to Roosevelt and loyalty to the President, was worried because Taft was "white-looking and his pallor does not seem healthy." It was, Butt wrote, "hard on any man to see the eyes of everyone turn to another person as the eyes of the entire country are turning to Roosevelt. Everything is on the *qui vive* for the return of the Hunter. He is certainly the first citizen of the world today."

Taft was gracious—far too gracious, if anything. In February he had meditated the wisdom of going in person to New York to meet Roosevelt, but had been dissuaded when it was said that the gesture might be interpreted as an attempt to conciliate his predecessor. But the President detailed the naval yacht S.S. *Dolphin* to carry Captain Butt to meet Roosevelt's boat.

It was raining when, in the early morning of June 18, the *Kaiserin Augusta Victoria* dropped anchor off quarantine, yet a vast crowd waited at the Battery. A delegation of Rough Riders had brushed up their uniforms. Bands, whistles, flags, and enthusiasm greeted the returning hero.

"I have been away a year and a quarter, and I have seen strange and interesting things," Roosevelt said in a brief address. "I am ready and eager to be able to do my part so far as I am able in helping solve problems which must be solved if we of this, the greatest democratic republic, are to see its destinies rise to the high level of our hopes and its opportunities."

"Ready and eager": these were words that caused frantic discussion that day. Did this mean that Roosevelt planned to return to public life? In all probability, he meant nothing of the sort. To Taft, who had written another letter of welcome, Roosevelt replied:

I shall make no speeches or say anything for two months, but I shall keep my mind as open as I keep my mouth shut.

4

Self-control was a virtue expounded and admired by Roosevelt. But never, from the start of his public career, had he been able to turn a deaf ear to the Lorelei song of politics. He heard the song again in June, 1910. This time it was to result in an ugly, venomous, vindictive quarrel between two men who had been the closest of friends. The party under whose banner Roosevelt had risen from assemblyman to President, and which he believed to be the guardian of all progress, was to split into factions and sink from power while a crisis rocked the world.

"One thing I want now is privacy," T.R. said, as he landed. "I want to close up like a native oyster. I hope you representatives of the press will not come to Sagamore Hill because I have nothing to say."

Obviously, the newspaper correspondents could not remain away from Oyster Bay and of course Colonel Roosevelt could not be an oyster. A bitter fight was in progress in New York State over a direct primary law, the reform that was to have ended so many political evils. Within four days after landing, Roosevelt had forgotten his pledge of silence for sixty days. Those who declared him opposed to the direct primary, he announced, were eligible for the Ananias Club, which "already has a big waiting list." Within ten days he had conferred at Oyster Bay with Gifford Pinchot and Senator LaFollette of Wisconsin, two of the foes of the Taft Administration.

Before a month had passed, Roosevelt had received most of Taft's enemies. Naturally, Taft was worried when he read the newspaper accounts of the cordial manner in which his foes were greeted at Oyster Bay. Moreover, he felt injured because Roosevelt had declined, on the specious ground that an ex-President should not visit Washington, to stay for a night or two at the White House. The time had not yet come, however, for open friction. The demands of politics required outward harmony, and on June 30, Roosevelt called upon Taft at his summer home at Beverly, Massachusetts. It was not a successful visit. Both Taft and Roosevelt were ill at ease and at no time were the two men left alone.

The break was delayed. The restless energy of Roosevelt turned to the primary fight in New York for an outlet. This was the first mistake. This was the error that led to all the rest. Charles Evans Hughes, soon to resign as governor of New York for the Supreme Court, was a fellow celebrity at the Harvard commencement on June 29, 1910. The governor was pledged to the direct primary and had called a special session of the New York legislature to force its passage. At the luncheon in Memorial Hall which followed, Roosevelt introduced Hughes and said:

Our governor has a very persuasive way with him. I had intended to keep absolutely clear from any kind of public or political question after coming home, and I could carry my resolution out all right until I met the governor this morning, and after a very brief conversation I put up my hands and agreed to help him.

That evening, Roosevelt made public an appeal for passage of the primary bill. It had, however, slight effect on the outcome. By a large vote on July 1, the Republican machine killed the measure.

A more secure individual would have ignored this setback, particularly in view of his expressed opinion that Hughes was "utterly cold and selfish." But to Roosevelt vindication was essential. Defeat was in the air; a coldly calculating politician with an eye on the presidential nomination of 1912 would have suppressed any yearning to take part in a contest that was futile. Roosevelt blundered on. He would fight William Barnes and the other bosses who had decreed the death of the direct primary.

It was not a happy summer, for Roosevelt nor for Taft. The former, on a speaking tour through the West, made statements which, to the President, seemed unwisely radical. Taft continued to feel that he had been greatly wronged.

"If I only knew what the President wanted," Taft said, again using the title which revealed so much regarding his real attitude toward Roosevelt, "I would do it, but you know that he has held himself so aloof that I am absolutely in the dark. I am deeply wounded, and he gives me no chance to explain my attitude or learn his."

Another attempt to show harmony between Taft and Roosevelt was staged on September 19, when Roosevelt again called upon the President. As little came of it as before. A week later the delegates to the state convention were gathering at Saratoga and among them was Lou Payn, the ancient foe whom Roosevelt had removed as superintendent of insurance in 1900.

"If there is any new party," said Payn, "its nucleus will be the men who are making the fight now against Mr. Roosevelt. It will be a party of conservatism such as would appeal to the men who won't stand having the Republican Party handed over to a kind of Bryanism."

Roosevelt won a victory and suffered defeat. He was elected temporary chairman of the convention. He succeeded in obtaining a plank endorsing the direct primary. He was instrumental in bringing about the nomination of Henry L. Stimson, whom he had once appointed United States attorney, for governor of New York. He praised, much more definitely than he had done until then, the accomplishments of the Taft Administration. But John A.

Dix, the Democratic candidate, was elected governor when November came. Roosevelt's enthusiastic references to the great abilities of "Harry" Stimson failed to win votes. The issue, said the New York *World,* was Roosevelt as candidate for President in 1912. A vote for Stimson was a vote to that end. It was not really the issue. The people were weary of Republican rule. Dix was elected by over 50,000 votes. The House too went Democratic, and in New Jersey, most significant of all, Woodrow Wilson became governor of his state. In Ohio, a charming gentleman named Warren Gamaliel Harding, whom Roosevelt had endorsed, was defeated for governor.

Momentarily, the political siren's song was stilled. Roosevelt returned to Oyster Bay. "I have been almost ashamed," he wrote, "of the fact that I have been unable to keep from being thoroughly happy since election. I think that the American people feel a little tired of me, a feeling with which I cordially sympathize."

"The bright spot," he told Lodge, "is that I think it will put a stop to the talk about my being nominated in 1912, which was beginning to make me very uneasy."

Chapter IV

TRUE DEMOCRACY

Roosevelt's journeys into the West and South during the summer and fall of 1910 constituted the most curious of paradoxes. By accepting the platform of the Republican party in the New York State campaign, the ex-President endorsed the Taft Administration. At the same time the ideas expressed in one or two of his speeches were anathema to Taft and his advisers.

New influences had been shaping Roosevelt's views, or bringing to fruition the political philosophy that had started to germinate while he was still in the White House. Among these, Herbert Croly and his *The Promise of American Life* have been too much ignored by those who have traced the development of the Progressive party. Published in November, 1909, *The Promise of American Life* had a profound effect on the thought of subsequent political commentators. It was peculiarly suited to stimulate Roosevelt, for Croly's philosophy was, in a sense, an extention of his own. It is not difficult to imagine Roosevelt's approval when, as he first dipped into *The Promise of American Life,* he read Croly's declarations regarding "Jefferson's intellectual superficiality and insincerity." His criticism of the Constitution, as an obstacle on the path to pure democracy, might have been voiced by Roosevelt himself. Similarly, Croly believed in the need for a moral tone in democratic aspirations.

All this was to be summarized by Roosevelt in 1910 as the New Nationalism, a phrase that rightfully belongs to him, since he gave it popularity but which, in fact, may have been conceived by Croly. In starting the trip across the continent in August of that year, Roosevelt said that his speeches would "represent myself entirely, nobody else." This, of course, was manifestly impossible. It was an extraordinary trip to be made by an ex-President who had insisted in public and in private that he had no political aspirations. Before a week passed, twenty-five newspaper correspondents were on the special train. The crowds which greeted him were at least the equal of those when he was President.

What were Roosevelt's motives in thus departing on a tour that could be interpreted only in the light of the political situation of 1910? It may be doubted that he knew. When it had ended, he felt that he had been instrumental in "securing a fairly united party support for the Republicans" in the West. This was quite absurd. What he really did was to focus public attention upon himself, to the probable injury of Taft, and cause additional bitterness and worry at the White House. It was not in Roosevelt's power to escape the dramatic. Quite apart from his speeches, he so conducted himself that Taft sank once more into obscurity. At Chicago, for example, he refused to sit at the same banquet table with United States Senator William Lorimer, whose election had been tainted by accusations of fraud. In consequence, an invitation extended to the junior Senator from Illinois was withdrawn and a sensation resulted. A few weeks later, in St. Louis, Roosevelt went for a ride with Arch Hoxsey in one of the flimsy kites that passed for airplanes in 1910.

The first important address on this westward tour was before the state legislature at Denver, Colorado; it was an amplification of Roosevelt's displeasure toward the courts expressed in 1907 and 1908. The criticism this aroused was greatly heightened by the most famous and possibly most disastrous speech of the trip, at Osawatomie, Kansas, two days later. In its essential points, the Osawatomie address foretold the charter of the Progressive party. Roosevelt quoted Abraham Lincoln's statement that labor was "prior to, and independent of capital" and deserved higher consideration. "I stand for the square deal," he said. "But I mean not merely that I stand for fair play under the present rules of the game, but that I stand for having those rules changed so as to work for a more substantial equality of opportunity and reward."

Effective regulation of corporations was impossible while "their political activity remains." Supervision of capitalization was essential, of railroads as well as other corporations, for "I do not wish to see the nation forced into the ownership of the railways if it can possibly be avoided"; a reiteration of Roosevelt's lifelong fear of socialism. As for the tariff, "the big special interests and the little special interests" had been far too influential in the drafting of schedules. An expert tariff commission, free of political influence, was the only solution. To guard against "swollen fortunes," income and inheritance taxes should be instituted. Other problems to be solved were protection of labor, conservation of natural resources and aid for the farmer.

The state must be made efficient for the work which concerns only the people of the state; and the nation for that which concerns all the people. There must remain no neutral ground to serve as a refuge for lawbreakers of great wealth, who can hire the vulpine legal cunning which will teach them how to avoid both jurisdictions.

The betterment which we seek must be accomplished, I believe, mainly through the national government. The New Nationalism puts the national need before sectional or personal advantage. The New Nationalism regards the executive power as the steward of the public welfare. It demands of the judiciary that it shall be interested primarily in human welfare rather than in property.

Thus far, Roosevelt had not mentioned the initiative and referendum or the recall of judicial decisions. The Osawatomie address aroused wide interest for two reasons. The first was that the public mind was better prepared for the reception of such doctrines. The second was that one or two passages were alarmingly close to the socialism from which Roosevelt had always shrunk. Most radical of all:

We are face to face with new conceptions of the relations of property to human welfare. The man who wrongly holds that every human right is secondary to his profit must now give way to the advocate of human welfare, who rightly maintains that every man holds his property subject to the general right of the community to regulate its use to whatever degree the public welfare may require it.

Regulate the property of Mr. Morgan or Mr. Harriman, those generous campaign benefactors, in the interest of the people? Do this to "whatever degree" the public welfare might require? Even Roosevelt became a little alarmed by the storm his Denver and Osawatomie speeches caused. And Taft was, of course, both hurt again and shocked.

2

After the defeat in the New York State elections in November, Roosevelt's position was anomalous. He had further alienated the Old Guard. His support of Taft had horrified the insurgents. "To St. Helena!" proclaimed his enemies, as they predicted that the name of Roosevelt would be merely a memory in 1912. By all the precedents of political history, this should have been so.

It looked as though Theodore Roosevelt could now devote his time, as he pretended to desire, to his horses, to the writing of editorials for the *Outlook*, to an occasional serious historical work. The obscurity of 1911 was, however, merely an eclipse. Roosevelt was to emerge from the shadow and take the final steps which led to the wrecking of his party and the ascension to power of Woodrow Wilson. Partly, this was due to his hold upon the people. More, perhaps, it was due to the basic strength of the popular dissatisfaction and to the additional prophets who proclaimed a cure. Finally, it was possible because Roosevelt avoided an error he had made in 1908. He declined to state whether he would be a candidate for the presidency in 1912 and explained in a private letter:

I do not wish to put myself in the position where, if it becomes my plain duty to accept, I shall be obliged to shirk such duty because of having committed myself. As things are now, I feel convinced that it will not become my duty to accept. They have no business to expect me to take command of a ship simply because the ship is sinking.

If Roosevelt's had been the only voice sounding the principles of the New Nationalism, the Progressive party might never have been formed. Two other individuals were behind the program for reform, although they differed on some of the details. One was Woodrow Wilson.

The other was LaFollette, whom Roosevelt had once compared to Bryan. The relations between Roosevelt and Wilson, who were to become such bitter enemies, had once been cordial to the point of personal friendship. Their first meeting took place in Baltimore, Maryland, on March 3, 1896. Roosevelt, as police commissioner of New York and an advocate of civil service reform, had been invited to address the voters of Baltimore and "was given a magnificent reception." Wilson spoke from the same platform.

Apparently the two men liked each other. At all events, when Roosevelt became Assistant Secretary of the Navy in 1897, Dr. Wilson felt at liberty to make a plea for some deserving Democrat about to lose his post in the Navy Department.

Wilson, when still far from public office, was a liberal of whom Roosevelt approved. As governor of New York, he called one speech Wilson had made "admirable in every way." A few weeks later, he asked whether there was any prospect that the Princeton professor would be in Albany; there was "much I should like to talk over with you."

"As an American interested in that kind of productive scholarship which tends to statesmanship," Roosevelt wrote on June 23, 1902, "I hail your election as President of Princeton."

On December 2, 1905, the Army-Navy game was held at Princeton and Roosevelt, attending it, was met at the station by Wilson. They shook hands with great cordiality, and Roosevelt went to Wilson's home for lunch. Soon after, the ripening friendship died. Perhaps it was because Colonel George Harvey, at a dinner in New York in February, 1906, declared that Wilson of Princeton was well qualified for the Democratic presidential nomination in 1908. More probably, the President had heard rumors that criticism of "my policies" had begun to emanate from the scholarly seclusion of Princeton. In November, the president of Princeton expressed agreement with the trust-control program of Roosevelt in so far as it related to publicity for corporate earnings and capitalization. But he was doubtful that the solution for the problems which faced America lay in politics. He seemed to favor some council, divorced from those who held office, which would attempt to cure the evils in the body politic. As for Roosevelt:

I have not seen much of Mr. Roosevelt since he became President, but I am told that he no sooner thinks than he talks, which is a miracle not wholly in accord with the educational theory of forming an opinion.

Wilson subsequently protested that the interview had not presented his ideas very accurately, but he did not disavow the content. Undoubtedly, Roosevelt was shown the interview. "I have felt rather impatient with his recent attitude on certain matters," the President said regarding Wilson, in 1908.

By September, 1910, Wilson had abandoned his pedagogical distaste for politics. Accepting the Democratic nomination for governor of New Jersey, he ran on what Roosevelt's own *Outlook* called "a Western insurgent Republican platform." Wilson was elected by 49,000 votes, although New Jersey had, in 1908, given Taft a plurality of 82,000. The record of his first year as governor of New Jersey made him a probable candidate for the presidency in 1912. In place of Roosevelt's New Nationalism, Woodrow Wilson was to voice the New Freedom. He was no longer a friendly or visionary or hostile college professor. He was a rival.

Theodore Roosevelt did not propose that salvation of the country should come at the hands of a Democrat, however in agreement with the principles of the New Nationalism. And yet the voice of Wilson, sounding these reforms, had hastened the termination of Roosevelt's eclipse in 1911.

3

Roosevelt and Wilson, and Taft in the White House; these were the leading persons of the drama. There was a fourth, hardly less important. This was LaFollette, who had been born in the traditional log cabin, who found masochistic satisfaction in recollections of early hardship, who had been influenced by Henry George's *Progress and Poverty*, whose favorite couplet was Henley's "I thank whatever gods may be, for my unconquerable soul." In 1911, LaFollette dreamed that the fruits of his labors would be the Republican presidential nomination in 1912, a nomination made possible by the growing insurgency that he had fostered. He was to die believing that Roosevelt, in seeking the nomination for himself, had betrayed him.

LaFollette, too, accelerated the passing of the shadow between Roosevelt and the public. This was his tragedy. It lay in Roosevelt's power, as the events of those turbulent years unfolded, to make LaFollette the nominee. It is improbable that the Taft forces could have blocked his selection. But Roosevelt chose otherwise. To say, however, that he deliberately betrayed LaFollette is again to attribute to him characteristics of cunning which he did not possess. The factor that made him refrain from endorsing LaFollette was his uncertainty whether the Wisconsin senator was really the prophet of the New Nationalism. It is not to be expected that LaFollette could appreciate this. He received from Roosevelt endorsement of his program. He naturally concluded that he had been used by Roosevelt to test the battlements of the enemy, and then discarded. The evidence is conclusive, however, that Roosevelt did not commit himself to support LaFollette. It is equally conclusive that he gave aid and comfort to his candidacy.

The movement for the nomination of LaFollette began during the Christmas holidays in 1910. The relations between the Wisconsin senator and Roosevelt, at this point, were harmonious. Would not the Senator come to New York for a conference at his earliest opportunity? He added that his son Ted, who was working in San Francisco, was a LaFollette enthusiast. But Roosevelt did not propose to commit himself without the reservations that so often marked his public utterances.

The National Progressive Republican League had to be content with modified endorsement by Roosevelt in the pages of the *Outlook*. The editorial began with the statement that "wherever there is any reason for caution, we are not only content but desirous to make progress slowly and in a cautious, conservative manner." Roosevelt quoted his Osawatomie speech to show that he did not advocate overcentralization; that is, he quoted the parts of it which so stated and ignored the section that gave an impression exactly the reverse. He said nothing about the initiative, referendum, and recall, but he did declare that Wisconsin, under the leadership of LaFollette, had probably advanced "farther than any other state in securing both genuine popular rule and the wise use of the collective power of the people." This was followed, in May, by another article on the progress toward democracy shown by Wisconsin.

"I wanted especially to tell you," the Wisconsin senator wrote, "how much I appreciate your strong article."

4

All the while, the Taft Administration progressed steadily toward defeat. Roosevelt assisted in the process, although probably without intending to do so at first. Yet it was particularly thoughtless of him to choose the tariff for public discussion. This time downward revision took the form of a reciprocity agreement with Canada. In August, 1904, Roosevelt had analyzed this with the realism of a politician who saw the dangers that it entailed. No agreement to admit Canadian raw materials free and providing importation of American manufactured products into Canada without duty could be negotiated.

But in 1911, Roosevelt could safely say that "the protection which the tariff gives to special interests" must be abolished. He believed in a tariff commission and the "most complete measure of reciprocity to which Canada will consent." Taft, instead of ignoring reciprocity, called an extra session of Congress. When it was approved, Roosevelt's prediction in 1904 was fully borne out. The farmers of the West were angry because Canadian grain would compete with their crops. They were angry because the manufacturers of the seaboard would reap still greater profits from the importation of raw products at lower cost. In Canada, too, reciprocity was received with hostility and it never went into effect because of overwhelming popular disapproval. Sir Wilfred Laurier's government fell because of it, and Taft was further weakened.

Taft's second error lay in seeking arbitration treaties with France and England. It is not to be wondered that the President was puzzled when Roosevelt opposed a treaty with any other power except Great Britain. In his address at Christiania before the Nobel Prize Committee on May 5, 1910, Roosevelt had declared that "all really civilized communities should have effective arbitration treaties among themselves." His only reservation was that each contracting party must respect territorial integrity: ". . . all other possible subjects of controversy will be submitted to arbitration," he said, except "the very rare cases where the nation's honor is vitally concerned." Taft knew and said so, that with this exception no treaty would mean anything.

So the President, suggesting treaties with France and England whereby "all questions determinable by the principles of law and equity" were to be submitted to the Hague Tribunal, faced the first important break with Roosevelt. In May, 1911, Roosevelt wrote in the *Outlook* that a treaty between the United States and Great Britain was possible because neither nation would commit an offense which could not be adjudicated. With any other nation, this was impossible. Taft's treaties were rejected by the Senate. He persisted in his advocacy of arbitration and laid himself open to a deliberate insult at the hands of Roosevelt the following December. The President had agreed to attend a dinner in New York in behalf of international peace and Roosevelt crudely announced that he would not go. Instead, he wrote an editorial for the *Outlook* expressing his opposition to arbitration.

"It is very hard to take all the slaps Roosevelt is handing me at this time, Archie," said Taft to his military aide. "I don't understand Roosevelt. I don't know what he is driving at except to make my way more difficult. It is hard, very hard, to see a devoted friendship going to pieces like a rope of sand."

Actually, the friendship no longer existed. Long before December, 1911, it had crumbled. Month by month, Roosevelt was swinging further to the left and away from the principles he had once believed firmly conservative. Taft, meanwhile, had slowly turned to the right. Responsibility for the friction was not wholly Roosevelt's; Taft was also to blame. On October 24, 1911, Attorney General Wickersham filed suit against the United States Steel Corporation and specified that the acquisition of the Tennessee Coal and Iron Company, during the panic of 1907, was one reason for the dissolution proceedings. This was the gravest of errors. Taft must have known that Roosevelt was peculiarly sensitive about the deal put across by Gary and Frick, and therefore insistent that it had been honorable, righteous, and to the best interests of the nation.

Chapter V

BATTLING FOR THE LORD

✳

Toward the end of 1911, a chasm dividing Taft and Roosevelt, the prospects of LaFollette for the presidential nomination were dwindling. He had announced his candidacy on June 17 and began seeking delegations for the Republican convention. LaFollette then committed an error which, knowing Roosevelt, he should have avoided. He mistook an attitude of cordiality, combined with Roosevelt's reiterated statement that he would actively endorse no one, for tacit support. T.R. had often felt far from cordial. In 1906 he had branded the Senator a "shifty self-seeker." No available letter promised support. LaFollette, in so far as his papers show, wrote nothing to Roosevelt commenting on any pledge. "I have endorsed no man for 1912," Roosevelt said on June 7, 1911.

The LaFollette boom collapsed because Roosevelt assumed this tantalizing attitude of watchful waiting. His support disintegrated, contrary to the accepted theory, prior to the tragic night of February 2, 1912, when, his nerves raw from the beatings of disappointment, the Wisconsin Senator spoke endlessly at a dinner in Philadelphia, repeating himself over and over, while rude and pitiless diners called "Sit down!" from the rear of the room. That he had already been abandoned is proved by examination of contributions to the preconvention campaign funds of LaFollette and Roosevelt. Prior to January, 1912, Gifford Pinchot and his brother Amos had donated $20,000 to LaFollette's chest. On January 8, 1912, William Flinn of Pennsylvania gave $2,000. In October, 1911, Medill McCormick of Chicago made a loan of $1,000. But by the middle of January, these men had switched to Roosevelt. It was obvious in early January, 1912, that Roosevelt was a candidate, although he continued to insist that only overwhelming demand and duty would persuade him. Mrs. Robinson was in Washington on January 14, and sadly told Archie Butt that her brother would never forgive the aspersion upon him in the steel suit. Taft, walking with his aide later on that same day, admitted that the breach was beyond healing.

"But, Archie," he added, "I am going to defeat him in the Convention. He may defeat me for reëlection, but I think I will defeat him in the Convention."

Conferences without end were held. Watchful politicians, wondering whether Taft or Roosevelt would win and determined to ride upon the safer bandwagon, issued evasive statements. Roosevelt pondered the best means by which he could announce that he had once again bowed to the popular will. It is important to remember, however, that Roosevelt still felt he was sacrificing himself and believed that he would be beaten. Taft was weak, he wrote two days before Christmas in 1911. LaFollette had developed no real strength in the West. And yet, should he seek the nomination for himself, it would probably go to Taft. In addition, election of a Republican in November was almost out of the question. As the weeks and the months passed, the Progressive campaign, born of sacrifice, was to become almost a religious crusade in Roosevelt's mind.

First, practical matters had to be arranged. At a meeting in the *Outlook* editorial offices on January 22, 1912, it was recalled that various governors of the Middle West had been offering their support. How should the public demand, to which Roosevelt would accede, be staged? It was suggested, and Roosevelt agreed, that seven or eight governors should sign a letter petitioning him to heed the voices. Thus he would seek the nomination without, as he quaintly phrased it, "the slightest manipulation" on the part of anybody. He went to his private office to begin the task of drafting a reply. An emissary hurried for a train which would take him to the first of the governors.

On February 9, 1912, a messenger left Chicago bearing a petition signed by Governors J. M. Carey, Wyoming; William R. Stubbs, Kansas; Charles S. Osborne, Michigan; Herbert S. Hadley, Missouri; Chester H. Aldrich, Nebraska; Robert P. Bass, New Hampshire; and W. E. Glasscock, West Virginia. The appeal recited the history of the Progressive movement. It set forth that only Roosevelt could make effective the movement toward the New Nationalism. Three days later Taft lashed out against the men who "are seeking to pull down the pillars of the temple of freedom and representative government."

It was, then, to be war. Roosevelt started for Columbus, Ohio, where he was to make the first address. To a reporter at Cleveland, who did not consider the phrase important enough to telegraph it until two days later, he said, "My hat is in the ring." If Taft had been less gentle or less judicial, Roosevelt might still have been crushed. But he loathed the very idea of attacking his friend and benefactor. At about this time the President had a conversation with Henry White, who was Roosevelt's close friend. On March 3, 1912, White described this talk with Taft:

He said that nothing would induce him to say—or to allow anyone whom he could control to say—anything against you personally; that he had never ceased to avail himself of every opportunity to express his gratitude for all you have done for him; that you made him President, and that he never can forget the old and happy relations of intimacy. [He] said that he could not help hoping that when all this turmoil of politics had passed, you and he would get together again and be as of old.

2

If the thought of a third party entered Roosevelt's mind to any extent in early 1912, it was received with disapproval. T.R., tossing his hat into the ring, had no other idea but a fight to take the regular Republican nomination from Taft. The time for revolution would not come until the G.O.P., following the ruthless methods that had prevailed at every national convention in history, refused to seat contested Roosevelt delegations. Then arose Roosevelt's cry of fraud, and he decided to abandon the associates with whom he had marched, through all the years, down the middle of the road.

As a candidate for the party nomination, Roosevelt exhibited lamentable lack of the skill that had made him invincible in the past. Perhaps he had lost his master's touch. Perhaps he was already growing too excited. He had been drawn into this struggle without viewing, with his normal clarity, the political road ahead. The Republican party was still the party of conservatism. In a campaign year the right-wing influences were certain to be dominant. But Roosevelt, who once had believed that "it is a sign of the highest statesmanship to temporize," now alienated the influences that controlled the nomination absolutely.

Roosevelt had been hesitant on the recall of the judiciary since his return from Europe. Speaking at Columbus in February, 1912, however, Roosevelt hurled phrases, fine and courageous phrases, whatever their wisdom, which spelled doom to any thought that the respectables would again endorse him. "I believe," he said, "in pure democracy . . . that human rights are supreme over all other rights, that wealth should be the servant, not the master, of the people." Unless "representative government does absolutely represent the people," it was not worthy of its name.

The conservatives in the audience must have stirred uneasily as they listened. Three devices, in particular, frightened them, and these Roosevelt proceeded to endorse. The initiative and referendum on legislation, he said, were necessary to "make good legislative failure." The recall against elective officers should be provided with adequate safeguards. As for the judiciary:

Justice between man and man, between the state and its citizens, is a living thing whereas legalistic justice is a dead thing. Moreover, never forget that the judge is just as much the servant of the people as any other official.

Our aim is to get the type of judge that I have described, to keep him on the bench as long as possible, and to keep off the bench, and, if necessary, take off the bench, the wrong type of judge. Therefore the question of applying the recall in any shape is one of expediency merely. Each community has a right to try the experiment for itself in whatever shape it pleases.

Impeachment, Roosevelt added, did not in any way solve the problem of removing unfit judges. But recall should be a last resort. A more rational step toward true democracy was the recall, in the several states, of judicial decisions on constitutional questions. If "any considerable number of the people feel that the decision is in defiance of justice," they should have the right to bring the subject before the voters. If the court decision was not sustained, it would "be treated as reversed, and the construction of the Constitution definitely decided—subject only to action by the Supreme Court of the United States."

"The Colonel and I have long since agreed to disagree on a number of points," said Cabot Lodge as the barrage of criticism started. Even the insurgents were a little dismayed, and Senator Borah of Idaho, supposedly among their number, said that "the recall of judicial decisions is bosh." No situation in his political career had "made me so miserably unhappy," Lodge said. Roosevelt answered that "you could not do anything which would make me lose my warm personal affection for you." The Chicago convention was only a few months off.

One maneuver, worthy of Roosevelt at his best, lay unnoticed for the moment in his letter to the governors. The only possibility of victory, and he considered this remote, rested in popular support. The voters at large, of course, were quite impotent to make their choice known save through preferential primaries in which delegates would be directed to vote for Taft, Roosevelt, or LaFollette at Chicago in June. He hoped, Roosevelt told the governors, that the people would be given a chance "through direct primaries" to do this. By his advocacy of the primary, Roosevelt assumed the offensive. He could challenge the Taft forces, knowing that they dared not take this chance, to institute the primary before delegates were selected.

When Roosevelt was asked regarding rumors that he would bolt the party if Taft were nominated, he denounced them as "deliberate faking."

3

By April, 1912, Roosevelt was certain that Taft had been "disloyal to our past friendship, disloyal to every canon of ordinary decency." When the President said that he had not bowed to political bosses, he was guilty of "the grossest and most astounding hypocrisy." The violence of Roosevelt's denunciations of the man he had loved and admired approached hysteria. At the same time, Roosevelt denied assertions by Taft that he was seeking to minimize the recall of the judiciary, as advanced in his Columbus speech, although he was doing exactly that. He emphasized the less radical recall of judicial decisions. Roosevelt denied that he had, within recent weeks, changed front on Canadian reciprocity, although he had done that, too. As the primary campaign progressed, Roosevelt grew even more shrill, and Taft was pitiful. He had to violate the tradition which decreed that a President should not sacrifice his dignity on the stump. "This wrenches my soul," he said during a tour through New England. "I am here to reply to an old and true friend who has made many charges. I deny those charges. I deny all of them. I do not want to fight Theodore Roosevelt, but I am going to fight." What of the bosses? Was it true that Roosevelt now spurned their support? The President said that William Flinn, who was behind him, was "one of the worst municipal bosses" in the history of Pennsylvania. Walter Brown of Ohio, also a Roosevelt man, was "the only boss in full commission" in that state. Taft added, with admirable candor:

The truth with respect to me is the same as with respect to Mr. Roosevelt. When I am running for the Presidency, I gratefully accept such support as comes to me. Mr. Roosevelt has done so in the past; he is doing so now. I do not hesitate to say that it involves the most audacious effrontery to attack me because men he characterizes as bosses are now supporting me.

Effrontery it surely was. "Condemn me if you will," Taft said a day or so afterward, "but condemn me by other witnesses than Theodore Roosevelt. I was a man of straw; but I have been a man of straw long enough."

It did not matter that Taft had accomplished much toward progressive government. What Taft achieved, and it was a great deal, became obscured because he was, with rare exceptions, a gentle person, and the presidency is not a role for such. His capacity for saying the wrong thing was almost unprecedented. The obnoxious tariff had been the best in history, he had said. No, I did not mean that, he added; I wrote the speech hastily, between stations on a train.

"I am a man of peace," said the President of the United States in May. "I don't want to fight. But when I do fight, I want to hit hard. Even a rat in a corner will fight."

Meanwhile Roosevelt's speeches referred to "the most momentous struggle since the close of the Civil War." At first, the enemy seemed to be winning. In New York, the machine declared for Taft. Indiana supported the President late in March. Lodge held Massachusetts steadfast for the President. But then Roosevelt carried the primaries in Pennsylvania, Maryland, and California. Most astonishing of all, he won in Ohio. Finally Taft suffered the humiliation of hearing suggestions that he could not, after all, win the election in November and that some compromise candidate, such as Hughes, should be selected. Roosevelt as well as the President rejected this proposal.

"I'll name the compromise candidate," Roosevelt said. "He'll be me. I'll name the compromise platform. It will be our platform."

One by one, the friends who had stood with Roosevelt for so long dropped away. Root, whom he had admired most among all the members of his Cabinet, was to be temporary chairman of the convention and thereby to assist in what Roosevelt declared to be the theft of the nomination. Philander Knox, now Secretary of State in Taft's Cabinet, was insisting that Roosevelt was "prompted by whims," by "imperious, ambitious vanities and mysterious antipathies." And Stimson, the "Harry" Stimson whom Roosevelt had lifted from comparative obscurity to become candidate for governor in New York, had accepted the post of Secretary of War in the Taft Administration.

The earlier pretense that Roosevelt would abide by the decision of the convention, should his candidacy be rejected, was soon abandoned; by the end of May he said that "I will have a great deal to say, and I won't stand it for a moment" if "the discredited bosses and politicians decide against me." In May and early June, Roosevelt was the center of attention. He aroused frenzied devotion and equally frenzied opposition. Dr. Allen McLane Hamilton, in the columns of the New York *Times*, seriously pondered the question of his sanity, and Dr. Morton Prince, an early apostle of the new and sometimes Freudian psychology, wrote a lengthy paper in which he said that a subconscious desire to be elected in 1912 had spread its poison through Roosevelt's system before he had left the White House.

4

Unquestionably, Roosevelt was the choice of a majority of the rank and file of the Republican party. His strength in the primaries proved this. But Taft was certain to be the nominee. Theoretically, then, justification existed for the subsequent declaration that the nomination had been stolen. Actually, it had been accomplished by traditional means. The convention rules of 1904 and 1908 applied in 1912, and Roosevelt had been quite content to work under them before. The shift in viewpoint came when his own destiny was affected. As a matter of literal fact, Roosevelt had in 1908 vetoed one change that would have assured his nomination. The well-worn suggestion that representation from the Southern states was disproportionate was then made again. That time it appears to have been offered in a sincere attempt to remedy a situation that bred only corruption. Roosevelt, who controlled the 1908 convention from the White House, rejected the proposal. It would probably have been rejected without his aid, but had it gone through, Taft's strength in 1912 would have been greatly reduced. The President, through the national committee, had absolute power over these office-holding delegates.

The significant point in any attempt to weigh the 1912 G.O.P. convention is that the rules of the party specified the election of national committeemen and the appointment of committees at the conclusion of each convention. The important Credentials Committee had been chosen with Roosevelt's tacit approval in 1908. The new committeemen, friendly to Roosevelt in the quarrel now in progress, would not take their seats until the Chicago convention had ended. Such was the law of the party, but Roosevelt ignored the party law, which was, at best, ridiculous. The Republican National Committee met on June 6, 1912, at Chicago and on the following day the work of deciding contests in favor of Taft began. The outcome was obvious from the start and Roosevelt, in his rage, said that the action of the committee was "dangerously near being treason to the whole spirit of democratic free government." On June 14 he left for the scene of the carnage.

"This has come down," he said when he arrived, "to be a fight of honesty against dishonesty." On the following night, addressing a huge meeting, Roosevelt declared that "we have a large majority of the legally elected members of the convention." He concluded with typical drama:

What happens to me is not of the slightest consequence; I am to be used, as in a doubtful battle any man is used, to his hurt or not, so long as he is useful and is then cast aside and left to die. It would be far better to fail honorably for the cause we champion than it would be to win by foul methods the foul victory for which our opponents hope. But the victory shall be ours, and it shall be by clean and honest fighting for the loftiest of causes. We fight in honorable fashion for the good of mankind; unheeding of our individual fates; with unflinching hearts and undimmed eyes; we stand at Armageddon, and we battle for the Lord.

All of which was exciting, and in the main, sheer nonsense. Roosevelt had no such clear majority, even among the honestly elected delegates, as he supposed. It may be set forth, as a matter of political realism, that the Republican National Committee would have seated enough Taft men, whatever the facts, to insure Taft's nomination.

It was Roosevelt's intention to bolt the party when he arrived in Chicago. He wholly forgot his earlier declaration that he would "bow cheerfully" to an adverse verdict. Headquarters were established at the Congress Hotel. A newspaper correspondent located the colonel after the first session of the convention on June 18. The sentiment of the meeting, and the vote for temporary chairman, which had resulted in the election of Root by 558 to 502, demonstrated the impossibility of Roosevelt's nomination. Why did he continue to remain in Chicago?

"I intend to see," he said, "that Mr. Taft is nominated."

The inference was that no compromise on some other liberal, such as Governor Hadley of Missouri, would be tolerated by Roosevelt. Former nominee Bryan, again a correspondent, heard with amusement and some elation the cries of "Teddy, We Want Teddy!" that came from the balconies and which foretold a possible Democratic victory. The hysteria did not, however, communicate itself to the leaders. The Credentials Committee went into session on the afternoon of the second day to endorse the earlier action of the national committee in seating the Taft delegates. The minority members said they would appeal to the convention against its ruthless action and when, at two o'clock on the morning of June 20, they reported their intention to Roosevelt, he made the announcement that was to result in the election of Woodrow Wilson.

"So far as I am concerned I am through," he said. "If you are voted down [in the convention] the real and lawful majority will organize as such. I went before the people and I won. Let us find out whether the Republican Party is the party of the plain people or the party of the bosses and the professional radicals acting in the interests of special privilege."

On Saturday night, June 22, the Roosevelt followers, including 344 delegates who had refrained from voting at the convention, pledged their support to him at a meeting at Orchestra Hall.

"If you wish me to make the fight, I will make it," Roosevelt said, "even if only one State should support me."

5

On July 2, 1912, Woodrow Wilson was nominated by the Democrats at Baltimore and the more realistic among Roosevelt's supporters must have known that victory in November was the most remote of possibilities. The Democratic platform was liberal. At first, it was not certain that the third party would be started. A few of the Roosevelt followers were discouraged. Others, such as Borah of Idaho, publicly announced their decision to remain within the party, and there conduct their fight for liberal government. Some deserted to Wilson. The difficulties in the way of a successful independent convention at which Roosevelt would be nominated were enormous. In most of the states no organization whatever existed. The party, as yet, had not even a name. Roosevelt, however, burned with high endeavor. The time for revolution, so rare indeed, had finally come. Munsey, Perkins, and a few others had agreed to finance a campaign, and on July 7 a call was issued for delegates to a convention in Chicago on August 5, 1912.

It was a novel political gathering. The delegates and alternates were required to pay their own expenses, and yet from many states two or three times the required number arrived. The convention opened at noon on August 5, with a long and ornate oration by Senator Beveridge of Indiana which reviewed the principles behind the Progressive party, the name finally selected. About 10,000 people were present when the address began and their enthusiasm mounted under the spell of Beveridge's musical voice.

Roosevelt spoke on August 6. His "Confession of Faith," as the address was called, was a voluminous document running to 20,000 words, which had to be cut in half in the spoken version. It branded the old parties as "husks, with no real soul within either, divided on artificial lines, boss-ridden and privilege controlled."

All this had been changed. The new party, Roosevelt said, would "put forth a platform which shall be a contract with the people and we shall hold ourselves under honorable obligations to fulfill every promise it contains as loyally as if it were actually enforceable under penalties of the law." The address covered in detail every reform for which Roosevelt had fought as President, every reform he had advocated since 1909. The platform that followed set forth these views. It called for woman suffrage, to which Roosevelt had become a recent and somewhat bored convert. It said nothing about the recall of judges, recommended in the Columbus speech, but it did include recall of judicial decisions. Among the other planks were: easier amendment of the Federal Constitution, social welfare legislation for women and children, workmen's compensation, limited injunction in labor disputes, farm relief, revision of the currency to assure elasticity, health insurance in industry, inheritance and income taxes, improvement of inland waterways, and limitation of naval armaments.

It was an impossibly ambitious platform, in the light of Roosevelt's statement that a party platform was an obligation with the force of law. Enactment of all these recommendations was beyond the realm of hope. Indeed, the Progressive platform had to be discounted along with the Democratic platform and that on which Taft was running. The puzzled liberal, wandering in this lumberyard of political planks, found it difficult to make a choice. All three platforms pointed to utopia. All were insincere. For all the bellows of the Bull Moose, however, the Progressive party was still Republican in its essential beliefs. It favored a protective tariff, with vague recommendations that this should be for the benefit of the wageworker. The Democratic party called for a tariff for revenue only.

There existed, also, a fundamental difference in the philosophy of government. This went deeper than mere state rights versus centralization. Roosevelt had wandered far from his early convictions that individual man must solve his own destiny. He called for protection by the Government, for a high degree of paternalism. Woodrow Wilson, who was also to change with the stress of the years, emphasized freedom for the people, rather than guardianship. He asked for competition in industry rather than some central agency which would decide whether a trust was bad or good.

6

The Progressive Convention adjourned with hymns, with banners flying. Its members repaired to their battlements feeling that the contest just ahead might possibly result in defeat but that victory would some day surely come. But Roosevelt, their leader, began a long and exhausting campaign that confirmed in his mind the earlier doubts which had haunted him. To Roosevelt, it was an old, old story; monotonous hours on the train, forced enthusiasms, crowds, too many speeches, factional quarrels that had to be ironed out, idiotic local politicians and fanatics who had to be seen. And behind all this lay the depressing realization of defeat. Victory was not in the air in 1912, although the crowds sang "Onward, Christian Soldiers." Wilson, to whom it all was a novelty, was fresh and vigorous and effective.

"Your old friend Theodore," wrote Henry Adams to Cecil Spring Rice, "has dropped us all, and has gone in pirating on his own account. I much fear that our dear Theodore is a dead cock in the pit. Everyone tells me that all interest in him or the election has passed. Woodrow Wilson is President until next advices."

Nor was discord entirely absent from the garden of idealism. Hiram Johnson of California, the Bull Moose candidate for Vice-President, felt that he had been ineffectively used by the Progressive National Committee. Roosevelt's throat bothered him and he complained, to his confidants, of being weary. During a trip through the Middle West and the South reports reached headquarters that his speeches were not as effective as they once had been, and that his throat was growing worse. It is not improbable that the condition of his voice might have made further speeches impossible.

Roosevelt reached Chicago on Sunday, October 13, from Iowa. It had been necessary to cancel addresses in Indiana and Wisconsin because of the candidate's throat. He insisted, however, upon making a scheduled speech in Milwaukee on Monday, October 14, and on the evening of that day, as he was leaving the Gilpatrick Hotel to go to the hall, Roosevelt was shot in the right breast by a fanatic, John Chrank, who shouted something about a third term. The crowd fell on the assassin and would probably have lynched him had not Roosevelt directed that the man be brought before him. "The poor creature," he said, and turned away.

The extent of the wound was not known. It might have been fatal, as far as Roosevelt knew. He was very white, as the crowd pressed about him. But when physicians said that he must go at once to the hospital, he brushed them aside and ordered the automobile, in which he had been standing when he was shot, to proceed to the hall.

"I will make this speech or die," he said. "It is one thing or the other."

It was found that the bullet had passed through the right breast, and had caused a wound that might be serious. He again insisted on speaking and went to the platform while the audience sat, rigid with horror and alarm, and heard an announcement that the colonel was wounded but would speak. He started in a low tone. "It is true," he said. "I am going to ask you to be very quiet and please excuse me from making a long speech. I'll do the best I can, but there is a bullet in my body." He paused for a second. "It is nothing," he added. "I am not hurt badly. I have a message to deliver and will deliver it as long as there is life in my body."

The speech was not important. It was delivered rather haltingly, while frenzied members of his party interrupted from time to time and begged him to stop. It is doubtful whether ten men in the audience had the faintest comprehension of his words. Yet Roosevelt's conduct was important. Men did not judge it histrionic or childish. The public imagination soared again, while both Wilson and Taft telegraphed their regret and said that the campaign must halt until Roosevelt's condition was known. An examination at the hospital disclosed that the bullet had entered the right lung, its velocity spent by passing through an overcoat, a spectacle case, and the folded manuscript of the speech he was to make. No alarm need be felt for Roosevelt's condition, the doctors stated on the following day.

"It matters little about me but it matters about the cause we fight for," Roosevelt said, in a statement to his followers. "If one soldier who carries the flag is stricken, another will take it from his hands and carry it on. Tell the people not to worry about me, for if I go down another will take my place. For always, the army is true. Always the cause is there."

A degree of lethargy in the campaign shifted to sincere sympathy for Roosevelt and admiration for his courage. He announced from Sagamore Hill, where he rested, that he would make one more address, at Madison Square Garden on October 30. This he did, and the rally had all the fervor of a Roosevelt meeting of days that had passed. He seemed strong and well. His face was ruddy. His voice, sounding again the principles of the Progressive party, carried to the far corners of the Garden and 12,000 people cheered and stamped their approval. Another informal speech or two followed before Election Day, but the result was in accordance with the prophecies. Wilson was elected with 435 votes in the Electoral College. Roosevelt won 88 votes and Taft, who had never really desired the presidency, carried only Vermont and Utah with their eight small votes.

Roosevelt, however, received 4,126,020 popular votes as against 6,286,124 for Woodrow Wilson and 3,483,922 for Taft. It was an impressive showing. "I accept the result with entire good humor," he said. "As for the Progressive cause, I can only repeat [that] the cause in itself must triumph, for this triumph is essential to the well-being of the American people."

Roosevelt had no illusions. War was to crowd new interests into his consciousness—new interests and new hatreds. By 1916 one object, the defeat of Wilson, loomed so large that it obscured all others. In all probability, Roosevelt would have turned his back on the Progressive party even had these changes not come. Soon after 1912 a friend called at Sagamore Hill and talked of victory in 1916.

"I thought you were a better politician," Roosevelt answered. "The fight is over. We are beaten. There is only one thing to do and that is to go back to the Republican party. You can't hold a party like the Progressive party together. There are no loaves and fishes."

Chapter VI

DRUMS OF WAR

❋

Between the Progressive campaign and the First World War, Roosevelt was at loose ends. He had no adequate outlet for energies which were as furious as ever, although the flesh was weaker. In 1912, and for the year or so which followed, Roosevelt believed again that his career had ended. "When it is evident that a leader's day is past," he wrote, "the one service that he can do is to step aside and leave the ground clear for the development of a successor." If Roosevelt gave much thought to 1916 and 1920, if he considered his own future except with profound gloom, his letters give no hint of it. In December, 1912, he was writing a lecture called "History as Literature" for delivery before the American Historical Society.

"None of its members, by the way, believe that history is literature," he wrote Cabot Lodge with asperity and accuracy, as he resumed the lifelong correspondence that had been interrupted by the last campaign.

To Roosevelt's undoubted relief, the period in which he combined a degree of scholarship with the activities of public sage and country gentleman was brief. During the comparative rustication one diverting controversy loomed. This was the libel action brought by Roosevelt against George J. Newett, the editor of an obscure weekly newspaper, *Iron Ore*, published at Ishpeming, Michigan. The suit was based on a preposterous item printed on October 12, 1912:

According to Roosevelt, he is the only man who can call others liars, rascals and thieves; terms he applies to Republicans generally. But if anyone calls Roosevelt a liar, he raves and roars and takes on in an awful way; and yet Roosevelt is a pretty good liar himself. Roosevelt lies and curses in a most disgusting way; he gets drunk, too, and that not infrequently, and all his intimates know about it.

Until they became particularly virulent during the Progressive campaign, Roosevelt ignored the repeated assertions that he was a heavy drinker. In 1912, however, the unfounded gossip achieved unprecedented volume because of the bitterness of the three-cornered contest for the presidency. The evidence is irrefutable that he was, if anything, overcautious. T.R. would sometimes sip from a wine glass, but rarely finished it. His closest approach to spirits appears to have been a very infrequent mint julep after a tennis game at the White House and then, if one may judge from the account by Archie Butt, Roosevelt participated largely in substantiation of his half-facetious claim that he too was a Georgian. And yet, untrue as they were, some basis existed for the whispers that Roosevelt drank to excess. It seemed impossible that such vitality could be natural. Men looked at his ruddy face, at his continued enthusiasms, at his gusts of anger or mirth or delight, and concluded that these were induced by alcohol. Too, he was inclined to joke about it. He recalled an occasion or two when he had declined a cigar and, asked whether he had any bad habits, had replied: "Yes, prize fighting and strong drink." During the Bull Moose drive, however, Roosevelt justifiably lost patience. He suggested that a libel suit be filed when the opportunity came. *Iron Ore* presented it, and action was taken.

The case was brought to trial on May 26, 1913, at Marquette, Michigan. Lasting for five days, while witness after witness testified to the plaintiff's abstemiousness, it was a complete triumph for Roosevelt. Finally the foolish editor of *Iron Ore*, unable to produce a single witness, admitted that he had been mistaken. Roosevelt said that he had not gone into the suit for money or "for any vindictive purpose"; he wished only to "deal with these slanders, so that never again will they be repeated." In accordance with Roosevelt's request, nominal damages—six cents—were assessed against Newett.

2

In the spring of 1913 Roosevelt made plans for a trip more dangerous than the excursion into Africa, and the disease and the hardships which he encountered hastened his death. The receipt of invitations to speak in Brazil and Argentina renewed a desire to explore the jungles of South America. By February and March of 1914 the party was descending a river that flows northward through the Brazilian jungle, an untraveled stream called the River of Doubt. If anything, Roosevelt's health was worse than it had been in Africa. For a man of his age and physical disabilities, the voyage was perilous in the extreme, and it nearly ended in disaster. The River of Doubt was filled with rapids and whirlpools. Roosevelt hurt his leg against a rock in attempting to extricate two of the canoes, which had become jammed against the rocks. An abscess developed, and on April 4, 1914, he contracted a form of jungle fever. He struggled on with the portage, however, although his heart pained him severely. A day or two later, he called his son Kermit to his tent.

"I want you to go ahead," he said. "We have reached a point where some of us must stop. I feel I am only a burden to the party."

The other members of the expedition, of course, would have endured any torture rather than leave Roosevelt to die. They brought him down the river and ultimately to safety, although he was so weak that most of the time he was prostrate.

Roosevelt's return in May, 1914, found him confronted with the old, old temptation to take part in politics. To petitions that he accept a Progressive party nomination for governor of New York, Roosevelt was emphatically and properly negative. For some time, however, he had watched with interest attacks being made on Boss Barnes of New York, who had led the forces for Taft at the Chicago convention. Roosevelt had worked with Barnes, as he had worked with Penrose and Quay and the other corrupt Republicans whose support had been essential to his program. In July, 1914, however, at a conference with minor political leaders, Roosevelt said he would sponsor no state ticket dictated by Barnes. On the other hand, it was time for the two wings of the Republican party to reunite; if the organization nominated "a Governor who would war on Republican crookedness just as much as upon Democratic crookedness," Roosevelt declared, he would support him. Then he issued a statement declaring that Boss Barnes and Boss Murphy of Tammany Hall were corruptly allied:

The interests of Mr. Barnes and Mr. Murphy are fundamentally identical. It is idle for a man to pretend that he is against machine politics unless he will openly and by name attack Mr. Barnes and Mr. Murphy.

Barnes had to answer Roosevelt if his power was to continue. On the following day, July 23, 1914, he brought suit for libel. The usual delays followed, but Roosevelt's enemies were elated as the trial, scheduled for April, 1915, at Syracuse, New York, approached.

"I am going to nail Roosevelt's hide to the fence," announced William M. Ivins, chief of counsel for Barnes, to Elihu Root a day or so before the trial started.

"Ivins," answered Root, "let me give you a piece of advice. I know Roosevelt and you want to be very sure that it is Roosevelt's hide that you get on the fence."

To their sorrow, the attorneys for Barnes learned that Root was right. They discovered that Roosevelt, a very self-confident witness who made speeches and orations until halted by the court, was not in the least dismayed by inconsistencies and contradictions in his career. He talked freely about his relations with Tom Platt. He admitted that he had been inclined, when Barnes first rose to power, to believe that he would make an honest leader. Their relations had been cordial during the period of the presidency:

Q. So you were acting as a monitor of Mr. Barnes in the effort to develop his political character and make a good and useful citizen of him; is that right?

Roosevelt: Only to this extent, Mr. Ivins; that with [most] men whom I met, I felt that they had two characters, a good character and a bad character. There were a few of them that were absolutely straight and upright and disinterested. There were a few that were hopelessly vile. Most of them were of a mixed character. My constant effort was to appeal to the side that was decent and to get the man to act rightly. I never broke with him, with any man, until I became convinced that it was hopeless to get the good side out of him.

Q. And you regarded Mr. Barnes as, in a measure, a Dr. Jekyll and a Mr. Hyde?

Roosevelt: I did; as most of them were.

The defendant, apparently unconcerned by the possibility that the jury would decide in favor of Barnes and return heavy damages, dominated the court room. The verdict on May 22, 1915, declared Roosevelt's criticism of Barnes truthful, which meant the gradual retirement of the New York leader from public life. At Oyster Bay, some months later, George Meyer, who had been in Roosevelt's Cabinet, mentioned the case. He could not remember, he said, the extent of the damages Roosevelt had received. The colonel grinned with delight.

"Would you mind saying that again?" he demanded, and Meyer did so.

"My dear fellow!"—Roosevelt's voice rose to its highest pitch—"*I* was the de-fen-dant!"

3

Then came the war. By August 4, the German armies were pressing toward Paris through Belgium, and President Wilson proclaimed the neutrality of the United States. The former President's confusion and contradictions are, in retrospect, astonishing and dismaying. On the irrefutable testimony of Associate Justice Felix Frankfurter of the Supreme Court, then soon to join the Harvard law faculty, Roosevelt was violently pro-Ally and anti-German at a gathering at Sagamore Hill on August 4. The jurist was at the meeting and remembered clearly, forty years later, how T.R. had shouted and gesticulated and had branded Germany an aggressor which must be halted. This was, of course, a private utterance which did not reach the newspapers. Yet the very next day, August 5, Roosevelt was quoted by the New York *Times*, and never denied the report, to the effect that the American people would support any chief executive who saw that this country came "through this crisis unscathed."

The unhappy fact is that Roosevelt could not, as the world tragedy opened, decide what he believed. On August

8, four days after the tirade against Germany at Oyster Bay, he wrote privately to Hugo Münsterberg of Harvard, an emphatic defender of the Kaiser. This curious letter said that, "in dire need, the statesmen of a nation" might "disregard any treaty, if keeping it may mean the most serious jeopardy to the nation." This, although Roosevelt would surely have denied it, was an exact summary of his own rejection of the sanctity of treaties.

It was during this period that Roosevelt wrote articles which he greatly regretted and altered before he permitted their publication in final form. The theory that he was influenced by friendship for the Kaiser toward pro-Germanism is without basis. While he was in the White House, as his presidential papers definitely prove, Roosevelt preferred Great Britain to Germany, although suspicious, to an extent, of both countries. If the statements of August to September, 1914, prove anything, it is that Roosevelt was still at heart a militarist. Roosevelt probably favored the cause of the Allies from the start. But those who supposed that the invasion of Belgium would move him were wrong. The first extended statement, after the private and public confused ones, appeared in the *Outlook* on August 22, 1914. This reiterated his pledge to stand by the Wilson Administration, with reservations relating to its future conduct. He continued:

I am not now taking sides one way or the other as concerns the violation or disregard of these treaties. When giants are engaged in a death wrestle, as they reel to and fro they are certain to trample on whomever gets in the way of either of the huge straining combatants.

In September, the Belgian Commission visited the United States, and Roosevelt wrote that the invasion had been justified because "disaster would surely have attended her [Germany's] arms had she not followed the course she actually did follow as regards her opponents on her Western frontier." There could be "nothing but praise and admiration due a stern, virile and masterful people, a people entitled to hearty respect for their patriotism and far-seeing self-devotion." All of which cannot be reconciled with his August 4 statements at Oyster Bay.

Germany admitted, Roosevelt said, that as "a matter of abstract right and wrong," the invasion of Belgium could not be justified. He then repeated his refusal, omitted from the final version of the essay, to pass judgment on Germany. He refused, in another passage subsequently censored, to pass judgment on the Antwerp air bombardments or the destruction of Louvain. Most important of all, in view of Roosevelt's eventual criticism of President Wilson, he wrote:

A deputation of Belgians has arrived in this country to invoke our assistance in the time of their dreadful need. It is certainly eminently desirable that we should remain entirely neutral. We can maintain our neutrality only by refusal to do anything to aid unoffending weak powers which are dragged into the gulf of bloodshed and misery through no fault of their own. Of course it would be folly to jump into the gulf ourselves to no good purpose; and very probably nothing that we could have done would have helped Belgium.

This passage, too, had been changed when Roosevelt's first book on the war appeared early in 1915. In its place appeared the following:

President Wilson has been much applauded by all the professional pacifists because he has announced that our desire for peace must make us secure it by a neutrality so strict as to forbid our even whispering a protest against wrong-doing, lest such whispers might cause disturbance to our ease and well-being. We pay the penalty of this—supine inaction on behalf of peace for ourselves, by forfeiting our right to do anything on behalf of peace for the Belgians.

4

Essentially, of course, the change in Roosevelt's views reflected the change in public opinion, but little of it heightens his reputation as a leader of public thinking. At first, the United States was indifferent as to the outcome, but this did not last. Great Britain and France were democracies; Germany an autocracy. The invasion of Belgium filled the newspapers with lengthy descriptions of the horrors of war. The British, moreover, were skilled in the uses of propaganda and their White Paper, published in August and setting forth the viewpoint of the Allies, was extremely well received in the United States. Germany, on the other hand, was guilty of an extreme blunder when, after waiting almost six weeks, she issued a White Paper of her own which was evasive and inadequate. By the end of October, Germany had become the villain.

All this undoubtedly accelerated Roosevelt's partisanship for the Allies. A second influence was his growing hatred for Woodrow Wilson, the consuming passion of the closing years. No opinion that Roosevelt held, no action which he took, can be considered apart from that hatred. It began immediately after his return from South America, in May, 1914, when he heard of the treaty, negotiated with Colombia by Secretary of State Bryan, which offered apology and an indemnity of $25,000,000 for the secession of Panama. This assault on the accomplishment of which Roosevelt was most proud was unquestionably the primary cause of his anger. On July 11, 1914, Roosevelt announced his retirement as associate editor of the *Outlook*. He felt "in honor bound to stand in strong opposition to the administration" which, in international relations, has "meant the abandonment of the interest and honor of America."

The animosity toward Wilson was revealed in Roosevelt's first speeches in 1914. The President had effected no small measure of the legislation advocated in the Progressive party platform. Roosevelt, however, could find no word of endorsement for the man who had countenanced an apology to Colombia. The Wilson Administration meant "the abandonment of every sane effort to secure the abatement of social and industrial evils." Roosevelt referred with heavy sarcasm to the "magniloquent vagueness" of the New Freedom which President Wilson had sounded. This had no meaning at all, he said, unless it was "the old license translated into pleasant rhetoric."

Roosevelt took exception, also, to Wilson's efforts toward international peace. Colonel House had been abroad during the summer of 1914 and had been talking with the important figures of Europe to that end. With the emotional assistance of Secretary of State Bryan, the President had been pressing for renewal or continuation of the arbitration treaties and had informed Congress, with ill-founded optimism, that "signs multiply about us of an age of settled peace and good will." Roosevelt had opposed the arbitration treaties during the Taft Administration. In nearly all of his references in 1914 to the World War he opposed them again, and it was in this connection, as much as with reference to Belgium, that Roosevelt said that treaties, in the event of war, were not "worth the paper on which they are written."

Such, perhaps, were among the reasons which led Roosevelt to shift from advocacy of neutrality and partial defense of Germany to his demand that the United States intervene. There was another, less tangible, cause. It, too, was behind the detestation for Wilson, which became almost psychopathic. Wilson believed that the President should act in a given situation only when the public support was with him. Roosevelt's conception was that a President should lead that public opinion toward endorsement after the action had been taken. The difference is profound. It filled Roosevelt with fury to see Wilson wait for the people to demand participation in the war.

And yet these two men really sought the same end. "England is fighting our fight," said Wilson. "I will not take any action to embarrass England when she is fighting for her life and the life of the world." By February, 1916, through the memorandum between Sir Edward Grey and Colonel House, the President had agreed that the United States would enter the war on the side of the Allies if peace overtures were blocked by Germany. Roosevelt and Wilson, each with the attributes of greatness, might have worked together. Instead Roosevelt blazed with anger and Wilson, whose seat was the seat of power, looked down with amused and lofty contempt.

By February, 1915, Roosevelt was "sick at heart over the actions of Wilson and Bryan." That month, Germany announced her submarine policy. In May, 1915, the *Lusitania* was sunk. This, said Roosevelt, was "murder on the high seas." His attack on Germany was scathing and bitter. His attack on President Wilson, whose unfortunate phrase— that a nation might be "too proud to fight"—inspired Roosevelt's vehement scorn, was hardly less vigorous. He called for seizure of all of Germany's interned ships and an edict against all commerce with Germany.

"I do not believe," he concluded, "that the firm assertion of our rights means war, but, in any event, it is well to remember there are things worse than war."

Wilson, rightly or wrongly, believed that the country did not yet desire war with Germany. Spring Rice felt that he was right. He told Sir Edward Grey that the "great mass of people here are deeply anxious not to be involved," that Wilson, on a visit to New York City, had been received with "a greater degree of popularity than has been given to anyone since Roosevelt." But Roosevelt said that loyalty to the administration meant "disloyalty to our self-interest," and demanded universal military service modeled after the Swiss system. To those who had urged preparedness, he said, the President had answered "with a cheap sneer, with unworthy levity. Thanks to the administration, the United States has been faithless to its duty." At heart, T.R. exploded, Wilson was "an abject coward."

"From the very outset," he explained, "I felt that the administration was taking the wrong course. I spoke only

when it became imperative under penalty of tame acquiescence in tame failure to perform a national duty."

Contempt for Wilson's action became an obsession as the
President continued to send protests against Germany's
submarine policy, instead of declaring war. At Sagamore
some weeks after the *Lusitania* outrage, Mrs. Longworth
looked at her father and observed mildly that another note
had been sent to Germany. Roosevelt's face reflected his
scorn.

"Did you notice what its serial number was?" he asked.
"I fear I have lost track myself; but I am inclined to think
it is No. 11,765, Series B."

The campaign of 1916, however, was really a referendum on the leadership of Wilson and of Roosevelt.

5

The war killed other things besides men. It killed the New
Nationalism for which Roosevelt had battled. It killed the
New Freedom of Woodrow Wilson. Any hope that Roosevelt would continue his devotion to the Progressive party
disappeared in the face of his opposition to the President.
He was "the worst President by all odds since Buchanan
with the possible exception of Andrew Johnson." Roosevelt
worried over rumors that Taft might receive the 1916 nomination. However, "it does not seem to me that I could support Wilson even against Taft." In November, 1915, he
spoke of the need for "trying to unite all the anti-Wilson
forces into a coherent whole" and hoped that the once-
despised G.O.P. would make it possible for the Progressives
to come back into the fold.

It was inevitable that Roosevelt should receive consideration as the nominee of the Republican party. This time,
he did nothing whatever to advance his chances. Roosevelt,
meditating a return to the party, disavowed any movement
for his own nomination that entertained any compromise on
the issues he believed important: opposition to Wilson, and
preparedness. He went to the incredible length of threatening that he would support Wilson if the party compromised
with honor and bowed to the influences that sought conciliation with Germany.

"And, by Godfrey, I mean it," said Roosevelt, convincing
himself, for the moment. "If there is a mongrel platform
adopted, I'll stump the country for him."

How inextricably mingled were Roosevelt's unlovely contempt for Wilson and his fine patriotism? It is impossible to

say. Both reached new heights during 1915, as Germany's policies drove the United States closer and closer to war. With the sinking of the *Lusitania*, the President started a drive for preparedness, but his program was far from satisfactory to Roosevelt. "Wilson has come to the conclusion that there is a rising popular feeling for preparedness," he sneered, "and, seeing votes in it, is prepared to take it up."

Roosevelt's great services toward preparedness were marred by his attitude regarding Wilson, who had, after all, the responsibility. He admitted himself, on at least one occasion, that the public was behind Wilson, that the antiwar sentiment was far the stronger. But his letters showed no tolerance, no trust—only hatred. At Plattsburg, New York, where the first of the officers' training camps had been started, Roosevelt made a speech on preparedness on August 25, 1915, which observed the proprieties. Then, as he boarded his train later in the day, he said that the President deserved support only when he served the country well. Wilson was not sincere; he uttered "weasel words" when he pretended to favor preparedness.

Meanwhile, Roosevelt backed steadily away from another nomination at the hands of the Progressive party, a nomination which would again insure the election of Wilson. In March, 1916 he issued a statement, not wholly conclusive, in which he said that no factional fight for his nomination would be permitted and that "it would be a mistake to nominate me unless the country has in its mood something of the heroic"; in other words, unless it was ready for war. The regular Republicans met in Chicago on June 7 and when delegates from the two wings of the party attempted to unite on a compromise candidate, the efforts failed. Roosevelt was nominated by a moth-eaten Bull Moose on June 10, and on that same day the G.O.P. chose Charles Evans Hughes. Roosevelt declined the Progressive party nomination by telegraph, although reserving the right to change his mind should the Republican platform be silent on the important issues of the war. He declined formally in a lengthy letter on June 22, 1916. So ended the Battle at Armageddon.

"I shall strongly support Mr. Hughes," Roosevelt announced.

It was not that Roosevelt liked Hughes, but that he disliked Wilson. In 1908, when the Republican organization in New York protested against renominating Hughes for governor, Roosevelt agreed that he had "wantonly and recklessly insulted the party workers." But in 1908, the election of Taft was in Roosevelt's mind and he urged that Hughes be chosen despite these faults. In 1916, he thought chiefly of defeating Wilson. Although Hughes was "not an attractive personality—a very, very self-centered man," Roosevelt labored for him. In his desperate efforts to reunite the party factions, he went so far as to write former Senator Foraker, whom he had driven from public life:

Not only do I admire your entire courage and straight-forwardness, but I grow steadily more and more to realize your absolute Americanism. There is no use in raking up the past now, but there were some things told me against you which (when I consider what I know now of my informants) would have carried no weight with me at the time had I been as well informed as at present.

All through the summer of 1916, as the campaign began, Congress was busy with Wilson's war program. The regular army was increased. New battleships were authorized. A Council of National Defense was created. But the slogan of the party was "He Kept Us Out of War," while Justice Hughes, with lofty vagueness, stood for "the firm and unflinching maintenance of all the rights of American citizens on land and sea." The man whom Roosevelt had endorsed was indefinite on nearly all questions.

Roosevelt was not vague. While Hughes campaigned monotonously, the apostle of war stormed westward to the Rockies in behalf of preparedness and Republicanism. He returned convinced that Wilson would win. His final speech was in New York City on the night of November 3 and, as in all the rest, his bitterness toward Wilson was transcendent. Toward the end, Roosevelt tossed aside his manuscript and, trembling with emotion, pointed out that President Wilson was living at Shadow Lawn, the summer White House:

There should be shadows now at Shadow Lawn; the shadows of the men, women and children who have risen from the ooze of the ocean bottom and from graves in foreign lands; the shadows of the helpless whom Mr. Wilson did not dare protect lest he might have to face danger; the shadows of babies gasping pitifully as they sank under the waves; the shadows of women outraged and slain by bandits. Those are the shadows proper for Shadow Lawn; the shadows of deeds that were never done; the shadows of lofty words that were followed by no action; the shadows of the tortured dead.

Thus Roosevelt excoriated the man, elected again by a narrow margin, to whom he was to appeal, within a few months, for authority to lead a division in France. It is possibly not surprising that Wilson and his advisers felt that he lacked the degree of balance required for military leadership.

Chapter VII

THE FINAL BLOW

＊

On an afternoon in 1911 at Sagamore Hill, Theodore Roosevelt and Henry L. Stoddard, his journalist friend and supporter, idly discussed the subject of titles. Stoddard ventured to say that Roosevelt probably preferred to be addressed as "Colonel."

"Yes," answered Roosevelt, "there's a lot in that title for me. But if I were asked what title I would prefer, it would not be President or Colonel; it would be Major General in the United States Army in active service. Remember I say active service—no swivel chair for me. Active service, however, is not likely to come in my day, so I suppose 'Colonel' I'll remain to the end. That's good enough."

It had been so since Roosevelt, as a child, turned his back on the gentle life of a naturalist and started to build for himself a strong body. War had always been romantic to him. He always wanted to take part:

1886: I have written to Secretary Endicott offering to try to raise some companies of horse riflemen in the event of trouble with Mexico.

1896 [Regarding Altgeld in 1896]: Remember, sir, I may at any time be called upon to meet the man sword to sword upon the field of battle. When war does come I shall be found at the head of my regiment.

1898: We will have a jim-dandy regiment if we go.

1908: If a war should occur while I am still physically fit, I should certainly try to raise a brigade of cavalry, mounted riflemen, such as those in my regiment ten years ago.

1911: . . . if by any remote chance there should be a serious war, then I would wish immediately to raise a division of cavalry. If given a free hand I could render it as formidable a body of horse riflemen, that is, of soldiers such as those of Sheridan, Forest, and Stuart, as has ever been seen.

February, 1917: I have already on file my application to be permitted to raise a Division of Infantry, with a divisional brigade of cavalry, in the event of war (possibly with the permission to make one or two of the brigades of infantry, mounted infantry).

Long prior to any probability that the United States would enter the war—indeed, soon after he had changed his mind regarding the invasion of Belgium—Roosevelt began to ponder the part he would play in the greatest of military dramas. He ignored, as the struggle grew close, his obvious physical disqualifications. He was blind in one eye, and racked by Amazon fevers. Hardly five years earlier T.R. had described himself as "an old man, wholly unable to make exertions." Yet in the autumn of 1914, he conferred at the Harvard Club regarding a Roosevelt Division to consist of mounted infantrymen. In January, 1915, Col. Gordon Johnston, of the regular army, was summoned to Oyster Bay by Theodore Roosevelt, Jr., who said that his father seemed depressed.

"I found Colonel Roosevelt," Johnston recalled, "suffering from one of his attacks of fever. He mentioned how much he would like to have a part in the war, and that gave me a clue to make a suggestion, partly to divert his mind."

The suggestion was that Roosevelt begin at once the work of raising a division. Subsequently, at another interview, Colonel Johnston expressed doubt, not unreasonably in view of Roosevelt's attitude toward Washington, that President Wilson would give him authority to go.

"I am going to see Mr. Wilson," Roosevelt said, "and tell him that if he will give me this commission and authority to organize and take this division to France, I will give him my promise never to oppose him politically in any way whatsoever."

For a little while after the election in 1916, the possibility grew that the United States might remain at peace, even that the war itself would end. This was Wilson's overwhelming aspiration. The President continued to use phrases, however, which offered ammunition to his foes. In addressing the Senate on January 22, 1917, on the hope of peace overtures, he said that it must be a "peace without victory." This was true, as the impossible provisions of the Treaty of Versailles were ultimately to make only too clear. But the phrase, like the thought that a nation might be "too proud to fight," was greeted with sneers. After all, Wilson was wrong; war was coming. Even as Wilson spoke, the German Government was swinging rapidly toward its policy of submarine ruthlessness. On January 31, 1917.

Count von Bernstorff, German ambassador to the United States, notified the State Department of the institution of zones in the Mediterranean and around the British Isles where all neutral shipping would be destroyed if it carried contraband. Von Bernstorff had sought with desperation to delay this decree. On February 3, President Wilson told Congress that the German ambassador had been handed his passports.

The President still held to the forlorn hope of peace and spoke of "armed neutrality." On March 12 and again on March 19, however, American ships were sunk without warning. On April 2, Wilson appeared before the Houses of Congress and declared that a state of war existed. He had gambled for peace and had lost. He returned to the White House with the applause of Congress and the galleries in his ears.

"My message was a message of death to our young men," he told Tumulty. "How strange it seemed to applaud that."

2

The announcement by Germany of unrestricted submarine activity meant war. To Wilson this meant utter misery and suffering. But in Roosevelt it aroused all the slumbering traits of adolescence. On February 2, 1917, he wrote the first of a series of appealing letters to Secretary of War Newton D. Baker. He told Mr. Baker that plans for the division were already prepared. He was ready to ask for certain officers for the posts of chief of staff, chief surgeon, quartermaster general, and for brigade and regimental commanders. "No situation has arisen," replied Baker, too curtly, requring such a division. But his letter would be "filed for consideration should the occasion arise."

"I do not believe Wilson will go to war unless Germany literally kicks him into it," Roosevelt declared ten days later. "I cannot criticize him until this point is decided, because I have applied for leave to raise a division; and if he gives me one and sends me to the war, I shall serve him with single-minded loyalty."

After diplomatic relations had been broken with Germany, T.R. wrote Baker again; this time asking for the appointment of Capt. Frank McCoy as his divisional chief of staff with the rank of colonel. But Baker answered that no such action could be taken "without the express sanction of Congress." There was an ominous note, which must have chilled Roosevelt's heart, in the War Secretary's phrase that

Congress would arrange for volunteer troops and for the appointment of high officers "under its own conditions." This was reiterated a month later. Roosevelt then said that his division could sail for France after six weeks of preliminary training and would there receive intensive training. He would need one regular army officer for each eight hundred or one thousand volunteers. High commanding officers "for all volunteer forces," Baker answered on March 20, "are to be drawn from the regular army."

The correspondence with the Secretary of War grew less formally friendly late in March. Roosevelt resented Baker's declaration that "general officers" were to be drawn from the regular army:

I am a retired Commander-in-Chief of the United States Army, and eligible to any position of command over American troops to which I may be appointed.

The regiment, First United States Volunteer Cavalry, in which I first served as lieutenant-colonel, and which I then commanded as colonel, was raised, armed, equipped, drilled, mounted, dismounted, kept for two weeks on a transport, and then put through two victorious aggressive fights, in which we lost a third of the officers, and a fifth of the enlisted men, all within a little over fifty days.

"The patriotic spirit of your suggestion is cordially appreciated," answered the Secretary of War.

"The President is purely a demagogue," Roosevelt wrote on February 28, ". . . his extreme adroitness in appealing to all that is basest in the hearts of our people has made him able for the time being to drug the soul of the nation into a coma. I say nothing in public about Wilson now."

On April 2, 1917, came Wilson's speech before Congress. On April 6, 1917, a state of war between the United States and Germany existed. "The President's great message of April 2 was literally unanswerable," Roosevelt said publicly. "Of course, when war is on, all minor considerations, including all partisan considerations, vanish at once. All good Americans will back the President with single-minded loyalty in every movement he makes to uphold American honor, defend American rights, and strike hard and effectively in return for the brutal wrong-doing of the German Government."

It is to be noted that this was far from an unqualified pledge; that Roosevelt would be the judge of Wilson's success in upholding American honor and prosecuting the war successfully. Roosevelt's approval was to depend, it developed, on whether the President would consent to a division under his leadership in France. Late in March, it became apparent to Roosevelt that consent from Wilson was doubtful. He knew that no authorization for volunteer forces would be given except with the consent of Congress. Consequently, he directed Lodge to "see that no army legislation is so framed as to leave me out." In his fervor to storm the battlements, Roosevelt actually considered the possibility of going even if the President rejected his offer. He notified Ambassador Jusserand that if France would pay for it, he would take an American division to France "under the American flag."

"If his Government does not, I shall try whether Canada would like to pay for an American division (under our flag)—I understand that they need more men."

Under the imminence of failure, Roosevelt abandoned pride. He prepared to humble himself before the man who was a pacifist, who mouthed "weasel words," who was the worst President since Buchanan, who had sacrificed the support of his countrymen, behind whom stood only "the flubdubs and the mollycoddles."

3

On April 7, 1917, Assistant Secretary of the Navy Franklin D. Roosevelt, whose wife was a niece of Theodore Roosevelt and who was himself distantly related to the colonel, crossed from his own office in the Army and Navy Building at Washington to that of Secretary of War Baker. Colonel Roosevelt was in town, he told Baker, and was anxious for a conference. The Secretary of War said that he would be glad to see the former President at any time and promptly agreed, on further suggestion from the Assistant Secretary of the Navy, to call on Roosevelt at the home of Mrs. Longworth, where he was staying. Mr. Baker recalled:

I found the house filled with visitors on the first floor, most of them Senators and close friends of Colonel Roosevelt. The former President seemed to be in high spirits. He came out when I arrived and greeted me cordially, put his hand through my arm and took me upstairs to one of the bedrooms. He then described his hopes for leading a division in France.

"I am aware," he said, "that I have not had enough experience to lead a division myself. But I have selected the most experienced officers from the regular army for my staff."

The Secretary of War repeated his earlier assurances that the request would be carefully considered, but Roosevelt must have recognized the inevitable when Baker added that the war was not a matter of individual problems but one in which innumerable considerations had to be taken into account.

"I had a good talk with Baker," Roosevelt subsequently said. "I could twist him about my finger could I have him about for a while."

The court of final resort remained—the President whom Roosevelt detested—and an interview at the White House was arranged for April 9. Joseph P. Tumulty, the President's secretary and naturally ardently pro-Wilson, was seated a few feet away while they discussed the division. He felt that "nothing could have been pleasanter or more agreeable," that the two men met "in the most friendly fashion, told each other anecdotes, and seemed to enjoy what the Colonel was accustomed to call a 'bully time.' "

"Yes," Tumulty quoted the President as saying when Roosevelt left, "he is a great big boy. I was charmed by his personality. There is a sweetness about him that is very compelling. You can't resist the man."

"He received me pleasantly," said Roosevelt, "and we had an hour's talk. I complimented him upon his war message and told him it would rank with the world's greatest state papers if it were made good and I told him I wanted a chance to help him make it good. I found that there was a confusion in his mind as to what I wanted to do. I explained everything to him. He seemed to take it well, but —remember—I was talking to Mr. Wilson."

Undoubtedly the amenities were observed. But as they sat in the Red Room, which Roosevelt had once ruled, there was mutual distrust beneath the seeming affability. The President, outwardly so calm, was singularly resistant to the opinions of others, even when they were his friends and political allies. This man who boomed of the division he wished to lead, who said that the President's message had been splendid but must be made good, had uttered scathing things, cruel, insulting, and false things, in all too recent months. T.R. knew that Wilson, even if animated only by hatred, had only to say that the General Staff did not approve of a Roosevelt Division. He could strike and still remain imperturbably calm. His was the power Roosevelt once had wielded, and with it he could wreck the aspirations of the closing years.

"I have no hard feeling toward Theodore," said William Howard Taft, about a year later, when asked whether he would forgive the past. "And if I had—I certainly could wish him no worse luck than to be sick in bed while Woodrow runs his war."

The truth is that we do not know the motives which caused Wilson to reject the Roosevelt Division. Certainly logic was on his side, and military efficiency as well. At first, Roosevelt intended to be the divisional commander; this is clear from his letters to Baker. It was only after the visit to Washington that he indicated his willingness to go as a junior officer. By then, rejection of the plan was certain. Baker had informed Roosevelt on April 13, 1917, that the War College Division "earnestly recommends that no American troops be employed in active service" until after adequate training and that all officers of the army or the National Guard be used for that purpose.

Roosevelt continued to cite his services in the Spanish-American War, confusing his undoubted bravery with military skill. "You forget," he told Baker, "that I have commanded troops in action in the most important battle fought by the United States Army in the last half-century," a safe enough statement, since in that time the only other fighting had been skirmishes against the Indians. "I desire that you judge me on my record." He pointed to the undoubted effect of an immediate expeditionary force on the morale of the Allies.

All this did not move Wilson. "I am not playing politics," said the President heatedly when Governor John M. Parker of Louisiana, a Democrat, interceded for Roosevelt. "Colonel Roosevelt is a splendid man and a patriotic citizen, as you say, but he is not a military leader. His experience in military life has been extremely short. He and many of the men with him are too old to render effective service, and in addition to that fact, he as well as others have shown intolerance of discipline."

And yet the Allies, weary of war, desperately needed the stimulus of American re-enforcements on the Western front. Roosevelt, more than any other man alive, would have brought promise of a new day. Word that he was coming would have spread through the trenches, and tired men might have found strength to resist at its start the drive that marked the second Battle of the Marne. Clemenceau felt this. Hard-pressed, he sent Wilson a final appeal to have Roosevelt come. His name was the "one which sums up the beauty of American intervention. He is an idealist, imbued with simple, vital idealism. You are too much of a philosopher to ignore that the influence on the people of great leaders of men often exceeds their personal merits, thanks to the legendary halo surrounding them. The name of Roosevelt has this legendary force in our country . . . you must know, Mr. President, more than one of our *poilus* asked his comrade: 'But where is Roosevelt?' "

But Marshal Joffre, who had hurried to America to ask that troops be rushed overseas, admitted to Mr. Baker that it cost from ten to fifteen thousand lives to train a major general.

Two facts made the Roosevelt Division impossible. The first was Roosevelt's character. With the best intentions in the world, as he had demonstrated as Assistant Secretary of the Navy and in the Spanish War, he desired to be subordinate. It was not, however, in his nature. Roosevelt, in France, would have been a source of friction. To send him would have placed Pershing in an impossible position, and whatever the faults of Wilson and Baker, they did stand behind their commander of the A.E.F. The second fact is that the Roosevelt Division would have drawn heavily from the civilian officer-material so desperately needed to build an army in a land where none existed. In his memoirs, General Pershing made no mention of the probable friction with Roosevelt. To grant the request for a division would have "opened the door for many similar requests," he wrote. Besides, "in such a war it was necessary that officers, especially those in high command, should be thoroughly trained and disciplined." Finally, Roosevelt "was not in the best of health and could not have withstood the hard work and exposure of the training camp and trenches."

Too, war had changed. Against gas and machine guns, Roosevelt's cherished "horse riflemen" would have been helpless. War, said President Wilson on May 5, 1917, was now "undramatic, practical, and of scientific definiteness and precision." No bands would play. No hills would be stormed. No hats or swords were to be waved above heroic troops. The God of War had changed, as the age had changed. He had adopted machine methods for wholesale slaughter, and gallantry was dead.

Inevitably, Roosevelt concluded that the basis of his rejection was political. He had told the President, in the memorable interview at the White House, that he would never come back from France.

"If you can convince Wilson of that," said Root, when

Roosevelt repeated the remark during a gloomy conference at the Harvard Club, "he will let you go."

Root, of course, knew better.

4

Good and evil, high patriotism and anger born of searing disappointment, struggled for mastery in Roosevelt during the war. "As good American citizens," he said, when the decision of the President reached him, "we loyally obey." But the wrath that seethed in him could not be controlled. Roosevelt did his country, and himself, a distinct disservice by publishing, when he did, the text of the correspondence with Baker. This was in August, 1917, at the height of the war. It served no possible purpose except self-vindication. The fight of Roosevelt's friends for legislation that would authorize a division under his command delayed, in the Senate, the passage of the selective service law. The two weeks that were lost might have been even longer had not Roosevelt himself urged the passage of any law that would meet the situation. His first important utterance, in an address at Oyster Bay on July 4, 1917, was a bitter criticism of Wilson's prosecution of the war: ". . . the net achievement," Roosevelt said, ". . . is a cause for profound humility."

In publishing the Baker correspondence, Roosevelt said that the action of Wilson in rejecting his services had been

supported and applauded by the leaders and intelligent partisans of Germany and opponents of war with Germany in this country. President Wilson's reasons for refusing my offer had nothing to do either with military considerations or with the public needs.

But if Roosevelt, in his anger and chagrin, undermined public confidence in the President in time of war, he performed, at the same time, great services. Wilson, his mind too much occupied by dreams of peace in 1916, might have more effectively put through a program of preparedness. Roosevelt did much to change the early attitude that food or ships or dollars, but not men, would win the war. He spoke for a unified Americanism, for common effort on the part of citizens of all nationalities. Beginning in September, 1917, he toured the country in behalf of determination, speed, and a vigorous offensive in the war. Without the voice of Roosevelt in 1917 and 1918, the war would have lasted longer. His was the voice of high emotion; unfair, of course, and believing to the last incredible detail the stories of German atrocities that British propagandists sent out from the Western front. It was the voice of emotion, but it did untold service in arousing the American people from their lethargy. The verdict of history may well be that Roosevelt at home, unhappy and vengeful, was far more useful than he could have been in France.

His four sons were fighting bravely and well with the American Expeditionary Force. On July 17, 1918, Roosevelt received word that Quentin, the youngest, had been killed in an aerial battle and that his plane had fallen behind the German lines. This was nearly the end. Roosevelt himself wrote the tribute to his son:

Only those are fit to live who do not fear to die; and none are fit to die who have shrunk from the joy of life. Both life and death are parts of the same Great Adventure. Never yet was worthy adventure worthily carried through by the man who put his personal safety first. Pride is the portion only of those who know bitter sorrow or the foreboding of bitter sorrow. But all of us who give service, and stand ready for sacrifice, are the torch-bearers. We run with the torches until we fall, content if we can then pass them to the hands of the other runners. The torches whose flame is brightest are borne by the gallant men at the front, by the gallant women whose husbands and lovers, whose sons and brothers are at the front. These men are high of soul, as they face their fate on the shell-shattered earth, or in the skies above or in the waters beneath; and no less high of soul are the women with torn hearts and shining eyes; the girls whose boy-lovers have been struck down in their golden morning, and the mothers and wives to whom word has been brought that henceforth they must walk in the shadow.

These are the torch-bearers; these are they who have dared the Great Adventure.

Not much time remained; Roosevelt's own adventure was drawing to its close. He was taken ill in February, 1918, and at the Roosevelt Hospital in New York City he was treated for an abscess on his thigh and for abscesses in his ears. He remained there for almost a month, and when he returned to Sagamore Hill the hearing was gone from his left ear. He was now half deaf as well as blind in one eye. His vigor continued. His hatred for Wilson was not softened by news from the front that the Germans were falling back. He made two additional speaking tours, one in May and another in September, 1918, and by fall he was sounding the demand for uncompromising surrender, for peace with victory. On November 11, 1918, the day of the armistice, he again returned to the hospital. This time it was inflammatory rheumatism, apparently induced by the fever infection from South America, but he was again able to leave and on Christmas Eve was back at Oyster Bay. He seemed to be gaining after the holidays. But through all the years, he had drawn too heavily upon the reservoirs of his strength. He dictated an editorial for the Kansas City *Star* on January 5, 1919. He went to bed rather early that evening and to James Amos, his Negro valet, he said, "Please put out the light." At four o'clock in the morning, January 6, 1919, he died. The immediate cause was an embolism, or blood clot, in the coronary artery.

Few had known that Roosevelt was seriously ill; even his physicians had no apprehension that the end was so near. The darkness came suddenly, and he would have chosen to have it so. He was not forced, as most men are, to watch the creeping shadows. And yet he was too young—only sixty-one—to die. Part of the bitterness of the closing years had come because he had climbed the heights too soon. For a final time the name of Roosevelt flared in the headlines. Cables carried the news to far-off places, and on a hundred thousand masts the flag he had served and had honored fluttered down to its halfway mark of mourning. Through the Italian Alps, that morning, sped a regal train, the train of the King of Italy. In the royal coach were President and Mrs. Wilson. The President was in high spirits. It seemed as though his aspirations for an international league for peace might reach fulfillment. He had been hailed as the savior of Europe by hysterical millions who reasoned only that the war had ended. On the morning of January 6, 1919, the President was being borne toward Modena, where the train halted for a moment. Wilson remained in the railway carriage, while the newspaper correspondents strolled on the platform. They chanced to be directly opposite him, and could see him through the window, as a messenger arrived with a telegram.

They watched idly as he read it. They became interested as conflicting emotions played across the President's face. When he first glanced at the message there was surprise. Then came pity. Then came a look of transcendent triumph. A moment later, the correspondents learned that the telegram had announced the death of Theodore Roosevelt.

5

Had Roosevelt lived, he would have joined the battalion of death that killed the League of Nations. But had he lived, he might have been elected President in 1920 and

hen there would have been no era of shame and scandal
t Washington. These are opinions, not statements of fact.
As to the first, the evidence is both sparse and conflicting.
As to the second, political futures are always uncertain.

The fact that Wilson was behind the League must have
been proof enough of its sinister purpose. "For Heaven's
ake," he begged Ogden Reid of the New York *Tribune*
ive days before he died, "never allude to Wilson as an
dealist. He is a doctrinaire; he is always utterly and coldly
elfish. He hasn't a touch of idealism in him. He is a silly
doctrinaire at times and an utterly selfish and cold-blooded
politician always."

In an address in September, 1918, Roosevelt said that it
was wrong to "supplant nationalism by internationalism."
n the editorial written just before he died, Roosevelt said
hat a League of Nations was greatly to be desired. How-
:ver:

> The trouble with Mr. Wilson's utterances, so far as they are
> reported, and the utterances of acquiescence in them by Euro-
> pean statesmen, is that they are still absolutely in the stage of
> rhetoric, like the Fourteen Points. Would it not be well to begin
> vith the League which we actually have in existence, the League
> of the Allies who have fought through this great war? Let us at
> he peace table see that real justice is done as among these allies
> and that while the sternest reparation is demanded from our foes
> . . yet should anything be done in the spirit of mere venge-
> ance? Then let us agree to extend the privileges of the League
> as rapidly as their conduct warrants it to other nations. Let each
> nation reserve to itself and for its own decision to clearly [*sic*]
> set forth questions which are non-justiciable.

The conclusion cannot be avoided that he was closer to
he position of Cabot Lodge than to that of Root or Taft or
Henry White. On November 26, 1918, at the hospital in
New York, Root and Henry White, who was to be a member of the Peace Mission, sat at Roosevelt's bed and discussed the terms of peace. White felt that Roosevelt, who
said very little, had endorsed the general idea of a League
of Nations. Two points are certain, however: Roosevelt
had traveled far from his position of the Nobel Peace Prize
address at Christiania in May, 1910, when he spoke of "a
League of Peace, not only to keep peace among themselves,
but to prevent, by force if necessary, its being broken by
others." The second point is that his conception of a peace
of victory, in which the conquered would accept the terms
of the conquerors, was the antithesis of Wilson's lofty conception of a peace in which justice should rule.

At all events, the gospel of vengeance won, the gospel that Roosevelt disavowed and yet had nurtured.

Wilson returned from the Peace Conference to be overwhelmingly rebuked in November, 1920. Might Roosevelt have been the Republican candidate had he lived? It is unlikely but not impossible. "If the Republican Party wants me, and I can advance the ideals for which I stand," he said in 1918, "I will be a candidate. But I will not lift a finger for the nomination." The leaders would not have wanted him. Plans were under way for the return of the Grand Old Party to power. Plans were under way for years of plenty after eight years of exile. But perhaps Theodore Roosevelt could not have been shunted aside.

Instead, Warren Gamaliel Harding became President of the United States.

INDEX

Abbot, W. J., 114
Abbott, Lawrence, 328
Abbott, Lyman, 296, 334, 346
Abernathy, Jack, 347
Adams, C. F., Jr., 60
Adams, Henry, 19, 22, 23, 88, 90,
    118, 171, 268, 272, 347–48, 398
Africa, T.R. in, 346, 357, 358–60
African Game Trails, 360
Agassiz, Louis, 8
Alaska, boundary dispute, 198, 203–
    06, 248
Albany Evening Journal, 149
Aldrich, C. H., 389
Aldrich, N. W., 296, 299, 340, 375
Aldrich-Vreeland Act, 339
Alfonso XIII, 368
Algeciras. See Morocco.
Alger, R. A., 128, 137, 138
Alien Landholding Act, 290
Allison, W. B., 297–99
Altgeld, J. P., 106, 107, 113, 114,
    412
Alverstone, Lord, 204, 205
Alvord, T. G., 51
Amador, Maria de la Ora de, 229
Amador de Guerrero, Manuel, 226–32
Amaya, Gen., 229–30
American Federation of Labor, 55,
    186
American Sugar Refining Co., 178
American Tobacco Co., 300
Amos, James, 422
Ananias Club, 377
Anderson, Judge, 237
Andrews, A. D., 95, 103
Aoki, Count, 288
Arbitration, 386, 407; T.R. and, 196.
    See also Alaska boundary dispute;
    Venezuela boundary dispute, debt
    dispute.
Archbold, J. D., 240, 246, 252, 254,
    356
Arizona, 374
Armageddon, 145, 260, 395
Armour, J. O., 249
Armour Packing Co., 295
Arnold, Benedict, 7, 9, 113
Arnold, E. C., 327
Arthur, C. A., 43, 56, 57

Associated Press, 255, 283
Austria, 275, 279, 285. See also
    World War.
Authors, T.R. and, 333–35
Aylesworth, A. B., 204, 205

Bacon, Robert, 194
Bacon, Mrs. Robert, 30, 75
Bad Lands, T.R. in, 35, 38, 39, 61,
    64–74, 76, 89, 360
Baer, G. F., 186–88, 190–96
Bahia Hondo, 210
Bailey, J. W., 297–98
Baker, G. F., 308
Baker, N. D., 414–20 passim
Balkans, 196
Ballinger, R. A., 371, 374
Barnes, William, Jr., 148, 149, 378,
    403–04; libel suit, 150, 314, 403–
    04
Barrère, 107
Bass, R. P., 389
Beaupré, A. M., 218–20, 232
Beck, Carl, 131
Belgium, invasion of, 404, 406
    (T.R. on), 407, 413
Bell, Gen. J. F., 282–83
Belmont, August, 234, 249
Benton, Thomas H., Life of, 82, 158,
    351
Berkman, Alexander, 107
Bernstorff, J. H., Count von, 414
Bethmann-Hollweg, Theobald von,
    364
Beveridge, A. J., 299, 301, 396
Big stick, the, 149, 196, 360
Bigelow, Sturgis, 185
Billings, Rev. Sherrard, 24
Bimberg, "Buttons Bim," 155
Birth control, T.R. and, 332–33
Bishop, J. B., 343
Bismarck, 169
Björkö, 278
Black, F. S., 140, 143
Blaine, J. G., 38, 48, 56–91 passim,
    69, 81, 83, 84, 86, 118
Bliss, C. N., 109, 252
Blocksom, Maj. A. P., and report,
    324–25
Bo, Marius, 215

Bonaparte, C. J., 87, 91, 241, 311, 313
Borah, W. E., 391, 396
Boston *Advertiser*, 61; *Transcript*, 61, 62
Boyd, Federico, 232
Brisbane, Arthur, 96
Brodie, Lieut. Col. A. O., 139
Brooklyn *Union*, 61
Brown, Walter, 392
Browne, H. J., 327
Brownsville riot, 322–27, 353, 356
Bryan, W. J., 58, 103, 105, 107, 109, 111–14, 115, 156–59, 169, 174, 187, 248, 259–60, 290, 299, 336, 338, 355, 356, 357, 378, 383, 395, 407, 408
Bryan, Mrs. W. J., 111
Bryce, James, 65
Buchanan, James, 416
Bull Moose, 156; party. *See* Progressive party.
Bulloch, Anna (aunt), 8, 11; James (ancestor), 7; James Dunwoodie (uncle), 34; James Stephens (grandfather), 7; Jean Stobo (Mrs. James, ancestress), 7
Bullock, Seth, 347
Bülow, Count von, 266, 274, 276
Bunau-Varilla, Philippe, 211–35 *passim*; Mme., 227
Bureau of Corporations, 240–41, 246, 249–50, 253, 295, 313
Burlington R.R., 295
Burr, Aaron, 113
Burroughs, John, 330
Butler, N. M., 59, 182, 248, 294, 303, 337–38, 346
Butt, Archie, 40, 298, 358, 359, 367, 376, 387, 388, 401
Byrnes, Tom, 95, 96

California, Japanese in, 280–82, 285–87, 288, 290
Cambon, Paul, 274, 279
Campaign contributions, 249–52, 318–20, 339, 356, 357, 388
Canada, 117, 286, 386, 392, 416. *See also* Alaska boundary dispute.
Canal Zone, 286
Cannon, J. G., 161, 240, 241, 257, 291, 292, 300, 335, 339, 340, 370, 372–73, 375
Capron, Allyn, 190
Carey, J. M., 389
Caribbean, T.R. and, 199, 206, 222. *See also* Cuba; Puerto Rico; Santo Domingo.
Carlisle, J. G., 92
Carmack, E. W., 235
Carnegie, Andrew, 249, 252, 328
Cassini, Count, 264, 267, 269, 271
Castro, Cipriano, 198–200, 204
Central America, T.R. and, 199. *See also* Colombia; Guianas; Mexico; Nicaragua; Panama; Venezuela.

Centralization, T.R. and, 183, 300, 385, 397
Cervera, Admiral Pascual, 134, 137
Chamberlain, Joseph, 205
Chandler, W. E., 297
Chaucer, 331
Chicago & Alton R.R., 295
Chicago, Burlington & Quincy R.R. *See* Northern Securities Co.
Chicago *News*, 61
Child labor, 253, 302
Chile, 116, 119
China, 262, 263, 266, 268, 269, 276
Choate, J. H., 3, 118, 337
Choynski, Joe, 25
Chrank, John, 398
Christmas, 10
Churchill, Randolph, 81
Civil service reform, 22, 60, 77, 85–86, 242; T.R. and, 42, 53, 146, 147, 150, 383. *See also* Roosevelt, Theodore, Civil Service Commissioner.
Civil War, 8
Clapp Committee, 252
Clark, E. B., 330
Clark, E. E., 194, 195
Clark, W. F., 188
Clarkson, J. S., 242
Clayton Act, 300
Clayton-Bulwer Treaty, 204, 212
Clemenceau, G. B. E., 418
Cleveland, Grover, 48, 52, 53, 58, 60, 62–64, 69, 77, 82–83, 85, 91–92, 107, 109–10, 115, 116, 119, 122, 149, 178, 193–95, 196, 204, 248, 250
Clews, Henry, 167
Clowes, *History of the Royal Navy*, 45
Coal strike, 158, 168, 185–96, 243
Collier's Weekly, 359
Colombia, 216–33 *passim*, 407
Columbia University Law School, 33, 40
Commons, J. R., 187
Concha, J. V., 217
Congress and T.R., 257–58, 339–41, 353
Conkling, Roscoe, 48–49
Conlin, Peter, 96–97, 104
Conrad, Joseph, 328
Conservation, 371, 374; T.R. and, 173, 243, 248, 302–03, 381
Constitution, T.R.'s attitude toward, 105, 336, 397
Conyers, Boyd, 327
Coolidge, 24
Cornell, A. B., 49
Corollary of 1904, 206, 207, 210–11
Corporation control, 157, 158, 169, 172, 181, 374, 407; T.R. and, 146–48, 150, 172–73, 189, 195–96, 239, 248, 253–54, 259, 299–302, 310–11, 336–37, 355, 381,

383. *See also* Coal strike; Northern Securities Co.; Railroad regulation; Speculation.

Cortelyou, G. B., 241, 247, 249–52, 304, 308–09

Costello, "Mike," 49

Cowles, Anna Roosevelt (Mrs. W. S., sister), 4, 5, 12, 22, 37, 76, 89, 155

Coxey, Jacob, 107

Craig, William, 188

Crane, W. M., 188, 190, 239

Croker, Richard, 78–79, 118, 145

Croly, Herbert, 379–80

Cromwell, W. N., 212–38 *passim*, 357

Cuba, T.R. and, 173, 208, 209–11, 248. *See also* Spanish War.

Cudahy Packing Co., 295

Cullom, S. M., 320

Cumberland, Prince of, 368

Curran, Father J. J., 187, 188

Currency reform, 92; T.R. and, 241, 247, 248, 303–05, 339, 397. *See also* Federal Reserve Act; Free silver; Gold standard.

Curtis, G. W., 8, 60, 63

Curzon, G. N. C., Marquis, 365–66

Cutler, A. H., 17, 18

Czolgosz, Leon, 162

Dakota Bad Lands, *See* Bad Lands.

Daly, Judge J. F., 145

Dana, C. A., 120

Daniels, B. F., 139

Daniels, Josephus, 175

Darien, Isthmus of, 6–7

Davis, H. G., 248–49

Davis, Jefferson, 7, 9, 113

Davis, R. H., 89, 90–91, 133–34

Dawes, C. G., 161

Dawson, T. C., 207

Dayton, Isaac, 79

Debs, E. V., 107, 113, 318

Defoe, Daniel, 17

Delcassé, Théophile, 269, 277

Denmark, 197

Democratic National Conventions: (1896), 111; (1900), 157; (1904), 248–49; (1912), 396

Department of Commerce and Labor, 173, 239–41, 243, 247

Depew, C. M., 79, 140–41, 143, 151, 180, 318

Dewey, Admiral George, 124–25, 130, 156–57, 200–01, 203, 207, 315

Dickens, Charles, 328, 334

Dillingham, Commander A. C., 207

Diplomatic lauguage, T.R. on, 344–45

Direct primary, 377–78, 391

Divorce, T.R. and, 99, 333

Dix, J. A., 378–79

Dodd, S. C. T., 252

Dolliver, J. P., 371

Doyle, Sir A. C., 370

Dumas, Capt. Philip, 283

Dunn, Maj. George, 167–68

Dunne, F. P., 137, 172, 175

Duqué, J. G., 228

Durand, Sir Mortimer, 267, 268, 277

Earl, Judge Robert, 182

East, Far, 196, 262, 267, 276. *See also* China; Japan; Philippines; Russo-Japanese War.

Eaton, Howard, 66

Edmunds, G. F., 56–60 *passim*

Edward VII, 262, 278, 283, 359, 366–67; funeral of, 367–70

Egypt, T.R. and, 14–15, 360–61

Ehrman, Felix, 231

Elena, Queen of Italy, 363

Eliot, C. W., 18–19, 27, 60, 117, 345

Elkhorn Ranch, 67, 73

Elkins, Davis, 293, 296

Elkins Act, 239, 295

Elliott, Susan, 7

Employers' liability, 148, 302, 336, 339, 374

Endicott, M. T., 412

England. *See* Great Britain.

Equitable Life Assurance Society, 251, 317

Erie Canal frauds, 140, 143, 147

Erie Coal Co., 187

Europe, T.R. and, 196

Evarts, W. M., 77

Everybody's Magazine, 330

Fairbanks, C. W., 172, 248

Fall, A. B., 233

Farley, Archbishop J. M., 309

Farm relief, 381, 397

Farragut, Admiral D. G., 120

Federal Reserve Act, 304

Federalism. *See* Centralization.

Ferdinand I of Bulgaria, 368

Ferris, Joe, 66, 72

Ferris, Sylvane, 66, 67, 71

Field, C. W., 51

Fischer, Carl, 44

Fish, Hamilton, Jr., 133

Fisk, N. W., 162

Fiske, John, 160

Fitch, A. P., 105

Flinn, William, 388, 392

Folger, C. J., 52

Foraker, J. B., 59, 172, 244–45, 296–97, 324–27, 356, 411

Ford, John, 146

Foulke, W. D., 89

France, 262, 265, 273–80 *passim*, 282, 386. *See also* World War.

Francis Joseph I, 364

Frankfurter, Felix, 404

Frederick III of Germany, 84

Free silver, 103, 107, 108–09, 110–13, 157, 175; T.R. and, 108, 113, 158, 303–04

Free trade, T.R. and, 46, 56, 78, 79
Frick, H. C., 107, 252, 310–13, 387

G. P. Putnam's Sons, 39
Gage, H. T., 160
Gage, Lyman, 163
Garbutt, Philip, 54
Garfield, J. A., 43, 49, 53
Garfield, J. R., 241, 300, 371
Garrison, W. L., 60
Gary, E. H., 310–13
Gentlemen's Agreement, 286, 287
George I of Greece, 368
George V of England, 367, 368
George, Henry, 77–80, 81, 384
Germans in America, T.R. and, 101
Germany, 262, 264–85 passim; attitude toward, 16, 197–203, 404–06. See also Venezuela debt dispute; World War.
Glasscock, W. E., 389
Glavis, Louis, 371
Godkin, E. L., 62, 81, 157
Gold standard, 109, 110–14
Gompers, Samuel, 55
Gorki, Maxim, 334
Gould, Jay, 51, 149, 169, 176
Grant, F. D., 95, 103–04
Gray, Judge George, 194, 195
Great Britain, 6, 261–85 passim, 386; T.R.'s attitude toward, 90–91, 116–17, 197, 360–61, 366, 386, 405. See also Alaska boundary dispute; Venezuela, boundary dispute, debt dispute; World War.
Great Northern R.R., 295, 305, 316. See also Northern Securities Co.
Grey, Sir Edward, 278–79, 408
Griscom, L. C., 267, 342
Guam, 287
Guantanamo Bay, 210
Guianas, 222
Guiteau, 43

Hadley, A. T., 177
Hadley, H. S., 389, 395
Hague Tribunal, 199, 386
Hale, Eugene, 172, 287, 288, 341
Hale, W. B., 285
Half-breeds (Republican party), 48
Hall, Rev. Dr. John, 37
Halloran, M. F., 85
Hamilton, Dr. A. McL., 393
Hamilton, Alexander, 81
Hanks, C. S., 24
Hanna, M. A., 59, 84, 106, 109, 110, 112, 113, 116, 117, 125, 151–58 passim, 161–72 passim, 178, 180, 186–87, 189, 191, 214, 223, 224, 239, 243–46, 247; 302; death of, 245
Harding, W. G., 233, 379, 424
Hardinge, Sir Charles, 279
Harper, J. H., 60–61
Harper's Weekly, 121
Harriman, E. H., 177, 184, 251, 305,

316–20, 353, 356, 382
Harris, J. C., 329
Harrison, Benjamin, 84–88 passim, 89, 91–92, 109
Harvard College, T.R. and, 16, 18–28, 31–32, 40, 41, 46, 75, 117, 331, 345, 377
Harvard Advocate, 25, 31
Harvey, George, 9, 383
Haskell, C. N., 356
Hawaii, 116, 119, 173, 262, 286, 287
Hay, Del, 170
Hay, John, 70, 90, 116, 118, 139–40, 153, 163, 169–71, 181, 197–204 passim, 212, 216–28 passim, 245, 262–69 passim, 273, 275
Hay-Herran Treaty, 217–21, 224
Hay-Pauncefote Treaty, 169, 212, 217, 218
Hayes, R. B., 22, 49
Haywood, William, 318
Haymarket riots, 77–78, 81, 106–07, 186
Health insurance, 397
Hearst, W. R., 20, 121–22, 124, 240, 282, 318, 356
Heath, Perry, 241
Heintz, F. A., 307
Hendricks, Francis, 149
Henley, W. E., 384
Henry, Prince of Prussia, 197, 198, 342, 368
Hepburn, Peter, 296
Hepburn Act, 294, 296–99
Herran, Tomas, 217. See also Hay-Herran Treaty.
Herrick, M. T., 115, 214
Hess, Jake, 42–44
Hewitt, A. S., 77, 79, 80
Higginson, H. L., 306, 345
Hill, A. S., 31
Hill, D. B., 77, 118, 291
Hill, D. J., 341–44
Hill, J. J., 177, 178, 184, 293
History of New York (T.R.), 82
Hoffman, Medora von, 67
Holland, 279
Holleben, Baron von, 199–203
Holmes, O. W., 18, 183–85
Holstein, Baron F. von, 283, 284
Holt, Henry, 61
Homestead riots, 92, 107
Hooper, Mrs. William, 367
Hopkins, Henry, 3
Hopper, De Wolf, 124
House, Col. E. M., 407, 408
Hoxsey, Arch, 380
Hubbard, Commander John, 229, 231
Huertas, Gen., 228, 230–31
Hughes, C. E., 251, 317, 352, 377, 378, 393, 410–11
Humphrey, Capt. T. B., 225–26
Hunt, I. L., 34, 47–48, 49, 50, 53, 64
Hunting Trips of a Ranchman, 82
Hyde, J. H., 252

Immigration, 173
Imperialism, 157, 158, 177, 206, 209, 211, 256; T.R. and, 84, 92, 116, 119, 144, 344, 360, 366. *See also* Panama.
Income tax, 107, 111, 169; T.R. and, 336, 355, 381, 397
Independence party, 356
Indianapolis *News*, libel suit, 236–38
Indifference, Harvard, 23
Inheritance tax, 169, 336, 341, 355, 381, 397
Initiative, 381, 385, 390
Injunction in labor disputes, 374; T.R. and, 302, 337, 339, 397
Insurance scandals, 148–49, 317
International Harvester Co., 313
Interstate Commerce Act and Commission, 293–99, 305, 316–17, 339
Ireland, Archbishop John, 187, 320–22
Iron Ore (libel suit), 401–02
Irrigation, T.R. and, 173, 243, 248, 302, 303
Italy, 275, 277, 285
Ivins, W. M., 403

J. & W. Seligman & Co., 109
J. P. Morgan & Co., 159, 177, 220, 226, 237. *See also* Bacon, Robert; Morgan, J. P.; Perkins, G. W.
Jackson, Andrew, 83, 341, 347, 351
James, William, 27, 345
Japan, 119, 197, 263, 280–90, 299, 342. *See also* Russo-Japanese War.
Jefferson, Thomas, 158, 259, 380
Jesup, M. K., 3
Jetté, L. A., 204
Joffre, Marshal J. J. C., 419
Johnson, Andrew, 77, 409
Johnson, Hiram, 290, 398
Johnston, Col. Gordon, 413
Jones, "Hell Roaring Bill," 70–71
Jones, H. C., 23
Jones, Judge T. G., 174–75
Judiciary, T.R. and the, 40, 181–85, 336–38, 339, 380, 381, 390–91. *See also* Recall.
Jusserand, Jules, 267, 271, 276–77, 416

Kaneko, Baron Kentaro, 270
Kansas City *Star*, 422
Katsura, Count Taro, 270
Kealing, J. B., 237
Kettle Hill, 136, 255, 367. *See also* San Juan Hill.
Kiaochau, 197, 201
King, Clarence, 170
Kipling, Rudyard, 89, 91
Klondike, 203
Knapp, M. A., 305
Knickerbocker Trust Company, 307–09
Knight case, 178

Knox, P. C., 40–41, 178, 179–80, 188, 190–91, 192–93, 234, 296, 302, 393
Komura, Marquis Jutaro, 272
Korea, Emperor of, 185
Korea, 262, 264, 265, 269, 270, 285
Kuhn, Loeb & Co., 109, 176, 177, 234

Labor and labor unions, 55, 77–79, 107, 172, 353, 355, 357, 374; T.R. and, 45, 55, 78, 80, 144, 146, 147, 172, 183, 185–96, 242, 247, 253, 302, 337, 339, 357, 381, 397
LaFollette, R. M., 169, 294, 299, 377, 379–96 *passim*
Lambert, Dr. Alexander, 126
Lamont, D. S., 250
Landis, Judge K. M., 300, 336
Lang, C. G., Archbishop of York, 366
Lang, Gregor, 66, 71
Lansdowne, Lord, 199, 274, 278
Las Guasimas, 91, 129, 133, 134, 135
Laughlin, J. L., 25–26, 303
Laurier, Sir Wilfred, 386
Lawrence, William, 3, 306–07
Lawson, William, 327
League of Nations, 365, 422–23
Lee, C. H., 160
Lee, Fitzhugh, 123
Lee, G. C., 30
Lesseps, Ferdinand de, 212–13, 234
Lexow Committee, 94
Libel suits, 235–38, 401–02, 403–04
Limitation of naval armaments, 397
Lincoln, Abraham, 59, 169, 184, 254, 354, 370, 381
Little Missouri. *See* Bad Lands.
Llewellyn, Maj. W. H. H., 139–40
Lloyd, H. D., 187
Lodge, H. C., 8, 26, 56–103 *passim*, 108–18 *passim*, 128, 137, 139, 141, 144, 152, 153, 160, 162, 171, 174, 175, 183, 185, 188, 189, 191,194, 197, 204, 205, 233, 246, 256, 288, 296, 298, 299, 316, 322, 332, 338, 340, 370, 371, 372, 374, 379, 391, 393, 401, 416, 423
Loeb, William, 202, 310, 328, 353
Loewenthal, Henry, 51
Lôme, Dupuy de, 122
London, Jack, 330
London *Spectator*, 82; *Standard*, 361; *Star*, 361; *Times*, 106
Long, J. D., 117–27 *passim*
Long, W. J., 330–31
Longfellow, H. W., 8
Longworth, Alice Roosevelt (Mrs. Nicholas, daughter), 36, 38, 116, 197–98, 268, 320, 409, 416
Longworth, Nicholas, 320, 352
Loomis, F. B., 222, 225
Lorimer, William, 380

Louisiana Purchase, 158
Low, Seth, 105
Lowell, A. L., 19
Lowell, J. R., 8
Luffsey, Riley, 71–72
Lurton, Judge H. H., 183
Lusitania, 408, 409, 410
Lyman, Charles, 85
Lynch, T. R., 59

McArthur, Rev. R. S., 112
McCormick, Medill, 388
McCoy, Capt. Frank, 414
McCreery, James, 109
McKinley, William, 42, 59, 74, 84,
    95, 104–05, 107, 108–26 passim,
    127, 128, 131, 144–74 passim,
    178, 179, 209, 213, 214, 215, 241,
    255, 320, 321; death of, 162–63
MacVeagh, Wayne, 154
Mahan, Admiral A. T., 120, 263, 288
Maher, Peter, 25
Maine, 122, 123–26, 127
Malefactors of great wealth, 176, 306,
    353, 381. *See also* Corporation
    control; Railroad regulation; Specu-
    lation.
Malmross, consul, 232
Maltese Cross Ranch, 67, 70, 74
Manchuria, 262–66 passim, 269, 276,
    285
Mandan (Dakota) *Press*, 69
Manhattan Elevated Railway, 50–51,
    53
Maracaibo, 202
Marat, 107
Margarita Island, 197
Marlborough, Duke and Duchess of,
    82
Marroquin, J. M., 216, 217
Marshall, Edward, 133
Matthews, Brander, 27, 80, 90, 176,
    328–29
Medal of Honor denied T.R., 144–45
Medora. *See* Bad Lands.
Meiji (Mutsuhito), Mikado of Japan,
    271
Memphis *Scimitar*, 175
Merriam, C. H., 330
Merrifield, A. W., 66, 67
Merry del Val, 362
Metternich, Count, 199, 278
Mexico, 116, 119, 284, 286
Meyer, G. von L., 268, 271, 272,
    404
Middle West, T.R. in, 158, 181, 189
Miles, Gen. N. A., 314–16
Miller, W. A., 241–42
Miller, Warner, 56
Minot, Harry, 32
Mitchell, John, 186–87, 189–96
Monotno, 269
Monotombo, Mt., 215
Monroe Doctrine, 196–99, 206; T.R.
    and, 116, 120, 173, 196–212 pas-
    sim, 248

Moody, John, 312
Moody, W. H., 295, 297
Moore, J. B., 201, 222–24
Moore & Schley, 310, 312
Moosehead Lake, 12
Mores, Marquis de, 67, 71–73
Morgan, J. P., 158, 159, 167, 176–80,
    184, 186, 187, 189, 192–95, 226,
    246, 251, 304–11 passim, 382
Morgan, J. T., 213, 235
Morley, John, 260
Morocco, 262, 265, 269, 272–80
Morris, Gouverneur, Life of, 82
Morse, C. W., 307
Morton, L. P., 77, 79, 83, 234
Most favored nation, 286
Moyer, 318
Muckrakers, 300–01
Mugwumps, 62, 69, 81, 82
Mukden, 267
Munroe, H. S., 194
Munsey, F. A., 396
Münsterberg, Hugo, 405
Murphy, C. F., 102, 403
Murphy, Lieut. G. M-P., 226
Murphy, M. C., 49–50
Murray, Annie, 29
Murray, Joe, 40, 42–44, 96
Muscle Shoals, 303
Mutual Life Insurance Co., 251
"My hat is in the ring," 389
Myers, Rev. Cortland, 112

Napoleon I, 11, 34
Nast, Thomas, 60
Nation, The, 82
National Progressive Republican
    League, 385
Nature-fakers, T.R. and, 173, 328,
    329–30
Naval coaling stations, 209
Naval War of 1812, The, 26, 33–34,
    43, 45, 82
Negroes, 156, 353, 355; T.R. and,
    59–60, 242. *See also* Brownsville
    riot; Washington, B. T.
Neill, C. P., 301
Nelson Morris & Co., 295, 301
Netherlands, The, 279
New England, T.R. in, 65, 181, 188
New Freedom, 384, 407, 409
New Granada, Treaty of 1846,
    222–23, 225, 232
New Mexico, 374
New Nationalism, 380–82, 384, 385,
    409. *See also* Progressive party.
New Orleans *Times-Democrat*, 175
New York *American*, 240
New York *Evening Post*, 52, 61
New York *Evening World*, 102
New York *Herald*, 61
New York *Journal*, 114, 121–22.
    See also Hearst, W. R.
New York Life Insurance Co., 251
New York National Guard, 45–46,

127, 138, 144. *See also* Roosevelt, Theodore, chronology.

New York *Sun*, 54, 302

New York *Times*, 44, 51, 60, 61, 102, 151, 247–48, 404

New York *Tribune*, 113, 114, 147, 179

New York *World*, 80, 95, 96, 122, 147, 169, 247, 317, 379; libel suit, 235–38

Newett, G. J., libel suit, 401–02

Newfoundland fisheries, 204

Newlands, F. G., Newlands Act, 302–03

Nicaragua, 116, 119, 169, 212–19 *passim*, 224

Nicholas II, 262, 265, 268, 271, 272, 273, 285

Nicolay, J. G., 170

Nicolson, Sir Arthur, 273, 279

Nobel Peace Prize and speech, 196, 386, 423

Norris, Frank, 300

Norris, G. W., 373

North American Review, 9

Northern Pacific R.R., 316. *See also* Northern Securities Co.

Northern Securities Co., 177–80, 181, 183–85, 186, 247, 248, 299

Obaldia, J. D. de, 228–29, 230

Odell, B. B., 148, 154, 239, 319

Olney, Richard, 122

O'Neill, W. T., 49, 53

"Onward, Christian Soldiers," 398

Open door policy, 206, 248, 262–63, 275, 279

Osborn, H. F., 365–66

Osborne, C. S., 389

Ossa, Amelia de la, 228

Otto Heintz & Co., 307

Our Young Folks, 17, 26

Outlook, 375, 384. *See also* Roosevelt, Theodore, chronology.

Palma, T. E., 209, 210

Panama and Panama Canal, 169, 173, 209, 284; T.R. and, 119, 210, 211–38, 243, 248, 407

Panama libel suit, 235–38

Panic of 1907, 304–13

Pardo, Manuel, 344

Parker, Judge A. B., 153–54, 248–50

Parker, A. D., 95, 103, 104, 105

Parker, E. W., 194, 195

Parker, J. M., 418

Parkhurst, Rev. C. H., 93–94, 103, 104, 112, 118, 141

Paterson, William, 6

Pauncefote, Lord. *See* Hay-Pauncefote Treaty.

Payn, L. F., 143, 148–49, 378

Payne, H. C., 241

Payne-Aldrich Bill, 373–74, 392

Pelée, Mont, 215

Pellew, George, 23

Pendleton, G. H., 85

Penrose, Boies, 153, 155, 247, 353, 403

Penrose, Maj. C. W., 323

Pension increases, 242

Perdicaris, Ion, and wife, 273

Perkins, G. W., 194, 195, 308, 311, 313, 396

Perkins, J. B., 340

Pershing, Gen. J. J., 419

Peru, 344

Philadelphia & Reading R.R., 305; Coal and Iron Co. *See* Baer, G. F.

Philippines, 123, 124, 125, 131, 173, 206, 208, 209, 248, 256, 269, 284, 287, 288, 316, 321, 352, 361

Pichon, S. J. M., 369

Pinchot, Amos, 388

Pinchot, Gifford, 303, 370–71, 375, 377, 388

Pinkerton, R. A., 107

Pius IX, 10

Pius X, 321–22, 362

Platt, Frank, 147

Platt, O. H., 209

Platt, T. C., 22, 48–49, 53, 77, 84, 94, 105, 108, 110, 117–18, 140–52 *passim*, 154, 160, 239, 346, 358, 403

Platt Amendment, 209

Populist movement, 107, 258

Porcellian Club, 29

Port Arthur, 263, 264, 267, 269

Postal savings, 339, 374

Potter, Bishop H. C., 187

Preparedness, 409–10, 411, 420

Prescott, H. G., 228

Pribilof Islands, 281

Prince, Dr. Morton, 393

Proctor, J. R., 86

Progressive party, 169, 251, 259, 379, 381, 382, 387–400, 402, 409; conventions and campaigns: (1912), 313, 396–98, 401, 407; (1916), 410

Prohibition, 100–01, 355; T.R. and, 98–100

Puck, 46, 81

Puerto Rico, 131, 137, 173

Pulitzer, Joseph, 80, 102, 121, 169, 237, 249

Pullman strike, 107

Pure food bill, 301–02

Putnam, G. H., 39, 61, 62

Quay, M. S., 84, 153, 155–56, 161, 189, 193, 241, 247, 403

Quigg, L. E., 141

Rabelais, 333

Race suicide, T.R. and, 332–33

Railroad regulation, 60, 169, 324, 341; T.R. and, 173, 177, 239, 254, 260, 261, 292–99, 305, 316–

431

20, 336–37, 341, 353, 356, 381.
See also Northern Securities Co.
Raines Law, 104, 144, 146
Raisuli, 273
Rampolla, Cardinal Mariano, 321
Recall, 381, 385, 390–91, 392, 397
Reciprocity, 172, 209, 248, 386, 392
Reclamation. See Irrigation.
Reed, T. B., 85, 88, 89, 110, 159
Referendum, 381, 385, 390
Reid, Ogden, 423
Reid, Whitelaw, 277, 367, 368
Religion (T.R.), 28; in politics, 362
Republican National Conventions: (1884), 46, 56–60; (1896) 110–11; (1900), 154–56, 164, 213; (1904), 248; (1908), 351, 352–54, 394; (1912), 387, 389–90, 393–95, 403; (1916), 410
Review of Reviews, 177
Reynolds, J. B., 301
Rhodes, J. F., 9, 58, 125
Rice, Cecil Spring, 4, 76, 82, 89, 90, 110, 116, 118, 119, 197, 203, 257, 265, 267–68, 276, 278, 332, 341, 359, 366, 398, 408
Richmond Times, 175
Riis, Jacob, 29, 80, 95, 105, 108
River of Doubt, 402
Roberts, Elmer, 283
Robespierre, 107
Robinson, Corinne Roosevelt (Mrs. Douglas), 4, 5, 10, 15–16, 29, 35–36, 37, 75, 388
Robinson, Douglas, 36, 89, 142, 167, 235–36, 238
Robinson, E. A., 334–35
Rochester Post-Express, 61
Rockefeller, J. D., 240, 252
Rockefeller, J. D., Jr., 186
Romanes Lecture, 360, 365–66
Roosevelt, Alice Hathaway Lee (first Mrs. Theodore), 26, 28–38, 40, 41, 43, 55, 75, 331; death of, 37
Roosevelt, Archie (son), 338
Roosevelt, Edith Kermit Carow (second Mrs. Theodore), 29, 38, 39, 75–76, 85, 88, 89–90, 116, 126, 142, 153–54, 198, 334, 359, 360, 364, 367–68
Roosevelt, Elliott (brother), 4, 9, 10, 12, 14, 15, 16, 32, 36, 37
Roosevelt, Ethel (daughter), 89
Roosevelt, F. D., 262, 328, 336, 416
Roosevelt, James A. (uncle), 39, 142
Roosevelt, Kermit (son), 89, 354, 359
Roosevelt, Klaes Martensen van (ancestor), 6
Roosevelt, Martha Bulloch (Mrs. Theodore, Sr., mother), 5–11 passim, 15, 22, 31, 32, 34, 36; death of, 37
Roosevelt, Quentin (son), 38, 39, 126, 142, 421

Roosevelt, Robert Barnhill (uncle), 33, 49
Roosevelt, Theodore, chronology, ancestry, 6–7; birth, 3–4; education, 11, 15–28, 32–33; foreign travel, 4, 9–10, 14–16, 33–34, 358–70; first marriage, 32; studying law 25, 32–33, 40–41, 160; beginnings in politics, 33, 41–44; assemblyman (N.Y. state), 34–38, 39, 46–56, 93–94, 99, 182, (campaigning for), 18, 34, 40, 43–44; officer in New York National Guard, 45, 106; children, 38; ranching (cowboy), 39, 64–74, 360; deputy sheriff, 71; second marriage, 38, 76; candidate for mayoralty (N.Y. City), 78–81, 86; Civil Service Commissioner (U.S.), 39, 83, 84–92, 242, 320; police commissioner (N.Y. City), 92, 93–106, 383; Assistant Secretary of the Navy, 39, 45, 105, 115–28, 320, 383, 419; Colonel of Rough Riders. See Spanish War, T.R. and; governor (N.Y. state), 138 145–50, 317, 383, (candidate for), 141–45; Vice-President, 160–63, (candidate for), 73–74, 141 150–59, (inauguration as), 255 President, 70, 71, 125, 139, 145 163–357, (inauguration as), 5–6 255–57; on the Outlook, 303, 332 334, 346, 382, 385, 387, 405–06 407; wounded, 398; last illness and death, 421–22
Roosevelt, Theodore, characteristic and pursuits, 23–24; personal appearance, 4 15, 20, 27–28, 96, 97 dress, 15, 20, 27, 47, 68, 71, 96 128, 367–68; adolescence in man hood, 4, 127, 171, 345, 359, 414 athletics, 24 (boxing), 12, 24–25 30; beauty, love of, 68; confession of error, 328; contradictions, 60–64, 65, 331–32, 377, 392, 400–09; courage, 66, 136, 399; depression and pessimism, 10, 30–31, 33–34, 44–45, 65, 102, 108 178, 239, 241, 246, 400; dignity 173, 337–38, 355; drinking, 20 68, 401–02; energy, 345, 377 400, 401; enjoyment, sense of, 9 10; exhibitionism, 47; health, 3–5 11–13, 14, 65–66, 188–89, 358 360, 398, 402, (eyesight), 13 358; human contacts, 66; humor 14, 97, 322, 366, 368–69, 401 hunting, 12, 15, 32, 66, 69, 173 242–43, 268, 275, 306, 331, 346 358–60; impulsiveness, 49, 383 memory, 26; morality, concern with, 26, 295, 306, 331–34, 337 338, 365, 375, 380; naturalist 4, 9–10, 11–12, 13–14, 15, 21 25, 31–32; optimism, 65, 104

politics, interest in, 22, 41, 65, 376, 402; power, desire for, 178–79; radicalism, 145, 259–60, 295 (*see also* Progressive party); reading, 16–17, 333; self-hypnosis, 57; smoking, 20, 68; swearing, 68, 401; truthfulness, 25, 318–19, 401 (*see also* Brownsville riot; Panama libel suit); war, attitude toward, 119–21, 123, 126, 404–06

Roosevelt, Theodore, financial status, 32, 39, 45, 66, 76, 89, 126, 152, 346, 359; homes of: (New York City), birthplace, 7–8, (other), 32, 34, 35, (Oyster Bay), 13, 17, 35, (Sagamore Hill), 82, (Cambridge), 21, (Albany), 34, (Washington), 89 and White House; nicknames, 4, 13, 68

Roosevelt, Theodore, Jr. (son), 52, 89, 263, 333, 385, 413

Roosevelt, Theodore, Sr. (father), 3–16 *passim*, 22

Roosevelt, W. E. (cousin), 41, 42

Root, Elihu, 3, 16, 79, 142–43, 149, 152, 159, 163–64, 168, 170, 171, 179, 182, 186, 189, 192, 193, 205, 207, 209, 211, 222, 232, 239, 248, 266, 282, 285, 286, 287, 291, 299, 311, 315, 320, 322, 338, 342, 345, 352, 371, 393, 395, 403, 419–20, 423

Rosen, Baron, 272

Rouvier, Maurice, 277

Rough Riders, 42, 45, 74, 127–40, 143–44, 151, 154, 255, 256, 359, 360, 365, 367, 376

Round robin, 137–38, 145

Russia, 273, 275, 276, 278, 280, 282, 283, 285. *See also* Alaska boundary dispute; Russo-Japanese War.

Russo-Japanese War, 196, 261–72, 276, 278, 280–81

Ryan, T. F., 179, 249

Sage, Russell, 51

St. Paul R.R., 295

Sakhalin, 272

Saltonstall, Richard, 29, 30; Rose, 29

Sampson, Admiral W. T., 129, 137, 315–16

San Juan Hill, 126, 134, 135–37, 141, 143, 156, 314, 367. *See also* Kettle Hill.

Sandwich Islands, 283

Santa Fe R.R., 309, 316

Santayana, George, 21

Santiago, Battle of, 132, 135–37, 144, 314

Santo Domingo, 206, 208, 210, 268

Schiff, Jacob, 109, 176

Schley, Admiral W. S., 315–16

Schley, G. B., 312

Schmitz, E. E., 286

Schofield, Gen. J. M., 193, 194

Schurman, J. G., 221

Schurz, Carl, 60, 63, 87, 92, 109, 144, 157

Schwab, C. M., 167, 186

Scribner's Magazine, 359, 360, 366

Secret service and Congress, 339–40

Seligman, Isaac, 109

Sewall, W. W., 64, 65, 66, 347

Shafter, Gen. W. R., 134–35, 136–38

Shaler, Col. J. R., 229, 230, 231

Shaw, Albert, 221

Shaw, L. M., 304

Sheard, Titus, 54

Sherman, J. S., 318, 319, 320

Sherman, W. T., 58

Sherman Anti-Trust Act, 177–78, 179, 184, 188, 191, 299–300, 311, 313

Sherman Silver Purchase Act, 108–09

Ship subsidies, 173

Sibley, J. C., 246, 254–55

Sigsbee, Capt. C. D., 124

Sims, Capt. W. S., 284

Sinclair, Upton, 258, 300

Smith, Delavan, 237

Smithsonian Institution, 359, 360

Socialism, 187, 193; T.R. and, 55, 258, 260, 290, 294, 295, 381

South, T.R. and the, 6–7, 8–9, 161, 174–75, 261, 379, 398, 401

South America, T.R. and, 196, 199, 203, 206, 207, 211, 402, 422. *See also* Chile; Peru.

Southern Pacific R.R., 177, 300

Spain, 122, 274, 278, 279. *See also* Spanish War.

Spalding, Bishop J. L., 194, 195

Spanish War, 115, 117, 126–37, 143–44, 157, 197, 208, 211–12, 248, 314; T.R. and, 4, 45, 91, 119–38, 366, 412, 418, 419. *See also* Rough Riders.

Speculation, T.R. and, 176, 181, 303–13, 337

Spelling reform, 27, 174, 328–29

Spinney, George, 49

Spooner, J. C., 297, 299

Spooner Act, 216

Springfield *Republican*, 61

Square deal, 381

Stalwarts (Republican party), 48

Standard Oil Co., 246, 251, 252, 261, 293, 295–96, 300, 327, 336, 338, 356. *See also* Archbold, J. D.; Rockefeller, J. D.

State Trust Co. (N.Y. City), 149

Steffens, Lincoln, 108, 258, 294, 298

Sternberg, Speck von, 200, 202, 206, 209, 266, 267, 275, 276, 283, 341

Stewart, J. A., 109

Stillman, James, 246, 304, 308

Stimson, H. L., 237, 378, 393
Stobo, Rev. Archibald (ancestor), 7
Stock exchange. See Speculation.
Stoddard, H. L., 412
Stone, C. W., 193
Storer, Bellamy, 115, 116, 173, 320–22
Storer, Mrs. Bellamy, 115, 116, 173, 320–22
Stotesbury, E. T., 251
Strenuosity, Gospel of, 4
Strong, W. L., 94, 95, 103, 104, 105
Stubbs, W. R., 389
Suez Canal, 213
Sullivan, John, 97
Sunday closing (N.Y. City), 98–104
Sunday-school class, 28
Supreme Court. See Judiciary.
Sweden, 279
Swift & Co., 295
Swiss Family Robinson, 17
Switzerland, 279; T.R. in, 33

Taft, C. P., 235–36, 357
Taft, W. H., 40, 88, 115, 116, 139, 160, 179, 182, 209, 210, 223, 233, 236, 238, 259, 268, 269, 270, 275, 287, 288, 290, 294, 299, 300, 313, 325, 346–59 *passim*, 366–99 *passim*, 407, 409, 411, 417–18, 423
Taft, Mrs. W. H., 351, 354
Takahira, Baron Kogoro, 269, 271, 272, 286
Talmadge, Rev. T. DeW., 112
Tammany Hall, 8, 49, 51, 53, 79, 91, 93, 94, 102, 117, 143, 145, 146, 403
Tangier, 274, 275
Tarbell, I. M., 258
Tariff, 60, 82–83, 92, 113, 169, 248, 373, 392; T.R. and, 46, 56, 69, 83, 172, 209, 210, 241, 253, 254, 291–92, 373, 381, 397
Tennessee Coal and Iron Co., 310–13, 387
Tennis Cabinet, 347
Thayer, W. R., 23, 200
"There'll Be a Hot Time in the Old Town Tonight," 129, 257
Thomas, E. B., 187
Thomas, R. H., 309
Thompson, C. W., 375
Thompson, H. S., 86
Thompson, N. J., 303
Tilden, S. J., 22, 49, 149
Tillman, B. R., 296–98, 341
Tirpitz, Admiral Alfred von, 280, 289
Tobacco trust, 300
Tolstoy, 333
Torres, Colonel, 230, 231
Tovar, Gen., 229–30
Tower, Charlemagne, 284, 288, 341–43

Tower, Hiram, 332
Townsend-Esch Act, 294
Treaties, T.R.'s opinion on, 405, 40
Trevelyan, Sir George, 232, 259, 289, 368
Trimble, R. J., 43
Tripoli, 277
Trust Company of America, 308
Trusts. See Corporation control.
Tumulty, J. P., 414, 417
Turner, George, 204

Union Pacific R.R., 305. See als Northern Securities Co.
United Copper Company, 307
United Mine Workers. See Mitchell John.
United States Steel Corporation, 159 167, 177, 246, 310–13, 387

Van Amringe, Dean, 40, 61
Van Buren, Martin, 351
Van Schaack, Elise, 11
Van Wyck, Augustus, 143
Varley, Mr. and Mrs., 273
Vatican and T.R., 320–22, 361–6
Venezuela, 206, 222; boundary dis pute, 116, 196, 204; debt dispute 198–203, 206, 248, 289
Victor Emmanuel III, 363
Virgin Islands, 197

Walker, George, 139
Wall Street. See Speculation.
Wall Street Journal, 247
Wanamaker, John, 86–88, 91
Ward, Hamilton, 50–52
Washington, B. T., 161, 173, 174–76
Washington, George, 370
Watkins, T. H., 193, 195
Watterson, Henry, 90, 235, 261
Webster, Sidney, 317, 319
Weld, Minot, 29
West, Dr. Hilborne (uncle), 7, 1
West, T.R. in the, 116, 162, 238 242–45, 268, 275, 379. See als Bad Lands.
Westbrook, Judge T. R., Westbroo scandal, 50–51
Wheeler, Gen. Joseph, 132, 137
White, Chief Justice E. D., 238
White, Henry, 29, 170, 197, 205 268, 288, 290, 368, 370, 389 423
White, Horace, 61
White, W. A., 161
Whitney, H. P., 179
Wickersham, G. W., 387
Wilcox, Ansley, 163
Wilderness Hunter, The, 82
Wiley, Dr. H. W., 301–02
Wilhelm I, 84
Wilhelm II, 84, 197–203 *passim* and T.R., 16, 262, 265–85 *pas*

sim, 288, 303, 341–44, 364–65, 368–69, 405. *See also* World War.

Wilhelmina I, 364

Williams, Bill, 70

Wilmer, Dr. W. H., 13

Wilson, Gen. J. M., 195

Wilson, James, 301

Wilson, T. E., 301

Wilson, Woodrow, 233, 259, 290, 300, 382–84, 395, 396, 397, 398, 399, 404–24 *passim*

Wilson, Mrs. Woodrow, 422

Winning of the West, The, 82, 90

Winslow, Commander Cameron, 272

Wister, Owen, 27, 76, 145, 333, 334, 346

Witte, Count Sergius, 272

Wolcott, E. O., 157

Women, T.R. on equality and rights of, 29, 331–33, 397

Wood, Gen. Leonard, 127–37 *passim,* 209, 286, 287

Workmen's compensation, 253, 336, 341, 397

World association for peace, T.R. and, 365. *See also* League of Nations.

World War, 200, 233, 404–21; T.R. and, 16, 202, 346, 399, 404–21

Wright brothers, 258

Wright, C. D., 190, 194, 195

Yamamoto, Admiral, 288

Young, Gen. S. B. M., 132–33, 134, 135

Zola, Emile, 333

HARVEST BOOKS

The Waste Land and Other Poems, T. S. ELIOT   HB 1
Modern Man in Search of a Soul, C. G. JUNG   HB 2
Ideology and Utopia, KARL MANNHEIM   HB 3
Main Currents in American Thought, VERNON L. PARRINGTON
    Vol. I, 1620–1800, The Colonial Mind   HB 4
Main Currents in American Thought, VERNON L. PARRINGTON
    Vol. II, 1800–1860, The Romantic Revolution in America   HB 5
The Old Order, KATHERINE ANNE PORTER   HB 6
Language, EDWARD SAPIR   HB 7
The Oedipus Cycle of Sophocles, *English Versions by*
    DUDLEY FITTS AND ROBERT FITZGERALD
    Oedipus Rex, Oedipus at Colonus, Antigone   HB 8
The Acquisitive Society, R. H. TAWNEY   HB 9
The Common Reader, *First Series*, VIRGINIA WOOLF   HB 10
The Well Wrought Urn, CLEANTH BROOKS   HB 11
The Last Adam, JAMES GOULD COZZENS   HB 12
From the Ground Up, LEWIS MUMFORD   HB 13
Economic and Social History of Medieval Europe,
    HENRI PIRENNE   HB 14
Theodore Roosevelt, HENRY F. PRINGLE   HB 15
Practical Criticism, I. A. RICHARDS   HB 16
The First American Revolution, CLINTON ROSSITER   HB 17
Essays on Elizabethan Drama, T. S. ELIOT   HB 18
Aspects of the Novel, E. M. FORSTER   HB 19
The Modern Temper, JOSEPH WOOD KRUTCH   HB 20
Man Against Himself, KARL MENNINGER   HB 21
Theory of Literature, AUSTIN WARREN AND RENÉ WELLEK   HB 22
The Golden Apples, EUDORA WELTY   HB 23
The Second Common Reader, VIRGINIA WOOLF   HB 24